Putting the
TRUTH
to Work

Putting the TRUTH to Work

The Theory and Practice of
Biblical Application

Daniel M. Doriani

P&R PUBLISHING

P.O. BOX 817 • PHILLIPSBURG • NEW JERSEY 08865-0817

Page design by Tobias Design
Typesetting by Colophon Typesetting

Printed in the United States of America

Library of Congress Cataloging-in-Publication Data

Doriani, Daniel M., 1953–
    Putting the truth to work : the theory and practice of biblical
    application / Daniel M. Doriani.
            p.   cm.
    Includes bibliographical references and index.
    ISBN 0-87552-170-3 (pbk.)
    1. Bible—Use. 2. Christian life—Biblical teaching. I. Title.

    BS538.3.D67 2001
    248.4—dc21
                                            00-066938

Contents

Preface

In my first fifteen years of preaching, I had methods for interpreting the Bible, but none for applying it. I had the unsettling sense that while God might be using my preaching, I hardly knew how. Because I had no method, I never knew why one sermon worked and another failed (though disaster is easier to analyze). Every success seemed accidental, and every failure felt like a harbinger of the great unmasking: "Why, this charlatan has absolutely no idea what he is doing!" I had the discomfiting sense that few pastors were more advanced theoretically than I. The best preachers seemed to rely on raw skill, instinct, and a few heartfelt ideals, but, when asked, they offered little specific guidance.

Two experiences in the 1990s altered my situation and gave impetus to the present project. First, in 1991 I joined the faculty of Covenant Theological Seminary, a community that cultivates the theory and practice of preaching, and I began to hope for some guidance in the area of biblical application. Second, in 1995 I had a sabbatical to complete an earlier book on Bible interpretation. In preparing a chapter on application I found that, compared to the surfeit of excellent readings for prior chapters, the quantity and quality of readings dropped precipitously. Few scholars were writing about application.

Indeed, from 1950 to 1970, scholars such as Berkeley Mickelsen, Bernard Ramm, and Louis Berkhof offered just a few chestnuts on application: avoid legalism, heed the Spirit, find principles, know the culture.[1] In the 1980s, specialized works on poetry, parable, narrative,

---

1 Very few pages were dedicated to application: e.g., A. Berkeley Mickelsen, *Interpreting the Bible* (Grand Rapids: Eerdmans, 1963), 6 of 379 (359–64); Bernard Ramm, *Protestant Biblical Interpretation,* 3d ed. (Grand Rapids: Baker, 1970), 0 of

dialogue, and wisdom literature still passed over application.[2] Recent introductions to interpretation commonly add one chapter on application to their deliberations.[3] While popular volumes take more interest in application and serious scholars have begun to consider it, publications on the subject remain rare.[4]

Why this neglect? In an era of specialization, application falls through a crack separating exegesis, ethics, and homiletics. Homileticians stress communication, exegetes discover original meanings, and ethicists typically work with principles (love, justice, wisdom) and dilemmas (Can we "approve aborting the ninth, possibly retarded, child of a woman whose husband has just deserted her?").[5] Scholars pause before publishing outside their field, leaving the integration of exegesis, application, and ethics to others.[6] Critical exegetes hesitate to

---

290; Louis Berkhof, *Principles of Biblical Interpretation* (Grand Rapids: Baker, 1950), 0 of 166.

2 E.g., Gordon Fee, *New Testament Exegesis* (Philadelphia: Westminster, 1983), 3 pages of 136; Terence Keegan, *Interpreting the Bible: A Popular Introduction to Biblical Hermeneutics* (New York: Paulist, 1985), 0 of 172; Peter Cotterell and Max Turner, *Linguistics and Biblical Interpretation* (Downers Grove, Ill.: InterVarsity, 1989), 0 of 332. William Larkin describes the situation in *Culture and Biblical Hermeneutics* (Grand Rapids: Baker, 1988), 104–13.

3 Sidney Greidanus, *The Modern Preacher and the Ancient Text* (Grand Rapids: Eerdmans, 1988), 40 pages of 340; Grant Osborne, *The Hermeneutical Spiral* (Downers Grove, Ill.: InterVarsity, 1991), 25 of 435; William Klein, Craig Blomberg, and Robert Hubbard, *Introduction to Biblical Interpretation* (Waco: Word, 1993), 26 of 400; Dan McCartney and Charles Clayton, *Let the Reader Understand: A Guide to Interpreting and Applying the Bible* (Wheaton, Ill.: Bridgepoint, 1994), 30 of 290; James Voelz, *What Does This Mean? Principles of Biblical Interpretation in the Post-Modern World* (St. Louis: Concordia, 1995), 30 of 365; Robertson McQuilkin, *Understanding and Applying the Bible* (Chicago: Moody, 1992), 40 of 334.

4 The journals *Interpretation* and *Expository Times* run articles on the topic fairly often. See the latter's series "New Occasions Teach New Duties?" in 1994–95. Popular works include Jack Kuhatschek, *Taking the Guesswork out of Applying the Bible* (Downers Grove, Ill.: InterVarsity, 1990); Jay Adams, *Truth Applied: Application in Preaching* (Grand Rapids: Ministry Resources Library, 1990); Dave Veerman, *How to Apply the Bible* (Wheaton, Ill.: Tyndale, 1993).

5 Gilbert Meilaender, *The Theory and Practice of Virtue* (Notre Dame, Ind.: Notre Dame University Press, 1984), 4–5.

6 Theological ethics is an exception, but it has hardly influenced evangelical hermeneutics. Leading writers are ethicists more than exegetes, so the gap between

apply texts whose historicity or veracity they doubt. Perhaps unwittingly, evangelical scholars mimic the critics' model of detached scholarship, possibly hoping an air of objectivity will win them acceptance.

With trepidation, I attempt to fill the gap and to tread the seam between academic and pastoral theology. Because I teach New Testament and hermeneutics and preach or teach in the churches very frequently, I hope to speak to both church and academy. Pastors will be interested to know that I pastored full-time for six years, served as an interim five times, and have been auxiliary staff in my home church for eight years. Scholars should be aware that my conversation partners are listed in the notes.

I gladly confess the core beliefs behind this monograph. I believe Scripture was written by individuals inspired by God. Divine inspiration implies its historical, theological, and ethical veracity. Human authorship implies that Scripture will repay critical investigation of its grammar, history, literature, rhetoric, and society. Thus, I advocate a circumspect use of critical methodologies, especially if we watch for presuppositions antithetical to faith, such as the antisupernaturalism of the historical-critical method,[7] the historical agnosticism in some literary criticism, and the denial of the human author's capacity to control his text, a denial found in deconstruction and some reader-response criticism.[8]

Theologically, my evangelical, Reformed, grace-oriented tradition

---

biblical studies and Christian ethics persists. Further, critics such as Bruce Birch, James Gustafson, Richard Hays, Eduard Lohse, Thomas Ogletree, Paul Ramsey, Larry Rasmussen, and Wolfgang Schrage dominate the field, so that influence on evangelicals is slight. John Frame and David Jones represent evangelicals in the discipline.

7 V. Philips Long, *The Art of Biblical Narrative* (Grand Rapids: Zondervan, 1994), 110ff., 123–25, 134.

8 Conservative reader-response criticism explores the responses the author intended to elicit. Radical forms approximate deconstruction by stressing that texts are enigmatic, underdetermined, and "recalcitrant," so that readers, controlled far more by their community of interpreters than by the author, bring the text to completion. See Robert Fowler, *Let the Reader Understand* (Minneapolis: Augsburg Fortress, 1991); Wolfgang Iser, *The Act of Reading: A Theory of Aesthetic Response* (Baltimore: Johns Hopkins University Press, 1978); Stephen Moore, *Literary Criticism and the Gospels: The Theoretical Challenge* (New Haven: Yale University Press, 1989), 69–130; Anthony Thistelton, *New Horizons in Hermeneutics* (Grand Rapids: Zondervan, 1992), 515–55.

guides me. Linguistically, I believe authors can achieve their goals.[9] Therefore, I speak of authorial intent, knowing that critics of authorial intent still expect their readers to seek *their* intended meaning.[10] Thus, we rightly explore the significance authors ascribe to their work.[11] Valid applications for contemporary audiences will correspond to the applications the authors intended for their original audience.[12]

It is a burden to know that full-length treatments of application are rare. With few predecessors, I hope that friends and critics will stand on my pygmy shoulders, correct my shortcomings, and stride on. To shorten this book, I bypassed both the basic principles for interpretation (treated in the companion volume, *Getting the Message*) and the effects of literary genre on application.

For whatever is good in this volume, I thank teachers past and colleagues present, especially the readers who offered countless beneficial suggestions. I especially thank my colleagues at Covenant, Hans Bayer, David Calhoun, Bryan Chapell, Jack Collins, and Michael Williams. The counsel of Wilson Benton, Donald Carson, John Frame, Mark Futato, Dennis Johnson, Doug Madi, Scotty Smith, Kevin Vanhoozer, James Voelz, Bob Yarbrough, and many students proved invaluable. My able research assistant, Bryan Stewart, tracked down many sources. I thank the board of Covenant Seminary who granted a sabbatical for this project.

I bless my children, Abigail, Sarah, and Beth, who "let Daddy study when the door is shut"—and also knew when to disregard the guideline for a talk or a romp. I dedicate this book to my beloved wife Debbie, who as I wrote, mourned when I mourned and rejoiced when I rejoiced.

---

9   Kevin Vanhoozer, *Is There a Meaning in This Text?* (Grand Rapids: Zondervan, 1998); Thistelton, *New Horizons,* 558–62, 597–602. Stanley Fish argues the contrary in *Is There a Text in This Class?* (Cambridge, Mass.: Harvard University Press, 1980). See also William K. Wimsatt and Monroe Beardsley, "The Intentional Fallacy," in W. K. Wimsatt, *The Verbal Icon* (New York: Noonday, 1954, 1966).

10 See D. A. Carson, *The Gagging of God* (Grand Rapids: Zondervan, 1996), 102–3.

11 Nor do we seek meanings hidden in allegedly extraordinary traits of ancient Greek or Hebrew. See Moisés Silva, *God, Language and Scripture* (Grand Rapids: Zondervan, 1990), 87–107.

12 I give provisional assent to E. D. Hirsch's distinction between meaning and significance (*Validity in Interpretation* [New Haven: Yale University Press, 1967]), but will modify it in the discussion of Krister Stendahl, John Frame and fuzzy boundaries in chap. 1, pp. 22–27.

Introduction

IS THE BIBLE RELEVANT?

Sometimes the seeming mismatch between the hard questions of life and the teachings of Scripture leaves us disappointed. On the one hand, we have clear rules no one seems to need. For example, if we own a bull in the habit of goring, Exodus 21 urges us to find recipes for steak. Or if, as we sit down to a dinner, our host says, "Incidentally, I offered the meat in the main dish to Zeus earlier today," 1 Corinthians 10 guides us toward the vegetables. But how many of us own cattle or live near a temple of Zeus? On the other hand, rarely does a simple Bible verse answer our pressing ethical questions. For example, no Bible verse tells us what we owe telephone solicitors.

We debate the proper treatment of telephone solicitors at my house. View 1 says they are rude, since they deliberately call at meal-time, and deceitful, for they often conceal their intent. Therefore we owe them nothing. So, if someone calls and, butchering our name, says, "Hello! Is this the Dobraini residence?" we can say, "No, it is not the Dobraini residence. Good-bye." Or if the caller says, "Hello, Mr. Dorundi, I am calling on behalf of Weed Blaster Fertile World lawn care. We have noticed lots of weeds in your yard recently and wonder if we can help you with that," I can say, "It may look like weeds to you, but actually we are fostering biodiversity." View 2 says that solicitors are simply trying to make a living. They may hate it as much as we do. Besides, God made telephone solicitors in his image too. So treat them accordingly.

In a very different vein, does the Bible shed light on contemporary debates about masculinity? Should a man be tough, or should he know how to cry? Does God favor stoicism or expressiveness? And how can younger, expressive men make sense of their stoical fathers? My father belongs to a stoical generation that grew up in the Depression and served in World War II. My father loves me, but I do not remember hearing those words. He is proud of me, but his generation feared spoiling children with praise, so my brothers and I rarely heard any from him when we were growing up. Men who grew up in homes like ours often have an odd blend of self-sufficiency and disdain for flattery on one hand, and a desperate hope that someone loves and accepts them, warts and all, on the other. I tell my children I love them and am proud of them so often that I wonder if I say it too much; perhaps I should dole out the praise at peak moments, like people who for maximum effect wear their best jewelry just twice a year. Which is better, the tough stoicism that girds men to endure poverty and war, or the sensitive expressiveness that gives families two nurturers?

Can we expect the Bible to supply answers to questions about telephones, emotions, and such? Custom teaches us to say no. Men discuss such things, but pastors rarely assess them. To a certain extent, that is right. The Bible is not an answer book where we look up answers to life's riddles. The teaching ministry of the church should focus on God's salvation and kingdom, not our emotions.

Still, pastors can do better at offering practical counsel. In some churches, text after text elicits the same few applications: be holy, be faithful, be committed. Week after week, believers hear that they must serve more, witness more, study the Bible more, support the church more. Worse, some preachers are repetitive *and* shallow, addressing the same few subjects in the same few terms. Even if they avoid the ultimate crime of propagating falsehood, they commit the penultimate crime of making Christianity seem boring and irrelevant.

Both scholars and pastors contribute to the problem. Scholars confess that they give little serious thought to the relevance of Scripture. One remarked that skill in application is more caught than taught, then added, "But sound application often seems hard to find, let alone catch."[1] Another admits that scholars have neglected the field:

1 William Klein, Craig Blomberg, and Robert Hubbard, *Introduction to Biblical Interpretation* (Waco: Word, 1993), 403.

"Discussions on biblical hermeneutics have given us a fair amount of guidance on how to elucidate what the text said—its original meaning and significance for its original readers." But they have done little to move "from what the text said to what it says" today.[2]

Pastors bear responsibility too. Some, deceived by the apparent simplicity of application, give it less than their best effort. Gifted pastors, knowing Scripture and human nature, readily develop points from certain passages. But without a method, intelligence and instincts will not carry the difficult texts. Daily crises squeeze out study time and supplant the ministry of the word. Sometimes—for both pastors and professors—busyness masks intellectual laziness; sustained reflection on complex matters is harder work than attending meetings. Exegetical skills erode, but who notices, short-term, if we abbreviate the toil of interpretation?

When sermon preparation does begin, some decide in advance what the church needs to hear, then scan for a text suiting their purpose. Eager to develop *their* message, they pay scant attention to the text. If, on Friday, they find that the text doesn't "work," then so much the worse for the text. If the pastors' ideas remain broadly biblical, if they know their congregations, damage is reduced. Intuition allows even negligent teachers to deliver some valid messages. But what happens when intuition runs dry? Habitual negligence is toxic. Trendy and comfortable themes surface regularly, covered with a veneer of proof-texts. Sermons become repetitive, anthropocentric chats, catering to fallen cravings, ignoring the whole counsel of God.

The church deserves better. But to build afresh, we need better methods, resting on the right starting points or presuppositions. The bulk of this book will describe methods, but first we need to describe the three-faceted foundation upon which our grasp of the Bible's relevance rests. The three, assumed rather than explained in most of this monograph, are exegesis, covenant, and grace.

The Foundation for the Relevance of Scripture

Exegesis

Skillful application rests upon skillful interpretation. We cannot expect to discover the contemporary meaning of the Bible unless we

2 I. H. Marshall, "The Use of the New Testament in Christian Ethics," *Expository Times,* 105:5 (Feb. 1994): 136.

know its original meaning. Still, this book does not teach exegetical skills; it presupposes them. It does not perform exegesis or display the full process; it harvests the results. My decision to assume that readers possess exegetical arts and will use them to supplement my explanations does not mean I devalue those arts. By those arts, we move from the original meaning to the contemporary relevance of Scripture. If our quest for the relevance of Scripture leads us to leap to subjective questions—"What does this text say to me?"—we are sure to moralize, sure to find passages saying trendy or self-serving things. If time permitted, we would review all the steps in exegesis to ensure depth and variety in application. Instead, first, I pledge that I have exegeted the passages I cite, often in far more detail than appears on the page. Second, I urge readers who wish to refresh their knowledge of interpretation to turn to my companion volume on interpretation, *Getting the Message*.

Among the facets of exegesis, mastery of contexts is most foundational. "Context" has several meanings. Just now, we need to consider the redemptive-historical context of biblical events and writings. The redemptive-historical context locates word or event within the history of Israel, within the unfolding plan of revelation and salvation. When analyzing an event or a word from God's spokesmen, we should always ask how the original audience most likely understood it. This entails knowledge of their culture, their language, and their spiritual position. By "spiritual position" I mean, "Where did they stand in covenant history?"

Covenant

To know where people stand in covenant history, we must ascertain the history and texture of the era. What had God said or done recently? How had the people responded? How much revelation did the people have? Did they understand it? Appropriate it? Were they faithful or unfaithful, prosperous or oppressed? What alternative systems of faith and conduct tempted the people? Did they agree with their leaders or oppose them?

There are several ways to use the concept of covenant to classify people. The simplest (not to say least useful) is: (1) prefall; (2) fallen, unredeemed; (3) fallen, redeemed; (4) glorified. Or we can ask if a person lived or an event occurred under the covenant with Adam, Noah,

Abraham, Moses, David, or Christ. Of course, we can seek far more detail. For example, Elijah fits in the Davidic covenant, divided kingdom, northern kingdom, in the early (nonwriting) prophetic movement when Israel had, under Ahab, recently transitioned from false worship ostensibly dedicated to the true God and toward the worship of foreign deities. Pastors should know these things as eleven-year-olds know multiplication tables.

Valuable as it is to use the concept of covenant for historical location, its use for theological location is greater. Do the people in view stand inside or outside God's covenant of grace? If they are outside the covenant, the prime application is, "Repent and believe." If they are within, application begins with a reminder, "God loves you and called you into a relationship with him. His grace empowers you to follow him and motivates you to serve him."

People who are inside the covenant are reminded of the motives for obedience. At Sinai, before declaring the law, God says,

> You yourselves have seen what I did to Egypt, and how I carried you on eagles' wings and brought you to myself. Now if you obey me fully and keep my covenant, then out of all nations you will be my treasured possession . . . a kingdom of priests and a holy nation. . . . I am the LORD your God, who brought you out of Egypt, out of the land of slavery. You shall have no other gods before me. (Ex. 19:4–6; 20:2–3)

The apostles use similar language, declaring, "We love because he [God] first loved us" (1 John 4:19). Again, "The love of Christ constrains us . . . that those who live should no longer live for themselves but for him who died for them and was raised again" (2 Cor. 5:14–15, my translation). Thus God's grace both enables and impels us to live for him. Yet, there are ways to think about motivation that partially corrupt motives such as covenant and grace.

Grace

If we were to ask an ordinary group of Christians why they obey God, some answers might be: "Because he is God and we owe him obedience." "Because I love him." "Because sin leads to trouble." "Because I fear God's anger." "Because I want God to bless me." Each of these has the potential to turn in a noble or an ignoble direction. To see this clearly, we may label the motives for obedience as the ways of wisdom, trust, gratitude, merit, fear, and love.

The way of wisdom affirms that it is reasonable to obey God's law because he created all things and knows how they work. We expect God's commands to be effective, to bring us good.

The way of trust believes God loves us and would never mislead us. We behave as God directs, even when it may not make sense, because we trust him to make it work.

The way of gratitude judges that it is fitting to obey God without reserve because God first gave himself to us without reserve when he redeemed us. Because he has done so much for us, we should do much for him, from gratitude and from a sense of obligation to him.

Each of these motives is essentially valid, though each can have a selfish twist. In the first two, we may obey primarily for the benefits we expect to accrue; we may obey more for the gifts than for the giver. In the third, we may obey merely to discharge a duty. All three may share too much with the *way of merit,* where people obey God to compel his favor or avert his anger.

Some believe the *way of fear* is as flawed as the way of merit. As they see it, fear leads people to obey God solely to avert punishment. But in the Bible, fear is more than that. Those who doubt the value of fear rightly say that God often commands us to "fear not." They may also quote John's dictum, "There is no fear in love. But perfect love drives out fear, because fear has to do with punishment" (1 John 4:18). But other Scriptures commend the fear of God. Proverbs says the fear of the Lord is the beginning of knowledge (Prov. 1:7) and of wisdom (9:10). The Psalms often bless those who fear the Lord (e.g. Pss. 25:12–14; 33:18; 34:7–9; 112:1). In the New Testament, Jesus, Paul, the author of Hebrews, Peter, and John all command their hearers to fear God (Matt. 10:28; Luke 12:5; Rom. 11:20–21; Eph. 5:21; Heb. 4:1; 12:28; 1 Peter 2:17; Rev. 14:7). Amazingly, Hebrews 5:7 says Jesus' prayers were heard because of his "reverent fear."[3]

Classically, theologians resolve this riddle—Should we fear God

---

3 Curiously, the NIV translates all three texts in Hebrews without using the term "fear," although the Greek is clear enough, using *phobeomai* in 4:1, and *eulabeia* (reverent fear or awe) in 5:7 and 12:28.

or not?—by distinguishing servile fear from filial fear. The epitome of servile fear is a servant or slave who cowers before an angry master. Servile fear should be alien to genuine believers, since Jesus has freed us from all punishment.[4] Filial fear, however, is fear mixed with affection. Filial fear makes respectful children think twice before dishonoring their parents and makes students work harder for esteemed professors. Filial fear produces reverent obedience to God.[5]

The discussion of fear should also clarify the role of wisdom, trust, and gratitude as Christian motives. All four may take a selfish turn and pale next to the way of love. It is noblest to obey God for his sake alone, from love for him. As Bernard of Clairvaux said, we cajole the *unwilling* with promises and rewards, not the willing. Who offers men rewards for doing what they want to do? Do we pay hungry men to eat? So then, if we demand benefits to obey God, perhaps we love the benefits rather than God.[6] Yet, just as fear has a valid role, when covered by love, so wisdom, trust, and gratitude can be honorable motives for obedience if they are chiefly responses to his loving grace.

The way of merit is the one unredeemable motive for obedience. Take the men mentioned above, raised by fathers who never said, "I love you." These men hunger for praise from their fathers. They long to be so good or do such good that their fathers have to say, "I love you; I am proud of you." But perhaps their fathers cannot say those words. Perhaps their fathers are dead. Then no human can satisfy their hunger. Their remedy is in the gospel. It proclaims that their Father in heaven loves them, without conditions. When we alienated ourselves from him, he reconciled us to himself. He adopted us as his children, welcomed us into his family, and now proudly announces, "Here am I and the children God has given me" (Heb. 2:11–13).

To be motivated by grace is to serve God through a love evoked by his prior love. It is to give to God from the bounty he first gave us.

---

4 Of course, unbelievers would be better off if they had such a fear, rather than disdain for God. As Isa. 8 and Heb. 6, 10, and 12 show, those who falsely profess faith should fear God's wrath.

5 This motif is so strong in the Old Testament that fearing God can be virtually synonymous with obeying him (e.g., Deut. 5:29; 6:2; 10:12; Prov. 3:7; Isa. 8:12–15).

6 Bernard of Clairvaux, *On Loving God* (Kalamazoo, Mich.: Cistercian Brothers, 1973, 1995), 7.17.

His redemption liberated us from the power of sin. His justification cured the guilt and condemnation of sin. His reconciliation removed the estrangement of sin. His adoption solved the loneliness of sin.

I address the grace motivation for obedience here because it is essential to the proper use of all that follows. This is not a devotional book, yet I cannot submit a text on the relevance of Scripture without starting with grace, for grace is as essential to our sanctification as it is to our justification. Our disobedience condemns us, but without gospel motives, our "righteousness" will too. Salvation is by grace from first to last. We never outgrow our need for the gospel.

A PLAN FOR SHOWING THE RELEVANCE OF SCRIPTURE

The three principal elements in application are the text, the interpreter, and the audience. The interpreter is a mediator, taking the message of the text to the people (fig. 1, arrow 1; see chap. 4), but also taking the questions and real needs of the audience to the text (arrow 2, chaps. 5, 6, 12). The interpreter finds the meaning of the text by drawing on his or her interpretive skill (arrow 3; see Doriani, *Getting the Message*). But the text can operate effectively only when it exercises its authority over the interpreter, who heeds its message, whether it seems pleasant or not (arrow 4, chap. 3). The interpreter brings the message to the audience most effectively when he or she listens to the questions of the audience and distinguishes their real needs from their felt needs (arrow

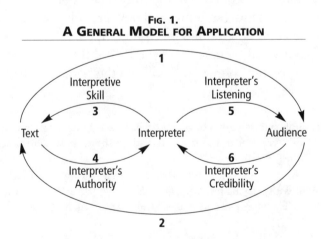

FIG. 1.
A GENERAL MODEL FOR APPLICATION

5, chaps. 3, 12). Finally, the audience profits most from its teachers when their character grants them spiritual credibility (arrow 6, chap. 3).

Chapters 1 and 2 establish certain theoretical foundations for applying Scripture. Chapter 3 explores the character traits and skills that enable interpreters to hear the Bible, understand the needs of audiences, and receive a good hearing. Chapter 4 explains the seven ways biblical texts generate applications: through moral rules, ethical ideals, doctrinal statements, redemptive acts in narratives, exemplary acts in narratives, symbols and songs and prayers. Chapters 5 and 6 show that sound application will answer the four classes of ethical questions people ask: (1) What should I do? (2) What should I be? (3) Where should we go? and (4) How can I discern right from wrong in a society with competing visions of morality?

Chapters 7–11 present methods for applying narratives, doctrinal passages, and ethical passages, and also establish theoretical foundations for the proposed methods. Those who want to pluck the how-to chapters out of this book will turn to chapters 7 (narrative), 9 (doctrine), 10 (ethics), and 12 (presenting Christ). If exegesis, grace, and covenant are the foundations of this monograph, the presentation of Christ is its capstone. In discussing that subject we will harvest highlights from preceding chapters and apply them to contemporary discussions about the best ways of proclaiming Scripture, to lead people to Christ.

To make the most of the how-to chapters, readers simply must know how to interpret the Bible, beginning with context. Interpretation most often goes awry when teachers wrench biblical teachings out of context to serve perceived needs. Of course, sermons ordinarily begin with illustrations that suggest the link between Scripture's world and ours, and rightly so. Pastors must show how Scripture addresses the fallenness and neediness of humankind. But even if a sermon begins by showing the relevance of its text, teachers must first have studied the text, beginning with its context. Indeed, if we master the several facets of context, we will avoid an array of errors and experience a cascade of interpretive virtues.

The term "context" has two distinct senses, which I call the literary and historical context.[7] The literary context, or "co-text," is the

---

7 Daniel M. Doriani, *Getting the Message* (Phillipsburg, N.J.: Presbyterian and Reformed, 1996), 29–59.

set of words, sentences, paragraphs, or chapters that precede and follow a text. Investigation of literary context examines the way a passage fits within the purposes of an entire book, how it plays off prior and ensuing sections, and how it amplifies or modifies the book's motifs. It tells us why a passage is here and nowhere else.

The historical context is the setting of a passage in culture, space, and time. The question "Where are we?" encompasses customs, languages, social structures, family patterns, economy, geography, climate, and architecture. It grounds biblical events and teachings in their time and place, showing how the Bible fits into and alters its world. It reminds us that there is no monolithic "biblical culture," for the land and people of Israel changed through history. For example, the population of Palestine increased greatly between Abraham's first sojourn and Joshua's conquest over five hundred years later. Similarly, Jerusalem was an isolated citadel in David's day, but a city with extensive Greco-Roman influences in Jesus' time.

Cultures are complex. It is mistaken, for example, to think that the scribes, Pharisees, priests, and Herodians constitute a monolithic group of Jewish leaders who were opposed to Jesus. There were rifts between groups and fissures within groups. Likewise, to understand 1 Corinthians, we must know the various parties within the church. Books like Numbers, Jeremiah, Galatians, and Corinthians also invite inquiry into the complex relationships between authors and their readers.

Further, God deals with his people through covenants that built upon one another. After the fall, God's promise to redeem humankind developed through God's call of Abraham and the subsequent growth of the Patriarch's clan in Canaan and Egypt. After numerical growth there, God led his people out of Egypt under Moses and constituted them a nation. God intended that Israel become his holy, treasured people—a light to the world. After Israel proved disloyal during the theocracy, God inaugurated a covenant with David: he and his progeny would rule in perpetuity through David's greater Son. But Israel continued to rebel against God. People worshiped idols, kings ruled unjustly, and priests stood by silently. So God chastised them, letting Israel divide into a northern and a southern kingdom. They weakened and sank into further rebellion. Then God punished the north, dissolving it through an Assyrian invasion, and disciplined the south through its exile in Babylon. Later, God restored Israel in part. Under the leadership of Nehemiah and Ezra, the people sampled the blessings of a promised new covenant.

Yet when John and Jesus began their ministries, the nation had barely tasted the restoration promised by the prophets. The Jews lived within the structures of the Mosaic covenant during Jesus' ministry, but when Jesus arrived, the new covenant—and the kingdom of God—began to break into this world. The death and resurrection of Jesus, together with Pentecost, constitute a cluster of events that establish a new covenant, a new phase in the life of faith. After them, every revelatory event and word falls within the particular redemptive-historical situation that prevails until the return of Christ.

1
The Nature of Application

Long ago, there was a kingdom called Bible-land. It was a fair country, well populated by kind and industrious people, but a river cut a ragged path through its entire length, dividing the country into two provinces. In some places the river was placid, so that the people crossed it freely and gained much from their conversation and trade. But elsewhere it raged with treacherous currents that carried away even the strongest swimmers and stoutest bridges. In some regions the swirling torrents carved canyons too broad, it seemed, for any span.

In these regions, though the separated people of Bible-land still honored each other, they found it difficult to trade, whether in objects or in wisdom. They did not become poor, precisely, but they were poorer, they knew, than their fellow citizens in places where the river was shallow and safe. Without the exchange of goods or ideas, they developed increasingly different ways of farming and manufacture, until as years passed, they could scarcely comprehend each other's ways on occasions when they did meet. Frustrated, some doubted that they should even attempt to cross the river. But wiser people trusted the reports of fine trade in other places, and they resolved to build bridges across even the broadest, ugliest ditches and deepest waters.[1]

This book is for those who want to cross a river representing barriers to the communication of God's word wrought by the passing of

---

1 From Gotthold Lessing, "On the Proof of the Spirit and of Power," in *Lessing's Theological Writings,* trans. and ed. Henry Chadwick (Stanford, Calif.: Stanford University Press, 1957), 55.

time and changes in cultures and language. In the language of the allegory, this book is more for builders than for architects, for communicators more than theorists. There will be theory in this book, but it will focus on texts.[2] But first things first. Let's begin with the God-centered nature of biblical application.

TO KNOW GOD AND CONFORM OURSELVES TO HIM

A God-centered approach to the relevance of Scripture has two foci: knowing the God who redeems and conforming ourselves to him. Jeremiah wrote,

> This is what the LORD says:
> "Let not the wise man boast of his wisdom
>   or the strong man boast of his strength
>   or the rich man boast of his riches,
> but let him who boasts boast about this:
>   that he understands and knows me,
> that I am the LORD, who exercises kindness,
>   justice and righteousness on earth,
>   for in these I delight,"
>   declares the LORD. (Jer. 9:23–24)

Jesus says, "Now this is eternal life: that they may know you, the only true God, and Jesus Christ, whom you have sent" (John 17:3). Paul says, "I want to know Christ" (Phil. 3:10). The goal is to know God, love him (Deut. 6:5; Matt. 22:37), believe in him (John 20:31), walk faithfully with him (Mic. 6:8), and increase in likeness to him.[3] The "old self . . . is being renewed in knowledge in the image of its Creator" (Col. 3:9–10). The goal of our redemption is to make us more and more like God, and ever more like Christ, who is the perfect image of God (Rom. 8:29; 2 Cor. 3:18; Eph. 4:22–24; Col. 3:9–10).[4]

Perhaps this seems obvious. Yet many Christians act as if there were

---

2 Strong theoretical texts include Roger Lundin, *Disciplining Hermeneutics* (Grand Rapids: Eerdmans, 1997); and Kevin Vanhoozer, *Is There a Meaning in This Text?* (Grand Rapids: Zondervan, 1998).

3 J. I. Packer, *Knowing God* (Downers Grove, Ill.: InterVarsity, 1973), 29–33.

4 Anthony Hoekema, *Created in God's Image* (Grand Rapids: Eerdmans, 1986), 28.

another center of application. For some it is law and obedience. But we must remember that the center of the law is God himself. "Love God," says the first command. "Love others as God loves," says the second. Even when we fail to obey, the law leads us to him, as we flee to Christ for mercy.

Others concentrate on health, happiness, maturity, or a meaningful life. But we know the futility of dwelling upon health, pleasure, or earth-bound significance. Whoever lives for physical pleasure will eventually agree with Marie Antoinette, "Nothing tastes." Living for health and existence becomes a tragedy; after a long slow decline, every hero dies at the end of his story. Living for meaning and history reads like theater of the absurd, tales full of sound and fury, signifying nothing.

We lose sight of the center of application when we promise happiness and maturity to the lost. Happiness and maturity are common *results* of life with God, but we dare not confuse results with the essence. While believers should expect to enjoy God's blessings and to find release from the self-entrapping nature of sin, the Prince of Peace also promises opposition and tribulation. He casts fire on the earth (Luke 2:34; 12:4–12, 49–53). True disciples do not seek the life of ease that pagans run after. In Jesus' day, pagans chased food, drink, clothing, and long life (Matt. 6:25–32). Today, pagans also pursue what is comfortable, popular, profitable, peaceful, and therapeutic. Jesus tells both, "Seek first the kingdom and its righteousness, and all these things will be added to you" (v. 33, my translation).

So Bible application promotes a relationship with God and conformity to him. We honor the law because we exalt God, who gave it and reveals himself in it. We honor virtue because virtue is conformity to God's character (not simply because no one can take it from us). This double goal of knowing God and conforming to him pervades Scripture, from Eden and Sinai to the teaching of Jesus and Paul. When God spoke to Adam and walked with him in the garden before the fall, Adam and Eve needed only to retain their conformity to God's character, for God created them in his image and likeness, holy, righteous, rulers of the world.[5] But the fall bespeaks Adam's failure to know God enough to trust him.

5 Hoekema, *God's Image,* 11–15, 28–31, 79–83; John Laidlaw, *The Biblical Doctrine of Man* (Edinburgh: T. & T. Clark, 1895), 182–95; G. C. Berkouwer, *Man: The Image*

At Sinai, God established a covenant with the newborn nation of Israel. The covenant begins with Israel's knowledge of her relationship with God: "I am the LORD your God, who brought you out of Egypt, out of the land of slavery" (Ex. 20:2). The first commands cement their relationship, one marked by love and honor. "You shall have no other gods before me" means Israel owes God exclusive loyalty. Any breach of that loyalty is "in his face," to use today's argot.[6] "You shall make no idols" means we must not fashion God in images of our choosing. God made one image of himself—humankind. Now he forbids that we make another. "You shall not misuse the name of the LORD your God" means, among other things, that we should never idly claim to worship God or to belong to him.

The later commands instruct the faithful to conform themselves to God's person and pattern of activity. This is clearest in the sixth through tenth commands.

- God says, "You shall not murder" for he is the God who gives life, physical and spiritual.
- He says, "You shall not commit adultery," for he is faithful to his people.
- He commands, "You shall not steal," for he is a giving God, sending sun, rain, and the fecundity of the earth to all.
- God commands, "You shall not give false testimony," for he is truth and his word is truth.
- God says, "You shall not covet," for he is generous, delighting to give gifts to his children.

Even the fourth and fifth commands require that our ways harmonize with his. We labor six days, then rest, because God labored six days and rested. We honor father and mother because God bestowed dignity and honor on humans, especially those who exercise authority for him.

---

of God, trans. Dirk W. Jellema (Grand Rapids: Eerdmans, 1962), 88ff., 100. Berkouwer denies that dominion is part of the image, pp. 70–72.

6 See, e.g., S. R. Driver, *The Book of Exodus,* rev. ed. (Cambridge: Cambridge University Press, 1929), 193; Godfrey Ashby, *Go Out and Meet God* (Grand Rapids: Eerdmans, 1998), 88; John I. Durham, *Exodus* (Waco: Word, 1987), 276, 284.

When Jesus instructed his disciples in the Sermon on the Mount, he, like the Father at Sinai, required his followers to conform themselves to him.[7] This is clearest in the Beatitudes, where Jesus blesses traits that the Gospels later attribute to him.

- Jesus blesses those who mourn. He mourned over Israel, a nation of sheep without a shepherd, a nation that would not let him gather her children under his wings (Matt. 9:36; 23:37).
- Jesus blesses the meek *(praüs);* he says, "I am meek *[praüs]* and humble," for he lays an easy yoke on his people (Matt. 11:28–30).
- He blesses those who hunger and thirst for righteousness. He received baptism, not from need, but to fulfill all righteousness (Matt. 3:15). He fulfilled the Law and the Prophets, personally and in his disciples, that their righteousness might exceed the scribes' and Pharisees' (5:17–20).
- Jesus blesses the merciful. His mercy and compassion (Matt. 14:14; 15:22, 32; 17:15; 20:30–31, 34; Mark 5:19; Luke 7:13; 17:13) moved him to aid the needy.
- He blesses the pure in heart. He was so pure his enemies could find no plausible charge to bring against him at his trial (Matt. 26:59–60), so pure he dared invite his foes to convict him of sin (John 8:46).[8]
- Jesus blesses peacemakers. He healed people and sent them off in peace (Mark 5:34; Luke 7:50). He bestowed peace on his disciples (John 14:27; 16:33; Luke 24:36) and authorized his disciples to bestow peace on Israel (Matt. 10:13), though not at any price (10:34).
- Jesus blesses the persecuted. He was persecuted unto death, despite his innocence.

Jesus only declined to ascribe one beatitude to himself, "Blessed are the poor in spirit." But if (as most interpreters believe) poverty of

7 See W. D. Davies and Dale Allison, *The Gospel according to Saint Matthew,* 3 vols. (Edinburgh: T. & T. Clark, 1988), 1:467; W. D. Davies, *The Setting of the Sermon on the Mount* (Cambridge: Cambridge University Press, 1964), 95–96.
8 At his trial the witnesses summoned to accuse Jesus were so unconvincing that the high priest finally had to ask him to incriminate himself (Matt. 26:57–66).

spirit is awareness of one's spiritual neediness, we see why.[9] For however far we progress toward Jesus, a gap remains between Creator and creature, between Redeemer and redeemed. Yet Jesus bridges that gulf by loving and identifying with the poor in spirit, by teaching, healing, and dining with them—with us.

Paul's letters propound the same ideal of knowledge of God and conforming to him. The Ephesians know the Son of God and become mature by attaining "the fullness of Christ" (Eph. 4:13). They have "come to know Christ"; thus they put on the new self, "created to be like God in true righteousness and holiness" (4:20–24). They are now "imitators of God," loving one another and forgiving one another as Christ did (4:32–5:2). Paul's goal is "to know Christ and the power of his resurrection and the fellowship of sharing in his sufferings, becoming like him in his death" (Phil. 3:10). Christians must follow Jesus' example and "do nothing out of selfish ambition . . . but in humility consider others better than yourselves"; they must watch out for others' interests, because that is how Christ lived among us (2:1–8). Our original design shall be our final destiny, for we shall be conformed to the likeness of the Son (Rom. 8:29; see also Phil. 3:21; 1 John 3:2). We have begun to progress in this, for we are being transformed into the Lord's likeness (2 Cor. 3:18). The whole of Scripture, then, focuses on a relationship with God and conformity to his character.

The process of becoming more Godlike begins and ends with his grace. By grace God formed Israel to receive the Messiah, who took flesh and offered himself to atone for sin. By grace Jesus came to seek and save the lost (Luke 19:10). By grace the apostles witnessed, proclaimed, and recorded his story. By grace God completed the good work he began in us (Phil. 1:6). Whatever we offer God is a response to his mercies (Rom. 12:1). It is all too easy for believers to lose sight of the grace of God in our sanctification. We return to the spirit of the older brother, who bragged and complained, "All these years I am slaving for you" (Luke 15:29, my translation). Like Peter, we ask, "We have left everything to follow you. What then will there be for us?" (Matt. 19:27). But bitterness and alienation corrupt any service that

9 Robert A. Guelich, *The Sermon on the Mount* (Waco: Word, 1982), 97–98; John Stott, *The Sermon on the Mount* (Downers Grove, Ill.: InterVarsity, 1987), 31–32, 38–39.

speaks with pride about years of *slavery* for God. And any time we ask, "What will we get for our service?" we run the risk of elevating the gift above the giver. If nothing else, the Pharisees show how dangerous "religion" and good works can be.

As we explore theories and methods for application, we must not lose sight of the main thing. Whatever else we say, a relationship with God is central. Still, we need theory, beginning with an understanding of what application is. We will proceed dialectically, moving from traditional definitions and views to my own position.

THEORIES OF INTERPRETATION AND APPLICATION

1. The Traditional View: First Exegesis, Then Application

The traditional view sees the application of the Bible as the last phase of biblical interpretation. In this view *interpretation* is the process of seeking and re-presenting the complete shareable meaning that authors intend to transmit, especially in difficult cases.[10] In interpretation we first understand a text or an utterance, then elucidate it, whether in words like or unlike the original, to convey its meaning.[11] In this view parts of Scripture are clear, but to navigate the world of the biblical history and poetry we also need specialized knowledge, much as ordinary citizens do when navigating the worlds of tort law or cricket. *Hermeneutics* is the theory behind interpretation. It provides strategies for a partial transcendence of our times and a reentry into the world of Scripture. One step removed from the text, it considers how interpretation takes place and establishes principles for proper exegesis and application.[12]

The traditional view says interpretation has two aspects (fig. 2). *Exegesis* is the exposition of Scripture. It discovers the meaning of a

---

10 The concept of "shareable" meaning excludes things neither print nor speech can fully transmit—the taste of apricots, the vista from a mountaintop, or the wonder of a miracle. See D. P. Fuller, "History of Interpretation," in *International Standard Bible Encyclopedia,* ed. Geoffrey W. Bromiley (Grand Rapids: Eerdmans, 1979–88), 2:863.

11 From Robert Morgan, *Biblical Interpretation* (New York: Oxford University Press, 1988), 1–2.

12 Gerhard Maier, *Biblical Hermeneutics,* trans. Robert Yarbrough (Wheaton, Ill.: Crossway, 1994), 15–20.

FIG. 2.
EXEGESIS PRECEDING APPLICATION

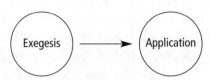

text—the author's intention—in its original setting.[13] *Application* rests upon exegesis. If exegesis determines what a text meant, application explores what it means. It articulates the *significance,* the implications, the relevance of biblical truth.[14] It describes the intended *effects* of the truth. If exegesis determines the "what" of a passage, application explores the "so what." If exegesis describes, application prescribes.

Krister Stendahl epitomized this view when he said, "When the biblical theologian becomes primarily concerned with the present meaning, he implicitly or explicitly loses his enthusiasm . . . for the descriptive task." Biblical theology can advance only when interpreters retain a sense of "the distance and the strangeness of biblical thought," and accept, he says, "that our only concern is to find out what these words meant" by using methods agreeable to "believer and agnostic alike." Only when interpreters refrain from mingling the two phases can "the Bible . . . exert the maximum of influence."[15] Conservatives will favor the position that we must determine the original meaning before shifting to contemporary uses, yet another view deserves a hearing.

13 An excellent defense of authorial competence and the possibility of communication is Vanhoozer, *Is There a Meaning in This Text?* Note that the critics' act of *writing* that "reliable communication through writing is impossible" is nearly self-contradictory. Even those who deny interest in authorial intent expect *their* readers to take interest in *their* intentions. All writing assumes that at least modestly effective communication is achievable.

14 I use "relevance" almost interchangeably with application and simply mean the significance or consequences of biblical truth. My usage is unconnected to the Church Growth Movement, whose legitimate goal of reaching seekers has bred both success and excess.

15 Krister Stendahl, "Biblical Theology, Contemporary," in *Interpreter's Dictionary of the Bible,* ed. George A. Buttrick et al. (Nashville and New York: Abingdon, 1962), 1:419–22.

2. A Counterproposal: The Meaning Is the Application

A counterview says that the traditional view of interpretation and application does justice neither to Scripture nor to the practice of its best interpreters. Of course, our concept and theory should describe, not rule out, what skilled teachers actually do when they apply Scripture.[16] The second view observes that Stendahl's sharp disjunction between interpretation and application breaks down in practice. For one thing, teachers begin to detect relevance before they finish interpretation. Interpretation and application coalesce and propel each other forward. When teachers note possible applications, they double their exegetical work as they seek to verify them. Second, Scripture itself links interpretation and relevance. On several occasions, Jesus rebukes Jewish leaders for what appears to be a failure to *apply* Scripture, but he actually chides them for failing to read (Matt. 12:1–8), to know (Matt. 22:23–33), or to understand it (Luke 24:44–47).[17]

John Frame proposes erasing the distinction between meaning and application altogether (fig. 3). He says, "The meaning of Scripture is its application."[18] That is, we understand Scripture only when we know how to use it. Try, for example, to separate the meaning from the application of the eighth commandment, "Thou shalt not steal." Suppose someone reproduces copyrighted materials, cheats on his taxes, and pads his expense account, yet claims he obeys the law, since he never "took" anything from anyone. We would not say that he failed to apply the command, but that he did not really *understand* it.[19] Indeed, Frame holds that the separation of meaning and application perverts the very nature of theology, since theology does not seek to discover abstract truth in itself. Theology is "the application of the Word of God by

16 Anthony Thiselton, *The Two Horizons* (Grand Rapids: Eerdmans, 1980), 357–58, 372. Cf. Ludwig Wittgenstein, *Blue Book,* 2d ed. (Oxford: Blackwell, 1960), 17–19; idem, *Philosophical Investigations,* trans. G. E. M. Anscombe (New York: Macmillan, 1973), 11, 14, 23.

17 Notice the implicit rebukes in John 5:36–40; 7:37–42; 10:24–39. Similarly, in Matt. 2 the scribes knew where the Christ was born from prophecy and the Magi, yet failed to go to worship him.

18 John Frame, *The Doctrine of the Knowledge of God* (Phillipsburg, N.J.: Presbyterian and Reformed, 1987), 67, 97.

19 Ibid., 82–83.

Fig. 3.
EXEGESIS EQUAL TO APPLICATION

persons to all areas of life" to meet spiritual needs and to promote godliness and spiritual health.[20]

Let's imagine how a teacher might expound Matthew 5:22: "Anyone who says to his brother, 'Raca,' is answerable to the Sanhedrin.
But anyone who says, 'You fool!' will be in danger of the fires of hell."
Naturally, the teacher is obligated to explain what "Raca" and "fool"
mean:

> The term "Raca" expresses contempt for the head. It means
> something like "Stupid idiot! Dummy!" "Fool" shows con-
> tempt for the character. It means, "You scoundrel." "Raca"
> means "You have no brains." "Fool" means, "You have no
> heart." Together, they imply, "You're worthless, good for noth-
> ing." Even Christian parents sometimes talk this way.
>
> When someone cuts us off in traffic and we mutter, "Idiot!"
> or when someone fails us and we whisper, "Worthless!" Jesus
> calls it murder. This is why; if we call someone a waste, a jerk,
> an imbecile, we pass judgment that he does not deserve to live.
>
> By this standard most of us are murderers—and the car-
> nage may not remain internal. Murder in the heart permits
> murderous actions such as abortion, euthanasia, and neglect of
> the poor. People take the lives of the unborn and refuse to help
> the needy because they make a judgment: "These lives have
> no value. The costs outweigh the benefits. They might as well
> be dead." Jesus says that such thoughts, even without action,
> make us liable to judgment.

Let me ask two questions: First, precisely where did exegesis end
and application begin in this explanation? Second, if someone said,

---

20 Ibid., 81–84.

"Okay, I won't call anyone 'Raca' or 'fool,' but I see no problem with 'good for nothing' or 'jerk,' " would we say that he had understood Jesus?

3. A Synthesis: A Permeable Barrier between Meaning and Application

The traditional view, described by Stendahl, best reflects work with difficult texts, where problems of language, culture, or other gaps in knowledge bewilder us. Stendahl inhibits subjective readers who rush to relevance before exegesis is complete. Surely, the better we understand a text in its original setting, the more accurately we see its current significance.[21] Frame, more mindful of straightforward texts such as laws, notes that the ability to paraphrase Scripture is not identical to knowing it. He rightly says that no one understands Scripture unless he can apply it in new situations.

We can learn from both Stendahl the exegete and Frame the theologian and ethicist. Stendahl rightly says sound application cannot occur without correct exegesis; there is a line between exegesis and relevance. Yet my study of both the biblical data and the way application actually occurs indicates, as Frame sees, that the line is thin and permeable (fig. 4). In the Bible's conceptual world, failure to apply usually includes a failure to understand *fully*. That includes a failure to respond to God, who represents himself in Scripture. If we cannot understand or heed *it,* we do not understand or heed *him*.

Frame's view does more justice to the way teachers actually operate. We do not exclude all thoughts of relevance until we complete our exegesis. While we interpret Scripture, Scripture interprets us. We scrutinize the text, and the text scrutinizes us, exposing our beliefs, experiences, and secrets. We might say Scripture applies itself to us. If we achieve sufficient awareness of this process, it will generate applications almost spontaneously, for the applications we sense usually touch matters that are common to humanity. We see our world afresh through the lens of Scripture, and verbalize our vision.[22] As we learn

21 Moisés Silva, *Explorations in Exegetical Method* (Grand Rapids: Baker, 1996), 197–99.
22 Lesslie Newbigin, *The Gospel in a Pluralist Society* (Grand Rapids: Eerdmans, 1990), 97–98.

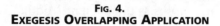

FIG. 4.
EXEGESIS OVERLAPPING APPLICATION

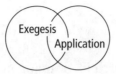

more of God through Scripture, we are impelled to declare his name, speaking from compulsion as much as calculation.

Fuzzy Boundaries around Application

Thus it is ill advised to draw a sharp line between exegesis and relevance, for the boundary between them is fuzzy and permeable. When C. S. Lewis writes that there is no contradiction in being a master of arts and a fool, people with postgraduate degrees catch their breath. Substituting their own highest degree, they understand and apply almost simultaneously.[23] Again, when a seminary professor tells his students, "Many a doctrinal deviation, many a heresy, began with an ill-advised quest for originality in a thesis," wise students ask, "Am I guilty of such a foolish quest?" One can hardly comprehend the words without beginning to apply them.

What begins as an exegetical remark may shade into relevance more gradually. Once, in preparing a sermon on Luke 14, I came to Jesus' words, "Take up your cross and follow me." I intended to peel away the layers of church talk that keep audiences from hearing "the cross" as Jesus' first audience did. But in probing ways to let the concept register today, I slipped into relevance:

> In Jesus' day, people knew what he meant when he said, "Take up your cross and follow me." Sometimes I wonder if we do. In America our lives are so comfortable that, by world standards, even the humble live in spacious homes, wear fine clothes, relax in soft furniture, and pray in splendid church buildings. Some days, the greatest struggle for those who live in the suburbs is heavy traffic or lower back pain. Real suf-

---

23   C. S. Lewis, *Mere Christianity* (New York: Macmillan, 1956), ix–x.

fering is as far from us as the ancient Middle East is from the modern West.

It is not wicked to live in suburbs and enjoy human comforts. But we must know the way our affluence influences us. We talk about suffering for Christ in ritualized ways, but when pastors drive to church in gleaming new cars, dress in impeccable suits, and speak from mahogany pulpits, the language of sacrifice can hardly register. Instead our language suggests how far we are from taking suffering seriously. For example, when people discuss their choice of a church or why they like their church, I hear lines like this:

- I love the preaching and teaching ministry.
- The people are so friendly.
- I love the music program; the choir is wonderful!
- I wanted a church with a strong ministry for youth, children, singles, etc.[24]

These sentiments are not evil; we *should* celebrate the strengths of our churches. Yet something is wrong if we choose a church chiefly for the programs and benefits it offers. Then the consumerist mentality is governing even decisions about our place of worship and service. I long to hear people say—not boastfully but candidly—"We joined this church because we believed they *needed* us. We joined because we saw a chance to pour ourselves out for the sake of the ministry here."[25]

There are no imperatives here, but as I scraped off the frozen phrases that keep people from hearing about "the cross" as Jesus' countrymen did, I passed the boundary into relevance.

A sermon my pastor recently preached on work had a similar structure. After an overview of the fundamentals—God works, requires

24 On the church's conformity to the culture's prevailing interest in consumption and entertainment, selfism and hedonism, see David Wells, *Losing Our Virtue* (Grand Rapids: Eerdmans, 1998), chaps. 2–4; Kenneth A. Myers, *All God's Children and Blue Suede Shoes* (Wheaton, Ill.: Crossway, 1989), chaps. 1, 9; D. A. Carson, *The Gagging of God* (Grand Rapids: Zondervan, 1996) 463–70.

25 Daniel M. Doriani, "Free but Costly: The Gospel in Luke," *Presbyterion,* 23 (Fall 1997): 76.

work, and created humankind to find fulfillment in work—he addressed several misunderstandings. For example, he urged us not to confuse kingdom work, such as evangelism, with work in our vocational calling. He elaborated:

> A student's work is studying, yet I have known students who picked the night before a test to walk down the hall in the dorm to engage Paul Pagan in a conversation rather than studying. Then, when our student does poorly on his test, he excuses himself by saying, "But I was up until two o'clock sharing the gospel with poor lost Paul."
>
> A stay-at-home wife and mother's work is running her household and managing her family, yet I have known mothers who prefer church work to housework. Then when things are falling apart at home and the children are running wild, she excuses the disaster by saying, "Know ye not that I must be about my Father's business?"
>
> I have known men who, rather than doing their job well, spend too much time discussing Christianity in a fellow employee's office. When the boss reprimands them for work not being done, the Christian thinks he is being persecuted for Christ's sake. But he is being reprimanded for doing poor work—work done in the name of Christ at that.[26]

Here too the shift from explication to application is gradual. God's view of work is described, then defective views of work, and finally the difference.

But sometimes Stendahl seems more apt than Frame, so that it is helpful to distinguish the *meaning,* the *significance,* and the *effects* of a text.[27] Sometimes the interpreter understands the meaning of a text but stumbles over its current significance—its application or relevance. Mosaic laws come to mind. We understand that someone who steals and resells an animal owes quintuple restitution for an ox and quadruple for a sheep. We comprehend the prohibition against sow-

---

26 Wilson Benton, August 30, 1998.
27 The following depends loosely on Vanhoozer, *Is There a Meaning in This Text?* 259–63, 367ff.

ing fields with two kinds of seed or charging interest on loans made to needy Israelites. But we wonder what they signify today.

Beyond the potential gap between meaning and significance, there is the question of what effects texts and ideas achieve in those who encounter them. Frame would say that a person who genuinely understands the truth, will think and act accordingly. If we truly understand that stealing, boasting, gossip, and lust are self-destructive and offend the almighty judge and king, we will renounce and discontinue them. But reexamine the sin list and see the problem. We may successfully resolve to stop stealing. But we often fall into boasting and gossip unawares, only afterwards realizing what we have done. And lust, like envy and irrational fearfulness, is a sin few want to commit. Think of Paul's words, "I have the desire to do what is good, but I cannot carry it out" (Rom. 7:18b).

Bad habits also illustrate the gap between meaning, significance, and effects. Imagine a conversation between a parent and a young person who habitually drops her towel on the floor after showering:

PARENT: Do you understand that we want you to hang up your towel after showers?

CHILD: Yes, I understand.

PARENT: Do you understand that it is more work for you to drop a towel, then bend over and pick it up, than it is for you to hang it up right away?

CHILD: Yes, I understand.

PARENT: But if you truly understood, you would hang it up.

CHILD: Dad, I truly understand. It's just a bad habit. Maybe it started when Mom picked up behind me when I was a kid. Maybe I'm just too rushed in the morning. I'll try to remember.

Wise parents understand that it is useless to redouble their efforts to explain the point with comments on kinetic economies or aesthetic theory as applied to bathroom care. (Though I "know" this, I sometimes do it anyway!) The child is right. We can "truly understand" yet forget or succumb to old habits. Indeed, we all suffer from compulsions, all become paralyzed by fears, so we cannot do what is right.

So then, understanding and application are separable but overlapping. There is a boundary, even if blurry. Sometimes biblical truth and its significance are so clear that conscious efforts to apply an idea are superfluous. Yet the very existence of this book implies that we can grasp the meaning of a narrative, a doctrine, or a command without seeing its contemporary significance. We need insight, but we can also profit from methods for finding the full relevance of narratives, doctrines, and laws.

Thus hermeneutics theorist Hans-Georg Gadamer says that we do not wholly understand a text unless we can apply it, since "understanding always includes application."[28] That is, a judge does not understand law and precedent if she cannot apply them to new cases, but a homeowner does understand a guide to household repairs if he uses it to fix things. Gadamer rightly says that if we truly understand, we apply. This nexus of understanding and application may occur either through immediate insight or through the painstaking use of methods.

IS A THEORY OF INTERPRETATION AND APPLICATION NECESSARY?

Many gifted preachers hardly think about theory. They operate instinctively. Perhaps, then, we need no theory of application. Perhaps we should tell the truth and let God do the rest. Or should we advance strategies for determining the significance of our exegesis? Let us consider three possibilities.

View 1. Application Is Subjective, Expressing Our Spirituality

The first view is that application is subjective and personal. Teachers apply Scripture through meditation not methods. As they probe Scripture, a point about fear or self-control strikes them. They think, "Yes, I need to challenge my fears," or "I need to control my desires." They apply the passage to themselves, unaware of the process. Later they ask, "Am I the only one facing this, or is it universal?" As one pastor put it, "In all my sermons, I preach to myself first; the congregation overhears."[29] If a preacher also keeps his congregation in mind as he prepares his sermon, what he knows about them "will suggest

28 Hans-Georg Gadamer, *Truth and Method,* 2d ed. (New York: Continuum, 1989), 307–11.

29 The quotations come from interviews with pastors from 1995 to 1998.

unexpected ideas and associations."[30] True application is the result of a "direct encounter between man and God."[31] God's grace, not a human plan, lets proclamation produce godliness.

Followed rigorously, this view makes theory superfluous. If we hear Scripture, we hear God and will know what to say. Techniques undercut spirituality. A book on the relevance of Scripture is as misguided as a mathematical formula for regaining balance on a bicycle. Application is better caught than taught. Novices learn by watching fearless preachers speak from the heart. Eventually, they will do the same.

This approach rightly gives prominence to the Master's voice in Bible interpretation. Too much technique can crowd God out of the study. Devotion to method can nullify delight in God and his word. Surely teachers need not take eight steps before they hear his voice. But this approach forgets that uncontrolled meditation has few safeguards. Those who meditate hear many voices, not all of them divine. Recent readings and events weigh heavily. Worse, our hearts deceive us. Sinful desires and petty grudges contaminate our meditations. We are too blind to our ego, too ignorant of others' needs, too prone to legalism, too dedicated to our own agendas to justify trusting our subjective impulses. The prowling mind can find evidence in almost every passage that what it wants, God ordains.

View 2. Application Is Problematic, Encouraging Legalism

A second view opposes methods of application on the grounds that talk of sanctification and morality threatens the gospel of justification by grace alone. Even messages on spontaneous, self-forgetful love of neighbor are "mostly hot air" because it cannot actually "be *produced* by us in any way."[32] Exhortations obscure the message of justification that we are simultaneously just and sinners. They make it too easy for the old nature to deny its death.[33] If sanctification is "the art

---

30 Karl Barth, *Prayer and Preaching* (London: SCM, 1964), 107.

31 Ibid., 66, 108–9.

32 Gerhard Forde, "The Lutheran View," in *Christian Spirituality: Five Views of Sanctification,* ed. Donald L. Alexander (Downers Grove, Ill.: InterVarsity, 1988), 14–16.

33 Ibid., 14–15, 23ff.

of getting used to justification," then teachers can speak of progress in grace, but not in character or obedience.[34]

According to this view, talk of growth and obedience naturally descends into works-righteousness or legalism.[35] If someone speaks seriously of Sabbath observance, Puritanism is thought to be knocking at the door. To dwell on the requirements of the law is to "support the . . . conscription of Christian conscience to some new drill-master." To define rules and set priorities (can one lie to save a life?) is to enter the Pharisees' world and to betray Christian freedom for a code.[36]

This view rightly fingers the danger of legalistic uses of Scripture. It knows that application must lead to a relationship with God, not with a legal code. It knows that eloquent talk can persuade people to change their behavior, but no human can change the heart. But it suffers from an unnecessarily negative view of the law and forgets that it takes work to apply biblical principles to new issues, such as technology-driven change or life in blended families. Further, few speakers truly leave application to God. If they spurn preparation, they will probably fall back on clichés and shirk the difficult questions.

View 3. Application Is a Gift and an Art, yet It Encourages Theory

Application is certainly a divine gift, but not all divine gifts are unmediated. We pray, "Give us this day our daily bread," yet we are also commanded to work for it (Matt. 6:11; Prov. 6:6–11; 28:19; 2 Thess. 3:6–12). Similarly, we both pray for wisdom and search it out (Prov. 2:1–8; James 1:5; 3:13). So too with application. It is a gift when God makes words strike their targets, yet he takes our words for his arrows.

Application embraces both method and art, with both technical and creative moments. No technique yields results apart from the skill

---

34 Ibid., 13, 27–32.

35 Lawrence W. Wood, "The Reformed View: A Wesleyan Response," in *Christian Spirituality: Five Views of Sanctification,* 84.

36 Karl Barth, *Church Dogmatics* (Edinburgh: T. & T. Clark, 1961), III.4.11–17. For analysis of this view, see Paul Ramsey, *Basic Christian Ethics* (New York: Scribner, 1950), 46–91; Edward LeRoy Long, "The Use of the Bible in Christian Ethics: A Look at Basic Options," *Interpretation* 19 (1965): 149–54; cf. James Gustafson, *Ethics from a Theocentric Perspective* (Chicago: University of Chicago Press, 1984), 2:298–300.

of the interpreter.[37] The art of application involves giftedness, a delight in God and his word, and knowledge of ways of captivating an audience. No set of techniques can transmit such things. Therefore no multistep plan guarantees stirring applications. Sound exegesis is necessary, but is not sufficient for valid application. Further, the role of method in exegesis is partly negative, reining in our wilder impulses.[38] Still, alongside meditation and prayer, techniques or methods can open new horizons; I intend to supply some.

When skilled preachers speak, when the air sizzles with their vehemence, the study may be invisible. But the message originated there as they inhabited the word, reading and meditating until a passion for the truth flamed. If asked to describe how they crafted their peroration, they may fall silent. They may say nothing more than "I discovered something and saw how it applied, first in my life, then for my people." Such an answer, while perfectly true, hardly helps a student. Indeed, gifted preachers probably do and know much better, but they are not accustomed to articulating their methods.

Their silence should not surprise us. When asked about the skills we possess, "How did you do that?" we often say, "I don't know, I just . . ." As Michael Polanyi said, "The aim of a skillful performance is achieved by the observance of a set of rules which are not known as such to the person following them."[39] One can be an accomplished musician, athlete, or artisan without understanding the theory of the craft. The instrument-making skills of Stradivarius, including his lost varnish recipe, that were born with his Amati masters, died unarticulated to his sons. Even if he had taken up the pen, he might have misrepresented his skills, as other virtuosos do.[40] Failure to understand skills occurs because we most attend to them when we begin to acquire them (learning to drive) or when something is amiss (a slumping athlete). Once a skill is established, our awareness of the

37 Don Browning, *A Fundamental Practical Theology* (Minneapolis: Fortress, 1991), 80–83.

38 Ernest Best, *From Text to Sermon: Responsible Use of the NT in Preaching* (Atlanta: John Knox, 1978), 110.

39 Michael Polanyi, *Personal Knowledge* (Chicago: University of Chicago Press, 1968), 49–57.

40 Charles Beare, "Stradivari, Antonio," in *New Grove Dictionary of Music and Musicians,* ed. Stanley Sadie (London: Macmillan, 1980), 18:193–96.

mechanics recedes. We focus on projects and subordinate our skills to them. The musician attends to the piece, not her left index finger. The speaker thinks of the next idea, not the pronunciation of the next vocable. Skills are, as Polanyi says, "personal knowledge," not theoretical knowledge.

If application is personal knowledge, a skill, one could argue that it is best learned from a master, even if the master can only partially explain it. If application is a skill, the church most needs an apprenticeship system, since apprenticeships best inculcate skills.

Yet there are still reasons to theorize about skills. First, there is not a master for every would-be apprentice. There are too many seminary students, too many isolated pastors, not enough excellent preachers, and not enough time. Second, by theorizing about the skills the church does possess, we can aid apprentices by cordoning off pitfalls, outlining procedures, and supplying illustrations of skillful application. Third, we do not want another Stradivarius to die with his secrets. Given that the knowledge of the masters may be unvoiced and semiconscious, we owe it to the church, and even the masters themselves, to distill their secrets and bring them to awareness. Finally, I believe the biblical data bearing on the relevance of Scripture await full exploration.[41] By creating a vocabulary and summarizing the masters' tacit skills, we can stimulate additional research.

NAIVE AND CRITICAL APPROACHES TO APPLICATION

To summarize, application is an intuitive skill *and* it demands theoretical training. To admit that pastors cannot explain their own practice implies that application is intuitive. But intuitive acts may invite theoretical reflection. Riding a bicycle does not invite it, for the skill is easily acquired, and the rewards of deeper study are few. But the skills of musicianship and athletics have sufficient complexity to invite practice, meditation, and coaching that contribute to excellence. Preaching is in their class.

Therefore, to alter the opening metaphor, sometimes the river runs dry, and we cross its gravel bed without knowing it. Yet to achieve excellence in application, we must labor. It takes exegetical skill to

---

41 Witness our lack of writing on the subject (see the preface).

comprehend an ancient text. We need critical skills to address our culture while immersed in it. The goal, then, is to steer between naive optimism and critical skepticism. The naive optimist says bridge-building is too intuitive to require serious study. The critical skeptic judges it impossible or unnecessary to build bridges at all.

Naive Optimists

Optimists think any bagatelle of sticks and ropes will suffice for bridge-building. They believe they can find a verse to address every perceived need. They trust their intuitions to correlate any passage to those needs. They are blissfully unaware of their tendency to read contemporary (Western) images of bread, water, clothing, darkness, choice, and freedom into the Bible. They do not consider how the West's individualist, materialist assumptions compromise their ability to hear Scripture. A comment on Jesus' "bread of life" discourse (John 6) illustrates:

> For us, bread is something that comes in fifty or sixty varieties, usually wrapped in plastic, and obtainable from the shelves of the local supermarket. For first-century Jews, it was one of two staples: without it, you died. Moreover, first-century Jews . . . understood that almost everything we eat is supplied by something else's death. Meat comes from a dead animal; bread comes from dead wheat. . . . Suddenly words like these take on new force: "If anyone eats of this bread, he will live forever. This bread is my flesh, which I will give for the life of the world." In the flow of the discourse, Jesus claims . . . to be . . . the one who gives his life that others may live. Without his death, no one lives. He is the "staple" of all spiritual life, and he achieves this by his death.[42]

The antidote to naiveté is not despair, of course. Naive readers ordinarily perceive at least the main thrust of a text. When we work with familiar topics in our own culture, interpretation is largely intuitive.[43]

---

42 Carson, *Gagging of God,* 121.
43 William Klein, Craig Blomberg, and Robert Hubbard, *Introduction to Biblical Interpretation* (Waco: Word, 1993), 4–5.

Happily, the Bible has enough that is universal that a marginally skilled adult reader can hardly misconstrue the central story.[44]

Still, without bequeathing interpretation to experts, there are reasons to get theoretical. First, even great scholars have imperfect knowledge of the biblical culture and language. Second, we assume our culture is universally valid. If we fail to detach ourselves from our culture, we read it into the text, domesticating it. Failing to encounter the otherness of Scripture, we miss the difference between the world in which we *do* live and the world in which we *could* live.[45]

Critical Skeptics and Subjectivist Conservatives

Skeptics understand cultural distance, but conceive it in ways that foster doubt about bridge-building. They say our knowledge of Jesus and Israel is minimal; they ask why ancient Jewish history should exercise authority over contemporary life. Gotthold Lessing said that the "accidental truths of history can never become the proof of necessary truths of reason" for only the necessary universal truths of reason can be binding.[46] Thus some skeptics seek to extract the timeless teachings of Jesus, the apostles, and the prophets, separating, as Thomas Jefferson said, "the diamonds from the dunghills" to find universal ethical principles based on love, justice, and mercy.[47]

Their low view of Scripture and of Christ leads skeptics to doubt the value of exegesis. Considering how toilsome exegesis can be, if one reaction to the Bible is as good as another, is it worth the trouble?[48] Why bother, if each faith commitment has the same value

---

44 Peter Cotterel and Max Turner, *Linguistics and Biblical Interpretation* (Downers Grove, Ill.: InterVarsity, 1989), 42–43.

45 Paul Ricoeur, "Metaphor and the Main Problem of Hermeneutics," in *The Philosophy of Paul Ricoeur,* ed. Charles E. Reagan and David Stewart (Boston: Beacon, 1978), 134–48; Charles E. Reagan, *Paul Ricoeur: His Life and Work* (Chicago: University of Chicago Press, 1996), 42–43.

46 Lessing, "On the Proof of the Spirit," 52. The gap between the accidental truths of history and the necessary truths of reason is the "ugly, broad ditch" Lessing could not get across.

47 Letter to John Adams, January 24, 1824, quoted in Stephen Mitchell, *The Gospel according to Jesus* (New York: HarperCollins, 1991), 4.

48 Mark Coleridge, "Life in the Crypt or Why Bother with Biblical Studies?" *Biblical Interpretation* 2 (1994): 139–51; and Carson, *Gagging of God,* 82–85, 105–6, 193–94.

before "god"? For example, feminist biblical scholar Elizabeth Schussler Fiorenza confesses that she searches the Bible for a "canon within the canon" that will support the heart of spiritual feminism, "the quest for women's power."[49] For her, a feminist critical hermeneutic "does not appeal to the Bible as its primary source but begins with woman's own experience and vision of liberation."[50] But when she says, "The Bible no longer functions as authoritative source, but as resource for women's struggle for liberation,"[51] we wonder: If the Bible is not authoritative, why sweat over exegesis? Why not meditate on experience and cull a few biblical ideas to support the result?[52]

Sadly, some conservatives agree that labor is superfluous. They trust the guidance of the Holy Spirit or the impulses of their spirit to lead them into all the insight necessary for right living.

Both the skeptical and the naive have their points. The story of Jephthah (Judg. 10–11) supports the skeptic; sometimes application is daunting. The Ten Commandments support the naive; one can hardly mistake their relevance. But ordinarily the truth lies between the extremes.[53] We have seen that it takes skill to separate the weight of "bread" in antiquity and modernity; but, that done, application follows readily, as we think, "Yes, Jesus is that bread, that staple, even for me."

THE AUDIENCE, CULTURE, AND APPLICATION

So far we have focused on the interpreter's work with Scripture. But communication depends as much on the audience's ability to receive a message as it does on the speaker's to generate it (fig. 5). Effec-

---

49 Elizabeth Schussler Fiorenza, *In Memory of Her: A Feminist Theological Reconstruction of Christian Origins* (New York: Crossroad, 1983), 13–19.

50 Elizabeth Schussler Fiorenza, *Bread Not Stone: The Challenge of Biblical Feminist Interpretation* (Boston: Beacon, 1984), 88.

51 Ibid., 14.

52 Schussler Fiorenza adds that the criteria for theological evaluation "cannot be derived from the Bible itself but . . . through women's struggle for liberation from all patriarchal oppression." The "experience of oppression and liberation must become the criterion of appropriateness for biblical interpretation and evaluation of biblical authority claims" (*In Memory of Her,* 32). Again, "The Bible is not the controlling and defining 'court of appeals' " (*Bread Not Stone,* 88).

53 Moisés Silva, *Has the Church Misread the Bible?* (Grand Rapids: Zondervan, 1987), 22–24, 80–92.

Fig. 5.
THE THREE MAIN ELEMENTS IN APPLICATION

Text ⟶ Interpreter ⟶ Audience

tive communication requires knowledge of the cultures of the Bible, the speaker, and the audience. Teachers must overcome two challenges in speaking in our culture, the problem of our immersion in it and the problem of our isolation from it.

Immersion in Culture

When we address our culture, we have the benefit of lifelong immersion in it. But alas, that blessing is also a curse, for like fish in water, we cannot see the medium in which we swim. It is hardest to see what is always before our eyes, hardest to remark on values everyone accepts.[54] We are embedded in a web of assumptions and experiences and inherit biases and blind spots from them. Most Americans *assume* that freedom is essential to happiness, that innovation is good, that contact with other cultures is beneficial, that water is abundant. Yet such assertions would seem patently false in many cultures.

We assume modes of thinking as well as facts and values. Someone teaches us what facts are worth knowing, what to look for in a text, what is interesting or difficult enough to merit explication, and what counts as a valid reply to a question. For example, when an earthquake struck Lisbon on All Saints' Day, 1755, the churches were full, so that perhaps thirty thousand died. Punctuating a period marked by Turkish invasions, internal wars, a rising slave trade, and greed for profit from the New World, the cataclysm brought widespread consternation. Why had this happened? Conclusions differed. Was it God's judgment on social sins? A sign of God's disapproval of Catholicism? A forceful call to repentance? Whatever the conclusion, the majority sought a spiritual explanation; few viewed the disaster simply as a natural phenomenon.[55]

54 Ludwig Wittgenstein, *Remarks on the Foundations of Mathematics* (Oxford: Blackwell, 1937–44), 1:141.
55 A. J. Conyers, *The Eclipse of Heaven* (Downers Grove, Ill.: InterVarsity, 1992), 12–18.

Today science explains disasters. Shifting tectonic plates cause earthquakes. Bacteria cause plagues. After catastrophes we call in scientists and grief counselors, not theologians. In the current majority culture, it is only marginally acceptable to suggest that God is involved with such events, except perhaps to mourn with those who mourn. Anything more clashes with the Western "plausibility structure," which says scientific explanations are what count.[56]

We cannot help but operate within our thought world in ways we may not detect. Like secularists, we have an affinity for scientific despiritualizing analyses that dominate normal conversation. Indeed, we are far enough from Lisbon's world that we struggle to understand why an earthquake caused a spiritual crisis.[57] If this is true for our understanding of a Western, Christian nation two or three centuries past, how much more of an Eastern, Jewish land two or three millennia past? Only by persistent mental discipline can we lay aside our assumptions.

Isolation from Culture

Many Christian leaders share the culture's sense that a theological analysis of an earthquake would make a peculiar television program. But we are farther removed from our culture on other points. For example, Americans largely assent to commonsense feminist ideas about the equality of men and women in gifts and energy. Paul's words about men teaching and wives submitting sound implausible, retrograde, offensive to secularists and even to many Christians.[58] Similarly, Western concepts of freedom and self-expression make even conservatives wonder if homosexuality is anything but an alternative lifestyle. If so, why deprive homosexuals of sex or marriage? Culturally isolated pastors overlook the extent to which Christians adopt secular views. Teachers can overcome these challenges by fostering dialogical communication.

---

56 Newbigin, *Gospel in a Pluralist Society,* 20–23, 52–65, 97–102. On plausibility structures, see Peter Berger, *The Sacred Canopy* (New York: Doubleday, 1967).

57 Conyers, *Eclipse of Heaven,* 15.

58 See Mary Kassian, *The Feminist Gospel* (Wheaton, Ill.: Crossway, 1992); Andreas Köstenberger, Thomas Schreiner, and H. Scott Baldwin, *Women in the Church: A Fresh Analysis of 1 Timothy 2:9–15* (Grand Rapids: Baker, 1995).

Dialogue

Conversations have an open-endedness, a life of their own. Neither party *leads* a true conversation; conversationalists are *led* down a path by the twists and turns of ideas. Study groups have a director and a direction, but they also allow unexpected detours. In books dialogue is suppressed, but active readers agree with, object to, and ponder implications as they work through them.[59] What differentiates dialogue from writing is that "in dialogue spoken language—in the process of question and answer, giving and taking, talking at cross purposes and seeing each other's point—performs the communication of meaning that, with respect to the written tradition, is the task of hermeneutics."[60]

During sermons people in the pew assent and dissent, lobbing silent questions and rejoinders into the air. I once sat near two women during a searing indictment of gambling. As they left the service, their previously unspoken dialogue with the pastor surfaced as they whispered, "Gambling is terrible, but we're okay. We set strict loss limits when we go to the casino." They agreed with the sermon's theology, but denied its relevance, thinking, "For me it's not gambling, it's entertainment" (again, a failure to apply is a failure to understand). Wise teachers invite spoken dialogue where appropriate, and unspoken dialogue when necessary. Monologues can elicit silent dialogue by anticipating possible objections, requests for explanation, and excuses. Malachi, Romans, and James all respond to anticipated questions and challenges from their readers. Thus preachers must exegete the congregation as well as the text.[61]

To exegete the congregation is to know its heart, its status before God. Preachers should take the joys and troubles of their congregation to the Bible. They can mentally survey a congregation and "ask the text questions they would ask," and those "they may not dare to ask," without projecting their own concerns onto the congregation.[62]

59   Gadamer, *Truth and Method,* 367–69, 383–88.

60   Ibid., 368. See also Martin Buber, *I and Thou,* trans. Ronald Smith (New York: Scribner, 1958).

61   See Leonora Tubbs Tisdale, *Preaching as Local Theology and Folk Art* (Minneapolis: Fortress, 1996), 19, 48.

62   Thomas Long, *The Witness of Preaching* (Louisville: Westminster/John Knox, 1989), 11–15, 24–36, 55–57, 70.

Exegeting the congregation means knowing that its history, social strata, age, region, and ethnicity create unique traits and recognizing that the thought world of pastor and congregation may differ. Exegeting the congregation means posing questions as modern local people do. (It also means no sermon is perfectly portable; if audiences change, sermons must too).

Of course, all humans share similar emotional experiences, biological characteristics, and spiritual traits, so we can reach people we do not know. But the universals of life come to expression in particular cultures and individuals. Good pastors answer the questions people have and address their felt needs, but also inform people when they should ask different questions and feel different needs. They speak to their people, both as insiders immersed in the community and as outsiders who see things the church cannot.[63]

By taking the particular audience into consideration, our application of Scripture will be "seriously imaginable" to them in their time and place.[64] If the exegesis of a congregation has been successful, it will find the message intelligible, defensible, plausible. In other words, the truth does not change, but explanations of its relevance do, because Christianity challenges the culture in ever-changing ways. Besides topics such as gender and sexuality, theological matters such as the holiness and wrath of God or salvation by faith in Christ alone also clash with popular notions. Our culture says religious convictions are matters of opinion or taste that cannot be true or false.[65] Decades ago, miracles and predestination were under siege. We must reply to today's contests.

Church planters and missiologists understand the importance of restating unchanging truth for new cultures.[66] Church planters know they must find fresh, locally viable expressions for eternal truths.[67] It is essential to "translate" theology into common English, as C. S. Lewis said, "The popular English language . . . simply has to be learned

---

63 Tisdale, *Preaching,* 11–53.

64 From David Kelsey, *Uses of Scripture in Recent Theology* (Philadelphia: Fortress, 1975), 170–74. While Kelsey speaks of theological constructions as seriously imaginable, the phrase is apt for application.

65 Newbigin, *Gospel in a Pluralist Society,* 13–15.

66 See the journal *Bible Translator* (published by the United Bible Societies).

67 George G. Hunter III, *How to Reach Secular People* (Nashville: Abingdon, 1992); Rick Warren, *The Purpose Driven Church* (Grand Rapids: Zondervan, 1995).

by him who would preach to the English; just as a missionary learns Bantu before preaching to the Bantus."[68]

Missiologists agree. They label the issue "contextualization," that is, "the translation of the unchanging content of the gospel . . . into verbal form meaningful to the peoples in their separate cultures and . . . existential situations."[69] Some missiologists say that once a translator has found language that communicates, application has almost begun. They say contextualization is the discovery of "the legitimate implications of the gospel text in a given situation."[70] Again, translation and exegesis determine what the author would say "if he were speaking to my audience," while contextualization determines how the original obligation "can be relived by my audience."[71]

SUMMARY

This chapter has attempted to lay out the prime issues in developing a coherent approach to the application of Scripture. We have stated the goal of application, to lead people to know God and conform themselves to him. We have described the nature of application, which has a definite but permeable boundary with the exposition of Scripture. (Perhaps the opening analogy should be the crossing of a *swampy* riverbed, where the borders are unclear.) The center of application is not *commanding* but expressing truth so that its relevance is obvious.

We have seen that application takes skill, intuition, and method,

---

68 C. S. Lewis, *God in the Dock,* ed. Walter Hooper (Grand Rapids: Eerdmans, 1970), 242–43.

69 Bruce J. Nicholls, "Theological Education and Evangelization," *in Let the Earth Hear His Voice,* ed. J. D. Douglas (Minneapolis: World Wide, 1975). See also Nicholls, *Contextualization: A Theology of Gospel and Culture* (Downers Grove, Ill.: InterVarsity, 1978), 20–55.

70 George Peters, "Issues Confronting Evangelical Missions," in *Evangelical Missions Tomorrow,* ed. Wade Coggins and E. L. Frizen (Pasadena, Calif.: William Carey Library, 1977), 169.

71 Grant Osborne, *The Hermeneutical Spiral* (Downers Grove, Ill.: InterVarsity, 1991), 332–38, 344–57. Cf. William Larkin, *Culture and Biblical Hermeneutics* (Grand Rapids: Baker, 1988), 139–41, 319–21.

so that theoretical study is justified. It is perhaps most like learning a musical instrument or a new sport. In sports there is a brief introduction to rules and equipment ("You hold it like this"), then the play begins. By watching experienced players and striving against them, by sensing what does and what does not work, skills increase. Yet if the goal is excellence, one must find a coach and become a student of the game. While talent, desire, mentors, methods, and feedback permit rapid progress in application, to become excellent, one must theorize too.

2
God-Centered Application

"All Scripture is God-breathed and is useful for teaching, rebuking, correcting and training in righteousness, so that the man of God may be thoroughly equipped for every good work" (2 Tim. 3:16–17). This statement rightly takes first rank in discussions of the relevance of Scripture, but it barely opens a theology of application. For one thing, it almost invites contradiction. After all, genealogies, imprecatory psalms, travel records, visions of dragons, and oracles for Edom hardly seem to enhance righteousness. What exactly is Paul claiming then? Does every passage bring at least one rebuke, one idea that engenders righteousness? What is a "passage" anyway? Further, no matter how significant 2 Timothy 3 may be, there is a wealth of subtler evidence about the way Scripture structures the life of faith. We need a theology of application, explaining how all Scripture equips the church for "every good work." Much of this book explores ways of putting Paul's promise into practice. This chapter explores how his promise is true.

We will see, first, that the Bible's claim of relevance, though apparently contradicted by genealogies and such, coheres with the nature and function of ordinary language. Speech acts have goals, which means they have relevance; Scripture simply functions like most language. Second, after sketching a biblical theology of application we will examine Jesus' use of the Scripture and see that he modeled *God-centered application*. Third, a study of 2 Timothy 3 will show that verses 16–17 are no mere proof-text but an anchor for a Christ-centered theory of application.

DOING THINGS WITH WORDS

Under ordinary conditions, communicators intend to *do* things with their words.[1] That is, when we speak or write according to the conventions of communication, we choose *words* to convey a *meaning* that our audience will find *significant* so that it will thus achieve some goal or *effect*. Speech moves and persuades.[2] With words we warn, encourage, promise, persuade, command, commission, pardon and apologize, embrace and reject. Pointless announcements annoy us. Chatterers embarrass themselves if they ask, "What was I saying?" or "What was I driving at?" We shake our heads at stories that go nowhere.

At home, even the simplest statements have intended effects. Suppose a father walks by a bathroom and observes, "There is a wet towel on the floor." If a wet-headed child peeks out of her room and says, "You're right, Dad; there *is* a towel on the floor!" and ducks back into her room, will the father be pleased at her agreement? No, for he meant that the owner and operator of the offending towel should move it.

Similarly, if before a family dinner the matriarch announces, "Dinner will be ready in five minutes," she means to *direct* everyone, "Wash up and begin to gather." When she performs the final inspection and

1 J. L. Austin, *How to Do Things with Words,* 2d ed. (Cambridge, Mass.: Harvard University Press, 1975); John R. Searle, *Speech Acts: An Essay in the Philosophy of Language* (Cambridge: Cambridge University Press, 1969); idem., *Expression and Meaning: Studies in the Theory of Speech Acts* (Cambridge: Cambridge University Press, 1979); François Recananti, *Meaning and Force: The Pragmatics of Performative Utterances* (Cambridge: Cambridge University Press, 1987); Kevin J. Vanhoozer, "The Semantics of Biblical Literature," in *Hermeneutics, Authority and Canon,* by D. A. Carson and John D. Woodbridge (Grand Rapids: Zondervan, 1986), 53–104; Anthony Thistelton, *New Horizons in Hermeneutics* (Grand Rapids: Zondervan, 1992), 283–312. These scholars, following Austin, distinguish locutionary, illocutionary, and perlocutionary speech acts. In a locutionary act, one utters words in a sentence with a certain sense and reference. The illocutionary act is what is done *in* the utterance, such as informing or ordering. The perlocutionary act is "what we bring about *by* saying something, such as convincing, persuading, deterring" (Austin, *How to Do Things with Words,* 94–121, esp. 109). I attempt to use the insights of these scholars by speaking more simply of the meaning (what the author intends to convey by his words) and the significance (what readers ought to get from his words).

2 Even apparent exceptions—speaking to annoy others or to repeat a mantra—have an oblique purpose.

declares, "There is no salt on the table," she expects one of her adjutants to fetch it. After prayer, Aunt Polly may pass a platter to Cousin Bob, whispering, "Here is the turkey." Cousin Bob would err, in this context, if he replied, "Yes, here it is," as if the goal were to confirm, by two witnesses, the location of the bird. Polly expects Bob to take the plate, serve himself, and pass it on. When the hostess later inquires, "Would you like ice cream or sherbet for dessert?" and someone replies, "You know, I haven't had sherbet for a while," she knows to place another tally by "sherbet."

Small talk is purposeful, too. When a mother says, "It's freezing out there," she directs her children to bundle up. When two strangers enter an elevator and one says, "It sure is hot out there," he acknowledges his fellow passenger. He means, "I acknowledge your humanity, please acknowledge mine so we can occupy this space more comfortably," knowing that if he actually said, "Sir, let us acknowledge one another's humanity so that we may settle into the ritual of staring at the floor buttons," his fellow passenger might leap out and take the stairs.[3]

Sometimes speech has multiple purposes. One Wednesday night at a church dinner my middle daughter and I lingered briefly over the end of our meal before we departed for our separate activities. Knowing our time was short, I was disappointed when a friendly interloper sat down and struck up an amiable but aimless conversation. When he paused, I put my arm around my child and said, "Did you know that this is the sweetest girl in the whole world?" With this remark I hoped to accomplish three things. First, I wanted to *assure* my daughter, "You matter to me; I will not stop paying attention to you every time an adult chats with me." Second, I showed that I wanted to *include* her in the conversation. Third, I sought to *affirm* my affection for her, declaring, implicitly, "I hold you in high esteem and gladly say so." Thus my words had three intended effects. They applied three ways.

Dialogue constitutes the easier part of the argument that language aims to produce an effect. When we turn to writing, there is no longer a speaker present to clarify ambiguities, to interpret furrowed

---

3 News media can obscure this, since they convey masses of apparently useless information—what can we *do* about hurricanes, riots, or train derailments in distant nations? But such reports, even factoids on asparagus harvests, at least entertain, and many have far nobler goals.

brows, to insist on his meaning or indicate its significance. Especially if the author is in no position to respond, readers have the ability to put texts to their own uses and can distort or pervert them. Nonetheless, this is not how we ordinarily play the game in written communication, especially when reader and writer hail from the same community, as is typically the case for Scripture. Writing does not elicit a response as directly as does conversation, but everything still has its purpose. Poetry ennobles. News reports inform. Lectures educate. Novels entertain. Essays shape opinion and policy. If, therefore, *all* language is purposeful, if people normally intend to do something with words, we must expect *biblical* language to be purposeful too.[4]

If the Bible were only ordinary language, it would all be relevant—even genealogies. But, of course, it is more than ordinary language. It is the true story about humankind, its plight and its redemption by the living God. It tells of God's redemption in every sphere of life, the spiritual, the physical, the intellectual, and the social. Just there, biblical genealogies are germane. Typical ancient Near Eastern genealogies were top-heavy with kings, gods, and heroes, but biblical genealogies are "bottom-dense" with lists of ordinary people. This reflects that God's plan was to create a "socially decentralized, non-hierarchical society" with interest in the "social health and economic viability" of its "lowest" units. And it suggests that we ought to strive for similar social effects today.[5]

A GENERAL THEOLOGY OF APPLICATION

One could lament the (apparent) clarity of 2 Timothy 3:16–17 since it functions as such a perfect proof-text for the relevance of Scripture that it permits us to ignore subtler evidence that all Scripture does indeed instruct in faith and righteousness. Later chapters will explore this evidence more thoroughly, but it is wise, early in our journey, to sketch a theology of application that further develops the twin goals of knowing God and conforming ourselves to him. We will note six themes, then explore Jesus' use (application) of the Old Testament at length.

4   The best defenses of the author and his intent are by E. D. Hirsch, *Validity in Interpretation* (New Haven: Yale University Press, 1967); and Kevin Vanhoozer, *Is There a Meaning in This Text* (Grand Rapids: Zondervan, 1998).

5   Christopher J. H. Wright, *Walking in the Ways of the Lord: The Ethical Authority of the Old Testament* (Downers Grove, Ill.: InterVarsity, 1995), 16–24, 152–53.

1. *Loving God.* The Bible is the story of salvation, the drama of a loving Father seeking estranged sons and daughters and restoring them to his loving family. After Adam's rebellion, God promises a child who will crush the deceiver who planted the thought of sin (Gen. 3:15). That child of Abraham will bless the world (Gen. 12:1–3); that Son of David will rule it forever (2 Sam. 7:8–16) until God fulfills the promise, "You will be my people, and I will be your God" (Jer. 11:4; 30:22; Ezek. 36:28; cf. Ex. 6:7). In Jesus the promise comes to fruition as he ransoms children from every nation and reconciles them to himself. The terminology varies, but the first theme of application is that God's prior love calls forth faith, obedience, and affection for the Father.[6]

2. *Responding to God.* When God acts and a biblical narrative records the event, the author usually pauses to report the response of the witnesses, whether it be faith, fear, penitence, astonishment, anger, or praise. By reporting how witnesses responded *then,* narratives indicate how readers should respond *now.* In the Gospels, some narratives explicitly commend faith (Matt. 8:1–13; 9:1–6, 18–36; 14:22–33; 15:21–28; Luke 7:36–50; 17:11–19; 19:1–10) or rebuke blindness (Mark 8:17–21). Others subtly lead readers to proper evaluations. When Jesus raises Lazarus, John juxtaposes the faith of Martha with the plots of the Jewish leaders (11:21–27, 45–53). Jesus also heals two chronically ill men by pools in Jerusalem on the Sabbath. Both times Jewish leaders criticize the healing. Both times Jesus seeks the healed man afterward. But one betrays him to the authorities (John 5:1–15), while the other defends and believes in him (9:1–38).[7] Get the point?

3. *Learning from biblical history.* Moses held Israel accountable to learn from her past. Each generation should see God's saving acts, recent or distant, as proofs of his covenantal love and authority and as summons

---

6   The idea that gratitude has no place in Christian life because it is a deficit motivation (based on owing something, rather than delight in giving it) conflicts with Heb. 12:28; Ex. 19:3–8; and Deut. 7:7–16. There are additional motives, but we do owe God obedience.
7   Whether the man from the pool of Bethesda was a traitor or a fool, he certainly identified Jesus to the authorities, who were incensed at the alleged violation of the Sabbath. Deliberate betrayal is at least a possibility.

to covenant loyalty. Thus, before entering Canaan, Moses told Israel that the covenant God made on Sinai forty years earlier "was not with our fathers . . . but . . . with all of us who are alive here today. The LORD spoke to you face to face out of the fire on the mountain. . . . 'I am the LORD your God, who brought you out of Egypt. . . . You shall have no other gods before me' " (Deut. 5:1–7). This is striking for, excluding Joshua and Caleb, all members of the desert generation were unborns or juveniles when Israel escaped Egypt. Moses knew that, of course, yet he says, "God made a covenant with *us*." In the divine economy, a covenant with the fathers remains in effect for the children.[8] Paul says Israel's history applies to the church. "Everything that was written in the past was written to teach us" (Rom. 15:3–4). Israel's dismal history of wilderness failures warns us "to keep us from setting our hearts on evil things as they did" (1 Cor. 10:6–11). Romans agrees with this principle, declaring that the accounts of Abraham's justification and David's forgiveness were not written for their sake alone, "but also for us, to whom God will credit righteousness" through faith (Rom. 4:1–8, 23–24).

4. *Imitating God.* At creation, God made man and woman in his image and likeness (Gen. 1:27). In redemption he re-created us "to be like God in true righteousness and holiness" (Eph. 4:24). Now we must be holy because he is holy, loving as he is love, just as he is just, merciful for he is merciful.

5. *Imitating Christ.* A believer's life follows the contours of Christ's. God destines us to become like Christ, "the firstborn among many brothers" (Rom. 8:29). Like Jesus we pass through hardship and tribulation before entering glory (Acts 14:22; Phil. 3:10–11). He says, "If

8 Notice multigenerational continuity again when each generation takes the first-fruits of Canaan to the house of God, confessing that God gave them the land. As the priest receives the gift, each Israelite must declare, "My father was a wandering Aramean and he went down into Egypt. . . . But the Egyptians mistreated us. . . . Then we cried out to the LORD . . . and the LORD heard our voice and saw our misery. . . . So the LORD brought us out of Egypt with a mighty hand. . . . He brought us to this place and gave us this land. . . . And now I bring the first-fruits of the soil that you, O LORD, have given me" (Deut. 26:1–11). Thus the past regulates Israel's present.

anyone wants to come after me, let him deny himself and take up his cross and follow me" (Mark 8:34, my translation). He washes his disciples' feet and declares, "Now that I, your Lord and Teacher, have washed your feet, you also should wash one another's feet. I have set you an example" (John 13:14–15). But our imitation of Jesus extends beyond suffering and service and sounds almost unlimited. "A student is not above his teacher, nor a servant above his master. It is enough for the student to be like his teacher, and the servant like his master" (Matt. 10:24–25).

6. *The path of blessing.* A lesser and more easily misconstrued theme intimates that if communities and individuals do things God's way, life ordinarily goes better. The world is set up to run God's way; thus, "The evil deeds of a wicked man ensnare him; the cords of his sin hold him fast" (Prov. 5:22). Again, "The righteousness of the blameless makes a straight way for them, but the wicked are brought down by their own wickedness" (11:5).[9] Those who obey the law find freedom and blessing (James 1:22–25). Further, God rewards obedience and punishes iniquity. All will render an account of their good or evil. Psalm 34:12–16 joins both themes:

> Whoever . . . loves life
> > and desires to see many good days,
> keep your tongue from evil
> > and your lips from speaking lies.
> Turn from evil and do good;
> > seek peace and pursue it.
> The eyes of the LORD are on the righteous
> > and his ears are attentive to their cry;
> the face of the LORD is against those who do evil,
> > to cut off the memory of them from the earth.

The "blessings of obedience" motif runs strongest in wisdom literature, which stresses the value of God's wisdom, whether gained from parents (Prov. 1–5) or from the word of God (Pss. 19, 119).

---

9 This theme appears in the law too. In Deut. 10:12–13 God gives Israel his commands "for your own good."

But two caveats are in order. First, the righteous can still suffer for doing the good (1 Peter 3:14). Second, even believers can return to a performance mentality. Forgetting that our obedience is never meritorious, we take off the white robe given to us by Christ and struggle to clothe ourselves in the rags of our own righteousness. Yet, if we avoid persecution and self-righteousness, obedience ordinarily brings blessing.

JESUS' THEOLOGY OF APPLICATION

Jesus' Use of Scripture

Jesus' reading of his Scripture, the Old Testament, is an important guide to our use of Scripture. With such a rich topic, we must be selective. Therefore, while making other points, I will emphasize that Jesus' use of Scripture highlights its testimony to him.[10] Further, his critiques of misuses of Scripture often pivot on a failure to recognize that testimony. We will see, therefore, that Jesus models theocentric application.

1. *Jesus and biblical law.* We anchor Jesus' legal use of Scripture in his affirmation that every stroke, every command of the law must be fulfilled (Matt. 5:17–20). His interpretations both deepen the demand and expand the scope of the law. He deepens the law's demand by addressing the motives behind overt sin (5:21–48). He bans murder and adultery, then forbids that we even harbor such thoughts. He rebukes narrow application of the law by applying it to new situations, such as dining habits and personal conflicts. When the Pharisees criticize Jesus for dining with sinners, he quotes Hosea 6:6, "I desire mercy, not sacrifice." When describing the way the church must resolve offenses, he uses Moses' law, "Every matter may be established by the testimony of two or three witnesses" (Deut. 19:15; Matt. 18:16). When the Pharisees censure his Sabbath observance, he pronounces the prime purpose of the day, "The Sabbath was made for man, not man for the Sabbath" (Mark 2:27).

The conclusion of Mark 2 registers Jesus' egocentric use of the law. He is the Lord of the law: "The Son of Man is Lord even of the

10 This section owes something to Craig Evans, who divides Jesus' use of the Old Testament into the legal, the prophetic, and the analogical ("Old Testament in the Gospels," in *Dictionary of Jesus and the Gospels,* ed. Joel B. Green, Scot McKnight, and I. H. Marshall [Downers Grove, Ill.: InterVarsity, 1992], 579–90).

Sabbath" (2:28). He keeps it perfectly:"Can any of you prove me guilty of sin?" (John 8:46). He interprets it definitively:"You have heard that it was said, but *I* say to you . . ."[11] Moreover, he invites those who cannot keep the law to turn to him for aid. He blesses the poor in spirit, who know their spiritual inability (Matt. 5:3). He offers his light yoke, in place of the heavy yoke of the law (11:28–30). He gives himself as a ransom for sinners (20:25–28).[12]

2. *Jesus and biblical prophecy.* Misconceptions about prophecy can impede our grasp of Jesus' use of prophetic Scriptures. We view fulfillment of prophecy as a proof of Scripture's veracity and God's sovereignty, and it is. Unfortunately, this "proof" concept leads some to regard prophecy as pious fortune-telling. The exact correspondence between forecast and event impresses readers; only God could orchestrate such agreements between prediction and history.[13] This slightly misguided mind-set can generate a dead-end exchange in some Bible studies:

Q: Why did Jesus ride into Jerusalem on a donkey?
A: To fulfill Scripture.
Q: But why did he fulfill this Scripture at this time?
A: Because it was prophesied.

This kind of (un)reasoning is inert because it nearly gets things backward. To overstate slightly, *Jesus did not do things because they were predicted; they were predicted because God ordained that he do them.* The prediction did not cause the action as much as the future action caused the prediction. Predetermined by God outside time, the action was presented by God to the mind of the prophet before its time, so that when the time arrived, the action would be recognized as the will of God.

This fulfillment motif is also egocentric. Jesus often predicted the events surrounding his death, saying that they fulfilled Scripture (Matt. 21:4; 26:54–56; 27:9; Mark 12:10; 14:49; Luke 18:31; 22:37; John 13:18;

11   The Greek, *egō de legō hymin* is emphatic six consecutive times (Matt. 5:22, 28, 32, 34, 39, 44).
12   Daniel M. Doriani, *Getting the Message* (Phillipsburg, N.J.: Presbyterian and Reformed, 1996), 180–83.
13   C. H. Dodd, *According to Scriptures* (London: Nisbet, 1952), 127.

18:32; 19:24–28, 36–37; 20:9).[14] The disciples struggled with this prediction before the event, but afterward they bent heart and mind to it. Grasping it at last, they followed Jesus' lead, searched Scriptures, and incorporated additional prophecies into their teaching. Such prophecies figure prominently in the apostles' sermons to Jews (Acts 3:18; 10:39–43; 13:32–33; 26:22–23). This motif admits that Jesus' crucifixion is repugnant to Jew and Greek, but explains that it follows the plan of God. Thus the proclamation of Jesus heralds his crucifixion and resurrection without shame (Rom. 1:16). It is the remedy for sin; it supports the most fundamental application, the call to faith in the risen one.[15]

3. *Jesus and biblical themes.* Jesus' work with biblical themes is so rich that we will investigate only the way Jesus uses Old Testament themes to call attention to his person and work. First, *Jesus surpasses and completes the ministries of Israel's leaders.* He declares that he is greater than Abraham, for he is eternal (John 8:53–56). He is greater than Jacob, because he is the gateway between heaven and earth (John 1:51; cf. Gen. 28:12) and because he gives a spring of water that wells up to eternal life (John 4:12–14). He surpasses Moses because he inaugurates a covenant of grace and truth rather than law (John 1:17) and because he offers the true, life-giving bread that comes down from heaven (John 6:32–35). He is greater than Jonah in his compelling call to repentance (Matt. 12:41). He surpasses Solomon in wisdom that attracts the nations (Matt. 12:42).

Second, *Jesus completes old covenant institutions.* He is greater than the temple, for he is the very presence of God (Matt. 12:6). He is the final priest, giving access to God (Heb. 7–10). He is the good shepherd, caring for Israel (Matt. 9:36; John 9:1–10:18; cf. Ezek. 34:1–16). He is the great prophet (Luke 7:16, 26). He is the great king, David's Son and David's Lord (Matt. 22:41–46). He is the final judge (Matt. 25:31–46), the wisdom of God (Luke 7:31–35).

14 He also predicts these events with the phrase "it is written" (Matt. 26:31; Mark 9:12; 14:21, 27; Luke 24:44–47; John 12:16; 15:25), and calls them a divine necessity (Luke 9:22; 17:25; 22:37, 24:7, 24–27).

15 *In New Testament Development of Old Testament Themes* (Grand Rapids: Eerdmans, 1968), F. F. Bruce shows how Jesus fulfills themes such as the salvation of God, the victory of God, the Son of David, the Servant Messiah, and the Shepherd King.

This sample of Jesus' development of biblical themes proves that, whatever else may be said, his interpretation concentrates upon Scripture's testimony to his supremacy. Jesus' reading and application of Scripture are relentlessly theocentric and egocentric.

Jesus' Critique of the Misuse of Scripture

Jesus' critique of Jewish misinterpretation of Scripture shows the same theocentric and egocentric character. Five times Jesus used the rhetorical formula "Have you not read?" to chide Jewish leaders for misreading Scripture.[16] Of course, Jesus was not inquiring after their literacy or reading habits; he meant that they failed to grasp the Bible's meaning.[17] On four of these occasions, they failed to understand Scripture's testimony to Jesus. A fifth text, which we will discuss first, chides the Pharisees for following the letter and failing to seek the intent of Scripture, as Jesus does.

In Matthew 19:3 the Pharisees ask, "Is it lawful for a man to divorce his wife for any and every reason?" Jesus replies, "Have you not read" that God created humans male and female, to become one flesh (vv. 4–6)? At least some of the Pharisees had *mis*read Moses, turning regulations intended to restrain divorce into permission for men to divorce their wives at their volition. Thus they misapplied Scripture, dwelling on the grounds for dissolution of marriage rather than ways of restoring it.[18]

---

16 The question appears ten times in the Gospels. It appears twice in one text and four times in parallel passages: Matt. 12:3, 5 (Mark 2:25; Luke 6:3); Matt. 19:4; Matt. 21:16 (Mark 12:10); Matt. 21:42; and Matt. 22:31 (Mark 12:26). The verb *anaginōskō*, ordinarily "I read," appears each time, but the phrasing varies slightly. It is *ouk anegnōte* in Matt. 12:3, 5; 19:4; 22:31; and Mark 12:26; but *oudepote anegnōte* in Matt. 21:16, 42, and Mark 2:25; *oude anegnōte* appears in Mark 12:10 and Luke 6:3.

17 The question has precursors in prophetic and rabbinic literature. Rabbis distinguished between reading and interpreting, between what a text says and what a reader learns. See David Daube, *The New Testament and Rabbinic Judaism* (Peabody, Mass.: Hendrickson, 1956), 427–32.

18 The *Mishnah* (trans. H. Danby, 1933) has about fifteen pages regulating divorce and ten regulating betrothals, but nothing about preserving or restoring marriage. Here is a law regulating bills of divorce (*Gittin* 2:5–6):

> It may be written with anything: ink, red dye, gum, copperas, or whatsoever is lasting; but it may not be written with . . . fruit juice or whatso-

The remaining cases turn on a failure to see that the Law and the Prophets testify to Jesus. First, in Matthew 12:2 the Pharisees charge him for permitting his disciples to pluck grain from fields they walked by on the Sabbath—not for stealing, but for laboring on the Sabbath. He replies, "Have you not read" how David and his companions entered the tabernacle and unlawfully ate the consecrated bread because they were hungry? That is, as human need outweighed sacrificial regulations in David's day, so something outweighs Sabbath regulations in Jesus' day. Further, Jesus asks, "Have you not read" that on the Sabbath priests toil in the temple and yet remain innocent? Jesus' point is twofold. First, the law knows priorities. Human need and service to the Lord supersede Sabbath regulations. But second, Jesus adds, "One greater than the temple is here" (12:6). That is, if priests are permitted to serve on the Sabbath in the space *representing* the presence of God, the disciples may do whatever is necessary to assist the anointed one who *is* the presence of God.

The other uses of "Have you not read" occur in controversies during Jesus' final week. In Matthew 21:14–15, some boys, seeing the healings Jesus performed in the temple area, sing, "Hosanna to the Son of David."[19] The chief priests and teachers become indignant when they hear this echo of the praise at the triumphal entry (21:9). But Jesus defends the children by quoting Psalm 8. "Have you not read," he asks, that from the mouths of infants and nurslings God has ordained praise? The children praise Jesus, he says, because they know the truth. Jesus'

---

ever is not lasting. It may be written on anything—on an olive leaf, or on a cow's horn (and he must give her the cow) or on the hand of a slave (and he must give her the slave). . . . All are qualified to *write* a bill of divorce, even a deaf mute, an imbecile or a minor. All are qualified to *bring* a bill of divorce, excepting a deaf mute, an imbecile, a minor, a blind man or a Gentile. . . . If it was received from the husband by a minor who (later) became of age, or by a deaf mute whose senses (later) became sound, or by an imbecile who became sane . . . it is still valid. But if (given by) one of sound senses who then became a deaf mute and again became of sound senses, . . . or by one who was sane who then became an imbecile and again became sane, it is valid. . . . If at the beginning and at the end an act is performed knowingly, it is valid.

19 The Greek, *tous paidas* is masculine. The neuter, *ta paidia* is more common (e.g., 18:3; 19:14).

use of Psalm 8 is also striking because he applies what was originally a hymn of praise to the Creator to himself. Is Matthew hinting that the children should have gone further? "Hosanna" is a shout of acclamation, and "Son of David" asserts messiahship.[20] But Jesus deserves even more praise, for he created and rules all. Crowned with glory and honor, he deserves worship (Ps. 8:2–8).[21]

In the fourth text, the priests and Pharisees complain that Jesus directs the parable of the wicked tenant farmers against them. They seem to have "never read" Psalm 118, that the stone the builders rejected became the capstone (Matt. 21:33–42). Psalm 118 praises God for delivering one who was despised and threatened on every side. This figure could be David, despised by his family and threatened by Goliath and Saul. Or it might be the nation of Israel, often scorned and attacked. But Jesus, the Son of David, the true Israel, recapitulates the suffering and vindication of his Old Testament types. Matthew's parable of the rebellious farmers would be cogent without the citation of Psalm 118, but Jesus wanted his disciples to see his rejection as the archetypal case of unjust rejection preceding public vindication (cf. Acts 4:11; Rom. 9:33; 1 Peter 2:6–8).

The final text, from Matthew 22, focuses on the Father. When the Sadducees deny the bodily resurrection, Jesus asks, "Have you not read what God said . . . , 'I am the God of Abraham, the God of Isaac, and the God of Jacob'?" (vv. 29–31; cf. Ex. 3:6). Jesus admonishes them for failing to "read" the verb tense—"I *am* the God of Abraham," not "I *was*." But more basically they failed to know God, the God of the living.

God-Centered Application

One might argue that the question "Have you not read?" is unfair in some cases. How, without assistance, could the Jews see Psalms 8 and 118 as testimonies to Jesus, when even well-trained Christian leaders struggle to comprehend? How could the Sadducees know the doctrine of God hangs upon verb tenses? But rabbinic sources show they

---

20 Robert Gundry, *The Use of the Old Testament in St. Matthew's Gospel* (Leiden: E. J. Brill, 1967), 41–43.
21 Following Dodd's idea (*Scriptures,* 104, 126) that New Testament writers cite Old Testament texts not as isolated quotations but as references to whole sections, I bring all of Ps. 8 into play.

were familiar with the minute scrutiny behind the "I am"/"I was" discussion. More important, even if Psalms 8 and 118 give cryptic testimony to Jesus' deity, the Jews certainly had enough evidence of Jesus' identity to override their objections to him (Matt. 21:33–46).[22] At other times Jesus chastises leaders for misinterpretation, citing their failure to see signs pointing to him (Matt. 16:1–4; Luke 24:45; John 5:39–40).

Jesus' pattern of applying Scripture to himself reminds us again that valid application begins with the knowledge of God. The Psalms can be comforting, narratives can be stirring, doctrine or ethics stimulating. But lessons that forget Jesus are sub-Christian, for they never transcend the goal of living well. The foundation of application is always the knowledge of God, Creator and Redeemer.

We see the foundational role of knowledge of God in many biblical dramas, as the protagonist's knowledge of God encourages faithfulness. Abraham offered Isaac on the altar because he knew that God provides (Gen. 22:8, 14). Joseph forgave his traitor brothers because he understood God's sovereign mercy: "It was not you who sent me here [to Egypt], but God" (45:7–11). Moses led Israel out of Egypt because he knew God remembered his covenant with Israel, because he knew God had more power than the armies or deities of Egypt (Ex. 3–15). David defeated Goliath because he knew "the battle is the LORD's" (1 Sam. 17).

Jesus expected his disciples to apply their knowledge of him to hard situations, too. Having seen his mastery of nature, how could they quiver with fear in a storm (Matt. 8:23–27; 14:22–31)? Having seen him feed a multitude, could they wonder where to find food (Mark 6:30–44; 8:17–22)? Thus faith is the starting point for all application. To this the prophets and apostles testify.[23] It is also essential to a true grasp of the great text on the relevance of Scripture, 2 Timothy 3:14–17.

---

22 Especially his implicit claims to deity—forgiving sins, receiving obeisance, etc. (see Daniel Doriani, "The Deity of Christ in the Synoptic Gospels," *Journal of the Evangelical Theological Society* 37 [Sept. 1994]: 340–43).

23 The Gospels constantly urge faith in Jesus. Each gospel *opens* with testimony to him. Matthew says he is the son of David and Abraham (1:1), Savior (1:21), Immanuel (1:22–23), king of the Jews and Messiah (1:1; 2:4). Mark 1:1 says Jesus is the Christ, the Son of God. Luke calls him the Son of the Most High, the Son of God (1:31–35), Christ the Lord (2:11), light for the Gentiles (2:30–32). John

2 TIMOTHY 3:16–17

In 2 Timothy 3, Paul famously declares, "All Scripture is God-breathed and is useful for teaching, rebuking, correcting and training in righteousness, so that the man of God may be thoroughly equipped for every good work."[24] Scripture as a whole—every book, section, and genre—has these traits. "Scripture" (graphē) is a collective noun, referring to the whole Old Testament (Matt. 26:54–56; Luke 24:27, 32, 45; John 5:39; Acts 17:2, 11; Rom. 1:2, 15:4; 1 Cor. 15:3–4).[25] Paul does not mean that every bundle of verses lends itself to all four: teaching, refuting, correcting, and training.[26] Rather, as Timothy leads the

---

says that the Word who was God from the beginning came to dwell among men (1:1, 14). In the *middle* of the various Gospels, as Jesus' fame spreads, the question often arises, "Who is this?" (Matt. 8:27; Mark 4:41; Luke 5:21; 7:49; 8:25; 9:9; John 12:34). Each gospel replies by recording two confessions at climactic points (Matt. 16:16; 17:5; Mark 8:29; 9:7; Luke 9:20, 35; John 9:38; 11:27). Each gospel also *ends* with Christ. In Matthew, believers baptized into the name of the Son will make disciples of the nations (Matt. 28:18–20). In Mark, as Jesus dies, a centurion confesses, "Surely this man was the Son of God" (15:39). In Luke, the risen Christ commissions his disciples to proclaim repentance and forgiveness in his name (24:45–47). John says he wrote so people might believe that Jesus is the Christ and have life in his name (John 20:31). Thus the call to believe in Jesus is the prime application of each gospel.

24 There is no verb in this sentence. The verb "is" must be inserted at one of two places: "All Scripture [is] God-breathed and useful," or "All God-breathed Scripture [is] useful." The second option is untenable for four reasons: (1) The translation "All inspired Scripture [is] useful" hints that some Scripture is not inspired, not useful, or both. Both thoughts are alien to Paul, the early church, and the Jewish world. They also undermine his argument. (2) It is logical to construe both adjectives the same way. In the first reading both are predicative, in the second one is attributive, the other predicative. (3) Attributive adjectives ordinarily appear before the noun, but here both follow the noun "Scripture." (4) The construction is exactly parallel to 1 Tim. 4:4, where both adjectives are predicative. See Kelly, *Pastoral Epistles,* 203, Knight, *Pastoral Epistles,* 446–47.

25 B. B. Warfield, *The Inspiration and Authority of Scripture* (Philadelphia: Presbyterian and Reformed, 1948), 234–39.

26 I concede that a case can be made for the view I resist, since *pasa* ("all") when joined with an anarthrous noun ordinarily means "every." See F. Blass, A. Debrunner, and Robert Funk, *A Greek Grammar of the New Testament* (Chicago: University of Chicago Press, 1961), 275.3; Nigel Turner, *Syntax,* vol. 3 in *A Grammar of the Greek New Testament* by J. H. Moulton (Edinburgh: T. & T. Clark,

church, Scripture is his first ally. This includes both Testaments. "Scripture" means the Old for Paul, but whether he intended to describe the Gospels and Epistles or not, his remarks suit them too.[27] Scripture is God-breathed *(theopneustos),* God's very word. What it says, God says, so it is useful for ministry.[28]

Paul's quartet—teaching, rebuking, correcting, training in righteousness—falls into two categories: creed and conduct.[29] Regarding *creed,* when Paul says Scripture is useful for teaching and refutation, he asserts that doctrine helps the church overcome error and grow in truth. Doctrine is practical; deviant ideas promote wickedness (2 Tim. 3:1–9; 4:1–5). Regarding *conduct,* Paul says Scripture both corrects wrongdoing and trains us in righteousness. Scripture rebukes sin and promotes godliness. This joint training in doctrine and conduct equips Christians for every good work. The church is healthiest when both theology and life are sound.[30] Indeed, they are inseparable.[31]

Some Christians act as if 2 Timothy 3:16–17 said, "Believe it or not, there is something useful in all of Scripture—even *doctrinal* texts!" But Paul constantly links doctrine and life. They form a twin antidote

---

1963), 199; A. T. Robertson, *Grammar of the Greek New Testament* (Nashville: Broadman, 1934), 771–72.

27 The concept that the Gospels and Epistles are Scripture arises within the New Testament itself. Second Peter 3:16 calls Paul's letters Scripture. Paul implies that new revelation has parity with the old when, in 1 Tim. 5:18, he places Deut. 25:4 and Luke 10:7 side by side and calls both Scripture. Paul also believes his message is the authoritative word of God (1 Cor. 7:17; 14:37, 2 Cor. 2:17; 1 Thess. 2:13), for he was taught by God (1 Cor. 2:13; Gal. 1:12). When Paul tells Timothy to "preach the Word" (2 Tim. 4:2), he means what Timothy learned from him. If Paul's oral message is authoritative for Timothy, then his written words are too (John Stott, *Guard the Gospel* [Downers Grove, Ill.: InterVarsity, 1973], 101; Knight, *Pastoral Epistles,* 448). On apostolic authority, see Herman Ridderbos, *Redemptive History and New Testament Scriptures,* 2d ed. (Phillipsburg, N.J.: Presbyterian and Reformed, 1988).

28 Warfield, *Inspiration,* 299ff.

29 Stott, *Guard,* 103; Knight, *Pastoral Epistles,* 449–50; Gordon D. Fee, *First and Second Timothy, Titus* (Peabody, Mass.: Hendrickson), 280.

30 Paul often exhorts the church to guard the gospel and shun false doctrine. Still, he declares the necessity of good works sixteen times: 1 Tim. 2:10; 3:1, 7; 5:10, 25; 2 Tim. 2:21; 3:17; Titus 1:16; 2:5, 7, 8, 10, 14; 3:1, 8, 14.

31 One can argue that orthodoxy is more foundational than orthopraxy, but Paul makes no such argument here. Certainly both dead orthodoxy and blind activism are problems (Rev. 2:1–7; Luke 10:38–42).

to godlessness and shallowness (3:2–9; 4:3–4). Timothy himself stands firm if he remembers Paul's *doctrine and life* (3:10). When doctrinal creed and moral code unite, people are equipped for good works. Paul grieves when people cease to put up with sound doctrine (4:2–4) for sound doctrine cures so many ills.

This ought to be obvious, even for churches professing disinterest in doctrine. Even if we just want Jesus to remove our griefs and fears, few things help us more than biblical anthropology. Where else can we find true self-knowledge? How else can we make sense of the grandeur and the misery of man? Or the way the judge of the earth, the great thinking machine, loses all reason when a fly buzzes his head? Only the fall can explain the glory and the refuse of our lives.[32] Just one thing matters more than a biblical self-understanding—the knowledge of God, of our guilt before him, and of his remedy.

Part of the problem is the habit of regarding application as something that *follows* exegetical and theological work. Second Timothy 3 implies that instruction in doctrine is already the beginning of application. When Paul says Scripture is useful for creed and conduct, it reflects the parity of his interest in doctrine and practice in 2 Timothy. In six passages (twenty-two verses) Paul urges Timothy to guard or proclaim the gospel (1:8; 1:13–14; 2:2; 2:8–14; 3:10–14; 4:4–5). In five passages (again twenty-two verses) he exhorts him to endure or watch his life (2:1–8; 2:15; 2:22; 3:5; 3:10–14). Doctrine and ethics are allies. Both equip the saints for good works.

From roughly 1850 to 1950, theologians obscured the relevance of doctrine by calling their discipline a "spiritual science"[33] or the science of religion[34] that systematically arranged the facts of Scripture[35] or the knowledge of God.[36] But an older concept of theology has returned. It views theology as a practical art that inculcates wisdom

---

32 I borrow from Blaise Pascal, *Pensées* (New York: Dutton, 1958), sections 135–47, 339–66, 425–35.

33 Abraham Kuyper, *Principles of Sacred Theology* (1898; reprint, Grand Rapids: Eerdmans, 1965), 92–105.

34 A. A. Hodge, *Outlines of Theology* (1879; reprint, London: Banner of Truth, 1972), 15.

35 Charles Hodge, *Systematic Theology* (1871–72; reprint, Grand Rapids: Eerdmans, 1952), 1:1–3, 10–19.

36 Louis Berkhof, *Systematic Theology* (Grand Rapids: Eerdmans, 1939), 19.

for living.[37] It says the knowledge of God and of self shape true godliness.[38] It says theology brings the truth of Scripture into "lively intersection" with the culture and the church.[39] It says, "Practical Christian living is based on . . . knowledge."[40]

SUMMARY

Paul's claim that all Scripture is useful appears to be undercut by genealogies and certain Mosaic laws and prophetic oracles. But Paul is right. Our study of ordinary language usage showed that normal speakers and writers always seek to "do things with words." *All* seek relevance; all seek effects. Scripture seeks the special effect of reconciling mankind to God and granting the blessings found in Christ. The prophets anticipated him, the apostles looked back to him, and he continually pointed to himself as he handled the law, prophecy, and biblical themes. In doing so, he declared himself greater than Abraham, Jacob, Moses, Jonah, and Solomon; greater than temple and priest, David and the kingship. He is the great prophet, the final judge, the wisdom of God. Jesus and his spokesmen have declared this. Now each generation of Christian leaders must restate the message. Several chapters explore ways to do so; the next chapter explores the character of interpreters who take up this mantle.

---

37 William Ames, *The Marrow of Theology* (1629; reprint, Grand Rapids: Baker, 1997), 77–78.

38 John Calvin, *Institutes of the Christian Religion,* trans. Ford Lewis Battles (1559; Philadelphia: Westminster, 1960), 1:4–9, 36–37.

39 David Wells, *Losing Our Virtue* (Grand Rapids: Eerdmans, 1998), 2.

40 Sinclair Ferguson, *Know Your Christian Life* (Downers Grove, Ill.: InterVarsity, 1981), 2; see also 1–8.

3

The Interpreter

A preacher is like a spiritual midwife, not giving birth but offering assistance as God creates spiritual life through the word. Like the midwife, the preacher is superfluous if all goes well. Men and women do come to faith by reading the Bible alone in dorm rooms, military barracks, or isolated cabins. But complications arise; people need assistance. So they need interpreters to mediate the ancient text message to modern audiences that have difficulty seeing its relevance. Thus, in the scheme of this book on the interpretation of the Bible, it is time to focus on the interpreter, the midwife.

GENERAL MODEL FOR APPLICATION

Returning to the model for interpretation presented in the introduction (fig. 6), this chapter examines the character of the interpreter, especially in its moral and spiritual dimensions. God works through the word, but teachers' character and training are among the means God uses to do so.

By dint of education and study of the geography, customs, language, and worldview of biblical ages, interpreters gain the knowledge that equips them to instruct novices. Like Philip with the Ethiopian eunuch, they ask, "Do you understand what you are reading?" and offer explanations of what puzzles the reader (Acts 8:30–35). But interpreters are more than conduits for data. They are embedded in their own culture. Their teachers have taught them "the facts" from the vantage points of their own distinct social and historical settings.

Fig. 6.
A GENERAL MODEL FOR APPLICATION

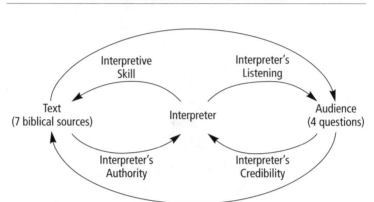

Hardly anyone will disagree so far, but I would suggest the more unsettling notion that, in ways we cannot fully detect, we Christians operate within the naturalistic thought world that we decry. We cannot fully transcend our culture's answers to questions such as (1) what matters are interesting or difficult enough to merit our attention, or (2) what counts as a valid reply to a question raised by accounts of the history or philosophy of centuries past. As noted earlier, like secularists, we have an affinity for scientific, despiritualizing analyses. Even for Christians, the scientific explanation is normal and the spiritual is exceptional. Thus the teachers who want to explain Europe's response to the Lisbon earthquake are not coolly dispensing abstract facts. They need the explanation themselves. Further, they may be so far removed from that thought world that they will struggle to attain "a wholly reliable understanding of what the Europeans of that day felt."[1]

If this is true for ideas and events from two or three centuries past, how much more for two or three millennia past? Take the case of the biblical teaching on gender roles. Since the rise of feminism, our culture has given almost monolithic assent to the commonsense feminist idea that men and women are equal in value, gifts, and energies. As a result biblical teachings such as "Wives, submit to your husbands," and "I do not permit a woman to teach or exercise authority over a man" sound problematic, even offensive. Traditional gender roles seem

1   A. J. Conyers, *The Eclipse of Heaven* (Downers Grove, Ill.: InterVarsity, 1992), 15.

vaguely implausible to vast numbers today. The exposition of Paul's teachings demands levels of explanation and defense that were unnecessary in A.D. 400, 1600, or 1900.[2] To teach effectively on gender, we need to know the biblical world and contemporary society and must also expect to struggle with the issue ourselves. (Conversely, with slavery and monarchy growing more distant in the West, the typical Christian reads of them, even in Scripture, with increasing detachment.)

Thus the questions people ask and the criteria for plausible answers vary (within limits) from one culture to another. What seems interesting and reasonable depends on our basic commitments, our worldview, our construal of reality, and the community within which we think.[3] Leaving these heady topics to others more skilled, let us focus on another subjective aspect of interpretation: the courage, character, and credibility of the interpreter.[4]

COURAGE

The Need for Courage

Preachers need courage—courage to let the Bible say what it means, courage to see the world as it is, and courage to address the

2 On these issues see Mary Kassian, *The Feminist Gospel* (Wheaton, Ill.: Crossway, 1992); and Andreas Köstenberger, Thomas Schreiner, and H. Scott Baldwin, *Women in the Church* (Grand Rapids: Baker, 1995).

3 For a start on theoretical apologetics, epistemology, pluralism, and postmodern construals of reality, see, among Christian writers, D. A. Carson, *The Gagging of God* (Grand Rapids: Zondervan, 1996); John Frame, *Apologetics to the Glory of God: An Introduction* (Phillipsburg, N.J.: Presbyterian and Reformed, 1994); Roger Lundin, *Disciplining Hermeneutics* (Grand Rapids: Eerdmans, 1997); Lesslie Newbigin, *The Gospel in a Pluralist Society* (Grand Rapids: Eerdmans, 1990); J. Richard Middleton and Brian J. Walsh, *Truth Is Stranger than It Used to Be* (Downers Grove, Ill.: InterVarsity, 1995); Nicholas Wolterstorff, *Reason within the Bounds of Religion,* 2d ed. (Grand Rapids: Eerdmans, 1984). Among secular writers, Thomas Kuhn, *The Structure of Scientific Revolutions* (Chicago: University of Chicago Press, 1962); Walter Truett Anderson, *Reality Isn't What It Used to Be* (San Francisco: Harper and Row, 1990).

4 I do not hereby minimize objective exegesis, to which my first volume was dedicated. But there is more to interpretation than skill. On faith and skill in interpretation, see Gerhard Maier, *Biblical Hermeneutics,* trans. Robert Yarbrough (Wheaton, Ill.: Crossway, 1994), 45–63; and Moisés Silva, *Explorations in Exegetical Method* (Grand Rapids: Baker, 1996), 197–215.

difference between the two. The temptation to cowardly silence assails us week by week, for week by week our preparations urge us to say things that may cause offense or raise doubts. If the subject is murder, we must say it is murder to call people morons, fools, jerks, or good-for-nothings, even if saying so indicts dozens in the audience. If the subject is sexual purity, we must say that extramarital sex is a thieving lie as well as adultery, since extramarital sex is a life-uniting act that has no life-uniting intent.[5] But will fear of scoffers silence us? Any time we speak on materialism, careerism, divorce, or abortion, we know that many visitors and church members will feel pangs of guilt, or will silently disagree. And some of those church members feed our families. The temptation to adjust our remarks to avoid offense can become intense. Imagine these scenes:

- Surrounded by homosexuals and their sympathizers, you are asked to explain traditional biblical morality.
- Invited to speak at a missions conference, you plan to say that a church's missions budget should exceed its building budget. You believe a building is essentially a gift a church gives itself. Therefore it is minimal, not radical, for a church to give others as much as it gives itself. But upon arrival, you see banners trumpeting a new building campaign.

I was once called upon to defend traditional gender roles at a theological meeting where there were twenty-five egalitarian feminists and only one other participant holding my view. Virtually everyone disagreed with me, and some attacked me personally, accusing me of misogyny or seeking to retain male power. With cameras rolling, the chairwoman asked me to respond. With my heart pounding and a nearly overwhelming desire to seem reasonable and likable, I began my response like this:

> I have read the feminist literature, have talked at length to feminist friends and relatives. I know the force of their arguments; I have heard their experiences. In fact, I believe I could state the feminist case convincingly, if I chose. My mother is an

5 Lewis Smedes, *Sex for Christians* (Grand Rapids: Eerdmans, 1994), 109–36.

ordained minister, and I have no sons but three daughters, so I lack no personal motive to advocate the feminist position. And of course, the feminist view seems more plausible, more humane in our culture. So, in some ways, I would prefer that the feminist case were true. But what I *prefer* is not the issue. The issue, finally, is whether the God of the Bible exists or not. If there is a personal, all-knowing God who wishes to communicate with his creation and has done so in the Bible, then that word has authority over us. When he speaks, it is our responsibility to understand and follow that word, whether we particularly like it or not. If that word runs against our preferences, then *so much the worse for our preferences.*

The conviction that there is a God who has spoken in the Bible is the root of all courage in preaching or teaching. If, when we preach, we share *our* thoughts about theology or morality, then we have reason to alter our remarks to avoid offense. But if we believe the one God has spoken through Jesus, the prophets, and the disciples, then we must state his message whether we think it will be well received or not. This includes the most scandalous thing a teacher can say— that Jesus is the only hope for sinners. This is the stance of faith and the source of courage.

The Source of Courage

In short, the root of the interpreter's courage is genuine faith, a trust in and commitment to the God of Scripture, the Savior and Lord. Of course, the posture I advocate is not the only option. There are three: readers may stand *over, beside,* or *under* the Bible (fig. 7).

1. *The reader over the text, as critic.* Critics may profess admiration or animosity for biblical religion. They may regard it as a noble spiritual system or as the naive product of a superstitious world to which modern minds cannot return. They may long for a simple precritical faith, or may wish to liberate society from the oppression of orthodox Christianity. But, they say, no thinking citizen can trust an alien authority that posits a three-story universe with angels in heaven, demons in hell, and humankind in between. In the world of the Bible, they say, miracles are common. No one controls his own life. Evil spir-

FIG. 7.
POSSIBLE RELATIONS BETWEEN READERS AND THE TEXT OF SCRIPTURE

1. Criticism: Reader over Text

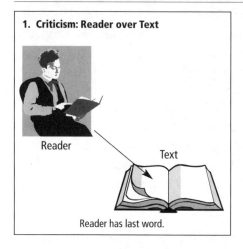

Reader

Text

Reader has last word.

2. Dialogue: Reader beside Text

Text

Reader

Reader still has last word.

3. Submission: Reader under Text

Text

Reader

Text (or God) has last word.

its may take possession of an individual, or God may grant him heavenly visions. For modern humanity, this mythical view of the world is obsolete and incredible.[6]

Moderns, critics allege, have lost their prescientific simplicity and cannot return to naive faith. If someone does decide to adhere to the Bible, it is that person's decision, but, like it or not, humankind retains the throne. So critics claim we are inevitably the final arbiters of truth, at least within our subjective world. I do not charge all critics with cowardice, but they have spurned the greatest source of boldness. They deny that a voice from outside themselves and their circle can speak authoritatively to them. Nothing can compel them to say something they would never choose.

2. *The reader beside the text, in dialogue.* Here the interpreter encounters past believers, and even God, through the Bible. In this view, when an interpreter hears Scripture, he or she enters its world, and a creative engagement can occur. One universe of ideas or one way of life meets another, and no one knows how it may end. The reader may be changed by the text, or he may, perhaps reluctantly, reject it.[7]

If we define a critic as someone who is willing, as a matter of principle, to say, "The Bible says X, and the Bible is wrong," the dialogue position is still "critical," since readers retain the right to accept or reject the biblical message. Yet this view shares the conservatives' belief in the power of the Bible to surprise, to transform, to lay the heart bare. Further, it holds, with conservatives, that while the Bible can insist on its authority, it ordinarily operates by "a non-violent appeal" to the imagination.[8] Thus this view stands between the pure critic and the pure conservative.

An aside is needed here: While dialogue is the wrong posture toward

6 Rudolf Bultmann, "New Testament and Mythology," *in Kerygma and Myth: A Theological Debate,* ed. Hans Werner Bartsch, trans. R. M. Fuller (New York: Harper & Row, 1961), 1–44; John Macquarrie, *Jesus Christ in Modern Thought* (Philadelphia: Trinity Press International, 1990), 70.

7 Hans-Georg Gadamer, *Truth and Method,* 2d ed. (New York: Continuum, 1989), 302ff; Anthony Thistelton, *The Two Horizons* (Grand Rapids: Eerdmans, 1980), 307–10.

8 Paul Ricoeur, "Toward a Hermeneutic of the Idea of Revelation," *Harvard Theological Review* 70.1–2 (1977): 37.

Scripture, a form of dialogue does suit the relation between pastor and church. Some leaders virtually equate their authority with that of Scripture. Yet the malign influences of sin, ignorance, and this age guarantee that our messages will mix truth and error. Therefore, the church must balance analytical independence (1 Thess. 5:21) with submissiveness to its leaders (1 Thess. 5:13; Heb. 13:7, 17; Gal. 1:8–9). We "obey [our] leaders" *and* we "test everything." Yet we test humbly, reticent to question pastors who have been called by God, then trained, tested, and approved by the church. Contrary to contemporary sensibilities, not all opinions are equal. The snap judgment of one who ponders a point for the first time cannot match the judgment of a seasoned leader who has pondered the roots, rationale, and results of the full array of opinions on a matter and has for years lived out the implications of his view.

3. *The reader below the text, in submission.* The submissive interpreter bows to the God who reveals himself in Scripture and accepts, in principle, whatever it says. If the Bible upsets a cherished conviction, we say, "I stand corrected," not "I wonder." Facing a difficult teaching, we may suspect that it has been misconstrued or otherwise hesitate. But if we confirm that it means what it seems to mean, then we bow—not to the text, but to the God who gave it.[9] So conservatives claim the highest willingness to submit to Scripture.

The difficulty with this view is that confessing, "I submit to Scripture," is one thing, while actually submitting is another. Further, this third view can be perverted by illogical thinking:

> I believe whatever the Bible says.
> Whatever the Bible says, I believe.
> I know what the Bible says.
> Therefore, what I believe is what the Bible says.
> Therefore, if the Bible seems to say something I don't believe,
>   it must not really mean that.

9 Critics sometimes accuse conservatives of biblicism—worshiping Scripture rather than God. This accusation makes sense to the critics since they separate God from the Bible. But if the Bible is indeed the word of God, then the charge of biblicism falls away. To submit to Scripture is to submit to the Lord who reveals himself in it. Believers respond to the Author through his book. It would be a deadly error if someone related to Scripture in itself and failed to see its reference to God.

This sort of thinking betrays a startling naiveté. Burdened with groundless self-confidence that they are knowledgeable and free from prejudices, people holding this view can distort texts so that they confirm prior beliefs and dismiss whatever does not fit their system. They profess the authority of Scripture but function as if impervious to it.

Paradoxically, the Bible may exercise more power over some who advocate the (inferior) "dialogue" position (view 2) than it does over many who claim to submit to it. A smug conservative thinks he has the message under control and seals his ears. Meanwhile, readers who claim the prerogative of a final no could be freer to hear the Bible's radical challenges and, perhaps, change as a result. If we would hear the Bible, we need a humbler syllogism:

I probably do not believe this passage as purely, as radically, as I should.
I probably do not understand this passage as fully as I should.
Therefore, I probably need this text to correct my understanding and deepen my faith.[10]

To further prevent self-deception, conservatives should distinguish between standing *on* the Bible and standing *under* the Bible, a distinction made by the evangelical German scholar Adolf Schlatter during a theological examination. A churchman asked Schlatter if he stood on the Bible. "No," he replied, "I stand *under* the Bible." That is, he would not use the Bible as a platform to build his own theology. He would observe the data of Scripture and allow them to determine his views.[11]

So belief in the God who speaks in Scripture fosters courage in the application of Scripture. Of course, critics can speak boldly and conservatives can deafen themselves to Scripture. Still, belief that God has spoken in the Bible and given us a message beyond our own wisdom moves us, in our speech, to please God rather than people. There

10 Dennis Johnson suggested this humbler syllogism as a corrective to the arrogant one.
11 W. Ward Gasque, "The Promise of Adolf Schlatter," *Evangelical Review of Theology* 4 (1980): 27.

is nothing that interpreters need more than faith. Yet they do need more than faith. They need skill and character.[12]

CHARACTER

The Need for Character

Robert Dabney said that if a speaker has intelligence but not integrity, "the plausibility of what he advances will be felt; but the more ability he shows, the more will the people fear to commit themselves to his opinions; for they have no guarantee . . . that he is not employing these forces of his genius . . . to . . . injure them." But if the people are convinced of a preacher's knowledge and affection and his desire for their benefit, then he has their ear. "Eloquence," Dabney concludes, "may dazzle and please; holiness of life convinces."[13]

Communication skills can create an ineffable aura that irresistibly draws audiences to some speakers. The texture of voice, confidence of manner, ease of gesture, liberty of gaze, and balance of energy and calm, all prepare an audience to listen expectantly. Yet perfect cadences disappoint if the content is only magnificent fluff. Delivery matters, but not half so much as content, and character deepens content.

1. *Character and listening.* Listening to others is essential if our messages are to meet real needs; several character traits foster this art of listening.[14] *Love* releases empathy, so we can see others as they are in their neediness. Love deletes the ego's persistent question, "What do they think of me?" and genuinely attends to others. To listen silently is to deny oneself, briefly. We give up the right to sound wise or clever.

---

12 Good interpretation demands the virtues of patience and self-discipline, but there is no intrinsic link between goodness or piety and exegetical skill. Character counts more in the subjective aspects of interpretation.

13 Robert Dabney, *Sacred Rhetoric* (1870; reprint, Carlisle, Pa.: Banner of Truth Trust, 1979), 261–63.

14 I sometimes wonder if Jesus' selflessness contributed to his ability to read minds (Matt. 9:4; 12:25; Luke 5:22; 6:8; 7:39–40; 9:47; John 2:25). Or was the reading of thoughts a manifestation of his omniscience? But he did not always make use of that prerogative of his deity (Matt. 24:36). Was it then a God-given prophetic insight? Or was he so selfless that he had a supreme "natural" ability to understand people? See John Wenham, *Christ and the Bible* (Grand Rapids: Baker, 1994).

We forgo our story, our last word, to put another's story or word first. *Courage* watches the culture and the church, without blinking, to address them as they are, not as we prefer to imagine them. *Wisdom* knows how to cut through blather and excuses until we hear the truth. *Mercy* listens tenderly, so that we diagnose in order to render aid, not to criticize. *Patience* listens quietly to the story of people just like us, and people utterly unlike us, old or young, rich or poor, simple or wise, smooth or broken, so we can tell them of Jesus.

These traits deepen our listening, so that our words acquire an authenticity that drills real issues in real terms, and so that people do not say, "I understand," or "I enjoyed your talk" (a troubling compliment for preachers who hope to create some constructive misery). Rather, they say, "I know exactly what you mean."

2. *Character and humility.* A preacher is a cardiologist who has survived a heart attack, a diagnostician who detects in himself a deadly yet curable disease. We who preach against sin commit the very sins we describe. The vain preach humility; the temperamental and the obese urge self-control. People think, "Look who's talking." But fear of accusations should not paralyze us. Instead, our tone and demeanor should cohere with our confession, "Like you, I am a sinner saved by grace. Here is what God says to all of us about sin and grace." We all "hold out the gospel in contaminated hands."[15] Of course, the pulpit should never become a confessional. Indeed, long, dramatic confessions may reveal a perverse pride: "See, even my sins are profound and interesting."[16] Yet candor regarding our sin liberates us to speak regularly, boldly, and penitently about it. It also gives our hearers the freedom to approach us and say, "I felt that you surveyed the landscape of my heart, and I must talk to you about it."

So humility serves communication. But it also deepens interpretation. The humble have space to grapple with sin, to confess their need of Jesus, to struggle for righteousness. Then, when we apply Scripture to ourselves, we press deeper, to the heart of a matter. When we have wrestled with sin, and lost a round or two, a realism, an awareness of

---

15   Cornelius Plantinga, "Preaching Sin to Reluctant Hearers," *Perspectives* 12 (Dec. 1997): 11–12.

16   Ibid., 12.

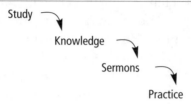

FIG. 8.
OLD MODEL: KNOWLEDGE PRODUCES ACTION

the difficulty of faithfulness, suffuses our work. The quest for righteousness elevates our capacity to locate the burden of a passage.

The Centrality of Character

Most of us have a simple, half-articulated model of the way teaching helps Christians grow. Ignoring the gaps that separate the library and the street, it suggests that we can move in a straight line from our study to knowledge to message to practice (fig. 8).

The old model has a valid insight: what we know influences what we do. The mind matters. As Paul says, "Do not be conformed to the pattern of this world, but be transformed by the renewing of your mind" (my translation). But the old model forgets that what we *do* also affects what we know. As Paul immediately adds, "Then you will be able to test and approve what God's will is" (Rom. 12:2). That is, when we try to obey the word, we put it to the test. When the word passes the test, we know it better because experience has confirmed it.

Thus, Jesus told some Jews who doubted his teaching that anyone who wanted to *do* God's will would recognize that his teaching came from God (John 7:15–17; see also Mal. 3:10; 1 John 2:3–4). There is no neutral vantage point for assessing Christ's claims. His truth is self-authenticating for those who commit themselves to it. Thus a renewed mind promotes godly action, but godly action also renews the mind. Consider how it works . . .

It is widely recognized that people gain knowledge gradually, by coming at something again and again. Two theologians, Friedrich Schleiermacher and Maurice Blondel, analyzed how the process works. Schleiermacher's contribution today has the label "the hermeneutical spiral."[17]

---

17 The original term (from Friedrich Schleiermacher, *Hermeneutics: The Handwritten Manuscripts* [Missoula, Mont.: Scholars, 1977], 113–16) was hermeneutical *cir-*

Fig. 9.
Hermeneutical Spiral

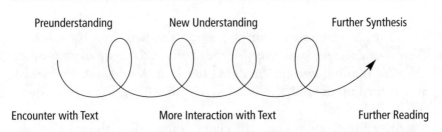

Preunderstanding	New Understanding	Further Synthesis

Encounter with Text	More Interaction with Text	Further Reading

1. *The hermeneutical spiral.* This phrase is designed to evoke the idea of open-ended movement from the world of a reader to the world of the text (and perhaps its author) (fig. 9). Texts open new vistas for readers by questioning their convictions and prejudices and introducing them to new worlds of thinking. Yet worldviews change slowly; a text (or speaker) cannot do all its work at once. Instead, readers spiral ever nearer to the author's meaning by refining their understanding whenever they return to it.

There is certainly truth in this idea, but some think of it in hyperintellectual ways. One scholar said, "I am . . . spiraling nearer and nearer to the text's intended meaning as I refine my hypotheses and allow the text to continue to challenge and correct those alternative interpretations, *then* to guide my delineation of its significance for today" (emphasis added).[18]

This idea has merit, but it sounds too narrowly cerebral. It misses the way life forces us to consider relevance long before we finish the mental process. For example, during a mission trip in northern India, we visited a deserted British cemetery in the southern Himalayas with our host, an experienced missionary. Suddenly a caretaker rushed at

---

cle. Unfortunately, it evokes the image of circular reasoning. Hermeneutical *spiral* better expresses the idea of refinement and movement. For an introduction to the spiral and the related new hermeneutic, see Thiselton, *Two Horizons,* 327–56; Grant Osborne, *The Hermeneutical Spiral* (Downers Grove, Ill.: InterVarsity, 1991), 6–8, 366–415; William G. Doty, *Contemporary New Testament Interpretation* (Englewood Cliffs, N.J.: Prentice-Hall, 1972), 28–51.

18   Osborne, *Hermeneutical Spiral,* 6. His position is subtler than this remark implies, but hermeneutical theorists sometimes leave the impression that protracted cogitation precedes application.

us, accosting us, "What are you doing here, you trespassers! How did you break in? This cemetery is closed. Get out of here, or I will set my dogs on you!"

To my astonishment, our polite host shouted right back at him, even as our accuser spoke, so that they bellowed on top of each other. "We did nothing wrong! We didn't break in. We drove here, parked, and walked up the hill. I've been here many times, and no one questioned us before."

After about one minute, the clamor diminished, though they still yelled rudely. In another minute, the tone became milder again. Momentarily, we had an invitation to tea! Astonished, I asked my friend to explain why he had shouted at the caretaker and how the roaring had calmed him. "The caretaker doesn't have much to do; it's his job to shout at us a little," he replied. "I yelled back because that's how you establish your sincerity and innocence here. If I had backed down, he would have decided that we *were* trespassers."

I had just been thinking about the proverb "A gentle answer turns away wrath," but this experience drove me to reconsider it. Obviously, my host had turned away wrath; his loud protest, paradoxically, served as a "gentle answer." Deliberately, not lacking self-control, he had yelled to make peace. Thus my friend's wise action led me to reexamine the proverb.

Whether we notice it or not, such reexamination is common. Sometimes we do "refine and correct hypotheses" and *then* "delineate their significance for today." But interpretation is fluid. We come to texts with our needs, questions, and heartaches. As we read, something touches upon a life issue, and we begin to apply the text to ourselves. Listeners, likewise, fasten upon incidental remarks if they connect with a life issue. A good sermon, many say, is one that gives them something to think about. That something is typically a life issue—our relationships, our aspirations, our secrets (thus creating a good reason for drifting off during a sermon). So interpretation is both a mental and a spiritual act. Attempts at heeding the word stimulate our ability to understand it.[19]

---

19 Some proponents of the hermeneutical spiral agree. Gadamer says that the understanding of a text is tested by one's ability to see its significance for new situations (*Truth and Method,* 277–305). Of legal and biblical law he says, "To understand the order means to apply it to the specific situation to which it is

2. *A spiral of heart and hands.* Blondel suggests that interpreters gain understanding of Scripture through attempts to apply it as well as added rounds of reflection. That is, we can begin to live by a text before exegesis is complete (fig. 10).

Blondel begins with the obvious point that humans both ponder and act. Aside from customary or habitual actions, we are planners. After planned actions we usually ask, "Did I act correctly? Did I obtain my goal or not? Could I have been more effective, more virtuous?" There is typically a gap between the goal and the result of our plans. In our sophisticated projects we rarely achieve precisely what we intend. This gap between our self-imposed demands and our actual level of success prompts us to ask, "What went wrong? How can I avoid repeating my errors? How can I build on my successes?" Finally, by working to close the gap between intentions and results, we progress toward the original goal.[20]

As believers read the Bible, they find many worthy goals—turning away wrath, doing justice, walking humbly with God. The attempt to fulfill a text by reaching its goals helps us see what it means. In this way our efforts at following a text help us understand it. The attempt to do what is right produces growth for both the will and the mind. Conversely, if we refuse to practice what we know, we sever this motive for learning. If anything, inaction causes us to avoid knowledge, because it stirs guilt. On the other hand, proper actions confirm halting steps in the right direction. An upward spiral develops as small successes breed confidence, and confidence prepares us for the next challenge.

This is not a common point, yet the best theologians are aware of it. Calvin said that pupils of Scripture must "apply themselves teachably" to the word and "reverently embrace" its witness. He concluded, "not only faith . . . but all right knowledge of God is born of obedience." So for Calvin the quest for obedience advances the

---

relevant" (p. 298). Of course, a strictly cognitive model is sometimes appropriate. See Ludwig Wittgenstein, *Philosophical Investigations* (New York: Macmillan, 1973), 151–55.

20 Maurice Blondel, letter to Père Auguste Valensin, quoted in Introduction to *The Letter on Apologetics and History and Dogmatics,* by Maurice Blondel, trans. and ed. Alexander Dru and Illtyd Trethowan (London: Harvill, 1964), 96; John Macquarrie, "Maurice Blondel," *Encyclopedia of Philosophy,* 1:323–24.

FIG. 10.
NEW MODEL: KNOWLEDGE AND ACTION STIMULATE EACH OTHER

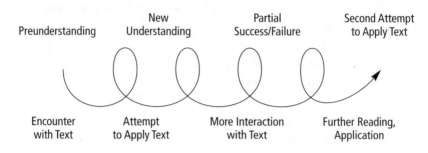

| New | Partial | Second Attempt |
| Preunderstanding | Understanding | Success/Failure | to Apply Text |

| Encounter | Attempt | More Interaction | Further Reading, |
| with Text | to Apply Text | with Text | Application |

knowledge of God and his word.[21] Similarly, Luther said interpretation requires "the experience of the heart" as well as skill with Scripture.[22] Wesley said that only the Bible could establish a doctrine, but that experience does "confirm a doctrine which is grounded on Scripture."[23]

More recently, Gordon Fee said, "The ultimate aim of all true exegesis is spirituality," first for interpreters, then for their hearers.[24] Before exegesis starts, we give the text permission to bring us up short, to astonish and admonish us. Through exegesis we invite the text and its Author to exegete our soul and the souls of our hearers.[25] Similarly, Moisés Silva said we cannot help but bring our failures and questions to the Bible:

> It is proper and even necessary to approach the Bible with a strong sense of our needs. The problems faced in the gospel ministry often alert us to truths in Scripture that might otherwise remain veiled to us. Proper exegesis consists largely of asking the right questions from the text, and the life of the church can provide us with those very questions.[26]

21 John Calvin, *Institutes of the Christian Religion,* trans. Ford Lewis Battles (Philadelphia: Westminster, 1960), 1.6.2.
22 Martin Luther, in Maier, *Biblical Hermeneutics,* 70.
23 John Wesley, *The Works of John Wesley* (Grand Rapids: Zondervan, 1972), 5:132–33; see also 129.
24 Gordon Fee, "Exegesis and Spirituality: Reflections on Completing the Exegetical Circle," *Crux* 31.4 (Dec. 1995): 30.
25 Ibid., 31, 34.
26 Moisés Silva, *Has the Church Misread the Bible?* (Grand Rapids: Zondervan, 1987), 22.

So spiritual formation both precedes and follows interpretation. A feedback loop connects knowledge and practice: knowledge guides Christian living, but Christian living also verifies knowledge. A passion for righteousness spurs teachers on to deeper study, and enriches the hermeneutical spiral.[27] As we speak hard truths in love, we learn what "speaking the truth in love" means (Eph. 4:15). When we respectfully submit to a difficult or foolish boss, we learn what submitting to harsh masters means (1 Peter 2:18). When we make peace with an irascible neighbor, we learn what "blessed are the peacemakers" means (Matt. 5:9). Furthermore, practical questions sensitize us to aspects of the text we might otherwise miss. Certainly, the question "How does this apply?" (What does it mean *now*?) drives us to the question "What did this text mean *then*?"

3. *Exploring the new spiral*. "Self-serving Bible knowledge" is an oxymoron. The Bible itself says knowing entails doing. After he washed the disciples' feet, Jesus said, "Do you understand what I have done for you? . . . Now that I, your Lord and Teacher, have washed your feet, you also should wash one another's feet. . . . Now that you know these things, *you will be blessed if you do them*" (John 13:4–17). James says, "Do not merely listen to the word, and so deceive yourselves. Do what it says." With diagnostic sarcasm, James extols those who affirm orthodox theology without acting on it, "You believe that there is one God? Good! Even the demons believe that—and shudder" (James 1:22; 2:19). The author of Hebrews chides his slow-learning readers when he says, "Solid food is for the mature, who by *constant use* have trained themselves to distinguish good from evil" (Heb. 5:11–14). That is, a failure to practice what they knew dulled his readers' minds, making it hard for them to grasp the teaching on Jesus' priesthood. They should have matured by applying their prior Christian experience to their current crisis.[28] If they had even tried, their imperfect attempts would have prepared them for their new struggle.[29]

As we saw in chapter 1, people do not really understand the Bible

---

27 Dan McCartney and Charles Clayton, *Let the Reader Understand: A Guide to Interpreting and Applying the Bible* (Wheaton, Ill.: Bridgepoint, 1994), 254–55.

28 William Lane, *Hebrews 1–8* (Dallas: Word, 1991), 131, 139.

29 John Frame, *The Doctrine of the Knowledge of God* (Phillipsburg, N.J.: Presbyterian and Reformed, 1987), 154.

unless they can apply it. If a congregation has a flawless ecclesiology but ignores visitors from other social and ethnic groups, they do not truly understand the church. If a couple memorizes Ephesians 5 but the husband attempts to domineer the wife who resists him at every turn, they do not "know" the passage.

The quest for righteousness also enhances interpretation by making us read the Bible expectantly. After a frustrating attempt at correcting one of our children, my wife declared, "She's too old to spank, and grounding punishes me as much as it punishes her. Take away privileges? She hardly watches television, and her activities are constructive. What is left?" That sort of question either drives us to despair or a deeper quest for knowledge. Weeks later, still hungry for an answer, I saw something new in the law "an eye for an eye, a tooth for a tooth." I knew that it forbids vindictive acts of revenge ("If you hit me, I'll kill you") and seeks perfect justice. But reading as a parent, I saw a principle that held promise for our disciplinary problem: *Let the punishment fit the crime and be proportional to it.*

The principle of proportional discipline implies that food crimes deserve food punishments. If a child acts wild at the dinner table and knocks over his beverages three consecutive days, he can drink water for dinner for three consecutive days. Property offenses deserve property discipline. If a child leaves her book bag on the floor four days, she can carry her books to school for four days (or bring them in a grocery bag). If children refuse to stay in bed, they can stay up, doing nothing, for ten minutes. The idea has worked for us; our children even see the justice in their discipline. In this view application is as much a skill (knowing "how") as a body of knowledge (knowing "that").[30] Knowledge of skills is experiential. We learn sports not by mastering the rules, but by playing the game. Again, we prove we know a musical instrument by playing it. To step closer to interpretation, judges demonstrate their knowledge of law by applying it justly to complex unprecedented cases.[31] Likewise, Christian leaders verify their skill with the word by applying it to difficult issues.

---

30 Gilbert Ryle, *The Concept of Mind* (New York: Barnes and Noble, 1949), 25–61; Michael Polanyi, *Personal Knowledge* (Chicago: University of Chicago Press, 1968), 53–55, 59–65.

31 Gadamer, *Truth and Method,* 277–305.

Consider again the proverb "A gentle answer turns away wrath." It is one thing to know *that* a gentle answer turns away wrath, another to know *how* to turn away wrath—how to deflect outrageous remarks, how to ignore insults, how to uncover the truth buried within an outburst, how to acknowledge the conviction that spurred the eruption. Whenever we learn more about turning away wrath, we better comprehend the text. "Knowing that" and "knowing how" connect.

CREDIBILITY

The Need for Credibility

The previous section asserted that the desire for a Scripture-shaped life enhances our grasp of the Bible. This section claims that the same quest deepens a teacher's credibility.

When leaders encounter their ignorance and folly and still persevere, that infuses their teaching with authenticity. When leaders engage spiritual issues themselves, it muzzles the blabber of glib solutions to superficially stated problems. But there is great loss if speakers indulge in sins rather than fighting them. If we let sin fester until its putrescence bursts open in public, our credibility suffers.

Suppose a counselor has casually divorced three women.[32] The first, he says, became a different person. The second he abandoned during a mid-life crisis. As for the third, "We both knew it was a mistake." A thrice-divorced man, drawing on his experience, could offer fine remarks about marriage and its troubles. Yet his failure to grasp the essence of marriage as a life-long covenant, for better or for worse, taints everything he says. The disadvantage for a single person who speaks on marriage is not the same. All teachers address topics beyond their experience. Those who never knew bereavement may be shallow or misinformed, but their remarks are not *corrupted* by their ignorance. The failure to exercise a Christian virtue *when the test comes* differs greatly from the failure to exercise a virtue because *the test never came.*

When we have struggled, prayed, and waited on God until the edge

---

32 I do not speak of those who suffer a divorce despite their best efforts and sorest sorrow.

of exhaustion, we cannot utter naive advice: "Your problem is simple; just take these easy steps." Our struggles teach us that every time we command, someone has the sinking thought, "I have tried and failed and cannot try again." If we have known defeat and God's power in the darkness, we grope not merely to find words we've read somewhere, but to articulate the soul's groanings.

Everyone knows that once they enter the ministry, pastors have to behave or suffer the consequences. Purity and sincerity are occupational requirements. Pastors can even learn to be content with a veneer of holiness. As one cynic said, "The one thing you really need in the ministry is sincerity, and if you can fake that, you've got it made."

Paul made character the first item in his profile of an elder in 1 Timothy 3:1–7. He seems more interested in leaders' tasks initially, since he begins, "If anyone aspires to be an overseer, he desires a noble *work*" (3:1, my translation). But he quickly switches to character: "An overseer must *be* . . ." (3:2). In the next sentences, Paul cites ten requirements of character but only two skills—the ability to teach and the ability to manage his family. So, for Paul, it is not enough to do the *work* of an elder; one must be the *person*.[33]

Paul's interest in an elder's family life underscores the point. For example, an elder must manage and take care of his children (3:4–5). Linking "manage" with "take care," we see that leaders validate themselves by serving their families. This connects with the requirement that elders' children obey them "with respect." Consider the way children obey their parents. Small children submit to parents because they are nearly powerless; they have no alternative. But the older children of harsh parents learn to obey with *disrespect*. Tardy obedience, a slouching torso, and rolling eyes—disdain oozes like an open sore. As they age, children submit willingly if they know their parents lead with love.

As with parents, the authority of church leaders depends more on the care they give than on the power they wield. Just as parents verify their right to respectful obedience by loving service, so leaders demonstrate their fitness for ministry by their service. But if a con-

---

33   The emphasis on character is noteworthy since 1 Timothy calls the leaders "overseers," a term that draws attention to the task of leading, rather than "elders," the term drawing attention to their maturity.

gregation concludes that its pastor is self-serving, it hesitates to grant him authority. People will ask, "Why did he say that? What does he want?" Like nothing else, sacrificial love earns trust.

Teachers know that people love illustrations, but they forget that their lives constantly illustrate their messages. When a pastor speaks about reconciliation, his patterns of conflict resolution illumine his sermon, for good or for ill. If we talk about loving the unlovely, we cannot glue ourselves to convivial folk and shun the awkward. Like it or not, the same holds for messages on any topic (self-control, the use of money) that we live out semipublicly. This has advantages, for no one can specify precisely what he means in every talk. If we practice what we preach, people may say, "I misunderstood you at first, but since I know you, I understand what you meant." Thus, a pastor's holiness gains him a hearing. Humans are imitators and pastors are role models. They should imitate Christ well enough that others could navigate by imitating them.

The Source of Credibility

Astute readers may object, "Does the credibility of the gospel really rise or fall with the moral attainment of the speaker? Is everyone justified by faith, except the preacher, who is justified by works?"[34] Someone could say this teaching has the potential, among pastors, to inflate the successful, intimidate the self-critical, and abet the hypocritical, who will learn to conceal their failings and trumpet their triumphs.

Indeed, an anthropocentric interest in a leader's holiness can undermine the church and the gospel. Moreover, we can overstate God's standards for leaders. The paradox is that God demands holiness, yet also supplies it though Christ. Leaders seize righteousness because God first seized them. We work out our salvation because God is already at work in us (Phil. 2:12–13).

So we seek holiness, yet we never outgrow the gospel message. First, God loves us no less when we fail to attain righteousness and he loves us no more when we do attain it. Indeed our achievements can separate us from the Lord through pride and our failures can unite us

---

34 See Leander Keck, *The Bible in the Pulpit: The Renewal of Biblical Preaching* (Nashville: Abingdon, 1978), 49–50.

to him, if we respond to them humbly. So we live in tension. Knowing our weaknesses, we stand by God's mercy. Yet we strive to model Christlike virtue. We know God's power is perfected in weakness (2 Cor. 11–12).[35] Thus God solves the problem of infinite demand with his gift of infinite succor.

SUMMARY

This chapter has explored the courage, character, and credibility of interpreters. As before, the analysis begins and ends with God. Faith in the God who speaks grants interpreters the courage to speak boldly against the preferences of their generation. Moreover, when we aspire to adorn our messages with a life that even roughly resembles our rhetoric, we know that if there be any purity of aspiration, if there be any progress in conduct, it is a divine gift.

If God gives a passion to live the truth, two things follow. First, the desire to practice what we discover improves our ability to understand and do the word. The attempt to live the word verifies sound ideas and exposes faulty ones. When we look squarely at our failures, and seek to remedy them, authenticity pushes its way into our messages. Partial successes purge errors and disclose more truth. Second, a wise life is beautiful (James 3:13). Like a flawed diamond, even a flawed holiness attracts attention. It grants us a hearing in church and society. Even partial goodness draws those who seek refuge from the storm of human corruption and brokenness (Isa. 32:2). The first visible marks of progress will adorn our words. As Paul says, if we watch our doctrine and our life, we will save both ourselves and our hearers (1 Tim. 4:15–16). So a preacher is like a spiritual midwife, needing skill with the word and with people. Yet more than skill, he needs faith in God, who works in him to create courage, character, and credibility.

---

35   See 1 Cor. 1–4; 2 Cor. 10–13; and Keck, *The Bible in the Pulpit,* 50–53.

4

The Seven Biblical Sources
for Application

My family moved to coastal North Carolina when I was fifteen. My next-door neighbor, also fifteen, delighted to show me the pleasures of life on the sound. One Saturday morning he ordered me, "Daniel, get you a basket and get on your bicycle. We are going oysterin'." Infected by his excitement, I obeyed, though I had no idea how I would recognize or collect the animals. We pedaled to a mud flat, a shell-covered inlet, at low tide. Hopping off, we ambled wordlessly toward the sun-dappled water. Waiting, watching, wondering for half an eternity, I finally broke the silence. "So," I asked, "where are the oysters? How do we get them?" My friend whooped and laughed. Bending over, he pried up an irregular shell and waved it at me. "Bud, you are standing right on top of them!" Indeed, thousands of oysters lay like half-sunken cobblestones around us, waiting for us to pluck them up.

Finding the relevance of Scripture should resemble the gathering of oysters. If we know where to look, there is an abundance in almost every text. Indeed, I believe most texts hold more potential applications than one coherent message could develop. The chief task, then, is not finding something to say, but fingering the one *chief* application that drives home the central theme of the text and arrays the subpoints around it.[1] Of course, genealogies, apocalyptic visions, and oracles

---

1 Sydney Greidanus, *The Modern Preacher and the Ancient Text* (Grand Rapids: Eerd-

against pagan nations prove more stingy than Romans or Psalms, but every text offers something on the life of faith.

Interpreters are the midwives of communication, hired especially for the difficult cases. The task of biblical interpretation, stripped to its essentials, is to mediate an ancient, authoritative message to audiences having difficulties grasping Scripture's meaning and relevance. Some interpreters think their task is one-directional, moving only from a text to an audience. But wise interpreters move the other way too, mediating the questions of their audience to the Bible. They know that most hearers approach the Bible with existential questions in hand. Thus interpreters can begin either with points the text generates, or with the questions people bring to it. This chapter presents seven ways that the biblical text generates applications. The next summarizes the four questions people bring to the text.

The Bible is not a set of instructions, but all of it is instructive. Every text is meaningful.[2] Biblical texts instruct us seven ways: through *rules, ideals, doctrines, redemptive acts in narratives, exemplary acts in narratives, biblical images, and songs and prayers.*[3] This list partially overlaps the various genres of Scripture, but we are not thinking of genre analysis. Each passage fits into one particular genre, but most passages include more than one of the seven sources of application.

RULES

Rules summon obedience to specific commands. They require definite actions in narrowly defined cases. We might expect rules to be easy to apply, but they pose challenges if the specific situation they

---

mans, 1988), 154–84; Douglas Stuart, *Old Testament Exegesis* (Philadelphia: Westminster, 1980), 46–51.

2 Richard Bauckham, *The Bible in Politics: How to Read the Bible Politically* (Louisville: Westminster/John Knox, 1989), 6; Richard Pratt, *He Gave Us Stories: The Bible Student's Guide to Interpreting Old Testament Narratives* (Phillipsburg, N.J.: Presbyterian and Reformed, 1990), 313–14.

3 This list owes something to Richard B. Hays, who suggests the quartet of rules, principles, paradigms (which seems to cover all uses of narrative), and symbol world (which includes what I call doctrine, symbol, and prayer) in *The Moral Vision of the New Testament* (New York: HarperCollins, 1996), and "Scripture-Shaped Community: The Problem of Method in New Testament Ethics," *Interpretation* 44

regulate no longer exists. For example, Moses said that if a "bull has had the habit of goring and the owner has been warned but has not kept it penned up and it kills a man or woman, the bull must be stoned and the owner also must be put to death" (Ex. 21:29). But how many people own bulls? To the automobile-driving crowd the rule seems utterly irrelevant. If we ever own a bull that has the habit of goring, we will know *precisely* what to do. But few do, so we are tempted to ignore Moses' rule.

Similarly, Paul tells the Corinthians that if an unbeliever invites them to a meal and tells them the meat has been offered to an idol, they should not eat it (1 Cor. 10:27–30). The rule is clear and relevant in cultures where people still worship idols, but how many Western Christians have been warned off a hamburger, "Before you start to eat, let me tell you . . ."? Even a simple command such as "Greet one another with a holy kiss" (Rom. 16:16) is complicated in North America by an unthinking consensus that it is passé. This entices us to ignore laws that fail to address familiar situations.

Of course, some rules do apply today just as they did two thousand years ago. For example, Jesus said that when one disciple sins against another, the offended party should go in private and correct him so as to win his repentance (Matt. 18:15). Again, Moses gave a relevant rule when he commanded judges to show no partiality and accept no bribe, since "a bribe blinds the eyes of the wise" (Deut. 16:19).

To apply Exodus 21, we must discern what, in our culture, resembles the case of the goring bull and apply Moses' principle to it. By contrast, Matthew 18:15 is so clear and relevant that, exegetically speaking, there is little to say.[4] But even here application entails more than stating commands. Teachers must also lead people through their objections and fears, through the obstacles that make obedience seem impossible. To put it another way, if Christians balk at rebuking a brother, the root may be a fear of rejection, an ugly scene,

---

(1990): 47–51. See also James M. Gustafson, "The Place of Scripture in Christian Ethics," *Interpretation* 24 (1970): 430–55; Richard Longenecker, *New Testament Social Ethics for Today* (Grand Rapids: Eerdmans, 1984), 1–15.

4 Matt. 18:16–18 has complexities that invite comment, but 18:15, by itself, is straightforward.

or a counterattack. These fears may overrun the desire to obey. When wise teachers proclaim such texts, they mention the impediments to obedience and motivate people to overcome them.

IDEALS

Ideals or principles guide a wide range of behavior without specifying particular deeds. Here is a sampler of ideals: "Love your neighbor as yourself" (Matt. 22:39); "Seek first the kingdom of God and his righteousness" (Matt. 6:33); "Be holy, for I am holy" (Lev. 11:44; 19:2; 20:7, 26; Heb. 12:14; 1 Peter 1:15–16); "If it is possible, as far as it depends on you, live at peace with everyone" (Rom. 12:18).

Like rules, ideals need not have the form of a command. For example, God says, "I desire mercy, not sacrifice" (Hos. 6:6; cf. Matt. 9:13; 12:7), an ideal that puts human welfare ahead of rituals. A related saying, "To obey is better than sacrifice" (1 Sam. 15:22; Prov. 21:3; Heb. 10:5), observes that it is better to do what is right immediately than to turn to God for mercy after failing. These ideals do not dictate specific action in a particular situation, but they guide a wide range of dispositions and deeds.

Ideals present their own challenges. For example, the principle "Honor your father and your mother" is simple *conceptually*. But the way we follow the ideal changes over the years. A four year old honors her parents by obeying them. A fourteen year old gives honor by obeying without rolling her eyes. A twenty-four year old honors by listening to her parents' directives carefully before gently explaining that she must make her own decisions now. A thirty-four year old respects his parents by maintaining a relationship in the hectic years of a young family and career. At forty-four or fifty-four, the parent-child roles reverse, as parents give bizarre advice, succumb to quixotic fears, and refuse to take their medications. In this situation, honor means the child now begins to lead, but gently, respectfully, without demeaning the parent. No single rule can guide us through these transitions. We need meditation, wisdom, observation, godly examples, and prayer.

DOCTRINE

Doctrines state the cardinal truths of the faith, the fundamentals of a Christian belief system. The form for applying doctrinal statements is, "If doctrine X is true, what follows?" Many judge doctrine to be impractical, perhaps because it is cerebral, perhaps because it seems that the only application is "Believe this." But few things are more practical than a good theory.

Above all, good theories and doctrines possess great explanatory power. They enable us to see the world as it is and ourselves as we are. Doctrine lets us see the world God's way—and few powers are more valuable. If we face one of life's riddles, and turn it over and over, awaiting an answer, a doctrine will be near the root when clarity finally comes. The Christian instruction of children is largely a matter of explaining what the world is like. For example, a biblical doctrine of humanity is crucial. It explains why some people lie, break promises, and behave cruelly, and why others show kindness and concern.

For instance, when one daughter lamented that a friend had become insufferably bossy and proud immediately after winning a spot on a cheerleading squad, I applied the doctrines of sin and of creation in God's image to help her understand and cope:

> This is not entirely surprising for an unbeliever. Since we are created in the image of God, we all have a drive for significance. But your friend doesn't know that. She has no sense of her identity and acceptance in Christ, so she has to find significance in something external, like cheerleading. Cheerleading gives her a new, higher status, and her fallen nature wants to get something out of it. That's why she can't handle her success.

Doctrine can also help children handle success without pride or confusion. If a child remembers that everything he has—both the raw ability and the desire to make the most of it—is a gift from God, pride evaporates. On the other hand, a self-effacing child is prone to deny or minimize her achievements. Here, too, we need doctrinal perspective. Parents might say to an excessively humble child,

> It gives us such joy to see you using the gifts God has given you. We know you have never thought of yourself as a great student or athlete, but maybe God has given you more abilities than you realize. He has also sent people into your life who

have helped you develop those gifts—a coach who helped you fulfill your potential at soccer, and a math teacher who explains concepts well. Some people become conceited when they earn honors and we're glad you don't. But it's also important for you to understand that you have these gifts so you will know how to honor God and help others with them.

In another vein, as doctrines take hold, they slowly change us. We should ask, "How would my behavior change if it came into conformity with my professed beliefs? How would the world change if the whole church acted on its beliefs?" When teaching doctrine, we should ask, "Who needs this doctrine most? In what times and settings? If someone were eager to put it into practice, where would he start? Who will resist, deny, or misunderstand it, and for what reasons?"

Let us return to cheerleading for a moment. If people are indeed created in God's image, the squad's sponsor will seek to turn down one candidate without demeaning her and approve another without suggesting she now has worth. Indeed, it is a constant challenge for everyone in authority—parents, teachers, managers, pastors—to learn how to deliver good or bad news, to children or adults, without giving wounds or causing pride.

Christians should also bear in mind that the promises of God are ultimately doctrinal statements, declarations of what God swears to do. When a judge says, "I sentence you to one year in prison," he means, "I decree and ensure it," not merely "I predict it." So God decrees and guarantees when he promises. That is, promises are more than predictions of what will happen. They are God's personal commitment to make things happen for those in relationship with him.[5]

REDEMPTIVE ACTS IN NARRATIVE

The central character in every Bible story is God, and some aspect of his redemptive purpose attaches to the main theme of every narrative. Therefore, while interpreters rightly draw moral lessons from

---

5 Christopher Wright says, "A promise is made *to* someone, whereas a prediction is made *about* someone" (*Knowing Jesus through the Old Testament* [Downers Grove, Ill.: InterVarsity, 1992], 65).

biblical history, theological lessons should come first. Thus the *chief* point of 1 Samuel 17 is not that David, a brave shepherd boy, slaughtered a giant, nor that we should be brave like David and slaughter our giants. Rather, both David and Goliath see their battle as a contest between their gods (17:43–47). When he cuts off Goliath's head, David says that the whole world will know "there is a God in Israel." This will happen, David pronounces, because "the LORD saves, for the battle is the LORD'S, and he will give all of you into our hands" (1 Sam. 17:47). Thus the moral lesson of the episode depends on David's grasp—and our grasp—of doctrinal truths concerning God's person and work.

When teaching narrative, therefore, we should focus first on the redeeming work of God and the divine self-revelation embedded in it. Old Testament narratives focus on God's covenants with Israel: his grace in establishing them, his faithfulness in upholding them, his justice and his mercy toward those who violate them. In some way, each gospel narrative points to Jesus' death and resurrection; some also hint at his restoration of all things. They also disclose the deity and the moral character of Christ—his compassion, righteousness, and wisdom.

Of course, narratives are not simply about God. They also recount faithful and rebellious responses to him. But even when men and women seize the stage, we should resist the temptation to hasten to use them as moral examples. Wicked acts are not just immoral; they constitute rebellion against God and his covenants. Likewise, noble acts are, above all, faithful responses to God's love as he initiated his covenants, endured infidelity to each one of them, and sent his Son to atone for our sins against him.

It is said that in a well-told tale "the whole story is the meaning," so that every element works together to produce the final effect.[6] The whole story of the Bible is that God is redeeming a people for himself. The effect is to disclose the darkness of our hearts and misery of our condition, and to draw us to God's remedy.[7]

---

6 Flannery O'Connor, *Mystery and Manners,* ed. Sally and Robert Fitzgerald (New York: Farrar, Straus and Giroux, 1957), 73–75; see also Leland Ryken, *Words of Delight* (Grand Rapids: Baker, 1987), 83.

7 We should note that some epistles and prophetic books have implicit and partial narratives. One can piece together a story from comments on half-reported events in epistles. Consider the conflict between Peter and Paul at Antioch

EXEMPLARY ACTS IN NARRATIVE

If some rush to draw ethical points from Scripture, others so fear moralism that they resist the idea of using narratives for moral lessons. But Jesus himself justifies the search for ethical principles from biblical narratives. In the temptation, his replies to Satan draw lessons from Israel's experience in the wilderness (Matt. 4:4, 7). Similarly, when the Pharisees questioned Jesus' Sabbath observance, he justified himself by drawing upon David's ritually illegal act in taking the priest's showbread when he fled from Saul. The needs of those on a divine mission, Jesus declared, take precedence over other moral obligations (Matt. 12:1–7).[8]

Biblical narratives generally *show* moral lessons rather than spelling them out. The books of Kings and Chronicles label the actions of kings "right" or "not right" before the Lord about twenty times, but otherwise the Bible rarely spells out its lessons. Instead of labeling things good or evil, it shows whether Israel was loyal or disloyal to the covenant and suggests comparisons with ethical precepts.[9] Immoral actions sometimes violate biblical laws so clearly that even marginally skilled readers know to take warning. In the Gospels the portrait of religious impiety is so compelling that none need say, "Don't be like the Pharisees."

Israel's decision to make the golden calf in Exodus 32 illustrates the way narratives work. Since the law of Moses forbids the use of idols for worship (Ex. 20:4–6), we know the act is sinful. Moses' punishing Israel's revelry confirms our judgment. But the whole narrative shows the event to be more than a single sinful act. The people despaired when Moses long remained with God on Sinai. Lacking

---

(Gal. 2), and the tensions between John, Gaius, and Diotrephes (3 John). Narrative elements are scattered through the prophets. See, e.g., Isa. 7–8; Hos. 1; Amos 7. The debates between God and man even give Habakkuk and Malachi a narrative component.

8 Jesus even rebuked the Pharisees for failing to draw the lessons implicit in the text.

9 On the indirect ways for narratives to affect readers, see Ryken, *Words of Delight,* 81–89; Robert Alter, *The Art of Biblical Narrative* (New York: Basic Books, 1980), 114–30; Tremper Longman III, *Literary Approaches to Biblical Interpretation* (Grand Rapids: Zondervan, 1987), 66–67, 75–100, 119–34.

faithfulness to the covenant, they asked Aaron to make them gods who would go before them (32:1). Aaron made an image of a golden calf, but steered the people to see the calf as a representation of the God who brought them out of Egypt. He even tried to turn the occasion into a festival to the Lord (32:4–8). He tried to avoid violation of the first commandment (no other gods) by tolerating a violation of the second (no images). But his plan failed. After the people offered their sacrifices, they immediately turned to revelry. The episode shows two things. First, Old Testament narratives invite their readers to compare the acts they see to the law of Moses. Second, the episode shows that sinful acts are not isolated misdeeds, for they rise from infidelity to God and covenant.

On the other hand, faithful acts in narratives can guide the life of faith. To return to David and Goliath, when David declares, "The LORD who delivered me from the paw of the lion and the paw of the bear will deliver me from the hand of this Philistine" (1 Sam. 17:37), we see the value of drawing on God's past faithfulness to meet present challenges. When David announces Goliath's doom, for "the battle is the LORD's," we sense the motivational power of faith (1 Sam. 17:47).

So biblical narratives do more than illustrate moral lessons. Some say we should never derive a moral lesson from a narrative unless another text states it explicitly.[10] Perhaps, but it is more important to see that stories teach in ways that plain prose cannot. One lesson of David's victory is that a proper view of God stirs courage. But the story says it better.

Or take Solomon's journey into folly. It is one thing to say, "Beware of small acts of unfaithfulness," another to see Solomon's all but imperceptible compromises fester into virtual apostasy. Recall Deuteronomy's ban on a king's multiplication of wealth, wives, and horses (esp. Deut. 17:14–17). Then observe that Solomon first makes stalls for horses (1 Kings 4:26), then buys horses and chariots in Egypt (10:26–29), gathers mounds of gold and silver for the temple (chaps. 6–10), and finally acquires numerous wives (11:3). Once we notice this, it grips us

---

10   R. C. Sproul, *Knowing Scripture* (Downers Grove, Ill.: InterVarsity, 1977), 71-73; with more nuance, Grant Osborne, *The Hermeneutical Spiral* (Downers Grove, Ill.: InterVarsity, 1991), 330; Walter Kaiser and Moisés Silva, *Introduction to Biblical Hermeneutics* (Grand Rapids: Zondervan, 1994), 202.

more than the words "Beware of compromise" ever could. Straight assertions cannot match the power of narrative to embody truth.

BIBLICAL IMAGES OR SYMBOLS

The Protestant church makes such slight use of religious symbols that even the best known, such as baptism, the Lord's Supper, and laying on hands baffle some people. But the Bible is laden with symbols and symbolic actions, especially in the ministries of Jesus and the prophets.

Hosea married a prostitute (Hos. 1–3). Isaiah went about "with buttocks bared" for three years (Isa. 20). Ezekiel cut off his hair, chopped it up with a sword, and burned it with fire (Ezek. 5).[11] In their historical contexts, these acts required little comment. Jeremiah smashed a clay jar before the elders of Israel, signifying that, for her sins, God would smash Judah like that jar (Jer. 19). Later, King Jehoiakim countered Jeremiah with his own symbolic act, slicing up a scroll of Jeremiah's prophecies and tossing it, a few lines at a time, into a fire (Jer. 36). Similarly, Malachi paints a word picture of Israel bringing blind and scabrous animals as sacrifices to the Lord. "Try offering them to your governor!" Malachi sneers, his words painting a thousand pictures (Mal. 1:7–8). These prophetic images shout, "God will judge. Be warned. Repent or suffer the consequences."

The laws of Israel involve images too. Regulations concerning feasts depict fellowship with God. The system of animal sacrifice visually presents the principle that the wage of sin is death.

Like the prophets, Jesus used symbolic acts to punctuate some lessons. He dined with sinners to embody his acceptance of them. His symbolic deeds hint that he is the Messiah. He chose twelve disciples, representing the restoration of the twelve tribes of Israel. He entered Jerusalem on a donkey, showing he is her peaceable king. He cursed a fig tree, a symbol of Israel, and cleansed the temple, acting as Israel's judge (Matt. 21).[12]

Symbolic speech should be explained, but not too much. Better

---

11 For more on symbolic acts see chap. 8, p. 210. Miracles frequently have a symbolic aspect.

12 For Jesus' symbolic words and deeds in his final week, see N. T. Wright, *Jesus and the Victory of God* (Minneapolis: Fortress, 1996), 489–519.

to leave room for imagination. Images capture the mind by making abstractions concrete. "God is compassionate and authoritative" is abstract; "God is our Father" is concrete. I once heard a sermon on sexual purity for teens based on Solomon's imagery for a young woman: "If she is a wall, we will build towers of silver on her. If she is a door, we will enclose her with panels of cedar" (Song of Sol. 8:9). "Be a wall, not a door—and certainly not a revolving door!" was the speaker's refrain. No one missed his point.

Biblical imagery creates what we might call an "aesthetic of application." Take, for example, Proverbs' picture of the sluggard:

> The sluggard says, "There is a lion in the road. . . . "
> As a door turns on its hinges,
>   so a sluggard turns on his bed.
> The sluggard buries his hand in the dish;
>   he is too lazy to bring it back to his mouth. (Prov. 26:13–15)

Now that's lazy, so lazy that Proverbs need not add, "Don't be lazy; don't be like the sluggard." We get the picture! We either resolve, "I will never play the sluggard," or ask, "Why do I look like a sluggard at times? How can I stop?" Here, too, the Bible does not *tell*, it *shows* the beautiful or ugly life.

Symbols and images may overlap with our prior categories, but have a life of their own. Consider the cross. Is it an element of the gospel narrative, a part of the doctrine of salvation, or a moral ideal ("Take your cross and follow me")? Perhaps all three. Once someone knows the doctrine, meditation on the cross may spur sacrificial service as much as would a regular command. The cross also questions us. Are we willing to suffer loss for God's cause? For any cause? Finally, it reminds us that God's atonement covers us if we fail the inquiry.

SONGS AND PRAYERS

Though they have a narrower scope than the other sources for biblical application, songs and prayers have their own voice in shaping the life of faith. For example, we know that the Psalms teach believers how to praise God, but they also teach us how to lament, give thanks, and even express anger. They speak the language of the heart, especially for the storms of life. The Psalms, Luther said, "teach us to speak with earnestness, to open the heart and pour out what lies on the bottom of it. They instruct us to speak earnestly amid storms and winds of every kind. Where does one find finer words of joy than in the psalms of praise?" Where does one find "more pitiful words of sadness than in the psalms of lamentation?" In the Psalter saints find words that fit their case and inform their emotional life.[13] By meditating on them, we also learn to treasure gratitude, praise, humility, awe, justice, and righteousness.[14] They invite us into a world that values something besides ceaseless activity. Biblical songs and prayers often contain doctrinal statements as well as symbols and ideals, yet their distinguishing mark—the direct address to God—gives them a special flavor.

Songs and prayers of praise may be most likely to touch the emotions or the spirit (not that the cognitive element is absent), but they have a second effect. If it is true that people learn to value what they behold, it is truer that people value what they praise. If we praise God for his justice, we prize justice. If we praise him for his loving-kindness, we cherish loving-kindness. By praising God for such qualities, we treasure them and are drawn to them ourselves.

UNDERSTANDING THE LIST

Two points should be made about our list of biblical sources for application. First, we do not claim that biblical texts generate applications in precisely seven ways, no more, no less. There are several ways to slice the pie. Seasoned scholars have presented shorter lists, especially when seeking simplicity.[15] Indeed, one could subordinate the last two categories to the first five; in fact, only the first five get full development in this volume.[16] Our list is longer to suggest the many modes

---

13 Martin Luther, *Word and Sacrament I,* ed. E. Theodore Bachmann, trans. Charles M. Jacobs, in *Luther's Works,* 55 vols. (Philadelphia: Fortress, 1955–86), 35:255–56.

14 Bruce Birch and Larry Rasmussen, *Bible and Ethics in the Christian Life,* rev. ed. (Minneapolis: Augsburg, 1988), 45.

15 See note 3 for Hays, Gustafson, and Longenecker. They take up the synthetic task of creating a biblical ethic. I stress the exegetical task of gathering materials for an ethic.

16 I decline to dedicate chapters to the last two categories because (1) I have little to add to what I said about songs and prayers in *Getting the Message* (Phillips-

the Bible uses to convey spiritual and ethical truth. It appeals most directly to the mind and the will in doctrines and commands. It appeals to the heart and imagination more by narrative, imagery, and songs.

Second, while I believe Scripture instructs through rules, ideals, doctrines, narratives of redemptive and exemplary acts, images, and songs and prayers, this list is not a catalog of the genres of Scripture, such as prophecy, poetry, parable, and narrative. The genres of Scripture only partially overlap the seven sources. Specifically, genre analysis is a more restrictive task, with the goal of categorizing a book or a section of a book as law (e.g., Deuteronomy), history (1 Samuel), or prophecy (Isaiah). The problem is not that most books contain several genres (although they do). The issue is that a passage may precisely fit one genre yet incorporate several of the seven sources for application. That is, a doctrinal text may contain ideals and images as well as doctrine. A narrative will describe redemptive and exemplary acts, but doctrines, prayers, and rules may also be embedded in it.

To illustrate, Luke 11:1–13 is clearly an ethical discourse on prayer, but readers should look for more than guidance on prayer per se. Let's closely examine some of the ways the text has relevance (see table 1).

Clearly, this text, divided into several lessons, offers several lines of application.[17] It contains an ideal pattern for prayer. It invites readers to reexamine their concept of God. Perhaps they harbor the fear that God is stingy, reluctant to offer aid. Even if he were, Jesus says, they should not give up prayer. God is a father who takes pleasure in giving his children good gifts. The problem, if there is one, is that an excess of potential ideas threatens to obscure the main point in a plethora of lesser ones.

A Range of Options

I hope that pastors and teachers will shift from the challenge of finding various applications to that of choosing the *best* among abun-

---

burg, N.J.: Presbyterian and Reformed, 1996), 239–42; and (2) though images function differently from regular prose, they do serve the other categories.

17   Luke 11:1–13 bears all the marks of a textual unit: one theme, one place and time, one set of characters, and distinctive language (such as the "God is Father" inclusio).

TABLE 1.
SEVERAL APPLICATIONS OF LUKE 11:1–13

Minor exemplary act: Jesus has a habit of praying. The disciples seek to pray as Jesus does.	11:1. One day Jesus was praying in a certain place. When he finished, one of his disciples said to him, "Lord, teach us to pray, just as John taught his disciples."
This looks like a rule—whenever you pray, do it this way; but it is actually an ideal for prayer. Image: God is Father and provider. Doctrine: He is holy, expects holiness. He provides. He is King; he forgives; he leads us through life.	11:2–4. He said to them, "When you pray, say: " 'Father, hallowed be your name, your kingdom come. Give us each day our daily bread. Forgive us our sins, for we also forgive everyone who sins against us. And lead us not into temptation.' "
A parable—an image—compares God to a stingy neighbor. Jesus anticipates that some will be reluctant to pray because they doubt that God will bother to answer. The parable invites reflection on the image of God as a cold neighbor. Even if he were cold, the story says, he would still answer your requests, either due to the petitioner's persistence or because a refusal to answer reasonable requests would shame him.[a] Doctrinally, the passage shows that God acts for his name's sake. Since God will not deny his people, his children should not fear.	11:5–8. Then he said to them, "Suppose one of you has a friend, and he goes to him at midnight and says, 'Friend, lend me three loaves of bread, because a friend of mine on a journey has come to me, and I have nothing to set before him.' "Then the one inside answers, 'Don't bother me. The door is already locked, and my children are with me in bed. I can't get up and give you anything.' I tell you, though he will not get up and give him the bread because he is his friend, yet because of [his shamelessness], he will get up and give him as much as he needs."

dant options. We will see in the next chapter that there are actually far more than seven paths for application. Specifically, while texts generate applications seven ways, people invite applications by asking four types of spiritual or ethical questions: questions concerning their duty, their moral character, their goals in life, and the need to discern the truth among competing worldviews. Since we can join all four questions with any of the seven avenues for texts, the result is not eleven

Doctrine: "It will be given" means *God will give.*[b] Therefore, this is a promise, a doctrinal statement about the way God proves his goodness.

11:9–10. "So I say to you: Ask and it will be given to you; seek and you will find; knock and the door will be opened to you. For everyone who asks receives; he who seeks finds; and to him who knocks, the door will be opened."

A second image compares God (accurately) to a generous father who gives all we need. We have a series of motives to pray that rests on doctrines about humanity, God the Father, and God the Spirit.

11:11–13. "Which of you fathers, if your son asks for a fish, will give him a snake instead? Or if he asks for an egg, will give him a scorpion? If you then, though you are evil, know how to give good gifts to your children, how much more will your Father in heaven give the Holy Spirit to those who ask him!"

a I prefer the second interpretation, believing the Greek indicates that the man inside the house rises and gives bread, not because of the knocking of the man who asks for help, but because of the desire to avoid the shame of violating social norms that require him to grant the urgent and reasonable request. See Joachim Jeremias, *The Parables of Jesus,* 2d ed. (New York: Scribner, 1963), 157–59, esp. n. 28; Kenneth Bailey, *Poet and Peasant* (Grand Rapids: Eerdmans, 1976), 125–33; I. H. Marshall, *The Gospel according to Luke* (Grand Rapids: Eerdmans, 1981), 465.

b When a passive verb does not specify the agent (no "it will be given *by* _____"), one should supply the name of God. It has been omitted according to the Jewish custom in the New Testament Era of avoiding use of the name of God if possible. Called the "divine passive," this construction appears over one hundred times in the New Testament. See Joachim Jeremias, *New Testament Theology,* trans. John Bowden (New York: Macmillan, 1970), 11; Robert Stein, *The Method and Message of Jesus,* 2d ed. (Philadelphia: Westminster, 1995), 63–64.

but, theoretically, twenty-eight areas to examine in searching for the relevance of a text (fig. 11). Of course, some categories, such as duty and rule or discernment and doctrine overlap, so that there are actually fewer than twenty-eight options. Still, it may help visual thinkers to portray all the options on a grid, as long as we view it as a guide for interpretation rather than a rigid template.

To sample how the categories might work together, take the begin-

FIG. 11.
TWENTY-EIGHT OPTIONS FOR RELEVANCE OF A TEXT

	Duty	Character	Goal	Discernment
Rule				
Ideal				
Doctrine				
Narrative (redemptive acts)				
Narrative (exemplary acts)				
Image				
Song or prayer				

ning of the *ideal* prayer, "Father, hallowed be your name." It is certainly our *duty* to open our prayers with concern for God's nature and honor. The category of *character* urges us to ask, "What kind of person is able to begin her prayers with petitions for God's glory and kingdom rather than her personal concerns, whether petty or great?" Jesus also suggests that we place God's honor ahead of our ambitions and needs. Further, it takes *discernment* to see that it is right to begin with God's glory and cause rather than our own. This is not to imply that every passage contains dozens of applications of every sort. Many of the slots will be empty for any text. But there are many options. An ideal, for example, can instruct us regarding our character and goals, not just our duties. Again, an image can affect our sense of duty or our goals, not just our discernment. Thus the seven sources and the four questions interact in various ways.

SUMMARY

Most biblical texts offer several lines of application. They typically manifest two or more of the seven ways a text can generate applications. Further, we can develop any of them through the four types of questions people ask. As a result, teachers should rarely struggle to find an application for a passage they cover. More likely, they should toil to find the central points among dozens of lesser ones. They should struggle not to *find* oysters, but to decide which ones to keep.

5

The Four Aspects of Application

In too many churches, people hear the same applications, in much the same words, week after week. Week by week they hear that they should pray more, evangelize more, serve more; be more holy, more faithful, more committed. Contaminated by traces of legalism, such messages grow dull and predictable. If the preacher's ultimate crime is to promote heresy, the penultimate crime is to make the faith seem boring. The problem rises largely from a tendency to equate application with telling people what to do. But application involves more than issuing commands (fig. 12).

According to our model for application, interpreters are mediators, responsible both to bring the Bible to the people and to bring the people to the Bible. Bringing the people to the Bible means showing them that the Bible answers their questions. Ethicists have long organized the moral questions people have in four categories. People ask, and the Bible answers, these four essential questions:[1]

---

1 My schema owes something to Bruce Birch and Larry Rasmussen, *Bible and Ethics in the Christian Life,* rev. ed. (Minneapolis: Augsburg, 1988), 35–65; and Thomas W. Ogletree, *The Use of the Bible in Christian Ethics* (Philadelphia: Fortress, 1983), 15–45. The Bible does address the four areas outlined, yet this is not the only way to slice the pie. Since Aristotle, inquiry has stressed duty, character (or virtue), and goals. With the rise of pluralism, relativism, and postmodernism, we need a fourth category, the ability to discern which voice to trust in the maelstrom of worldview options. See J. Richard Middleton and Brian J. Walsh, *The Transforming Vision* (Downers Grove, Ill.: InterVarsity, 1984); and *Truth Is Stranger than It Used to Be* (Downers Grove, Ill.: InterVarsity, 1995).

FIG. 12.
A SIMPLE MODEL FOR APPLICATION

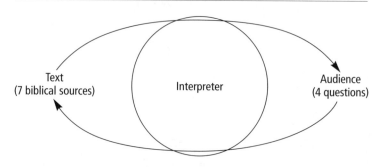

1. What should I do? That is, what is my *duty?*
2. Who should I be? That is, how can I become the person or obtain the *character* that lets me do what is right?
3. To what causes should we devote our life energy? That is, what *goals* should we pursue?[2]
4. How can we distinguish truth from error? That is, how can we gain *discernment?*

Christian leaders should use all four questions, not as a rigid template to be forced on every message, but as a guide to full-orbed application. They need not inject all four into every lesson, but they should see if the message invites them. If we consistently answer all four questions, we will escape the ruts of favored themes, and our messages will increase in variety and depth.

GOING BEYOND LAW

Many fall into predictable preaching by dwelling on duty or law—on what people should *do*—and neglecting other perspectives on the Christian life. The problem of a legal mind-set confronted me once when I was trying to help a couple rescue a collapsing marriage. Silent and exhausted at the end of a painful session, the husband suddenly had an idea. "Dan," he exclaimed, "why don't you just tell me what

---

2 I switch between singular and plural pronouns because the Christian life is both individual and communal.

to do? Specific commands for me as a husband and father. Write them on a card. Something like, 'Ten commandments for a Christian husband and father.' Then, if she will accept them, write down ten for my wife." I could not decide whether to applaud his willingness to try again, or to scoff at his naiveté. After a decade of constant quarrels, what made him think a new set of laws, points he had heard many times, could revive his marriage? Yet my friend set me wondering. Where had he gotten such an idea? From the culture? From his own activist mentality? From a past teacher? From me?

Few leaders would succumb to such a legalistic request. Yet, since Jesus' day, many religious teachers have thought that they could lead people into righteousness by prescribing, in detail, what to do in every situation. Rabbis living near the apostles' era specified the limits on Sabbath labor in minute detail: how far one could walk (one thousand yards), how much one could write (one word), and how much milk one could take out of storage (one small gulp).[3]

The challenge for Christian leaders is to promote obedience to the law while still resisting legalism. When necessary, Jesus compared his disciples to servants who should do as they are told (Luke 17:7–10; cf. James 1:22). Yet he scorched the Pharisees for making the law into a burden. It is easy to lose our equilibrium.

In combating antinomianism, even respected theologians have so stressed obedience to commands that they have squeezed out other perspectives. Harry Blamires said, "Because Christianity is a religion of revelation . . . it follows that the moral keynote of Christianity must be obedience." The center of Christian morals is "submission to demands," so that "God calls and man obeys."[4] John Murray, without denying the doctrine of justification by faith, declared, "The criterion of our standing in the kingdom . . . is nothing else than meticulous observance of the commandments of God in the minutial details of their prescription."[5]

---

3 See any edition of the Mishnah or the Talmud or secondary literature such as Emil Schürer, *A History of the Jewish People in the Time of Jesus Christ,* 5 vols. (Peabody, Mass.: Hendrickson, 1995).

4 Harry Blamires, *Recovering the Christian Mind* (Downers Grove, Ill.: InterVarsity, 1988), 109–10.

5 John Murray, *Principles of Conduct* (Grand Rapids: Eerdmans, 1957), 154; see also 14, 23–25.

What shall we say? Yes, it is good to submit to God's demands. But the Christian life is far more than meticulous submission to God's commandments. Believers should also seek to nurture the fruit of the Spirit, to develop their gifts, to dedicate themselves to kingdom projects, and to grow into maturity of character.

To see the limits of law, consider the decisions we face on a Sunday afternoon. We may take a nap, go for a walk, call a family member, meditate on Scripture, or visit a friend. *Since each is equally lawful, meticulous consultation of the law will not lead us to the right choice.* We will probably choose according to the most desirable goal—rest, fellowship, or spiritual growth. Thus, law sets the parameters within which to make a good decision, but to make decisions we need to consult more than the law.

There is more to Christian ethics than law-keeping. Making the same point, John Frame aptly summarizes ethics as "the application of a norm to a situation by a person."[6] Frame agrees, then, that obedience to norms (duties) is only one aspect of Christian living. Norms point out the choices people should make, but we must also consider the character of the person who makes the choices. Is he capable of making the right choice? Is he capable of seeing the situation clearly enough to apply the norm to it? Character reminds us that to *do* the good, one must *be* good. That is, good deeds flow spontaneously from a person transformed by God's saving grace. Goals are crucial, too, as they lead us to recognize the obstacles and find the best means to achieve what is good. Finally, using discernment we learn how to see the situation as it is, as God sees it, so we know which norms apply. Thus, to lead well we should use all four perspectives on the Christian life: duty, character, goals, and discernment.

Christian living is lawful and dutiful, but there is more. Above all, regeneration, faith, and repentance precede good works. Regeneration, the gift of a new heart, mind, and affections in Christ, is the root of obedience, especially if we define obedience as doing the right thing at the right time with the right attitude. The regenerate receive the Spir-

6 John Frame, "Doctrine of the Christian Life" (unpublished syllabus), 4–5. His categories differ slightly from mine. His "norm" equals my "duty"; his "person" equals my "character." My scheme divides Frame's "situation" into two parts, "goals" and "discernment."

it's illumination that they may see God and the world as they really are and that they may aspire to live for God in this age. Regeneration and illumination are preconditions for obedience to the law.[7] To use biblical language, because we have died to sin and been raised with Christ, we can crucify the flesh with its lusts (Rom. 6:1–12). Because God is at work in us, we can work out our salvation with fear and trembling (Phil. 2:12–13). So then, there is no profit in reacting to lawlessness by embracing a soft legalism that implies that we *gain* God's favor by grace through faith, but that we *retain* his favor by law-keeping.

Furthermore, the interest in the minute prescriptions and demands of the law hardly fits the way Christians ordinarily grow in holiness. We do not typically attain maturity by heeding laws or demands. First, it is impossible to state legal demands in enough detail to cover every situation. Second, even if it were, there is no guarantee that we could remember them all. In entering some moral situations Christians do wonder, "What is the right moral decision here?" But we also enter with character traits, insights, values, and habits that strongly predispose us to one option or another. If someone slams a door on our finger, we do not ponder whether a mild vulgarism is or is not lawful. What we say chiefly depends on our habits, on what is in us.[8]

To clarify, and perhaps to oversimplify, we can summarize the four ways of viewing moral situations. Again, wise teachers use all four perspectives:[9]

Duty says, "When individuals, perhaps Christians, encounter a moral situation . . ."

- They need counsel. They need to know—perhaps they need to be told—what to do.
- Key questions are, "What is our duty? What does the Bible teach us to do in this situation?"

---

7 For an excellent recent discussion, see Sinclair Ferguson, *The Holy Spirit* (Downers Grove, Ill.: InterVarsity, 1997), 118–73.

8 Regarding predispositions, see Stanley Hauerwas, *A Community of Character: Toward a Constructive Christian Ethic* (Notre Dame, Ind.: University of Notre Dame Press, 1981), 115.

9 For the key questions in the first three categories, I am indebted to Frame, "Christian Life," 4, 96.

- What they will do is unknown. They may go either way, to what is right or what is wrong. Each situation is something new, and anything may happen, depending on how people decide to respond to the law.

Character says, "When individuals, perhaps Christians, encounter a moral situation . . ."

- What they do is probably set in advance by their nature, by moral skills and predispositions formed over the years.
- Key questions are, "How must I change if I am to be holy? Who am I already, in Christ? How can I become more like him?"
- What they do is predictable. Mature moral agents are like wise salesmen, athletes, or counselors. Little is new to them; they see familiar patterns and use old skills.

Goal says, "When individuals, perhaps Christians, encounter a moral situation . . ."

- What they do depends on where they are going, what they might want to accomplish.
- Key questions are, "Where will I get a sense of direction? What are the best means for achieving godly ends? How can I seek to change the world so it conforms to God's plans?"
- What they do depends on where they want to go and what they want to achieve.

Discernment says, "When individuals, perhaps Christians, encounter a moral situation . . ."

- What they do depends on how they see the situation.
- Key questions are, "How can I gain discernment? How can I resist what is false in the mind-set and customs of this world? How can I gain wisdom from God and the church?"
- What they do depends on the options they can see. That in turn depends on their knowledge of Scripture and the ability of their Christian community to think and live as Christians.

It is clear that we have only begun to find the relevance of a Scripture when we formulate duties. We must use all four questions to deepen our application of Scripture.

Duty

Duties are the moral obligations that provide structure for human relationships. Duties tell people what they owe God and others. The concept of duty rests on Scripture—from the Ten Commandments (Ex. 20) to the Sermon on the Mount and the hortatory sections of the Epistles. The Mosaic law developed in Exodus 21–24 and Deuteronomy 5–26 was the constitution for Israel's national life. These passages both show *that* we have duties and tell *what* they are.

Duties are the laws or ground rules of human interaction. They may be universal commands or prohibitions governing all personal relationships. Or they may be particular and temporary. It is my duty to prepare lectures, to have devotions, and to spend time with my children.[10] When people do their duty, we call them obedient, righteous, or good. When they violate their duty, we call them disobedient, immoral, or irresponsible.

To illustrate duty, imagine a locker-room interview of a losing coach after a close football game. A naive reporter asks, "Coach, why didn't you put twelve or thirteen players in for that crucial fourth down play at the goal line at the end of the game?" A duty-oriented coach will reply, "Because we are playing *football,* sir. Extra players are against the rules of the game." Or suppose a woman is telling a friend about a job interview that ended when she confessed that she had scant relevant experience. Her friend replies, "Why didn't you just lie about it? You would have been experienced in a few weeks!" A duty-oriented woman will reply, "Because no one should treat people that way." Lying violates the rules for interviews.

As we saw above, duty readily shades into legalism, which can be attractive for the wrong reasons. It sounds bold, firm, and clear. It can enhance the control of authoritarian leaders. It may attract lazy

---

10 Our definition of "duty" includes what Kant called the categorical imperative, but also the Puritan sense of the term as the obligations falling to everyone according to calling or situation in life.

Christians who like to keep Christian living simple—just do what you are told.

Despite these dangers, duty has its place. The Ten Commandments do govern Christian behavior. By schooling people in their duty we establish a necessary minimum standard for conduct. Duty teaches that every person deserves respect, that we never gratuitously harm others, never treat them as mere objects, or as means to our ends, to be discarded when they lose their utility. Rather, we treat them as we would be treated (Matt. 7:12; Prov. 24:8–9). Dutiful people know that some things simply are not done, especially among those who know God (Gen. 34:7; 2 Sam. 13:12). Violations of duty constitute wickedness, not just mistakes or inappropriate behavior.

We usually reserve the word "duty" for universal principles such as "Do not murder" or "Do not lie." But there is indeed a place for meticulous scrutiny of the law for the details of our duty. It is our duty to refrain from murder, but the details include a ban on abusive language ("You fool," in Matt. 5:21–26). It is our duty to shun idolatry, but the details include a law against eating meat offered to an idol— if and only if someone takes time to tell us about the meat (1 Cor. 10:28). The specificity of such laws makes them intensely relevant when they match a current situation, such as the problem of abusive language. But when there is no obvious match, as with Paul's word about meat offered to idols, the specificity accentuates the differences between his day and ours and makes it hard to apply his words today.[11] Further, the more specific we become in our exploration of the detailed application of the law, the more we invite debate. Consider this progression toward ever more specific duties:

1. Be holy.
2. Be holy sexually.
3. Avoid sexual temptation.
4. If single, avoid spending long periods alone with attractive members of the opposite sex.
5. Leaders, warn people about the dangers of Western style dating and long engagements.

11 Victor Furnish, *The Moral Teaching of Paul*, 2d ed. (Nashville: Abingdon, 1985), 17–18; idem, "Belonging to Christ: A Paradigm for Ethics in First Corinthians," *Interpretation* 44 (April 1990): 146. Furnish says the more specifically a law addresses one situation, the less likely it is to apply directly to others.

The first three commands are broad and undebatable in orthodox churches. Numbers (4) and (5) are narrower and more subjective. They may register as wisdom or even as puritanical legalism rather than duty. Pastors earn their pay when they lead the church through such matters. Therefore, though prone to misuse, duty is a valid category. The best way to combat legalism is to join duty and character. Character balances duty by stifling the notion that Christian living consists in adherence to a set of rules.

CHARACTER

Character is the distinguishing nature or essence of a person. Character reminds us that Christian living is not just about doing right or wrong. "It is also about the kind of persons we ought to be, the kind of persons who . . . think issues of right and wrong really matter, who love the right and hate the wrong and can be counted on under stress to do the right thing."[12] Character is about the work God does, revivifying the heart and fashioning a new nature within us.

We must distinguish character from personality. Our personality is our disposition, our style. Shy or outgoing, quiet or talkative, cheerful or serious, cautious or risk-taking: these poles of personal style are not (necessarily) moral categories. Character differences have a more overtly moral and spiritual cast. Honest or shifty, resolute or erratic, humble or proud—these are moral categories. Further, the ability to be one or the other rests on our spiritual condition. (Of course, personality can have a moral component. Shy and quiet people can be prone to cowardly silence, or they may be the best listeners. The cautious may refuse to step out in faith or may demonstrate prudence and self-control. Risk-takers can be senselessly reckless or bold for God's cause. In short, personality traits bear watching because they predispose us to certain virtues and vices, though they are not good or evil in themselves.)

From start to finish the Bible addresses character. God formed and tested the character of men such as Abraham, Joseph, and Moses. The prophets lament Israel's hardheartedness—and promise that God will

12 David Jones, unpublished lecture for the faculty of Covenant Seminary, January 27, 1998.

make their hearts new (Jer. 9:26; 17:9; 31:31–34).The apostles penned thirty lists of virtues and vices, that is, positive and negative character traits. Jesus said a good character produces good deeds: "Every good tree bears good fruit, but a bad tree bears bad fruit. A good tree cannot bear bad fruit, and a bad tree cannot bear good fruit" (Matt. 7:17–18).[13] Paul agreed that good deeds are the spontaneous result of the Spirit's life in us, of a new heart and mind (Rom. 6–8; Gal. 5:22–23; Eph. 4:17–32).

Sports can illustrate the point. As a college freshman I played on an inept intramural basketball team. It had one excellent player, one half-decent player (me), and seven misfits whose motto was, "We may be small, but we're slow and lazy." After several crushing losses, I invited a skilled player from another team to watch a game and suggest how to improve our play, perhaps with a new offensive or defensive plan. After the game, my friend uttered just five words, "Dan, find a new team." Coaching schemes could not correct what ailed my team. It lacked the ability to execute them. Sadly, many spiritual coaches command people to jump higher when they lack the capacity.

Likewise, it is pointless, even nonsensical, to command secular people, "Store up for yourselves treasures in heaven" so that God will reward you (Matt. 6:20). Secular people *inevitably* store their treasures on earth. How could it be otherwise? How can they trust God to reward them when they deny his existence? Their unbelief destroys the capacity to obey. Similarly, nominal Christians will resist the statement, "No one can serve two masters. . . .You cannot serve both God and Money [or Mammon]" (6:24). The antithesis baffles them. They say, "But I have been serving two masters for years. Why *not* pursue God and money?" Until someone believes in the God who commands, no one heeds the law "Serve God, not money."

So the category of character entails the capacity to act on Christian instruction. Character considers the connection between who we are and what we do. The football interview may be instructive again: Why didn't the coach use thirteen players for the crucial play? The dutiful coach said, "It is against the rules." The character-oriented coach

13 In the Gospels see also John 15:1–16; Luke 6:43–44; Matt 3:8–10; 21:34–43. In the Epistles, Rom. 7:4–5; Gal. 5:22–23; Eph. 5:9; Phil. 1:11; Col. 1:6, 10; Heb. 13:15; James 3:17. There is also an obedience that is more vice than virtue (Matt. 19:20–24).

says, "Because I am not a cheater. I will not win at any price." In the job interview, because the character-oriented woman is not a liar, she will not fabricate a résumé. If duty says, *"No one should act that way,"* character says, *"I cannot act that way."*

If duty stresses what we ought to do, character stresses who we ought to be. Moral agency involves both being and doing, moral character and moral obligation. Duty says, "Do the right thing." Character says, "Righteous (and renewed) people do the right things." Duty tells what the right acts are. Character wonders who is and who is not disposed to perform the right acts. It examines the virtues that predispose people to do the right and the vices that predispose them to evil.

Character is "the chief architect of our actions and decisions."[14] It has an open-endedness; no one knows where a virtue such as courage or love may eventually lead, what adventures or sacrifices it may create. A courageous person is able to do courageous things, and regularly does so. We could say that the person of truly courageous character perfectly completes every duty that courage requires.[15] Yet in ordinary language we also say that someone courageous goes beyond the call of duty.

Virtues are moral skills or dispositions that suit people for life as a whole, not just obedience to a rule. They equip us "to respond creatively to new situations." The path of virtue is never mapped out in advance by the law; we must find our way.[16] Virtues resemble moral habits, habits of treating people with love and dignity, whether they deserve it or not. Yet virtues transcend habit. For when we encounter a difficult new situation, we enter it. What we see and do in it depends on who we are.[17] Our character lends some predictability to the scene, even if character may express itself in unanticipated ways.

---

14 Birch and Rasmussen, *Bible and Ethics in the Christian Life,* 81.

15 Again, the four questions overlap and may be different perspectives on the same thing. The man with the character trait of honesty readily fulfills all the duties of truth-telling. He achieves the goal of his yes being yes and his no being no, abetting the goal of a trusting society. He also discerns how to avoid deceptiveness. See Robert Roberts, "Virtues and Rules," *Philosophy and Phenomenological Research,* 51.2 (June 1991): 329ff.

16 See the account of virtue in Gilbert Meilaender, *The Theory and Practice of Virtue* (Notre Dame, Ind.: Notre Dame University Press, 1984), 7–9.

17 Hauerwas, *Community of Character,* 115.

Duty and Character

Some people debate whether the performance of good deeds (or duties) is the source of character, or whether character is the source of good deeds. Aristotle said that we attain virtues by exercising them, that we are what we habitually do. "We become just by doing just acts; temperate by doing temperate acts; brave by doing brave acts."[18] In the New Testament Era many rabbis believed every person has both a good and an evil tendency; the one who does the good, aided by the legal tradition, becomes good. For Aristotle and the rabbis, conduct determines character; we are what we habitually do.[19]

But in biblical theology, transformation precedes good works. Spiritual rebirth is the source of righteous deeds. When preachers address the character of their congregation, they go to the root of Christian conduct. Therefore, in preparing every message, we should ask, "Have I adequately addressed the heart, the character of my audience?"

This does not mean we should order people to change their character. We must not say, "Stop being fearful; be courageous." That may be nothing but a new law. Instruction in character begins with God. First, we tell believers they already have a new character through their rebirth by the Holy Spirit and by their union with Christ. They are a new creation, saints from the day of salvation (1 Cor. 1:2; Phil. 1:1). Second, because God is at work in us, we form our character as we work out our salvation with fear and trembling (Phil. 2:12–13).

Ignorance of duty is a problem that pastors must address, but most people have at least a sketch of their obligations. For most, inability or refusal to perform their duty is the fundamental issue. It is pointless to dictate commands to someone who cannot obey. One might

---

18 Aristotle, *Nicomachean Ethics* (section 1103), trans. W. D. Ross, in *The Basic Works of Aristotle,* ed. Richard McKeon (New York: Random House, 1941), 952–53.

19 E. P. Sanders doubts that the rabbis gave law and obedience priority over character. See his *Jesus and Judaism* (Philadelphia: Fortress, 1985), chaps. 9–10, and *The Historical Figure of Jesus* (London: Penguin, 1993), chaps. 4, 14. But I think the traditional view of first-century Judaism will win the day. See N. T. Wright, *Jesus and the Victory of God* (Minneapolis: Fortress, 1996), 376–83; Charles L. Quarles, "The Soteriology of R. Akiba and E. P. Sanders' *Paul and Palestinian Judaism,*" *New Testament Studies* 42.2 (April 1996): 185–95; Paul Ramsey, *Basic Christian Ethics* (New York: Scribner, 1950), 46–52.

as well shout to a drowning man, "Swim! SWIM!" That is precisely what he wishes, but cannot do. It is just as futile to bellow duties to people who cannot or will not do what they know they should. Thus issues of character—the ability and the motivation to obey—are the most fundamental ethical concern.

That said, we must recognize that there is another element, a feedback loop, in the relationship between duty and character, leading us to nuance the theme of "character first."

Consider a woman who always fulfills the duty of telling the truth, so that we call her honest. The honest woman believes in telling the truth and habitually does so. Nonetheless she may decide, just once, that it is justifiable to tell a lie to avoid a great evil. She may tell the lie with difficulty. Yet, if another pressing situation arises, she may tell a second lie more easily. If this happens repeatedly, we hesitate to call her honest. In time, she could even lie with such ease that we could call her a liar. Conversely, a dishonest woman could become disgusted with her deceits and their consequences. One act of courageous truth-telling may break the hold of her habit. She might even repent, by God's grace, and embrace honesty. In that fashion action shapes our consciousness and our character. By doing what is right, we begin to know what is right. As the saying goes, "Do and you will know."[20] Thus, while deeds proceed from character, they also affect character.

Character changes slowly, but change it does, so that no single action is absolutely predetermined by it. It *is* possible to do something that is out of character, and so to violate our nature. Yet when we do so, we may begin to change who we are. Aristotle, with pagan wisdom, says, "We become just by doing just acts." C. S. Lewis, with Christian wisdom, says, "Every time you make a choice you are turning the central part of you . . . into something different from what it was before. And taking your life as a whole, with all your innumerable choices, all your life long you are slowly turning this central thing either into a heavenly creature or a hellish creature."[21]

Because character is the root of a godly walk, efforts to proclaim

---

20 Adolf Schlatter, "The Theology of the New Testament and Dogmatics," in *The Nature of New Testament Theology,* ed. and trans. Robert Morgan (London: SCM, 1973), 127.

21 C. S. Lewis, *Mere Christianity* (New York: Macmillan, 1956), 86–87.

the relevance of Scripture must begin and end with character. That is a leading way to avoid the soft legalism we discussed earlier. But to work on character one also needs good goals and discernment.

GOALS

Goals are the causes and aspirations that direct our choices. We use our energy and skill to pursue them. A goal may be a small aspiration ("I want to plant a flower garden") or a life-shaping dream ("I want to be the governor of Virginia"). Our goals determine where we spend our life's energy. When we know our goals, we know where we are going and why. Goals "supply the reasons for committing ourselves to our chosen projects." They explain why we work on one thing but not another.[22]

Christian leaders are responsible to help people choose and fulfill wise goals. Thinking about goals is a primary element in the guidance pastors give. Goals and guidance operate within the parameters given by the law. When offering guidance, we assume people are fulfilling their basic duties and proceed from there. We never urge a young man to enter a career in gambling or smuggling, even if he seems to have the knack. Neither do we advise a single woman to insinuate herself into an unstable marriage to see if she can pry a man loose. Working within the limits set by the law, we help students choose programs of study and help adults determine whom to marry, where to live, or what job to take. This is the sphere of goals.

Still, some Christians hesitate to use goals in ethics. They fear lawlessness. They fear that a good end will justify any means. But the Bible encourages thought about goals. First, we are made in the image of a God who has goals for all creation and particular goals for his people. Second, the notion that one God created, structured, and now governs all things gives "a degree of confidence in the reliability and predictability of life in this world" that encourages the pursuit of goals, whereas polytheistic and magical worldviews do not.[23] Third, God gives unique goals to particular individuals. He ordained Moses, and

---

22 Ogletree, *Use of the Bible*, 19.
23 Christopher J. H. Wright, *Walking in the Ways of the Lord* (Downers Grove, Ill.: InterVarsity, 1995), 120–22.

no other, to lead Israel out of Egypt. He called Solomon, not David, to build his temple. Fourth, the idea of spiritual gifts shows that God has specific purposes for people to this day. Pastors know that complicated projects work best when team members have and use diverse gifts.[24] When each uses his or her God-given talents, we accomplish our goals with joy.

When we live within the law (and refrain from wasting our energy), goals guide our activities. Goals determine where we work and how we live. They structure our lives—when we get up, how long we work, where we shop, play, and go to church. Goals direct smaller decisions too. If we have free time, we will choose whether to golf with friends, eat out with the family, or catch up on work, according to our highest goal.

We can contrast goals with duty and character in four ways. First, the questions vary. If duty asks, "What should I do?" and character asks, "Who am I?" goals ask, "Where should I go and why? Where should our community go? What strategy might get us there?" Duty studies what we should do, character studies who we should be, and goals consider what we should accomplish. Second, the language varies. With duties we say, "You must," for they are imperative, nonnegotiable. But with goals we say, "You may," for many goals are optional, good for one person but not another. Third, the focus of attention varies. Character knows *how* it is going, but not always *where*. Goals know *where* they are going, but not always *how*. To exaggerate, character is about a *way* of living that can end up any*where;* goals are about an *end* of living that can be achieved any*how*. Fourth, to exaggerate differences again, the motivation varies: duty responds to the law's requirements; character responds to God's gifts; goal responds to worthy projects.

Goals offer a new perspective on sin and fallenness. If we fail to perform a duty, we have disobeyed. If we do not have a virtue, we may have a vice. If we have no goals, our lives are futile. Goals remind us

---

24 A mission trip to inaugurate a theological study center in the Caribbean was supremely successful because of the diversity of the team's gifts. There were an architect, a visionary, an administrator, a "talking-head" teacher, and an encourager. (His motto, "It is my calling to put the 'fun' back in fundamentalist," made me wonder whose calling it is to put the "mental" back in "fundamentalist.")

that some acts are innocuous but pointless. Watching television or playing marbles may be intrinsically harmless diversions. Even if someone pours hours into them, we hesitate to call them immoral. But thinking about goals reminds us that something is amiss if diversions cause us to neglect God's higher purposes. We must seize every opportunity to do good (Eph. 5:16) and drive to attain it. We know our God-given role and must fulfill it, even if we must pass by other perfectly good goals to get there. Remember, Paul acted on his calling to minister to the Gentiles (Gal. 2:9), building on no man's foundation (Rom. 15:20). As Paul says, "I press on to take hold of that for which Christ Jesus took hold of me. . . . Forgetting what is behind and straining toward what is ahead, I press on toward the goal to win the prize for which God has called me" (Phil. 3:12–14).

To return to football, if a reporter asked a goal-oriented coach why he did not use thirteen players for the big play, he might answer this way: "First, it wouldn't work. The referees would notice. Second, the glory—and entertainment value—of football lies in the play of man against man, skill against skill. Give one team a numerical advantage, and the glory—and the revenue—disappears." A goal-oriented woman might refuse to pad her résumé for similar reasons, saying, "It could work in the short run, but if the boss found out, he might fire me or decide he could never trust me. Honesty is the best policy." So goals focus on results.

Goals also direct our energies. When young adults ask what talents they have or what career they should pursue, they are searching for their life's goals. Later decisions about family planning, job offers, and kingdom responsibilities are goal-related too. Duty and character cannot answer such questions, because career choices, excluding counterfeiting, and marital options, excluding polygamy, are between good and good. If the various options being considered are honest, goals make the call, not duty.

Individuals or families that perform the same duties and pursue similar virtues may show blessed diversity if they have different goals. One family is musical: everyone plays an instrument, and recordings fill the air. Another is athletic: the sports schedule guides their free hours. Others love travel, gourmet cooking, or special Christian ministries.

Of course, all goals are not equal. Specialization declines into self-indulgence if a family strives only to collect antique cars, read mystery novels, or tend damask roses. Selfish goals violate the law of love. But if we caution against abuses, teachers can liberate a blessed diversity by helping people find the course of life and the causes that God has for them. When we discover those causes, we may stay up late at night, leap from bed in the morning, forfeit our leisure, and still exult in life. When people find that purpose, they feel, "For this God created me; this charges my life with significance." Pursuing the right goals, we improve our corner of the world and feel God's pleasure at our actions.

DISCERNMENT

Discernment is the insight, the understanding, the perception, to see things as they are from God's perspective. It is the ability to discriminate between biblical and unbiblical voices within competing worldviews and concepts of the good life. Discernment is a cousin to wisdom. If wisdom is, among other things, skill in the arts of living,[25] discernment is skill in the art of seeing. If wisdom is "the knowledge of God's world and a knack of fitting oneself into it," discernment is knowledge of the world and the ability to fit in or resist, as needed.[26] We develop discernment by using "control beliefs," that is, the fundamental convictions about God and the world that regulate or "control" many others. Control beliefs guide us as we grasp and test ideas, as we discriminate between competing worldviews.[27]

The story of David and Goliath portrays discernment at work. When the Philistine and Israelite armies stalemated in the hills of Judah, Goliath offered to fight a hero from Israel and let that contest substitute for a full battle. Though Saul had promised his daughter in marriage and release from all taxes, no one came forward because, the soldiers knew, dead men pay no taxes anyway. Lacking discernment, they

25 Bruce Waltke, "The Authority of Proverbs: An Exposition of Proverbs 1:2–6," *Presbyterion* 13 (1987): 70–75.

26 Cornelius Plantinga, *Not the Way It's Supposed to Be: A Breviary of Sin* (Grand Rapids: Eerdmans, 1994), 116.

27 Nicholas Wolterstorff, *Reason within the Bounds of Religion,* 2d ed. (Grand Rapids: Eerdmans, 1984), 22, 67–68.

wondered, "Who will dare to fight the giant?" But David's belief in God let him see things differently. When he arrived and heard the giant's defiance, he turned the question on its head, "Who is this uncircumcised Philistine that he should defy the armies of the living God?" (1 Sam. 17:26). David's victory began when he discerned that the question was not "Who will dare to fight the giant?" but "Who is fool enough to taunt the living God?" Striding into battle, Goliath scanned David and despised his youth: "Am I a dog, that you come at me with sticks?" But David saw that Goliath had despised God, not man. "The battle is the LORD's," he cried, as he ran toward his foe (17:42–48).

Duty stresses what we ought to do, character examines who we ought to be, and goals touch upon what we ought to seek; discernment explores the competing ideas about our duty, about godly character, and about suitable goals. Discernment helps Christians find their way among the competing answers to these questions. It enables us to see things God's way. It detects the corrupting influences in the self or the culture that lead us to misconstrue our duties, develop vices, and adopt foolish goals. Thus discernment is less a partner of duty, character, and goals than it is a servant of them. It aligns our perspectives with God's, so we can see duty, character, and goals as he does. If the opposite of duty is disobedience, the opposite of virtue is vice, and the opposite of sound goals is aimlessness, then the opposite of discernment is blindness, myopia, and folly.[28]

Discernment enables us to stand back and inspect the moral landscape. This standing back is not a full detachment from society and history. Postmodernists and Christians at least agree on this: the ideal of the autonomous, ahistorical, rational agent is a fantasy.[29] But even if we cannot escape our time, we must attempt a partial transcendence. Each age has its insights, blind spots, and spirit. It behooves every pastor to analyze the assumptions and critique the spirit of his age. Some

---

28 Plantinga, *Breviary of Sin,* 119–27; see also pp. 1–27 for more on the terminology of sin and disruption.

29 According to the Enlightenment and existentialist ideal, "To be a moral agent is . . . precisely to be able to stand back from any and every situation in which one is involved, from any and every characteristic that one may possess, and to pass judgment on it from a purely universal and abstract point of view that is totally detached from all social particularity." Alisdair MacIntyre, *After Virtue* (Notre Dame, Ind.: University of Notre Dame Press, 1981), 30.

of the best men of the age—Innocent III, Bonaventura, Thomas Aquinas—fully supported the Inquisition, which included execution by torture or burning. Sadly, many Reformers agreed that heretics deserved to die. Here the theologians had no discernment.[30]

Discernment is particularly needed in the area of dating and courtship, which varied cultures view quite differently. The dominant Western culture sees dating as innocent fun or a coming-of-age ritual. Others see it as needless temptation. The dominant culture sees dating and cohabitation as practice for marriage. Others see breaking up as practice for divorce. Or take abortion. Some see abortion as the excision of a cluster of cells, the removal of the "product of conception." Others see violence against the defenseless.[31] One sees women gaining control over their lives. Another sees children losing their lives. One sees a woman gaining her body. Another sees a woman losing her soul.[32]

The language of discernment is less "You must" and more "Have you ever noticed?" When inculcating discernment, teachers help people listen and see better. Think of Proverbs and the refrain "Listen, my son" (1:8; 4:1; see also 2:1; 3:1; 4:20; 5:1) and of Ecclesiastes' "I saw" motif (3:16; 4:1; 5:13; 6:1; 8:9; 9:13). Discernment stands aside, like the conscience or the social critic, to free us from our prejudices and from our culture's contamination.

To return to our hypothetical football interview, a reporter with discernment might marvel at the entire scene. How odd for fans to careen from agony to ecstasy over the exploits of overgrown, unknown teenagers. How strange for men to care more for spectator sports than for their own fitness. How peculiar that we give extensive media coverage to the formulaic postgame utterances of winning and losing coaches.

Discernment enables the church to halt its creeping conformity

---

30 Philip Schaff, *History of the Christian Church* (Peabody, Mass.: Hendrickson, 1996), 5:515–25.

31 On the basis of the biblical mandate to care for the weak, Richard Hays, *The Moral Vision of the New Testament* (New York: HarperCollins, 1996), 451ff., argues against abortion.

32 Frederica Matthewes-Green, "Wanted: A New Pro-Life Strategy," *Christianity Today*, 12 Jan. 1998, pp. 27–30. She pleads for dialogue that stresses the harm abortion does to the hearts of women.

to the age. Unless Christians can critique their culture, its prevailing mood will undermine the convictions that clash with it. For example, when everything is organized along rational, bureaucratic lines, when every problem seems open to a scientific and technical solution, belief in a God who miraculously intervenes to change the world seems less plausible. No one need *argue* against divine intervention; the pattern of daily life makes it seem implausible.[33]

Experience exerts great influence on discernment. One person thinks it harmless to drink wine or beer in moderation; another will never touch alcohol. Perhaps the one experienced wine at meals, and the other had an alcoholic parent. Community also shapes discernment because most people are followers. They see moral situations as their culture or subculture does. The community defines what is customary, and what is customary seems moral or appropriate. Even those who reject the culture's dominant view remain in contact with it, whether by reacting to it or by joining a countermovement.

Discernment matters because, as speakers know, whenever they address a controversial point, a portion of their audience silently resists. Some disagree because they see life another way, perhaps as the dominant culture does. If hearers reject the leader's view of the situation, they will also reject his guidance. Teachers, therefore, must sniff out the spirit of the day and address it.

OATHS: A TEST CASE

With our survey of the four commonly asked questions complete, it is fitting to see how they relate to the seven ways texts create applications (chap. 4). We can do so through a case study of Jesus' teaching on oaths.

---

33 Sociologists say that three aspects of modernity tend to make Christianity less plausible to the ordinary person: (1) functional rationality leads to disenchantment with Christianity; (2) cultural pluralism undermines the exclusive claims of any religion; (3) structural pluralism splits life into public and private spheres, leading to the privatization of religion. See James Davison Hunter, *American Evangelicalism: Conservative Religion and the Quandary of Modernity* (New Brunswick, N.J.: Rutgers University Press, 1983), 9–17; Peter Berger, Brigitte Berger, and Hansfried Kellner, *The Homeless Mind: Modernization and Consciousness* (New York: Random House, 1973), 12–16.

Again, you have heard that it was said to the people long ago, "Do not break your oath, but keep the oaths you have made to the Lord." But I tell you, Do not swear at all: either by heaven, for it is God's throne; or by the earth, for it is his footstool; or by Jerusalem, for it is the city of the Great King. And do not swear by your head, for you cannot make even one hair white or black. Simply let your "Yes" be "Yes," and your "No," "No"; anything beyond this comes from the evil one. (Matt. 5:33–37)

If time permitted a full exegesis, we would explore the customs and reasoning behind Jesus' teaching. Happily, the main point is clear, even if questions remain. First, in terms of the seven ways texts create applications, did Jesus intend the prohibition of oaths to be a rule, absolutely forbidding oaths, or an ideal? Second, since we restrict oaths to formal settings today (weddings, courtroom testimony, etc.), does Jesus' teaching apply beyond those events?

Despite appearances, the prohibition of oaths is an ideal, not a rule. Since God himself takes oaths to confirm his promises (Gen. 22:16–18; Pss. 95:11; 132:11; Heb. 7:20–28), we cannot absolutely prohibit oaths. Further, in the Old Testament, God regulates Israel's oaths rather than forbidding them (Lev. 19:12; Num. 30:2; Deut. 23:21–23).[34] Further, while most oaths taken in the New Testament are rash (Matt. 14:7; 23:16–18; 26:72; Acts 23:12–21), Jesus himself spoke under oath once (Matt. 26:63–64).[35] Thus divine usage proves that oaths are not intrinsically wicked. Disciples may take oaths in some settings, even if that is less than ideal.

In calling the prohibition of oaths an ideal rather than a rule, we neither annul nor weaken it, for we must strive to fulfill God's ideals.[36] To prevent deception, the law of Moses urged the regulated use of

34 Early Anabaptists took the prohibition literally; some literalists remain today.
35 When the high priest charges, "Tell us if you are the Christ," and Jesus replies, "You have said it" (my translation), the witnesses immediately respond to it as an affirmative answer. On the use of uptake in the interpretation of dialogue, see Jack Dean Kingsbury, *Matthew as Story,* 2d ed. (Philadelphia: Fortress, 1988), 95–103, esp. 97–98.
36 To cite another case, no divorce is an ideal, not a rule. Divorce is sometimes permitted, though it is never ideal (Matt. 5:31–32; 19:7–9; Deut. 24:1–4).

oaths. Jesus proposed a more daunting ideal, that a disciple's words be so reliable that the need for oaths withers away. He supported the ideal with images (heaven as God's throne, earth as his footstool) and implicit doctrines (God reigns over everything, over heaven and earth, even our hair).

Jesus' teaching also has a positive thrust. Ideally, disciples will be so faithful to their word that oaths and similar conventions will wither away in their circles. The phrase "similar conventions" reminds us not to be literalistic, but to seek contemporary analogies to oaths. Promises figure prominently here. Consider the father who tells his children, "If you help me clean up the yard today, I will take you out for ice cream tomorrow." The children clean the yard, but tomorrow passes without requital. Confronted later, the father moans, "Something came up" or "Sorry! I forgot. You should have reminded me." Eventually, wise children learn to have their parents solemnize their words with promises if they want their reward. Thus, when a child asks, "Do you promise?" she condemns us by testifying that our yes has not always been yes. The ideal of no oaths implies no promises either.

Thus Matthew 5:33–37 is an ideal, supported by images and implicit doctrines, requiring disciples to be so true to their word that oaths, promises, and similar conventions disappear. Some might think the exposition of the ideal is now complete: we understand and must now obey the ideal. But no, for of our four questions, we have addressed only duty, leaving character, goals, and discernment untouched.

To recapitulate, a disciple's *duty* is to prove so faithful to his word that oath-taking atrophies. But this ideal also probes our *character*. We know we should keep our word; what prevents us from doing so? Why do we make promises we scarcely intend to keep? Is it a shallow desire to please others? A device we use to get out of difficult conversations? Or do we falter through folly more than malice—perhaps by failing to anticipate foreseeable obstacles? Yet there is a dark side to broken promises. Most of us violate words spoken to the powerless (our children) more than the powerful (our boss). Again, we break an invisible commitment, such as nursery duty, more than a visible one, such as leading a meeting. But there is good news too. The truth-telling God is remaking his people in his image, giving us a capacity for veracity. He who took oaths to convey his reliability to unreliable people is making us reliable enough that oaths will atrophy among us.

Next, our *goal* is to fashion a home, church, workplace, and society where yes means yes, so that oaths and promises wither away. Our goal is to promote an atmosphere where a word is enough, where we truly become promise keepers, where, at length, people stop requesting promises and vows.

Last, *discernment* asks why people take words so lightly in our culture. Older businessmen lament the end of the era when one's word was his bond. Do we think a word written carries more authority than a word spoken? Perhaps we say so much, so casually, about so many topics, that we can hardly pay attention to what we say. Our culture's recklessness with words has affected us, until we must struggle to regain God's view of words.

This look at oaths suggests a basic model for application. First, we established what Jesus' command meant, concluding that it was an ideal rather than an absolute law. Second, we built a bridge from the original meaning (oaths) to a contemporary parallel (promises). Third, we expanded the discussion beyond the category of duty, moving to character, goal, and discernment.

It remains to show the theocentric and gracious elements in Jesus' teaching on oaths:

1. The teaching on oaths has a theocentric context. As part of the Sermon on the Mount, it describes the will of the King for his realm, for his disciples as they come to him (Matt. 5:1–2).

2. The standard of the realm is the King's person, not just his law. For the King who forbids oaths is a truth-teller. Indeed, when he must vouchsafe his word, he does not *swear* that he speaks truth, he *declares* it, saying, "Truly I say to you" (5:34). He does not swear, for there is none by whom to swear. He rewards good and requites evil.

3. Yet God does condescend to swear oaths when necessary for *our* sakes, to guarantee his word. So God's action answers the question, "Must a Christian never swear, or may we take oaths on special occasions?" May we take oaths when testifying in court? Upon entering government office or military service? While some say not, the majority, consulting the whole of Scripture, distinguish public and private swearing. They say that although we always seek the no-oaths ideal, we, like God, may condescend to take oaths for the sake of our auditors. Thus, courts counter the temptation to lie both by making perjury a crime and by having witnesses swear an oath, with God as wit-

ness, to ensure truthfulness. If called to testify, therefore, disciples might say, "I will tell the truth regardless, but because you do not know that I am trustworthy, I will take the oath."

4. But Jesus' teaching conveys divine grace as well as divine standards, a grace we need because we fail to meet Jesus' standard. Indeed, given our propensity to careless or deceitful words, we may need oaths more than we care to admit. Jesus introduces this grace twice in Matthew 5. At the beginning, he blesses the poor in spirit, for they know their need of grace (5:3). At the end, he says, "You shall be perfect, as your heavenly Father is perfect." This climaxes a section of increasingly stringent demands of disciples. First, Jesus requires fidelity to the one nearest to a man, his wife ("Whoever divorces his wife . . ." [5:31–32, my translation]). Second, he asks for fidelity to every word spoken in our society ("Let your 'Yes' be 'Yes' . . ." [5:33–37]). Third, he demands restraint toward those who insult and assault us ("Turn the other cheek . . ." [5:38–42]). Fourth, he insists that we love our enemies (5:43–47). This is daunting enough, but 5:48 is infinitely harder: "Be perfect, therefore, as your heavenly Father is perfect." Some say (correctly) that the Greek word for "perfect" *(teleioi)* means mature or complete, not sinless. So then, we need not be perfect, only as mature and complete as God! But that is a small comfort. It seems that Luther was right. The sermon's legal demands drive us first to despair, then to Christ. Yet there is hope even in the demand "You shall be perfect." While the intent is certainly imperatival, the form is a future indicative *(esesthe)*, which in both English and Greek can predict as well as demand. Since the sermon has eschatological promises—the blessed will be comforted, will inherit the earth, will see God—readers may read the future indicative as a promise: "You will be perfect." It will happen.[37]

---

37 The future indicative is imperatival in Matt. 5:48, but predictive in Matt. 5:4–9. English is similar. Parents can escalate their commands this way: "I would like you to clean your room," then, "Clean your room," and finally, "You *will* clean your room." See Leon Morris, *The Gospel according to Matthew* (Grand Rapids: Eerdmans, 1992), 133; also Nigel Turner, *Syntax*, vol. 3 in *A Grammar of New Testament Greek* by J. H. Moulton (Edinburgh: T. & T. Clark, 1963), 86; Max Zerwick, *Biblical Greek Illustrated by Examples* (Rome: Editrice Pontifico Istituto Biblico, 1990), 94–95; C. F. D. Moule, *An Idiom Book of New Testament Greek* (Cambridge: Cambridge University Press, 1971), 178–97.

5. Further, the command comes from God the Father in heaven. "Father" conveys his nearness to us. "In heaven" conveys his power for us. He is our Father; what is more natural than for children to resemble their parents? By God's grace, a disciple's highest requirement is to resemble the Father in heaven.

SUMMARY

If a teacher's ultimate crime is to propound heresy, the penultimate crime is to make biblical truth sound boring. Many teachers weary their hearers with predictable, repetitious talks. We can do better. If the Bible generates applications seven ways—through rules, ideals, doctrines, redemptive acts in narratives, exemplary acts in narratives, images, and songs and prayers—and if people bring four kinds of questions to that material, then there are numerous potential avenues for applying any text. This chapter has focused on the four types of questions people ask: (1) What is our duty? (2) What is a noble character, and how can we obtain or develop it? (3) What goals should we pursue? (4) In a cacophony of competing voices, how can we distinguish right from wrong? When teachers address all four questions, they escape soft legalism and the other ruts that can impede their work. Using all four, we should find a blessed variety and depth in our Bible application.

Yet issues remain to be addressed. Are the four questions grounded in Scripture? Are they open to abuse? How can we use them in preaching?

6

Using the Four Questions

The last chapter described the four questions people ask: What should I do? Who should I be? Where should I go? How can I distinguish truth from error? Most teachers favor one or two of these questions and neglect the others. The goal of this chapter is to equip Christian leaders to use all four questions to develop deeper applications in three ways: (1) by expanding the rationale for the questions, (2) by explaining the use and misuse of each one, and (3) by offering concrete suggestions for their use.

To introduce our exposition, picture a Christian family halfway through supper on a fall evening. As the food disappears from their plates, conversation swells until their youngest child, recently matriculated into kindergarten, punctuates a remark with an epithet straight from the gutter. The parents suffered no illusions about sheltering their child from the effects of sin when they sent her to school, whether public or Christian, but they cannot mask their dismay. The patter of conversation and the percussion of utensils cease at once. The child, astute enough to know something is wrong but naive enough to not know what it is, falls silent, eyes downcast. As gently as possible, mother and father open a line of inquiry, "Did you just say what we think you said, and do you know what it means?" Head bowed, stifling tears, she nods a confession, then wags a denial. Yes, she said it, but no, she did not know it was naughty. "I just heard it on the playground. I didn't know. . . ."

Duty

Duty in the Christian Life

A child's naive use of rude language illustrates the need for parents and teachers to tell people their duties. Parents must explain the ground rules for speech in the home: "Dirty words" offend people. Insulting words—"Shut up, you idiot, you liar"—wound people. Blasphemous words and the vain use of God's name insult him. The goal is to proclaim God's moral will in its concreteness, yet avoid legalism.

In recent years the sweet wind of grace has blown through evangelical Christianity, liberating many from the bonds of legalism, guilt, and doubt. My community counts it a blessing to promote this message of grace. But this movement, like all others, has its enthusiasts and simplifiers, some of whom drift, unwittingly, toward antinomianism. They forget that grace is more than the general benevolence of God. They forget that the second stanza of "Amazing Grace" starts, "'Twas grace that taught my heart to fear," before continuing, "And grace my fears relieved." Grace teaches that sin is a plague so virulent, with consequences so dire, that it defies human remedy. Only the cross of Christ can save anyone from it.

The words "grace" and "salvation" carry implications. Salvation is always *from* something; grace is ever *despite* something. God's grace saves us from death, despite our unworthiness, at the cost of the lifeblood of the Son. Thus God says, "Be holy, because I am holy," for "[we] were redeemed from the empty way of life . . . with the precious blood of Christ" (1 Peter 1:16, 18–19). Grace teaches us to live a new life. Having completed his survey of God's gift of salvation, Paul declares what Christians, in joyful gratitude, ought to give God: "Therefore, I urge you, brothers, by the mercies of God, to present your bodies as a sacrifice, living, holy, and pleasing to God" (Rom. 12:1, my translation). We should lay aside particular sins and generic sin (Heb. 12:1). "You were bought at a price. Therefore honor God with your body" (1 Cor. 6:18–20).

Grace teaches believers to delight in God and his gifts, but that pleasure is more than sentimentalism. It requires us to learn every lesson of grace. If we delight in God, we delight in One who finds sin repugnant. Thus Paul says, "The grace of God the Savior has appeared to all men, instructing us, as we renounce godlessness and worldly desires, to live wise, just, and godly lives in this age" (Titus 2:11–12, my translation).[1]

It follows, therefore, that commands and prohibitions also belong in churches that center on Christ and his grace. Fear of legalism should not foster a nebulous idealism that never actually says, "Do this, not that." Generalized beneficence toward others ("Everybody, I love you!") is not love. The law of God indicates which acts are loving and which are not. Love fulfills the law (Rom. 13:10; Matt. 22:37–40). The Bible is neither a philosophical system of ethics nor a handbook of ethical law, but it does mark God's interest in daily conduct as our field of service. Romans 12 does not begin, "Offer your heart," or "Offer your mind," but rather "Offer your *body*," evoking the need to serve in the concreteness of daily life. God takes people into his service as they are, in all their relationships and capacities.[2] Therefore, Scripture does not hesitate to put forth "single injunctions in almost casuistic fashion." It knows ethical principles will not lead to proper conduct in every case; we still need specific instruction.[3]

Some think Christian ethics is exhausted by a denunciation of good works and a "definition of the grace which imparts moral energy."[4] They think they need nothing but the command to love God and neighbor, guided by subjectivity. Even though it can invite lawless-

1 The Greek *(Epephanē gar hē charis tou theou sōtērios pasin anthrōpois paideuousa hēmas, hina arnēsamenoi tēn asebeian kai tas kosmikas epithymias sōphronōs kai dikaiōs kai eusebōs zēsōmen en tō nun aiōni)* invites comment. First, *paideuousa,* translated "instructing," often has the sense of discipline or correction, an overtone that fits here. Second, grace primarily instructs us positively, *hina . . . zēsōmen,* that we should live a certain way. The modal or instrumental participle *arnēsamenoi* in the subordinate clause suggests that the way we live properly is by "denying" or "renouncing" godlessness and wordly desires.

2 Ernst Käsemann, "Principles of the Interpretation of Romans 13," in *New Testament Questions of Today,* trans. W. J. Montagne (Philadelphia: Fortress, 1969), 197.

3 Writing in the Apostolic Era, the Roman philosopher Seneca entertains the possibility that one who knows principles also knows how to apply them in every situation; but he concludes, on the contrary, that one must add particular precepts, encouragements, and illustrations to philosophical principles in order to improve conduct. See Seneca, *Moral Epistles,* 94 and 95, trans. Richard M. Gummere (Cambridge, Mass.: Harvard University Press, 1962), 13–19, 65–67, 79, 99.

4 Ernst Troeltsch, *The Social Teachings of the Christian Church* (New York: Macmillan, 1931), 1:198.

ness under the rubric of grace, they approve the Lutheran motto, "Love God and do as you please." But Jesus says, "If you love me, you will keep my commandments" (John 14:15, my translation). Further, knowledge of God's commands equips people to test alternative sources of moral direction—custom, conscience, tradition, civil law, and even spontaneous impulses.[5]

Someone will say, "When we focus on law, we take our eyes off Jesus." But Jesus himself says, "You are my friends if you do what I command" (John 15:14). He tells his followers to make disciples of the nations, "teaching them to obey everything I have commanded you" (Matt. 28:20).[6] We see then why John Murray stresses observance of "the detail of the divine prescription."[7] Further, even the law's prohibitions lead to Christ, as their stringency alerts people to their inability to obey. Law exposes the sinfulness of sin and our need of Christ (Rom. 7:5–13; Gal. 3:21–24).

So then, when God reclaims the heart, he requires "specific obedience—not only in the form of a universal appeal to the moral conscience, but in concrete injunctions."[8] The principle "Honor God with your body" needs particulars: flee immorality; shun prostitution (1 Cor. 6:15–20). A good tree bears good fruit (Luke 6:43; Matt. 7:16–20), but believers need to know the content of good fruit as the whole Bible articulates it. Similarly, repentance spells the end of *particular sins*. Therefore, the prophets uttered general calls to repentance, yet also denounced specific sins, such as vain religiosity and oppression of the poor (Isa. 1:14–17; 10:1–4; Jer. 7:3–10; Amos 2:4–12; Mal. 1:6–14; 2:10–16). Likewise, Paul told the Ephesians to put off the old self and put on the new, then urged them to put off particular sins—falsehood, theft, and unwholesome speech—and to put on righteousness—truthfulness, generosity, and edifying speech (Eph. 4:20–32).

Sabbath observance illustrates the point. Many Christians do not

5 Richard Mouw, *The God Who Commands* (Notre Dame, Ind.: University of Notre Dame Press, 1990), 8–9.
6 The Greek *(didaskontes autous tērein panta hosa eneteilamēn hymïn)* could be translated "teaching them to observe every last thing I commanded." Matthew's gospel contains the greatest quantity of Jesus' moral instruction.
7 John Murray, *Principles of Conduct* (Grand Rapids: Eerdmans, 1957), 154–55.
8 Wolfgang Schrage, *The Ethics of the New Testament,* trans. David Green (Philadelphia: Fortress, 1988), 44.

know that it brings peace and pleases God if we rest and lay aside ordinary work on the Lord's Day. Teachers should tell them so, yet without entering into minute regulation of the day. How? When pressed for guidance on Sabbath observance, I refrain from commanding but share what I do and why, blending principles and particulars. So, I will go for a walk or play catch, but for several reasons will not engage in competitive sports:

In Casual Activity	In Competitive Sports
We delight in creation and embodied life.	We delight in defeating an opponent.
We enjoy embodied life.	We discipline our bodies and battle them.
We forget the tyranny of the clock.	We watch the clock for time spent or left.

In making these points, I refrain from the legal act of commanding. Rather, I unfold the logic of my perspective and urge my hearers either to accept it or to formulate another, so that, as Paul says (of another debated point), "each one may be fully convinced in his own mind," for "each of us will give an account of himself to God" (Rom. 14:5, 12). The goal is the development of my hearers' moral judgment, not the surrender of their moral judgment to mine.

Thus, a focus on God's grace in Christ limits but does not annul the need for moral instruction. We have seen the folly of dwelling exclusively upon the law. But the refusal to command is no cure for legalism. Teachers must still tell people what God requires, sometimes with an unabashed "You ought to." The idea of obedience to God's law and conformity to his will, through general principles and particular precepts, pervades Scripture.

A Misuse of Duty—Legalism

Teachers should explain the God-given duties of humankind, commanding when Scripture is clear, advising where mists linger. Yet we must remember the temptations of legalism even as we affirm the place of commands. To understand this danger we must first define legalism, a term with several meanings and an offense with several forms.[9]

Most perniciously, "legalism" is the hope of attaining or retaining salvation by works. It performs good works in order to gain God's favor, whereas the Bible says we perform good works because we have his favor. This type of legalism makes God the rewarder of works, "the patron of achievement."[10]

"Legalism" can also mean the act of fabricating new laws. Whether the source is religious tradition or misinterpretation of Scripture, they do not come from Scripture. This type of legalism takes two forms: (1) it may forbid that which is permissible, such as playing cards; or (2) it may require that which is advisable, such as morning devotions. These regulations have the appearance of spiritual zeal, but in reality *it is as pernicious to add to God's commands as it is to subtract from them.* Both acts violate God's will by usurping his authority. Again, it is just as rebellious to forbid what God permits as it is to permit what God forbids (on adding laws, see Matt. 15:3–9; 1 Tim. 4:1–3; Col. 2:16–19).

In popular language, "legalism" can mean an exceptional concentration on law and obedience to the exclusion of other facets of Christian living. The various forms of legalism may run together; certainly the latter types are more common among evangelicals.

Legalism grows from defective theology and misguided moral fervor. It holds that God loves and favors us more if we behave well. Certainly, obedience pleases the Lord and iniquity grieves him. But how could he love us more than he already does? As Paul says, "God demonstrates his own love for us in this: While we were still sinners, Christ died for us" (Rom. 5:8).

Legalists also misconstrue the motives for obedience. They motivate by guilt: If you don't obey, God will be angry or withhold his blessings. They motivate by fear: If you don't obey, he will punish you. Legalists encourage devotions by saying, "Don't skip morning devotions if you want to have a good day," and by threatening the fires of hell for unconverted children.[11] They promote missions by asking

---

9 See also chap. 12, and Stephen Westerholm, *Israel's Law and the Church's Faith: Paul and His Recent Interpreters* (Grand Rapids: Eerdmans, 1988), 132–34, on the meaning of "legalism."

10 Leander Keck, *The Bible in the Pulpit* (Nashville: Abingdon, 1978), 104.

11 For the problem, see Richard Baxter, *A Christian Directory*, in *The Practical Works*

Christians, "If you do not evangelize, who will? On the last day, the unevangelized will cry out against you, 'Why did you not tell us of our eternal peril?' Their blood will be on your heads."

A Neglected Use of Duty—Casuistry

A proper concept of casuistry can help preserve what is good in the consciousness of duty while avoiding its excesses. "Casuistry" is almost an epithet in some circles due to past Roman Catholic abuses and its reputation as rules for getting around the rules. Yet casuistry may be defined justly as the art of applying abstract moral principles to discover the correct course of action in concrete and (especially this) difficult ethical cases.[12] Casuistry carves the trails that unite code to conduct.

Consciously or not, we are all casuists in the sense that we apply fixed principles to the riddles and "shifting circumstances of daily life."[13] Casuistry is an inescapable facet of moral choices. The choices may be wrenching: Should a woman with small children leave a husband who strikes her occasionally? When is it time to turn off a respirator? What do we owe to beggars? Or the choices may be mundane: must we obey the irritatingly low speed limits for smooth, deserted ribbons of blacktop in Kansas?

Casuistic questions appear in the Bible: What are the grounds for divorce (Matt. 19; 1 Cor. 7)? Must we pay taxes to Caesar (Matt. 22)? May Christians eat meat that has been offered to idols (1 Cor. 8)? Some cases persist, while others change. The Pharisees asked, "Is it lawful to heal on the Sabbath?" We ask, "Is it lawful to go shopping on Sunday?" The Pharisees asked, "Must I tithe the seeds from my garden?" We ask, "Should I tithe before or after taxes?" But the choices do matter. If the motive of casuistry is a desire to obey God and to live out what the Spirit is still saying through the word, if casuistry does not promote a relation to the law in itself, it serves discipleship.[14]

of the Rev. Richard Baxter (London: Duncan, 1830), 4:105–16, 190ff. For the cure, see Jerry Bridges, *The Discipline of Grace* (Colorado Springs: NavPress, 1994), 13–27.

12 Thomas F. Merrill, introduction to: *William Perkins, 1558–1602: His Pioneer Works on Casuistry* (Nieuwkoop B. De Graaf, 1966), 10.

13 Geoffrey W. Bromiley, "Casuistry," in *Baker's Dictionary of Christian Ethics,* ed. Carl F. H. Henry (Grand Rapids: Baker, 1973), 85.

14 J. I. Packer, "Situations and Principles," in *Law, Morality, and the Bible,* eds. Bruce Kaye and Gordon Wenham (Downers Grove, Ill.: InterVarsity, 1978), 155.

Biblical principles do not fully answer most such questions. Some questions elude the Bible's attention; no rule covers the case. Or several norms apply, but seem to point in different directions.[15] In the search for answers wise pastors enlist the person bringing the question, for we seek to develop their moral judgment, not to coerce their surrender to ours. Moreover, no set of rules can erase the need for prudent judgment by mature moral agents.[16] Therefore, we devalue lists of exceptions and priorities, since they cannot engineer correct decisions. Pastors find the haven between legalism and antinomianism when they offer guidance without forcing their judgments on others.

The Puritans' fearless—and perhaps uncritical—use of duty and casuistry is instructive. The Puritans were accused of lapsing into morbid introspection and fostering legalism. The truth is, the way they proliferated duties, they at least invited the charge of creating and requiring submission to new laws not found in Scripture.[17] But we can only praise the enthusiasm for holiness that led them to formulate specific decisions about living for a righteous God.

For example, at a time when virtually every Englishman was a member of the Church of England, William Perkins considered this difficult case: "May someone who is taking another to court take the Lord's Supper, or is the lawsuit a sign of sin and refusal to forgive?" That is, are lawsuits between Christians morally permissible? A positive answer invites the spectacle of Christians taking communion side by side on Sunday and squaring off in court on Monday. A negative reply would virtually advocate the closure of the nation's civil courts. Perkins answered by distinguishing three classes of forgiveness and urging Christians to practice all three: (1) laying aside hatred and the lust for revenge; (2) refusing to inflict punishment for wrongs done;

---

15 This is frequently the case in medical ethics. See Mark Kuczewski, "Casuistry," in *Encyclopedia of Applied Ethics,* ed. Ruth F. Chadwick et al. (San Diego: Academic, 1997), 1:425–30.

16 Thomas W. Ogletree, *The Use of the Bible in Christian Ethics,* rev. ed. (Philadelphia: Fortress, 1983), 26–27.

17 See, for example, William Gouge, *Of Domesticall Duties* (London, 1622); Paul Baynes, *An Entire Commentary upon the Whole Epistle of St. Paul to the Ephesians* (London, 1643; and Edinburgh, 1866), 336–73 (on 5:21–6:9); Nicholas Byfield, *An Exposition upon the Epistle to the Colossians* (London, 1615 and 1868), 346–69 (on 3:18–25); Daniel Doriani, "The Godly Household in Puritan Theology, 1560–1640" (Ph.D. diss., Westminster Theological Seminary, 1986), 201–3.

(3) giving others the benefit of the doubt when evaluating their conduct. This trio notwithstanding, Perkins concluded that believers may seek a remedy and defend themselves legally when wronged.[18]

Another Puritan, William Ames, answered questions of conscience. For example, if we have a sinful thought, should we keep it to ourselves or express it? Ames made careful distinctions. If one maintains silence in order to commit the sin more easily, then it is evil. Or if someone utters an evil thought to bring it to completion, it is evil. But if someone keeps a thought silent because it is evil and shameful, the silence is good. Ames also considers troublesome thoughts that might lead to sin. An evil thought, he notes, is not a sin until the mind approves it. But if "we begin to nibble upon it and are tickled with it," if we contemplate it with delight or complacency, then we sin. If we roll impure thoughts in our minds and entertain them with pleasure, we have approved the evil, even if there is no intent to act upon it.[19]

Whether we fully agree with Ames and Perkins or not, we cannot dispute the pastoral value of such deliberations. We are true to Scripture when we shine its light on our most personal questions. We should meditate upon our thought life. Many believers seek guidance there. Casuistry may look like excessive rigor or introspection to the spiritually inert. Indeed, casuistry does nourish legalism if it seeks to specify conduct for all situations, or if it elevates its judgments from counsel to law code. But the godly recognize meditative casuistry as a friend, not an enemy, of holiness.

The church, not to mention society at large, hardly invites this kind of pastoral work today. As the value of private judgment soars, "judge not" has become the Bible's most quoted aphorism. Excess interest in duty and casuistry does invite legalism and morbid introspection. But abuse does not negate the proper use of duty and law.

Proper Use of Duty

Pastors should use duty to inform their people of God's will in two areas. First, in a morally chaotic age, preachers must instruct their people in both the law's principles and its particulars. Life has baffling

---

18 See *William Perkins, 1558–1602*, 137.

19 William Ames, *Conscience with the Power and Cases Thereof* (1639; reprint, Norwood, N.J.: Walter J. Johnson, 1975, book 3, chap. 20, 94–96.

moments, and people cannot always differentiate right from wrong. Teachers should expect to give moral guidance.

Second, in an individualistic age, duty reminds us that societies operate within parameters, and obligations and limitations come with the privileges of membership. If we want to enjoy the public roads, we must follow their rules. If we live in a family, we can't crank up the stereo whenever we please.[20] We can flesh out the proper use of duty with several dos and don'ts.

Do
1. Give concrete direction based on biblical directives. A sermon on Matthew 18 should say what to do when a brother sins against us. A sermon on spiritual gifts should tell people how to find and use theirs.
2. Give concrete guidance based on your best wisdom. Pastors should suggest how to lead family devotions, or how to be faithful stewards of wealth.
3. Tell people what may go wrong when they seek God's way. Know that an attempt to correct a sin may be rebuffed. Children may squabble and yawn during devotions.
4. Find duties in all seven types of biblical sources for application, not just moral passages. Remember the moral thrust of doctrine, narrative, and imagery ("Like one who seizes a dog by the ears . . .").
5. Make circumspect use of casuistry in sermons, classes, and conversations.
6. Distinguish between biblical mandates and wise counsel.
7. Relate all duties to our life in Christ and the internal work of the Spirit.

Don't
1. Stress duty to the neglect of character, goals, and vision.
2. Convey a "just do it" attitude. Admit that the fulfillment of duty can be complicated.
3. Give the impression that you have the answer for every situation.
4. List strings of duties, especially if they stand alone, without motives or reasons.

20 Eight of the ten commands of the Decalog are negative, suggesting we must first know what God prohibits.

CHARACTER

Return with me to the little girl who used a rude word at the table. In fact, that girl is my daughter. She is eleven now, and all evidence indicates that she has never used that word again. She still loves to collect and disburse new words. (When I recently asked her to clear the table, she replied, "Yes, my liege.") But she experiments with polysyllables, not rude language, because she prefers to surprise people with an arcane lexicon, not a lewd one.

It doesn't always work that way. Some children become addicted to the odd power of vulgarity. It may start with a desperate desire to fit in or a slip of the tongue that looses an obscenity on the playground—to the thrill of certain classmates! Cursing brings acceptance, and it continues precisely because it is against the rules. In fifth grade I did a lifetime of cursing in six months for those very reasons until it became tedious and I quit (permanently). A lesson on the rules stopped my daughter's rude talk, because she wanted to please her parents. But the rule against cursing spurred me on, for I wanted to please my crude mates. The illegality was the chief attraction (Rom. 7:8–11).[21] Character explains why some people, upon learning what the dirty words are, immediately long to use them, while others eschew them.[22] It explains why some seek to fulfill their duties while others shun them.

Character in the Christian Life

To understand character, we must distinguish it from personality and virtue. I define personality as social style or disposition. Introverted or extroverted, witty or plodding, cheerful or pensive—these are categories of personality, not morality, though they do predispose to some strengths and flaws. For example, the extrovert, may, given his nature, serve his community by welcoming newcomers and telling hard

---

21 Augustine recalled the night when he and his hooligan friends stole some pears, not to eat them (they fed them to pigs), but "to enjoy the actual theft and the sin of theft. . . . We did this for the reason that it was forbidden." *Confessions,* trans. John K. Ryan (New York: Doubleday, 1960), 2.4 (p. 70).

22 Thus, even in our self-analyzing culture, we can be surprised by evaluations of our traits, whether good (humility, generosity, patience) or evil (avarice, pride, gossip), that are perfectly clear to others. Traits become invisible because they are part of us. The good wells up and evil oozes out almost effortlessly.

truths, but he may dominate and wound others. The introvert may be a gentle encourager, but may hold her silence when a word is needed. Because basic personality changes little, the same relative strengths come easily and the same errors dog us all our lives. Character traits, by contrast, have an overtly moral cast. Honest or shifty, resolute or erratic, humble or proud—these categories have links with personality, but they are fundamentally moral traits.

To facilitate some later points, let us also exaggerate the difference between character and virtue. Let us call virtues the good traits, habits, and patterns of life that are accessible to anyone. Virtues are discrete, even atomistic predispositions to goodness and can be defined as the pleasing mean between two extremes. Courage is the mean between cowardice and foolhardiness; temperance is the mean between profligacy and stinginess. By custom, personality, nurture, or habit one can acquire these virtues without being, in God's eyes, a good person. Thus a politician may be generous but also a liar and an adulterer. The atomistic nature of such goodness is essential to virtue as we will use the term. By contrast we will call character the coherent moral goodness that comes from a good heart and ultimately from God himself.

In biblical theology, character has two aspects—character as *definitive gift* from God and character as *progressive work*. The definitive gift renders believers saints from the moment of salvation, whatever their failings (1 Cor. 1:2; Phil. 1:1; Heb. 10:14). It is the believer's heritage through a relationship with the God who justifies sinners and reconciles them to himself by grace (Rom. 4:5; 5:6–8). It resonates with those psalms that ask, "Who can discern his errors? Forgive my hidden faults" (Ps. 19:12); and, "If you, O LORD, kept a record of sins, O Lord, who could stand?" (130:3; 51:1–12). Using this gift is not an arduous task but the habit of returning to "that perfectly passive moment" when God declared us right in his sight.[23]

The progressive aspect of character is the holiness we attain by cul-

---

23 Gerhard O. Forde, "The Exodus from Virtue to Grace: Justification by Faith Today," *Interpretation* 34 (1980): 39. Forde, in a distinctly Lutheran moment, says the steps of self-discipline have an inverted relationship with holiness. Christians travel not from partial to complete righteousness, but from complete righteousness, as gift, to partial righteousness, as God purges sin so virtue can spring forth.

tivating our new life in Christ. Progress here is partial, gradual, arduous. James has this in mind when he says, "A person is justified [vindicated] by what he does and not by faith alone" (2:24).[24]

Christian and Secular Concepts

Contemporary ethics, pagan ethics of the first century, and biblical ethics all share an interest in virtue, even if they conceptualize it differently. The New Testament has about thirty lists of virtues and vices. The longest vice list, in Romans 1:29–31, charges unbelievers with wickedness, evil, greed, depravity, envy, murder, strife, deceit, malice, gossip, slander, and willful iniquity.[25] The fruit of the Spirit in Galatians 5 (love, joy, peace, patience, kindness, goodness, faithfulness, gentleness, and self-control) is the longest virtue list.[26]

New Testament virtue lists share some terms from Hellenistic lists, showing that Christian and pagan concepts of virtue partially overlap. The cardinal virtues of wisdom, temperance, courage, and justice and the cardinal vices of foolishness, licentiousness, injustice, and cowardice, led Cynic and Stoic lists in the first century and remain on many Christian lists to this day.[27]

But there are differences too. First, the Greeks say that we get

---

24 Gilbert Meilaender, *The Theory and Practice of Virtue* (Notre Dame, Ind.: Notre Dame University Press, 1984), 105–22, especially 119–20.

25 For shorter vice lists, see Matt. 15:19; Mark 7:21–22; Rom. 13:13; 1 Cor. 5:10–11; 6:9–10; 2 Cor. 12:20–21; Gal. 5:19–21; Eph. 4:31, 5:3–5; Col. 3:5–8; 1 Tim. 1:9–10; 2 Tim. 3:2–5; Titus 3:3; 1 Peter 2:1; 4:3, 15; Rev. 21:8; 22:15. That no single term appears in every vice list suggests that the lists are somewhat ad hoc and at least sometimes adapted to local situations. See B. J. Oropeza, "Situational Morality: Paul's Vice Lists at Corinth," *Expository Times* 110.1 (Oct. 1998): 9–10.

26 Other virtue lists include 2 Cor. 6:6; Eph. 4:2–3, 32, 5:9; Phil. 4:8; Col. 3:12; 1 Tim. 4:12; 6:11; 2 Tim. 2:22; 3:10; 1 Peter 3:8; 2 Peter 1:5–7.

27 Catalogues of virtue and vice also appear in Qumran's Manual of Discipline (1QS 4:3–6, 9–11) and in the Didache (2.1–5.2) and the Epistle of Barnabas (18–20), both of the latter from the second century. For a literature survey, see Eduard Lohse, *Theological Ethics,* trans. M. Eugene Boring (Minneapolis: Fortress, 1991), 83–88; and H. D. Betz, "Excursus: a Catalogue of Vices and Virtues," in *Galatians* (Philadelphia: Fortress, 1979), 281–83. For Paul and Stoicism, see David de Silva, "Paul and the Stoa," *Journal of the Evangelical Theological Society* 38.4 (Dec. 1995): 549–64; also, Apocalypse of Peter 21–34.

virtues by exercising them: "We become just by doing just acts."[28] Virtue is accessible because it is simply the mean between extremes of behavior. But Christians see character as a supernatural gift, the work of God in his children. Second, the contents of the lists differ. Christians esteem humility and patience. But Aristotle esteemed pride as the mean between the vices of vanity and humility. The proud man is "one who thinks himself worthy of great things, being worthy of them"; he rightly makes great claims.[29] Further, "the proud man despises justly" since his opinion is valid, whereas Paul forbids the strong to despise the weak (Rom. 14:3).

The Beatitudes demonstrate the difference between Christian and pagan conceptions. The four cardinal Hellenistic virtues are wisdom, temperance, courage, and justice; also praised are integrity, generosity, and endurance. Many Christians treat the Beatitudes as if they were a list of seven or eight virtues, but are they? Jesus begins with three beatitudes of weakness and neediness (fig. 13). He blesses the poor in spirit, that is, those who recognize their spiritual poverty. Almost absurdly, he blesses those who mourn. But it is good to mourn over sin in oneself or others. He blesses the meek—those who spurn ambition and self-assertion—because they know their spiritual poverty deprives them of any ground for asserting themselves. Knowing their poverty, and humbled by it, they hunger and thirst for righteousness. God promises to satisfy that hunger, matching each beatitude of need with a corresponding strength. Thus the Beatitudes are not a set of virtues, but a sketch of disciples who know their needs and hunger for God's remedy.

Gaining Character

But how precisely can this hunger for righteousness be satisfied? One can attain discrete virtues in the sense of practicing generosity or honesty. But no one can become a better person by a simple resolution. Unbelievers, cut off from the source of virtue, inescapably suffer from self-centeredness and related vices. Believers, by contrast, have

---

28 Aristotle, *Nicomachean Ethics* (section 1103), trans. W. D. Ross, in *The Basic Works of Aristotle,* ed. Richard McKeon (New York: Random House, 1941), 952–53 (book 2, chap. 1).

29 Aristotle, *Nicomachean Ethics,* 991–95 (book 4, chap. 3).

FIG. 13.
THE BEATITUDES

A Blessed Character

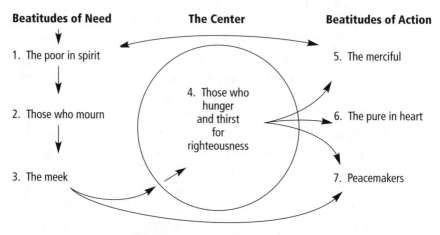

Beatitudes of Need

1. The poor in spirit
2. Those who mourn
3. The meek

The Center

4. Those who hunger and thirst for righteousness

Beatitudes of Action

5. The merciful
6. The pure in heart
7. Peacemakers

World's Responses (Matt. 5:11–16)
1. Persecution
2. Evidence of being influenced (by salt, light)
3. Praise to God because of good deeds

the resources they need to grow in character. Given the scope of this book, we can only list a number of those resources.[30]

1. God himself works among us, increasing our love and justice. The One who calls to holiness makes us holy (1 Thess. 3:12–13; 5:23–34; Phil. 2:12–13).

2. United to Christ, we are a new creation. We who died with Christ rose with him to a new life. Reconciled to God by him, we become the righteousness of God in him (Rom. 6:1–4; 2 Cor. 5:18–21). This is no legal fiction but a divine decision that is both judicial and mystical.[31]

---

30 Richard B. Hays, *The Moral Vision of the New Testament* (New York: HarperCollins, 1996), 16–185; David Jones, *Biblical Christian Ethics* (Grand Rapids: Baker, 1994), 37–58; Lohse, *Theological Ethics*, 25–60, 105–30; Ogletree, *Use of the Bible in Christian Ethics*, 135–73; Schrage, *Ethics of the New Testament*.

31 C. E. B. Cranfield, *The Epistle to the Romans* (Edinburgh: T. & T. Clark, 1975), 1:316–17.

3. The Spirit works in us, liberating us from sin and transforming us into the glory and likeness of him whom we behold (2 Cor. 3:16–18). He clothes us with power (Luke 24:49; Acts 2:17–18). Right acts proceed from men and women made new (Matt. 7:17–20).[32] Saying this is not to deny that disciples must resist the devil, flee temptation, and obey hard commands. The Christian life is a struggle, a war. But we fight because God has enlisted and outfitted us, not vice versa. Good deeds are fruit. They are also our obedience (Rom. 16:19; 2 Cor. 9:13, 10:6; Philem. 21; 1 Peter 1:22)!

4. We live under the authority of Christ the Lord. His kingdom has broken in, though this age continues. He has all authority; he is with us always; he has bought us with a price. We prove our allegiance by living in obedience to him (Matt. 7:21–23; John 13:13–14).

5. God has renewed the minds of believers, removing the veil that prevented understanding and giving us the mind of Christ, so that we take every thought captive to him (1 Cor. 2:10–16; cf. Isa. 40:13; 2 Cor. 10:5; Phil. 1:9).

6. We have, in Christ, a model of sacrifice for others. He is an exemplar who illumines and beautifies the path of obedience (Matt. 20:25–28; Phil. 2:1–11; 1 Peter 2:21–25).

7. The day of judgment approaches. Christians should live out their heritage, lest we miss the blessings and reap the curses of the covenant (Matt. 24–25; Heb. 12; Rev. 1–3, 18–22).

8. The church is a family that shares a life of worship and love (Acts 2:42–47; 4:32–35). This community has a cohesive identity as the true Israel of God (1 Peter 2:4–10).

Each of these motifs merits extended attention. We will focus, however, on linking the first four under the rubric of the indicative and the imperative as a motive for the Christian life.

For Paul, the capacity to fulfill one's duty by acting righteously depends upon God's prior renewal of the character. Paul's *indicative* statements of what God has done in believers constitute the founda-

---

32   Paul most fully develops the idea that good works begin with the Triune God's good work in the Christian, but it originates with Jesus. He said that the Father, Son, and Spirit dwell within his disciples, so that those who abide in God bear fruit (John 14:16–23; 15:1–16). He also said that good trees bear good fruit, and that the good man brings good things out of the good stored up in his heart (Matt. 12:34–35; Luke 6:43–45).

tion for *imperative* statements of what God requires of them.[33] Raised
with Christ, they are to offer themselves to God as his instruments for
righteousness (Rom. 6:19–23). Good trees, they are now to bear the
fruit of the Spirit (Gal. 5:22), the fruit of the light (Eph. 5:9), the fruit
of righteousness (Phil. 1:11), and to walk worthy of God (Col. 1:10).[34]
Christians perform good works because they are redeemed; therefore
it is fitting that the Epistles typically feature a theological account of
human need and divine deliverance before commandments appear.

The indicative-imperative pattern is most striking when the same
idea appears as an indicative in one place and as an imperative in another: "Do not let sin reign in your mortal body . . . for sin shall not
be your master" (Rom. 6:12–14, 22). "You have clothed yourselves
with Christ" and "Clothe yourselves with the Lord Jesus Christ"
(Gal. 3:27; Rom. 13:14). Sometimes indicative and imperative are side
by side: "Since we live by the Spirit, let us keep in step with the Spirit"
(Gal. 5:25; see also 1 Cor. 5:7).

The indicative-imperative pattern has been understood several
ways. Critics have viewed it as a contradiction or a moment of for-
getfulness in which Paul fails to realize that he calls the same thing a
gift in one place and an obligation in another. But how could Paul
not know he put both elements side by side on occasion? Others
remove the difficulty by emphasizing one pole at the expense of the
other. Thus the indicative represents an ideal from which proper
behavior would eventually spring; the imperative is, then, a necessary
concession to the immaturity of Paul's churches, "a kind of starter to
get the motor of ethical conscience running."[35]

But Paul intends a tension, expressing the paradox that the kingdom has arrived and is yet to come. In Christ, the old age is ending, yet
the new age is just dawning. The interplay of indicative and imperative
shows that the dialectical interaction of this age and the age to come

33 Paul Furnish, *Theology and Ethics in Paul* (Nashville: Abingdon, 1968), 224–27;
    Schrage, *Ethics,* 168–72; Herman Ridderbos, *Paul: An Outline of His Theology,* trans.
    John DeWitt (Grand Rapids: Eerdmans, 1975), 253–58; Ernst Käsemann, " 'The
    Righteousness of God' in Paul," in *New Testament Questions,* 168–82, esp. 176.
34 The Synoptics, John, Paul, Peter, and James agree that faith without works is
    dead. See Luke Timothy Johnson, *The Letter of James* (New York: Doubleday,
    1995), 60–61.
35 Schrage, *Ethics,* 168–69 (not his own view).

defines the Christian life. Paul speaks to those who have been justified in Christ, but who are "still pilgrims in the new life that is theirs."[36]

Theologians may use the slogan "Become what you are" to express the link of the indicative and the imperative, but it permits distortions. "Become what you are" allows an anthropocentric reading, as if God has done his part and now the task of self-realization is ours, as we perfect what he gave in principle. But we must not separate the gift from the giver, as if the new life is our personal treasure. In a way, the supreme gift is the giver himself. The oscillation from indicative to imperative implies that what is a gift from God is also a command from him.[37] "One is not freed from sin, and then, perhaps, also put under a new Lord"; a man is saved "because he has a new Lord."[38] We have a gift, freedom from the power of sin, but we must grasp it again and again. In this way we verify the grace given to us. The indicative signifies that the reign of God has begun, the imperative means that the defeat of evil is incomplete.

Thus Paul's indicative-imperative tension expresses the gospel's tension: "the kingdom is present; the kingdom is future." The tension says, "Persevere with Christ. You belong to him and he to you." The Pauline formula "We died to sin. . . . Count yourselves dead to sin" (Rom. 6:2, 11) means, "Recognize what the truth of the gospel declares you to be. See yourself as you are revealed by the gospel and live accordingly."[39] Christ is Lord, but his lordship is contested in this age. Christ is Lord indeed for the one who actually serves him.

Pastors should bless their people by describing their inheritance in Christ, because it brings such encouragement. On a typical Sunday morning most congregants know their duties—and know the weaknesses that keep them from fulfilling them. Of course, God can remake people even if they have no knowledge of their union with Christ. But wise preachers offer hope of growing in obedience, as the children of God appropriate his work within themselves.

36 Ibid., 170; George Ladd, *A Theology of the New Testament* (Grand Rapids: Eerdmans, 1974), 57–104, 524–25.

37 Ernst Käsemann, *Commentary on Romans,* trans. Geoffrey Bromiley (Grand Rapids: Eerdmans, 1980), 172–76; Furnish, *Theology and Ethics,* 151–56, 225–26.

38 Robert Tannehill, *Dying and Rising with Christ* (Berlin: Töpelmann, 1967), 82.

39 Cranfield, *Romans,* 315.

The Misuse of Character

Despite the clarity of the biblical teaching on character, some theologians are uneasy. They think first of the danger that disciples will boast in their accomplishments, depriving God of his glory and slipping into self-reliance. The greatest danger, however, is not egotism, but putting confidence in the flesh, turning away from God to one's own strength.[40] Lutherans especially warn that "our own personal righteousness" is as dangerous to the soul as is vice, for it threatens to pervert the gospel of justification by faith. The very concept insinuates that humans can attain merit before God. Luther says the exodus of the redeemed is not from vice to virtue, but "from virtue to the grace of Christ."[41] The "most vital enemy of righteousness is not the 'godless sinner' but the 'righteous' who think in terms of progress or movement."[42] Many strive to achieve a virtuous life, but their virtue never cares to glorify God. Such natural virtue owns no true merit. Such virtue is the splendid vice of the rich young ruler, who always obeyed God, but never loved him. Such virtue brings harm, since it puffs up human pride and "insane confidence."[43]

This critique observes that confidence in one's virtue conveys a false sense of peace. A stress on the small, disciplined steps toward virtue threatens to obscure the infinitely greater leap from human sinfulness to divine mercy. Far better to know our sin and still find a peace grounded in God's grace. As one poet-theologian put it,

> I pray incessantly
> for the conversion
> of the prodigal son's brother.
> Ever in my ear

40 Furnish, *Theology and Ethics*, 137–38, 150. In the New Testament, boasting, almost entirely restricted in usage to Paul and James *(kauchēsis, kauchēma, kauchaomai)*, is used less for bragging than for turning to self, to creation, and away from the Creator.

41 Martin Luther, *Lectures on Romans*, trans. and ed. Wilhelm Pauck (Philadelphia: Westminster, 1961), 3–5.

42 Forde, "Exodus from Virtue to Grace," 37.

43 John Calvin, *Institutes of the Christian Religion*, trans. Ford Lewis Battles (Philadelphia: Westminster, 1960), 2.3.3–7 (292–99); 2.5.6–8 (323–26); 2.7.3–6 (351–55).

rings the dread warning:
"This one has awoken
from his life of sin.
When will the other
awaken
from his virtue?"[44]

Another critic of virtue observes, "How predictable that an interest in virtue should rise now, in a culture consumed with self-development theories and narcissistic self-absorption." Virtue can deconstruct into a moral good that we *possess* and admire in ourselves. If someone acts generously because it fits and confirms his image of himself as a generous person, for whose benefit is he acting generously?[45] So virtue devours itself when its attention turns in upon itself and away from the one who is treated generously. It collapses into a fitness program for the soul: "A little sacrifice may be good for you." At its worst, it salves the professional who does some pro bono work for the sake of image or the drinking club that performs a public service to ease its conscience.

Yet we should hesitate to condemn entirely this aspiration for virtue.[46] Suppose a stingy woman wants to think of herself as a generous person. Initially, her generosity lacks spontaneity; she has to ask herself, "What would I do if I wanted to act generously?" If she answers this question correctly and acts on it, not once but many times, she may learn to see the path of generosity more readily, may acquire the habit of acting generously, until she finally is a generous person.[47] In such cases, the line between hypocrisy and aspiration blurs unexpectedly. C. S. Lewis recognized this in his autobiography. Impressed by the virtue of a World War I army friend, Lewis in his pre-Christian days began first to admire, then to feign virtue in his presence. Lewis comments,

44 Dom Helder Camara, *A Thousand Reasons for Living,* trans. Alan Neame, ed. Jose de Broucker (Philadelphia: Fortress, 1981), 71.
45 Meilaender, *Virtue,* 13–16.
46 For an analysis of concern for one's virtue, see Bernard Williams, "Utilitarianism and Moral Self-Indulgence," in *Contemporary British Philosophy,* ed. H. D. Lewis (London: George Allen and Unwin, 1976), 306–21, esp. 313ff.
47 Meilaender, *Virtue,* 14–15.

If this is hypocrisy, then I must conclude that hypocrisy can do a man good. To be ashamed of what you were about to say, to pretend that something which you had meant seriously was only a joke—this is an ignoble part. But it is better than not to be ashamed at all. And the distinction between pretending that you are better than you are and beginning to be better in reality is finer than moral sleuthhounds conceive.[48]

If Lewis is right, then even the underbelly of virtue has value. Virtue may preen for the mirror, but perhaps it is better to preen than to be indifferent to one's appearance. Of course, an interest in the appearance of virtue or in feeling better about oneself is fatal *if it ends there.* But interest in the appearance of virtue may be the first tangible sign that God is working, convicting of sin, bringing the spirit a discontent with its darkness, and stirring a desire for true righteousness.

The Proper Use of Character

Character balances duty by stifling the thought that the Christian walk is nothing but rule-keeping. It reminds us that duty cannot cover every situation. We do not learn to respond to life's vagaries by consulting the rule book. Yet character needs duty and habit. Duty's sense of obligation and habit's benign lack of self-awareness both keep virtue from promoting pride and vain introspection.

We must hold the two aspects of character, the definitive gift and the progressive work, in creative tension, lest our striving invite narcissism, and lest the passive receipt of the gift invite complacency.[49] The gift comes first, then we strive to lay hold of it. We aim to become in deed who we already are by grace. Even Calvin, the prophet of

---

48 C. S. Lewis, *Surprised by Joy: The Shape of My Early Life* (New York: Harcourt, Brace, 1956), 191–93. Lewis continues, "I was, in intention, concealing only a part: I accepted his principles at once, made no attempt internally to defend my own 'unexamined life.' When a boor first enters the society of courteous people what can he do, for a while, except imitate the motions? How can he learn except by imitation?"

49 Pietists criticize other Protestants for collapsing moral and spiritual regeneration into one another, thereby breeding passivity and complacency rather than striving and working. See James Gustafson, *Christ and the Moral Life* (New York: Harper and Row, 1968), 63–72.

human inability, said, "No one shall set out so inauspiciously as not daily to make some headway, though it be slight. Therefore, let us not cease so to act, that we may make some unceasing progress in the way of the Lord. And let us not despair on account of the smallness of our success. . . . When today outstrips yesterday, the effort is not lost."[50]

As with duty there are guidelines for preaching character.

Do
1. Remind people that they are a new creation in Christ.
2. Show that the concepts of God, redemption, and regeneration capture who the Christian is, and that Christian living grows out of our union with Christ.
3. Urge people to examine their character and motives. Induce them to probe the reasons behind their actions. Ask why right living sometimes seems easy, sometimes impossible.
4. Help people see discipleship as the spontaneous manifestation of a renewed heart first and as the result of moral striving second.

Don't
1. Reduce character to noble traits we acquire by our own effort.
2. Reduce character to a new law: Go be more merciful, just, faithful.
3. Imply people can change by resolve and determination.

GOALS

The Concept of Goals

No one would call the Reformers pragmatists; nonetheless their history includes tales of men who did whatever it took to advance their cause. When Calvin, driven off his preferred route by war, first visited Geneva, Farel, the preacher there, saw in him the man to perfect the reform he had begun in that unruly city. When Calvin deflected Farel's pleas for aid and prepared to resume his trip to Strasbourg for solitary study, Calvin says that Farel "went so far as an imprecation, that it might please God to curse the rest and quietness

---

50 Calvin, *Institutes*, 3.6.5 (688–89).

I was seeking, if in so great a necessity I withdrew and refused aid and succor." This so horrified Calvin that he remained.[51]

When, after Luther's condemnation at the Diet of Worms, it became clear to the German prince, Frederick the Wise, that Luther's life was in danger, he ordered armed horsemen to attack Luther's party as it returned to Wittenberg. With curses and displays of violence, they abducted Luther and dragged him to a hiding place unknown even to Frederick, so he could honestly tell the pope and emperor that he knew not where Luther was.[52] We could question the legal propriety of the acts of Frederick or Farel, but law was not on their minds when they made their plans. They sought a goal, the protection and advance of their fledgling movement.

The stories of Frederick and Farel illustrate the way goals work. The mind turned toward goals is directed to accomplishment, to results, to the achievement of ends. It seeks to benefit individuals (Luther) or societies (the city of Geneva). As it does so, it presupposes a knowledge of duty and character. That is, all humans (so I would argue) answer to the same duties, and all should desire the same character. But whereas duty and character are the same for all, goals are individualized. Goals are about diversity in gifts, callings, interests, and circumstances.

Christian leaders should give more attention to goals in their application of Scripture. Some Christians will resist this notion. The very stories of Frederick and Farel explain why they hesitate. When goals drive actions, we can become calculating, anthropocentric, and willing to manipulate. Therefore, some say, we should follow the law and let duty and habit guide our decisions. But consider; don't goals drive the choices that call habits into existence? Career goals guide our education and work patterns. Personal goals give direction to our marriages and homes and worship. We may awaken at 6:00 daily and drive to an office with no deeper thought than arriving on time. Yet the job we hold and the commute we endure stem from choices directed toward fulfilling our goals.

---

51 François Wendel, *Calvin: The Origin and Development of His Religious Thought,* trans. Philip Maret (New York: Harper & Row, 1963), 48–49.

52 Roland Bainton, *Here I Stand: A Life of Martin Luther* (Nashville: Abingdon, 1950), 149–50.

Goals are especially important when we stand at life's crossroads, confronted by mutually exclusive paths, but they also direct routine social and economic decisions. The goal of a better society drives policy debates. The goal of prosperity governs economic policy. But goals guide smaller decisions too. For example, I once asked my wife why she was ordering a stack of greeting cards. "Because we are almost out," she replied.

"But why not run out and be done with it?" I teased.

"Because cards are polite," she answered. "They show we care about our friends and family." Thus a goal (nurturing friendships) fashions a custom (keeping a stock of cards).[53]

The Neglect of Goals

Despite the prominence of goals in daily life, pastors neglect goals in their teaching. The biblical data exists, but several factors limit our attentiveness to them. First, the terminology for goals is poor; the small repertoire of key terms, such as "purpose" and "plan," limits awareness. Second, the separatist impulses of some Christians militate against setting goals. If the world is beyond redemption, why bother with great projects? Third, personal and social experiences lead some to avoid goals. Burned by unfulfilled dreams, some individuals prefer to aim low and drift along in a safe routine. Socially, two world wars and the failure of the great isms of the nineteenth century (Marxism, nationalism, and naturalism, to name three) may explain why people were wary of grand projects for most of the twentieth century. Fourth, ethical systems that judge morality on the basis of whether goals are met are liable to devastating criticisms (see appendix A, at the end of this chap.).

The Biblical Warrant for Goals

Despite these difficulties, there are four reasons to use goals in biblical application. First, God himself is purposeful. He forms plans and

53 Plato divided the good into three categories: (1) harmless transitory pleasures (which today would include gourmet desserts, entertaining movies); (2) things that bring both pleasure and benefits (knowledge, health, friendship), and (3) things valued solely for the benefit they bring (medical treatment, unpleasant jobs). See *The Republic,* trans. Francis Cornford (London: Oxford University Press, 1941), 42ff.

executes them according to his free will and sovereign purpose. He stood under no obligation to create humanity or, after the fall, to redeem it. God orders all things according to his purpose and will (Eph. 1:11; Rom. 9:11). He even has purposes in allowing pagan rulers to prosper. To display his power throughout the earth, he raised up Pharaoh (Ex. 9:16). He chose Babylon to punish Judah for her disloyalty (Isa. 46:9–11; Hab. 1:1–11).

God's goals also drive his covenants and redemptive plan. After the fall, he promised a seed of the woman to crush the serpent's head (Gen. 3:15). To that end, he initiated a covenant with Abraham, to bless all the earth through him (Gen. 12:1–3; 18:18–19). To preserve the covenant family during a famine, he allowed Joseph's brothers to sell him into slavery (Gen. 45:5–7; 50:20). He called Israel out of Egypt to create a people to be his treasured possession (Ex. 19:5–6). Time forbids that we tell this story in full. God even used the disasters of the old covenant to prepare for the incarnation at the right time (Gal. 4:4–6). Each phase of Jesus' ministry served its own goals and the final goal—his death and resurrection in Jerusalem. This was God's set purpose; and though sinful men executed it (Acts 2:23–24), it was a divine necessity that Jesus die and rise in Jerusalem (Luke 9:22; 13:33; 17:25; 22:37; 24:7).[54] Since God is purposeful, since he created humans in his image, we have a warrant to pursue goals.

Second, the Bible's authors wrote with goals in mind. John wrote his gospel that his readers might believe that Jesus is the Christ and have life in his name (John 20:31). His first epistle seeks to assure the redeemed that they have eternal life (1 John 5:13). Luke wrote his gospel to grant his readers certainty of the things they were taught (Luke 1:1–4). Proverbs guides its readers away from the consequences of folly and toward the way of wisdom (1:18–27; 5:1–14, 22–23; 6:27–29; 9:10–18).[55] The laws of Exodus and Deuteronomy create a new identity for Israel as the holy people of God.

---

54 Of the New Testament's 98 uses of *dei* ("it is necessary"), 40 appear in Luke-Acts, generally at crucial junctures in Jesus' story. See I. H. Marshall, *Luke: Historian and Theologian* (London: Exeter, 1970), 106–11; Jack Dean Kingsbury, *Conflict in Luke* (Minneapolis: Fortress, 1991), 55–56, 115; W. Grundmann, "dei," in *Theological Dictionary of the New Testament,* ed. Gerhard Kittel and Gerhard Friedrich, trans. Geoffrey W. Bromiley (Grand Rapids: Eerdmans, 1964–76), 2:21–25.

55 Gordon Fee and Douglas Stuart, *How to Read the Bible for All Its Worth* (Grand

Third, God lays goals on his agents. He commissioned Moses to lead Israel out of Egypt. He charged Joshua to lead the conquest of Canaan. He called the prophets to summon Israel to repent. He ordained the apostles to proclaim and teach the true faith, assigning Peter to the Jews, and Paul to the Gentiles (Gal. 2:7–9). In his zeal for evangelistic goals, Paul said, "I have become all things to all men so that by all possible means I might save some" (1 Cor. 9:22–24); he also said that Timothy could learn from "my teaching, my way of life, my *purpose*" (2 Tim. 3:10).

Dozens of biblical statements suggest goals for which every disciple should strive. The psalmist aspires to "dwell in the house of the LORD all the days of my life" (Ps. 27:4). Paul commands, "If it is possible, as far as it depends on you, live at peace with everyone" (Rom. 12:18). Hebrews says, "Let us consider how we may spur one another on toward love and good deeds" (10:24), and "Let us run with perseverance the race marked out for us" (12:1–2). The motif of calling also sets forth God's purposes for believers. God calls Christians into fellowship with Christ (1 Cor. 1:9) and to peace (1 Cor. 7:15), freedom (Gal. 5:13), holiness (1 Thess. 4:7), conformity to Christ (Rom. 8:29; 1 Peter 2:21–23), and eternal life (1 Tim. 6:12; 1 Peter 5:10).

Fourth, God's bestowal of spiritual gifts is intended to lead individuals and groups to pursue unique goals.[56] He blesses the honing of particular skills, which others may appreciate without personally desiring them. Romans 12:8 hints that Christians may take pleasure in the exercise of gifts: leaders are to govern with zeal, the merciful are to act with gladness, and benefactors are to give with simplicity, that is, without thinking of recognition or repayment, but with joy in the giving itself.[57]

Rapids: Zondervan, 1982, 196–99; Derek Kidner, *Proverbs: An Introduction and Commentary* (London: Tyndale, 1964), 36–37, 53–55.

56 A spiritual gift is a capacity and a desire for ministry given for regular use in the church and the kingdom.

57 The Greek reads *ho metadidous en haplotēti, ho proïstamenos en spoudē, ho eleōn en hilarotēti*. Commentators taking "simplicity" this way include Cranfield, *Romans,* 2:625; and James D. G. Dunn, *Romans 9–16* (Dallas: Word, 1988), 730. See also B. Gärtner, "Simplicity, Sincerity, Uprightness," in *New International Dictionary of New Testament Theology,* ed. Colin Brown (Grand Rapids: Zondervan, 1975–78), 3:571–73; O. Bauernfeind, "haplous," in *Theological Dictionary of the New Testament,* 1:38–87.

The Proper Use of Goals

If goals do deserve consideration in our reflection on Christian living, there are three implications for pastors. First, we should liberate a blessed diversity within the kingdom. Second, we should give more attention to guidance in formal, not just private settings. Third, an awareness of goals motivates Christians to press beyond doing the right thing and to seek to do the right thing so as to obtain the right results.

First, then, *goals liberate blessed diversity.* The doctrine of spiritual gifts implies that Christians should set varied goals for kingdom service in the church and in the wider world. Individuals and groups feel God's pleasure when they cultivate their highest gifts and passions. The sense of a God-given purpose frees people to concentrate on one task and ignore others without guilt. To put it another way, as important as it is to discriminate between good and evil, perhaps more decisions hinge on separating the good from the best. A strong sense of goals and gifts permits choices between the projects that compete for our energy.

Beyond kingdom service, teaching on goals implies that pastors should help believers think through their vocations and avocations. Pastors know that God blesses all honest vocations. Yet the church does little to flesh this out—to discover the bearing of the faith on engineering, business, farming, medicine, or sales. Pastors lack competence to speak to some of these fields, but they can suggest the first principles for serving Christ in each realm. And they can help Christians in various fields find each other and probe for truth together, even apart from church groups. We could also comment on avocations. Though the biblical testimony is minimal, there is enough to warrant our attention.

Second, teachers should use the pulpit, not just private meetings, to help Christians find God's particular purpose for their lives. In the past, theologians suggested how Christians might achieve their goals. The Puritans gave guidance on how to find a suitable spouse, how to find a fitting vocation, and how to hire a servant, sometimes issuing step-by-step directions. Even the most learned did not consider it beneath them to help the faithful achieve godly goals.[58] Marriage, vocation, and hiring remain worthy topics. Pastors can also help their

---

58 See William Perkins, *Works* (London, 1604), 3:669–700; Thomas Gataker, *Cer-*

flocks fulfill some of the ideals we discussed in earlier chapters. How should adult children honor their parents? How can we craft a gentle answer to turn away wrath? To illustrate, let me suggest some ideas that dissipate wrath and help frame a healing reply (using 1 Sam. 25:1–34; Prov. 9:8–9; 12:15; 13:20; 14:16; 15:5; 17:10; 20:3; 25:12; 26:4–5; 29:11, 20; James 1:19; 1 Peter 2:21–23):

1. The ability to stay calm under fire is a precondition for success.
2. To turn away wrath, one must understand it. If someone is angry, hear him out.
3. Be slow to defend yourself, lest the attack be doubled.
4. However exaggerated the anger, there is probably an element of truth in it.
5. Thank foes for constructive criticism. Apologize however honesty permits.
6. Remember that whatever the intent, valid criticisms offer a chance to grow.
7. One need not reply to every charge, but be quick to answer attacks against personal integrity.
8. Observe peacemakers to distill their wisdom.

Third, goals remind us to shift from simply seeking to do the right thing to the objective of doing the right thing so as to obtain the right results. True, there are times to do the right thing and let the chips fall where they may. But there are also times when we cannot afford the luxury of indifference to consequences. Then we must *do the right thing the right way at the right time to achieve the right results.*

Suppose, for example, that a newly married man, John, appears too controlling with his wife. Suppose, further, that John is defensive, so that he may be impervious to a rebuke that lacks solid evidence. Because the goal is to help John and his wife, we cannot simply issue a rebuke and declare our duty complete. Compassion requires us to plan, to anticipate consequences. An early intervention could prevent trouble, but without evidence, John might dismiss the rebuke and with-

taine *Sermons* (London, 1635); William Gouge, *Of Domesticall Duties;* John Dod, *A Plaine and Familiar Exposition of the Ten Commandments* (London: 1612); cf. J. I. Packer, *A Quest for Holiness* (Wheaton, Ill.: Crossway, 1990).

draw. Or we could wait for irrefutable evidence of the problem. But while we wait, John may settle into his destructive patterns. Duty says, "Say something," but goals say, "Do it when you can win John." Here are some suggestions for preaching goals:

Do
1. Become attuned to the Bible's statements about goals.
2. Help individuals and the community to find God's unique gifts and callings.
3. Urge people to find goals and causes larger than themselves. Such goals can relate to family, church, and society.
4. Help people fashion concrete strategies to accomplish goals in all areas of life.
5. Urge perseverance. Every great project meets obstacles.
6. Analyze and critique the goals our culture values.
7. Help people separate both the good from the best and God's general will for all from his particular will for them.

Don't
1. Imply that we may ignore God's revealed will to achieve worthy goals.
2. Allow thinking about goals to foster individualism and narcissism.

DISCERNMENT

Discernment in the Christian Life

Everyone who studies the Holocaust wonders how the citizenry of a civilized, ostensibly Christian nation could either cooperate or fail to protest the extermination of the Jews, Gypsies, the handicapped, and more. Why, when the Nazis came to round up the Jews, did most people do nothing, while a few towns risked everything to save them?

Le Chambon, in southern France, was a risk-taking village. Its pastors led a community that gave refuge to hundreds of Jews and smuggled them to safety in Switzerland at great personal cost. Years later, when interviewed about their willingness to risk everything for the Jews, the pastors insisted they had done nothing heroic; they had to help, it was only natural.[59] Le Chambon was a Huguenot community with a long history of religious persecution. Its citizens saw the Jews as a persecuted religious minority like themselves. Once they saw the Jews as people like themselves in a season of great need, it was not even, in their eyes, an act of bravery to help them. With restored vision (which is almost interchangeable with discernment), they readily applied the biblical principle "Love your neighbor" to the crisis.

Discernment is the ability to step back from our culture, customs, experiences, and prejudices, and see the world as God does. It is the ability to discount the familiar and see issues from God's perspective. Without vision we are bound to the values of our culture, as modified by personal experience.

Discernment is a precondition for reform, but it usually takes a critical mass of visionary people to effect change. An individual standing alone can do little. Discernment led Francis of Assisi to initiate evangelism of the Muslims with a mission to the king of Egypt in 1219. The medieval church knew Scriptures that motivate missions, of course, but did not apply them to the Muslims, whom some regarded as subhuman. Once Francis saw their humanity, his mission was logical. Yet little came of his initiative, in part because few shared it.

When, like Francis, leaders propose ideas that clash with prevailing customs, they should persuade and explain until they gather a critical mass of people committed to a new course. Suppose an American questions the propriety of Western-style dating. He wonders: Is it an innocent coming-of-age ritual, or is it a needless temptation to put attractive young people alone with each other late at night, in the dark, without a chaperone? He wonders: Is the growth of serious relationships practice for marriage, or is breaking up practice for divorce? He knows how rare Western dating is in world history; even today half the world thinks dating is insane. But he also knows how odd his views sound locally. Further, to denounce or attempt to banish dating would accomplish nothing (he is working toward a *goal*). He must gather ideas, invite parents and youth to question dating, then persuade them of his view. To win the youth and their solicitous parents, he must also propose alternatives and persuade a critical mass of people to support them.

59   Philip Hallie, *Lest Innocent Blood Be Shed* (New York: Harper and Row, 1979), 20–27.

Through such a process, one generation's radical ideas become the next generation's options and even habits. The role of community in effecting change indicates that people make most decisions without thinking, for the right seems obvious. *One of the tasks of a leader is to make the right things seem obvious.* Ideally, the right will become customary and wickedness will look absurd.

The Bible has more testimony to the importance of discernment and its cognates, wisdom, understanding, and insight, than one might think. It praises the wisdom of Solomon, Daniel, and Abigail. It offers wisdom (Prov. 1–10; James 1:5) and commends the man of understanding (Prov. 10:23; 11:12; 15:21; 17:27). The law of God enables us to discern hidden faults (Ps. 19:12) and gives its adherents insight (119:99). The prophets mock pagans who are so blind that they worship images they fashioned with their own hands (Isa. 44:9–20), then grieve for Israel's leaders who do the same (Isa. 56:10–12; 59:9–10; Ezek. 5–9).

Jesus' parables offer a new way to see the kingdom and discipleship. The parable of the sower (Matt. 13) depicts the kingdom as something unobtrusive yet potent as a seed. The parable of the good Samaritan (Luke 10) offers a new perspective on strangers in need: the priest and Levite saw the potential for defilement and loss of income if they touched a dead body; Jesus and the Samaritan saw a neighbor.[60] The parables of Luke 15 show that God loves the lost and celebrates their return, even if they smell of pigs and look as if they have been with prostitutes. Such stories invite the Pharisees to see themselves in the older brother, whose self-righteousness keeps him out of God's celebration.

Paul describes (Eph. 4:17–24), prays for (Phil. 1:9–11; Col. 1:9–11), and commands (Rom. 12:2) the renewal of the Christian mind. Hebrews helps its readers see persecutions in the light of the supremacy of Christ and God's faithfulness to past saints (Heb. 11). John commands his readers to test the spirits (1 John 4). Revelation lets Christians see their suffering as part of a cosmic conflict between God and Satan (Rev. 12–14). Each of these texts promotes godliness by helping us see reality God's way.

---

60   Kenneth Bailey, *Through Peasant's Eyes* (Grand Rapids: Eerdmans, 1980), 43–46.

The Misuse of Discernment

Each of the four aspects of biblical application has weaknesses if isolated from the others; discernment is no exception. Duty by itself declines into legalism, character becomes vague principles, and concentration on goals succumbs to lawlessness. The discerning can be arrogant, proud of their insight, aloof, despising provincials who cannot transcend their culture (though they think they do). Content to see what is right, they detach themselves from the world of action.[61] At worst, vision succumbs to relativism, "You see things your way, I see them mine. If we had the same experiences, we might agree." Discernment seeks dialogue, but in the effort to listen well, to respect another viewpoint, one can forget persuasion and passion. If one lays passion in a drawer, it dissipates.

The Proper Use of Discernment

Dangers notwithstanding, discernment contributes to pastoral work in at least five ways. First, *discernment equips believers to resist and engage non-Christian thought.* Pastors should offer tools to foster the critique of secular worldviews. They can train their analytical people to ask questions that will reveal someone's worldview:

- What is the nature of humanity? (Or, who am I?)
- What is the nature of the world and all reality? (Or, where am I?)
- What is wrong with the world? (How can we account for brokenness?)
- How can it be fixed? (Is there a hope for redemption?)
- What is the basis of morality?
- What is the meaning of human history?[62]

Second, *discernment fosters deliberation and self-criticism.* It teaches believers to pause and analyze situations before rushing to action, to ask how others see things, and to inquire into the deceits of sin that

---

61 I owe this point to Clay Smith and his contribution to a hermeneutics seminar at Covenant Seminary in 1996.
62 This list is mine, but the questions are well known. Cf. J. Richard Middleton and Brian J. Walsh, *The Transforming Vision* (Downers Grove, Ill.: InterVarsity, 1984), 35; James Sire, *The Universe Next Door* (Downers Grove, Ill.: InterVarsity, 1976), 17–18.

blind church and society.[63] It increases the aptitude for self-examination, teaching that the customary way is not the only way.

Third, *discernment helps the church reach secular people.* It inculcates humility, a willingness to give an account for our actions and justify them to others.[64] It supports a readiness to hear out the convictions and questions of agnostics and seekers.[65] It hones skills in dialogue necessary to engage alien voices while still using control beliefs to articulate a Christian response. Denunciations of sin may galvanize the faithful, but they rarely persuade those who differ. Discernment encourages careful listening and measured replies.

Fourth, *discernment helps Christian leaders maintain integrity.* Many leaders face a quiet, relentless pressure to support the status quo, to vindicate the established ways of church or society. The church is powerful, and people want its approval. Perhaps unconsciously, they reward leaders when they "prophesy smooth things" and punish them when they do not. Discernment helps leaders challenge conventional morality and resist the pressures to conform. Since "morality" often means behavior according to custom, we must see beyond custom in order to change it.

Fifth, *discernment galvanizes leaders to cause constructive trouble.* Jesus and the prophets frequently subverted their culture's values while false religious leaders affirmed them. Both Jesus and the rabbis told parables, but only the rabbinic parables reinforced conventional values. For example, the parable of the "exceptional laborer" describes one who accomplishes much and receives a large reward. But Jesus told the parable of a generous employer who pays every worker the same amount, regardless of their labor (Matt. 20:1–16). The Jewish parable is conventional and pleasing; Jesus' is unsettling. The parables sug-

---

63 James F. Childress, "Scripture and Christian Ethics: Some Reflections on the Role of Scripture in Moral Deliberation and Justification," *Interpretation* 34 (Oct. 1980): 375–76.

64 Richard Niebuhr, *The Responsible Self* (New York: Harper and Row, 1963), believes the ability to justify an action is essential to theoretical ethics. See also Childress, "Scripture and Christian Ethics," 372–74; Edward LeRoy Long, "The Use of the Bible in Christian Ethics," *Interpretation* 19 (1965): 158–59.

65 For a list of secular convictions, see George G. Hunter III, *How to Reach Secular People* (Nashville: Abingdon, 1992), 43–54.

gest how disruptive Jesus' teaching must have seemed at first, and should still today, if we hear it afresh.[66]

Discernment is a gift God gives all of the redeemed, but we can take steps to develop it. In general, we need to discount our private experience and realize that customs and presuppositions vary widely from one age and culture to another. Therefore, we must cultivate challenging relationships, so as to hear all kinds of people, yet without simply trading ideas. We should also seek ideas outside our generation and social orbit, reading a variety of secular literature. Here are some concrete suggestions:

1. Read church history to gain insight from the church in other lands and times.
2. Listen to people a generation older and younger than yourself. Savor radical friends.
3. Read social critics, Christian and otherwise, to gain their perspectives on society.
4. Know the times. Read widely. Watch television, noting what it values and what it skewers.
5. Develop a conscience that distinguishes righteousness from wickedness.
6. Study the Bible, fearlessly following its lead, refusing to read familiar ideas into the text.

SUMMARY

People ask four classes of spiritual questions. Following our survey in chapter 5, we have now offered both theological rationale for their validity and practical ideas about their use. We have covered a great deal of ground, but have always sought to equip Christian leaders to expand their concept of the relevance of Scripture. With our analysis of the way our questions generate applications complete, we turn to the task of finding applications in several genres of Scripture.

---

66 Harvey K. McArthur and Robert M. Johnston, *They Also Taught in Parables* (Grand Rapids: Zondervan, 1990), 58, 199.

APPENDIX A:
A SHORT CRITIQUE OF UTILITARIANISM

The ethical school that judges the morality of actions by their consequences is known as utilitarianism. Classical utilitarianism claims that the only reason for performing an action is that it causes more happiness than would the alternatives. Thus, the test of an action's goodness is this: does it produce the greatest happiness (or least pain) for the greatest number of people? More precisely, "The only reason for performing some action A, rather than various alternative actions, is that A results in more happiness (or more generally, in better consequences) for all mankind . . . than will any of these alternative actions" (J. J. C. Smart, "Utilitarianism," in *The Encyclopedia of Philosophy*, ed. Paul Edwards [New York: Macmillan, 1967], 8:206–12; for the classic account of utilitarianism, see John Stuart Mill, "Utilitarianism," in *The Philosophy of John Stuart Mill*, ed. Marshall Cohen [New York: Modern Library, 1961], 321–98, esp. 328–52). From the beginning, utilitarianism has invited criticism on four grounds (grounds already known to Mill; see "utilitarianism," 344–51).

1. Utilitarianism founders on human ignorance, our inability to predict and control the consequences of actions. To calculate the consequences of an act fully, one must be omniscient, since a deed that initially seems beneficial may later have disastrous consequences. (Witness, for example, the decision to bring starlings to America for insect control, which resulted in the elimination of regional cherry crops and the extinction of a dozen native bird species.)

2. Utilitarianism supposes that humans act from "generalized benevolence," that they are as interested in the happiness of the greatest number as they are in their own (Mill, "Utilitarianism," 339–44; Smart, "Utilitarianism," 8:208). But people are naturally egocentric (as even the pagans knew; see Plato, *Republic*, 43–45). Further, even if they intend to act in the general interest, the capacity for self-deception remains. Lofty ideas may camouflage base motives.

3. Utilitarianism decays into lawlessness if people do whatever it takes to achieve their purposes. Lawlessness is a consequence so devastating that one should never violate a moral norm in order to achieve a goal, however laudable it may appear.

4. Utilitarianism invites situation ethics. If, for example, a situa-

tionist is alone with a dying friend and promises to care for the children, why should he keep his word if he meets two other needy children who are brighter and more responsive to him? He would still serve a neighbor, and do greater good, so why keep the promise? If a greater benefit would come from breaking the promise, strict consequentialism will say, "Break it." But the very concept of promising, something fundamental to society, is annulled if it can be laid aside so readily.

This case suggests how readily utilitarianism declines into egocentricity, and how it has difficulty explaining why people should keep onerous vows. Take marriage as an example. Why should a man keep a promise to love and cherish a wife who has become irritable and demanding, if a more pleasing woman becomes available? Marriage vows do not mean, "My calculations indicate that I will be happiest if I marry this person." Paul Ramsey correctly says that if marriage rested on such a calculation, it would be "an almost untenable wager . . . on the persistency of present feelings," a wager against the depredations of time and the sinful and transitory nature of humans ("The Biblical Norm of Righteousness," *Interpretation* 24 [1970]: 426–29). Utilitarian thinking obscures the essence of marriage as the union of two lives through a pledge of permanent fidelity; marriage vows are not a bet on happiness (see James Olthuis, *I Pledge You My Troth* [New York: Harper and Row, 1975]).

Refined forms of utilitarianism have appeared in recent decades, and some give duty a prominent place. "Rule utilitarianism" especially seeks to safeguard duty, stressing that societies experience the greatest good when they follow moral rules, even if the rules sometimes cause pain or injustice in the short run. Thus it is best to tell the truth, even when an immediate good could apparently be achieved by telling a lie; for lies sow incalculable distrust (Smart, "Utilitarianism," 208). But this hybrid form of utilitarianism is not prevalent. (See David Lyons, *Forms and Limits of Utilitarianism* [New York: Oxford University Press], 1965.)

A Brief Reminder on Interpretation and Context

In making the transition to the most practical chapters, the most "how to" elements, we pause to remind ourselves again that the study of the relevance of Scripture builds on skillful interpretation. Though the boundary between interpretation and application is blurry, teachers must master exegesis if they wish to move correctly from the original meaning to the contemporary relevance of Scripture. If we leap to the subjective question, "What does this text say to me?" we are sure to moralize, sure to find the text saying trendy or self-serving things.

Thus it is imperative that both before and during the application process we keep in view the textures of biblical times. We must remember how much revelation the people had and how they were appropriating it. Sensitivity to the original context is especially important for topical studies. When teachers seize a text that answers a significant question, then proceed to cross-references and concordance studies, it is all too easy to ignore the text's setting. No one has time to analyze every passage that is cited, but pastors should at least note the epoch of the main text for thematic studies.

Beyond knowledge of the general culture, we must consider the relational context of books. Do author and readers share a common outlook, or does the author adopt a critical position? What are the author's goals and motives in writing? Finally, because authors of historical books often wrote decades (the Gospels, Acts) or even centuries (Genesis, Chronicles) after the events they recount, we must take into consideration the culture both of the event and of the writer.

Awareness of a book's genre, whether history, poetry, prophecy, vision, wisdom, lament, letter, or sermon, is another crucial facet of context and interpretation. For example, genre studies teach us not to equate proverbs with promises. Proverbs distill truths in pithy statements, but they do not commit God to guarantee results, as promises do. Again, a lament records how a believer mourned and suggests how we might do so, but not every lament immediately leads to a point in systematic theology. Technically, each genre merits special attention, but because fine introductions to genre issues are available elsewhere, the following chapters discuss only narratives, doctrinal passages, and ethical texts. The discussions of narratives and ethical texts have two chapters each, the first outlining a plan for application, the second assessing the underlying theoretical issues.

When this book was first outlined, the intent was to recapitulate the entire process of interpretation, since skillful application depends on skillful interpretation. Though the book's length forbade it, I still believe skill with contexts, analysis, grammar, and the rest is essential for depth and variety in application. Athletic coaches like to inculcate "master tips." With master tips, if we do one thing right, we necessarily avoid an array of errors. Similarly, if we master the several facets of context, we will avoid an array of errors and benefit from a host of interpretive virtues that will immeasurably enhance our efforts at application.

7
A Plan for Applying Narrative

Whenever we go to Grandma's house, the children head for the photo albums, pore over the pictures, and beg, "Tell us a story, Daddy, tell us a story 'bout when you were little." Children love stories, and one well-chosen story about when we were little can do more to break the hold of contemporary culture than can three lectures on the evils of the age. Narratives can be touchstones for adults, too. The story of how Grandpa nursed Grandma back to health during her long illness, knowing it would cost him the professional advancement he craved, can direct the married lives of his heirs more effectively than can a hundred imperatives about fidelity.[1]

Teachers know stories move people; that is why they constantly search for illustrations. How strange, then, that we are so eager to use contemporary stories in our preaching yet so reluctant to preach on the stories of the Bible. About 35 percent of the Bible is narrative, but a survey of model sermons in leading preaching journals showed just 8 percent expounding a biblical narrative.[2] People love a good story, so I doubt that the problem lies with the audience. Why then do pas-

---

1 Robert Roberts, "Virtues and Rules," *Philosophy and Phenomenological Research* 51.2 (June 1991): 328.
2 My research assistant, Bryan Stewart, found that 9 of 114 sermons surveyed (7.9 percent) expounded a narrative (more used a narrative topically). In *Preaching* 3 of 39 sermons published from July 1997 to June 1998 expounded a biblical narrative. In *Pulpit Digest* 6 of 75 sermons published from January to December 1998 expounded a narrative.

tors prefer discourse—epistles, psalms, and law? Several answers come to mind:

- Structural problems. Narrative does not lend itself to traditional propositional preaching or to three-point outlines.
- Length. Since the length of narratives varies from a few verses (short miracles) to several chapters (Absalom's rebellion), they may not fit into local ideas of proper sermon length.
- Familiarity. Beloved narratives are well known. How can we say anything new?
- Pedantry. Narrative preaching can bog down in explanations: "To understand this, you have to know the ancient Israelite custom. . . ." No one wants a sermon to devolve into history lessons or tales of old, unhappy, far-off things, and battles long ago.

But I suspect a more fundamental problem. Teachers hesitate to expound narratives because they know how much can go wrong in exposition and application. It is possible, for example, to ignore the very nature of narrative and treat stories as "golden casket[s] where gems of truth are stored."[3] We might seize upon golden doctrinal maxims. We find, "The Glory of Israel does not lie or change his mind" (1 Sam. 15:29), and proclaim the veracity and immutability of God. We may read Peter's declaration, "There is no other name under heaven given to men by which we must be saved" (Acts 4:12), and deliver a gospel message. Or we interpret moralistically, reading Daniel 6 and urging imitation of Daniel's faith. Scanning Genesis 27 and 28 we may declare that liars always fall into trouble, as Jacob did. None of this is entirely wrong, of course. Biblical narratives do convey moral and theological truths. But it is a mistake to treat narratives as if they were *chiefly* repositories of such lessons.

On the other hand, we may let the story stand but allegorize, moralize, or spiritualize the details, thereby undermining the main thrust of the narrative. Not long ago I heard a sermon illustrating these crimes. A message on missions, it appealed to Jesus' call of the disciples after

---

3 William How, in Edmund Clowney, *The Unfolding Mystery: Discovering Christ in the Old Testament* (Colorado Springs: NavPress, 1988), 11.

the great catch of fish in Luke 5:1–11. The speaker, a reputable Christian leader, made six points, reporting, explaining, and applying each event.

1. *Report:* Jesus encountered Peter when he was washing his nets (5:2). *Explanation:* Washing and mending nets are the boring and repetitive aspects of being a fisherman. *Application:* We all have boring, repetitive tasks (doing dishes, commuting). But God speaks to us in our drudgery.
2. *Report:* Jesus encountered Peter at a moment of professional failure; he had no fish (5:2–5). *Explanation:* Even fishermen don't always know where the fish are. *Application:* We all fail from time to time. Don't be afraid to fail. Nothing ventured, nothing gained.
3. *Report:* Peter let Jesus sit in his boat near the shore, in the shallow water, but Jesus wanted to go into deep water (5:3–5). *Explanation:* We have let Jesus enter our boat, but sometimes we want to stay in shallow, safe water near shore, in our comfort zone. *Application:* When Jesus gives the command to take the boat into deep water, do it. Take a few risks.
4. *Report:* Jesus made an unreasonable request to let down the nets (5:4). *Explanation:* If there were no fish all night, why should there be fish now? *Application:* Expect your bosses to make unreasonable requests, too.
5. *Report:* Peter went into the deep water and let down his nets (5:6). *Explanation:* Although the request was unreasonable, Peter was teachable, submissive. *Application:* We should be teachable, too.
6. *Report:* When the fishermen let down the nets, they had a great catch of fish (5:6–7). *Explanation:* Peter took a risk and received a joyous reward. Peter learned that Jesus is Lord. *Application:* Be like Peter; take risks for the Lord. Be fishers of men.

The speaker's pleasing manner spread a thin blanket of plausibility over his remarks, and he probably captured the imagination of those who suffer from repetitive tasks and unreasonable bosses; but even a novice interpreter groans at the techniques. The trouble, as anyone who has ever been pressed into service as a referee knows, is that it is easier to critique another's errors than to do it right yourself. Therefore, let us outline a plan for interpreting and applying narratives.[4] We will draw upon the flaws in the preceding sermon to explain certain points.

In Luke 5, Jesus demonstrates the power, omniscience, and goodness that enable disciples to trust him. But the first five themes of the sermon only superficially related to the miracle's main point. Risk-taking, drudgery, and unreasonable requests are not Luke's interests. The sermon drew moral lessons from elements of the narrative that set up the main point, but missed the main lesson itself. To be sure, disciple-making entails risks, but Luke 5 does not even hint at them; if anything, it does the opposite, given the powers Jesus employs. In the sermon's first five points, the main action was always Peter's. Because the message neglected Jesus' power and goodness until the last phase, it necessarily became anthropocentric. In the final analysis, it said, "Do this for a better life. Do this so you can accomplish something for God." The sixth point did touch the chief idea, but in a way that still focused on Peter—what he learned about Jesus—more than on who Jesus is. So the message focused on man rather than God.

But sound interpretation of a biblical narrative always focuses first on the acts of God. God is always the main character, the main actor, in biblical narratives. Indeed, the Bible is one long drama that begins when God creates heaven and earth, and ends when he restores them (Gen. 1:1; Rev. 21–22). The intervening chapters describe God's activity, God's grace, God's achievement of his aims; they do not focus on human activity or humans reaching out to God. In fact, "scriptural history implies that God's story advances despite the deeds of the people of God . . . as often as through them." For example, Genesis dwells more on God's dealings with Abraham and Sarah "than on the way Abraham and Sarah relate to God."[5] Even if a segment omits mention of God's hand, the larger work makes God's role clear. First

---

4 On interpreting biblical narrative, see Robert Alter, *The Art of Biblical Narrative* (New York: Basic Books, 1980); Mark Powell, *What Is Narrative Criticism?* (Minneapolis: Fortress, 1990); Leland Ryken, *Words of Delight* (Grand Rapids: Baker, 1987). They stress elements of literary analysis such as setting, plot, and characterization.

5 John Goldingay, *Models for Interpretation of Scripture* (Grand Rapids: Eerdmans, 1995), 56–58.

Samuel mentions God roughly four hundred times as judge, deliverer, and director of Israel; will anyone quibble if he fails to appear in one pericope? Therefore, let sermons focus on God's actions and self-revelation.[6]

After we see God's work clearly, discerning the way it advances his redemptive purposes, we should consider how men and women responded to it. Knowing that the friends and foes of God have responded in roughly similar ways through the ages, we should see his work through the eyes of the disciples, unbelievers, and fence-sitters who were present that day. Few Christians would reject this notion, but we need methods to facilitate theocentric interpretation.

THE BASIC INGREDIENTS IN NARRATIVE ANALYSIS

Types of Narrative

It will be beneficial, first, to define what we mean by narrative. Scholars distinguish three types of narrative, each of which must be interpreted differently.

1. *Dramas* are narrative accounts with sufficient length and detail to create vivid characters and dramatic tension as the story unfolds and moves toward a resolution. Biblical dramas include the near sacrifice of Isaac (Gen. 22), Gideon's victory over Midian (Judg. 6–7), the escape of Daniel's friends from the fiery furnace (Dan. 3), and the resurrection of Lazarus (John 11).[7]

2. *Reports* are brief records of events such as battles, building projects, dreams, or reigns of minor kings. Reports describe simple events and lack full characterization and dramatic tension. By itself, a report

---

6 Goldingay adduces a series of reasons to believe biblical narratives regard God as the main character: (1) The disinclination to record the thoughts of characters in narratives, the elusiveness regarding their designs, de-emphasizes them and leaves room for God. (2) The New Testament is reluctant to use the Old Testament for examples to be avoided, in part because it knows the examples will not actually be avoided. (3) It is often difficult to tell if what people do is right or wrong; if the purpose of narrative were to provide moral examples, that would be clearer. See Goldingay, *Models,* 41, 56–61.

7 We will focus on dramas because they do more to advance the story of redemption than reports do and because speech stories are often better suited to discourse analysis.

may reveal little, but taken together, a series of reports imparts much about the works of God. For example, we might wonder about the significance of the reports of Isaac's well-digging activity (Gen. 26:15–32). But when we notice that he lost wells three times (vv. 15, 19–22) but stayed in the area, as God had commanded (26:3), then dug two more wells, which he finally held, we see the digging as obedience and perseverance in the promises and commands of the covenant. A pattern emerges: God commands and promises, Isaac perseveres, and God reaffirms the promise (26:24).

3. In *speech stories* the main event is a speech given in a historical setting. We see speech stories when the apostles preach sermons or defend themselves at trials (Acts 2, 3, 13, 24–26), when prophets appear before kings (Isa. 7; Amos 7), and when Jesus explains his miracles at length, especially in John (John 5, 6, 11). A speech story is a hybrid genre that may be ill suited to narrative analysis. There is no substitute for mature judgment here, for stories often fall on the border between dramas and speech stories. For example, in the Gospels Jesus may punctuate a miracle with a terse lesson.[8] But the speech often dominates the passage so that it is better to study it as doctrinal or ethical instruction.[9]

The Phases of a Drama

The primary goal of narrative analysis is to discern the activity of God as he achieves salvation. Next we notice the responses of the faithful and the unfaithful. The teacher presents God's work so that we first see what God has done, then consider how the children of God and the world responded to him. Short as they are, biblical dramas exhibit the same six phases as do all dramas (fig. 14). The six phases lead preachers to the main point, the God-centered lesson, of the narrative.

1. *Setting the stage.* Examine both the literary and the cultural contexts of the drama.[10] First, note the location of the story in its literary context, that is, in the narrative of the book in which it appears. Second, note the time and place of the story. Determine the spirit of

---

8 Scholars sometimes call these "pronouncement stories."

9 See Daniel M. Doriani, *Getting the Message* (Phillipsburg; N.J.: Presbyterian and Reformed, 1996), chap. 6.

10 See Doriani, *Getting the Message,* chaps. 3 and 4.

FIG. 14.
SIX PHASES IN A DRAMATIC NARRATIVE

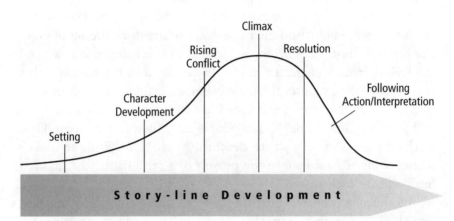

the day and its place in redemptive history. How much revelation do the people have? What are the issues of the hour?

2. *Character development*. List all the characters, stating what is known about their history, interests, and motives, whether from Scripture or external sources. Look for an individual or a group that believes, and for someone who is unbelieving or (apparently) uncommitted. Expect to learn the characters' traits more from their words and deeds than from comments by the narrator.

3. *Conflict*. The narrative begins to move when a problem arises, whether it is a physical need, a spiritual quest, or a military threat. Conflicts commonly have several phases as events escalate toward a conclusion.

4. The *crisis or climax*. At the moment of greatest tension we hold our breath and wonder, "What will happen now?" When Abraham raises his knife, when David rushes at Goliath, when Elijah summons fire from heaven, we have reached the climax. Here we must suspend our knowledge. We know how each story turns out—we've heard it so many times! But the characters in the story do not. They are "future-blind," and we should pretend to be if we wish to relive the power of biblical narratives.

5. *Resolution*. If at the climax of the story the witnesses to the event were holding their breath, the resolution permitted them to release it. When Abraham spares his son, David slays his foe, or fire falls from

heaven, we have a resolution. We release our breath when we see that *God* spared Isaac, defeated Goliath, and sent fire.

6. *Following actions or sayings.* At the nexus of the climax and the resolution we usually find the main point of the story, the act of God. But the main point can be elusive. In that case, it helps to seek a word from God, from a character in the drama, or from the narrator, that comes just before or after the main event and explains its significance. In the case of the near sacrifice of Isaac we twice hear that the Lord will provide (Gen. 22:8, 14). But people can misconstrue events. They ascribed the power of Jesus to demons (Matt. 12:24) and the snake's bite of shipwrecked Paul to the pursuit of a criminal by the goddess Justice (Acts 28:3–6).

Proficiency at charting the six phases of a drama demands practice, since biblical narratives may skip phases, have double climaxes or stories within stories, or otherwise stray from the norm. Further, authors develop their own styles. Acts has several speech stories that straddle the boundary between narrative and discourse; 2 Kings features terse reports and high dramas. The narratives of the Pentateuch, Judges, and Samuel often sprawl over multiple chapters, while the Synoptics use short intense stories. But whatever the book, teachers should seek the main point at the climax-resolution nexus and in the following sayings.

The Fundamentals for the Application of Narrative

Once again, in expounding narrative the prime responsibility is to discover the way God accomplishes salvation and reveals himself. Here the preacher must embrace the repetitive aspect of God-centered preaching. Teachers must dare to be boring. That is, they must dethrone the demigods of innovation and novelty and never weary of proclaiming the main thing—God's love, grace, and holiness, retold with freshness and conviction.

Of course, we cannot repeat the same few ideas endlessly. First, the forms of human need vary greatly, as does the grace that meets those needs. Second, there is diversity in peoples' responses to God. The men and women who originally witnessed God's acts showed the same doubt, denial, and anger that unbelievers manifest to this day. Even among the faithful there is variety: faith may be weak or strong, timid or indomitable.

To multiply applications, first list every character in the story and view the episode through each one's eyes. Look for the following:

- God or his agent accomplishing an aspect of his redemption
- believers showing faithful responses to God or the failures common to God's children
- unbelievers manifesting one or more of the paths of rebellion
- neutral parties exemplifying the way people put off decision and vacillate

Teachers usually have preliminary hunches about the way the application of a message will go. But we must be patient and establish the main, God-centered point first. Then we can determine whether proposed secondary ideas, drawn from the way the human characters respond to God, truly develop the main idea or take flight from it. When teachers focus on the human characters in themselves, they inevitably shift toward moralistic lessons. But a focus on God and human responses to him can revivify even the most familiar narratives, such as the stories of David and Goliath and of the Magi.

SPECIFIC EXAMPLES OF NARRATIVE ANALYSIS

David and Goliath

Sadly, one must introduce the story of David and Goliath with a word of caution, for it is oft abused. Scores of sermons reduce David to a moral exemplar: "Be courageous and fight your giants as David did." In Sunday school, children learn that even little ones can do big things, if God is with them. But even well-informed adults miss aspects of the narrative.[11]

Both 1 and 2 Samuel identify David as Israel's warrior king (1 Sam. 16:18), to whom God gives strength and victory (1 Sam. 2:10; 2 Sam. 22:51). Knowing this, and with eyes sensitized to battle more than some other matters, we identify David's declaration "The battle is the LORD's" (1 Sam. 17:47) as the theme of the episode. That is valid since the statement appears at the climax of the narrative, as David advances

---

11 Almost all commentators notice the theme of God's honor, but none makes it a major focus.

to slay the giant. God does save, delivering Israel from a major invasion. But there is more.

The context reveals young David to be the Lord's anointed (1 Sam. 16), whom he now introduces to Israel.[12] The king-in-waiting, chosen instead of tall, impressive Eliab, David is the man after God's own heart (16:13). Like Jonathan (14:1–15), he rekindles faith in Israel and demonstrates what God can accomplish through a faithful servant.[13]

The narrative focuses on God, but it creates avenues for relevance when seen through the eyes of believers (David), unbelievers (Goliath, the Philistines), and supposedly neutral parties (Saul, the Israelites, David's brothers).

In 1 Samuel 17:1–25, the Philistines invade Judah, driving deep into its territory, until an Israelite army meets them, creating a military impasse. Goliath, a giant, offers to settle the conflict through a battle between two champions, and taunts the quivering Israelites daily. Saul and his army seem to be neutral bystanders, but their inaction proves their faithlessness. The Israelites are God's army and Saul his anointed, yet they do nothing while a pagan shames them and their God. Lacking David's zeal and faith, they cannot see the situation God's way. With worldly wisdom, they are afraid and wonder who will dare to fight the giant (v. 25).

God brings David to the camp just in time for Goliath's taunt (v. 23). He arrives, hears, and grows incensed that "this uncircumcised Philistine" should disgrace Israel, should "defy the armies of the living God," and heap shame on them (vv. 10, 26, 36).[14] David recognizes the affront to God and offers to fight Goliath in the name of his dishonored Lord (vv. 32, 45). Because the other Israelites have lost sight of God's honor, they cannot fathom David's motivation to fight

---

12 David is old enough to kill wild animals (17:36) and bear armor at Saul's court (16:21), but he apparently had not reached twenty, the age for entry into Israel's standing army (Num. 1:3; 26:2).

13 Robert Bergen, *1, 2 Samuel* (Nashville: Broadman & Holman, 1996), 187, 194; S. G. De Graaf, *Promise and Deliverance,* trans. H. E. Runner (Phillipsburg, N.J: Presbyterian and Reformed, 1977), 112.

14 The Hebrew *ḥrp* may mean "defy, mock, or heap shame." See John Hartley, "ḥrp," in *New International Dictionary of Old Testament Theology and Exegesis,* ed. Willem A. VanGemeren, 5 vols. (Grand Rapids: Zondervan, 1997), 2:281–82; see also Bergen, *1, 2 Samuel,* 190.

(vv. 28–37).[15] Eliab, David's oldest brother, accuses David of coming to see blood (vv. 28–30), but we hear the sibling jealousy—an old theme, which the previous chapter prepared (16:6–7).[16]

Reports of David's resolve work their way to Saul, who investigates. He hesitates to let David attempt an apparent suicide mission (17:31–33), but not for very long (17:37–38). Armed only with a staff and a sling against a fully armed, armor-draped giant, David advances (v. 40).[17]

The text of the verbal conflict preceding the battle exceeds that of the conflict itself. Goliath insults his handsome foe, curses him by the Philistine gods, and promises to feed his shamed carcass to the birds (vv. 43–44).[18] But the giant's jeers cannot match David's inspired insults (vv. 45–47):

> You come against me with sword and spear and javelin, but I come against you in the name of the LORD Almighty, the God of the armies of Israel, whom you have defied. This day the LORD will hand you over to me, and I'll strike you down and cut off your head. Today I will give the carcasses of the Philistine army to the birds of the air and the beasts of the earth, and the whole world will know that there is a God in Israel. All those gathered here will know that it is not by sword or spear that the LORD saves, for the battle is the LORD's, and he will give all of you into our hands.

Now we know that the contest between David and Goliath is a contest between the gods. If David strikes down Goliath, his Lord is vindicated. If not . . .

The battle itself is almost anticlimactic. David runs, reaches into his bag, slings, and strikes before the giant moves. Goliath is face-down and dead in twenty-seconds' reading time.

15 David does have a secondary interest in rewards (v. 26). Is this meant to set up Saul's subsequent repudiation of the reward? Or does it prepare for a far deadlier egoism in our hero (2 Sam. 11)?
16 The "jealous older brother" theme in the Old Testament includes Cain and Abel, Jacob and Esau, and Joseph and his brothers in Gen. 4, 27, and 37, respectively.
17 Goliath's scale armor weighed 125 pounds; his spear point 15.
18 To die and go unburied is nearly the ultimate disgrace.

Sermons that escape the moralizing praise of David and blame of Saul seize upon the statement "The battle is the LORD's."[19] That exclamation does capture the main idea. Yet there is more. Observe the prominence of God's honor at the beginning (v. 10), the turning point (vv. 23–26), and the climax of the drama (vv. 45–46). Goliath insults the honor of Israel, God's army, hence the honor of God himself. No one rises to God's defense, not regal Saul the anointed, not impressive Eliab. No one stirs until David arrives.

David's courage is no accident. He already knows God as his deliverer (vv. 34–37). He is already anointed as king. Love for God and his honor gives David discernment that makes him burn at Goliath's offense to God.[20] The narrative is, therefore, theocentric. God raised up an anointed, zealous servant-king, God brought him to the battle line at the right moment, God inspired him to see the issue as it was, God empowered him to defeat the foe. Thus God defended his honor and turned back the invading army.

These points form the bedrock for the first set of applications of 1 Samuel 17. This narrative instructs us to know, honor, and trust the God who empowered David to defeat his enemy and defend his dignity. *Application 1:* Expect God to defend his honor. He says, "Those who honor me I will honor, but those who despise me will be disdained" (1 Sam. 2:30); and he will back his words.

Beyond the lesson concerning God's honor, we see his redemptive power. David's victory is significant in itself, for it thwarted an invasion that reached deep into Israel. David defeated forces bent on destroying God's people. His action preserved the integrity of the nation. David's survival of the battle matters too. As God's anointed, he risked his life to save his people. *Application 2:* Know that God ever protects and defends his people. In victory, David foreshadows Jesus' defeat of Satan.[21] Zeal for God's honor consumes both David

---

19 The poems that open and close the books of Samuel state the major themes (1 Sam. 2; 2 Sam. 22–23). Hannah says, "It is not by strength that one prevails; those who oppose the LORD will be shattered. . . . He will give strength to his king" (1 Sam. 2:9–10). David sings, "The LORD is my rock, my fortress, and my deliverer. . . . You armed me with strength for battle" (2 Sam. 22:2, 40).

20 See Bruce Malina, *The New Testament World: Insights from Cultural Anthropology* (Philadelphia: Westminster/John Knox, 1981), 25–50, esp. 37–39.

21 David is never called a type of Christ in the New Testament, and the books of

and Jesus. Both deliver God's people from a destroying foe. Both deliver from a position of weakness. Both display God's power.

David's heroism elicits diverse responses, as God and his agents always do. From Eliab David gets skepticism, from Saul suspicion, from Jonathan loving acceptance (1 Sam. 18:1–4). God's actions elicit the same responses to this day. The gist of *Application 3:* God's redemptive work leads some to faith but leaves others in unbelief.

God is the central character in 1 Samuel 17; the subsidiary characters bounce off him. David is an active believer. Goliath and the Philistines are unbelievers. To call Saul and his army neutral would be generous. They are cowards, especially Saul, who is the anointed king and the tallest, best-armed man.

May a preacher warn against behavior reminiscent of the army's inaction, Eliab's jealousy, and Saul's cowardice? It all depends on how it is done. If we simply admonish, "Don't be inactive when action is required," or "Don't be jealous of your siblings," or "Don't let others volunteer to carry out your tough responsibilities," we are moralizing, focusing on men in themselves. These points are not so much false as rootless, cut flowers that shall wither and die. We must get to the root. *Application 4:* Unbelief breeds culpable inaction and cowardice in every Israelite agent but David. It freezes Saul and the army. It lets Eliab castigate David for blood lust (v. 28), and prompts Saul to worry about David's lack of armor (vv. 33–40). Faithlessness deprives them of the insight that the battle is the Lord's. The failures of Saul, Eliab, and the army illustrate the consequences of unbelief. Their inaction proves that neutrality toward God is not a genuine option. We are for God or against him.

David is the sole active believer here, but he is more than an example of courage. Samuel makes deeper points: God is a warrior, the protector of his people. He calls, anoints, and nurtures agents to deliver them.

But there is a subtler theme in David's role. Notice first that the

Samuel lack any explicit expectation that a future ruler from David's line will restore his house. Nevertheless, (1) David is anointed as (2) the greatest king, yet (3) he is a flawed sinner who needs a redeemer. (4) David is one of a few who, like Jesus, functioned in more than one office, as king and prophet. (5) The Gospels often call Jesus "the Son of David."

death of Goliath is not David's sole motivation. He does not volunteer saying, "I believe I can beat the giant." David *knows* he can and will do so to defend God's honor and remove Israel's disgrace. We abuse the narrative if we say Christians must fight giants as David did. The vapid song of the women of Israel (18:6–9) shows that praising the man misses the point. Instead, we should ask what motivates David and see that it is his relentlessly theocentric outlook. His zeal for God liberates courage.[22] He burns to remove Israel's disgrace because the world must know there is a God in Israel. He fights in God's name, in God's strength, for God's honor (17:45–47). David explains in Psalm 69,

> I endure scorn for your sake. . . .
> I am a stranger to my brothers . . .
> for zeal for your house consumes me,
>   and the insults of those who insult you fall on me. (vv. 7–9)

Zeal for God's honor is the face of faith in 1 Samuel 17. The catapult for the story is the giant's defiance of that honor and the inability of Israel to defend it. Saul's promise of his daughter's hand in marriage and release from taxes moved no one, because, apparently, the soldiers knew that dead men pay no taxes anyway. Discernment, however, let David turn the question on its head. "Who will dare to fight the giant?" became "Who is this uncircumcised Philistine that he should defy the armies of the living God?" (v. 26).

Notice the theme of defiance. The Philistine says, "I defy the ranks of Israel" (v. 10). David arrives as Goliath shouts "his usual defiance" (v. 23). The Israelites say, "He comes out to defy Israel" (v. 25). David asks who Goliath is to "defy the armies of the living God" (v. 26). Then David announces to both Saul and Goliath himself that the giant must die for defying God (vv. 36, 45–46). Both the repetition of the term and its use in pivotal dialogue underscore its prominence.[23] Goliath's insult combines with David's eye for the Lord's honor to rouse David.

---

22   Significantly, the language of courage, bravery, valor, and heroism never appears in the narrative.
23   Alter, *Art of Biblical Narrative,* 69ff.

Application 5: David's zeal to guard God's dignity probes us. What stirs our passions? What makes us angry? We become offended at minor snubs or acts of disrespect. We rage at people who cut us off in traffic or stretch yellow lights already quite red. We are quick to anger at personal offenses, but calm over offenses to God's name and holiness. We say, "What do you expect of sinners?" But there is a place for indignation over sin: "The deeds of faithless men I hate. . . . Every morning I will put to silence all the wicked in the land" (Ps. 101:3, 8). There is a place for grief over sin: "Streams of tears flow from my eyes, for your law is not obeyed" (Ps. 119:136).

One day I was playing basketball in the gym of a Christian college when a couple of strangers invited themselves into our game. We were willing to accept them, but soon, contrary to our code of conduct, they began using obscene and blasphemous language whenever they made a mistake. It set the Christians on edge, but no one said much until, after an extraordinary expletive, the man in charge ignited. "Listen," he roared, "You can say ### and you can say @@@ and you can say ★★★. I don't care much; they're just rude. But you either stop using the name of my Lord like that or get off this court!" I am not sure whether the vehemence or the rarity of the speech impressed us more, but we witnessed zeal for God's honor that day.

Let us pause to review the steps to be taken in explaining the story. First, we identified the main, theocentric point. We drew on the literary context (the anointing of David) and historical context (the political importance of the conflict). We used standard methods to analyze the drama. Repeated reading called attention to the prominence of God's honor at crucial points.

Second, by seeing zeal for God's honor as the unique thrust of this tale of faith, we can bring stray exegetical data from 17:26–28 into focus.[24] David's insight that the question is not "Who will dare to fight the giant?" but "Who does this Philistine think he is . . . ?" no longer appears to be an unrepeatable flash of intuition. It has a source—zeal

---

24 Critical scholars who doubt everything in the account except perhaps the idea that David killed a Philistine warrior are pressed to explain why the narrator added these ideas to the tale. Critics tend to explain such details in terms of David's rise to kingship. Typically, Eliab's bitterness proves David was the only fit king from Jesse's line, and Saul's cowardice shows why his line was rejected. See P. Kyle McCarter, *1 Samuel* (New York: Doubleday, 1980), 296–97.

for God's honor. Our emphasis on honor also makes more sense of the moment when Eliab berates David. We know better than to make it into a cautionary tale about sibling rivalry (hardly Samuel's concern!). Eliab shows that a person who loses sight of God's honor can fall into a misguided concern for his own. Similarly, the interview with Saul shows the consequences of his faithlessness but also his lack of interest in protecting God's people and name. These themes get at the roots of sin and provide material for relevant application that far surpasses lists of dos and don'ts.

Third, we can now relate the story to the theoretical material of earlier chapters. With regard to the sources of application (chap. 4), this passage is chiefly a narrative of redemptive and exemplary acts, but there is also instruction in the doctrines of faith and God's honor. As for the four questions people ask, we hesitate to read the passage as a call to duty to act as David did. David's victory rests on his character, God-given boldness, and his fidelity to God. David had a goal too, removing God's shame. Finally, David discerned that his earlier victories over wild animals were signs of God's care and that the Philistine campaign was an assault on the Lord.

The Adoration of the Magi

Our second test case will be shorter and will develop the technique of watching the responses of the various witnesses to God's action. In Matthew 2:1–12 God acts by announcing the birth of Christ. He fulfills his promise to "raise up to David a righteous Branch, a King who will reign wisely" (Jer. 23:5). This servant will "bring back those of Israel [God] has kept" and will be "a light for the Gentiles" to bring "salvation to the ends of the earth" (Isa. 49:6). Four characters in the drama respond to the announcement: Herod, all Jerusalem, a group of chief priests and teachers, and the Magi.

First, we see *the anger of Herod,* who attempts to kill Israel's true king by murdering the infant males of Bethlehem. This act marks him as a foe of God, an antiking, an antichrist, who would do Satan's work for him. Herod also illustrates the folly of wickedness. He hears the oracle, corresponding to a prophecy, that the king of the Jews is born. If Herod believes it is true, why does he think he can slay God's Messiah? But if he believes it false, why bother killing the infants? Both the murder and the folly typify the foes of God. Yet the Father protects his Son and his covenant of salvation by sending the Magi a timely dream.

Very few are as hateful as Herod, but there are other types of failed response. Second, then, we note *the anxiety of Jerusalem*. When Jerusalem's citizens hear the report of the Magi, they are disturbed, for they know that Herod's distress could mean their pain. There is, however, no desire to investigate if this is indeed the birth of God's Messiah. They only ask if the news might harm them. Alarmed, they do nothing. There remains today a class of humans whose concern for spiritual things goes just far enough to ask if the reports of Jesus could somehow interfere with them.

Third, we see *the apathy of the chief priests* and teachers of the law. Upon hearing the Magi's report, Herod tries to avoid being deceived by interrogating these two antagonistic groups of Jewish experts about Jesus' birthplace. They answer well, aptly citing Micah. Their elegant quotation formula, "Thus it was written through the prophet," evokes both the divine origin and human agency of prophecy. Yet, surprisingly, we see no more of these leaders. They expected the Messiah and now hear a promising report. But they are satisfied to quote Scripture and do nothing. Content with their expert knowledge, they neither praise God nor join the Magi in worship. Their initial inertia later became aggressive opposition. Today, no one stands precisely where the priests and teachers did, yet many rest content in their knowledge, as if information about God could substitute for worship.

In *the adoration of the Magi* we see God fulfilling his purpose to bring the nations to himself: "Nations will come to your light, and kings to the brightness of your dawn" (Isa. 60:3). God's surprising love for Gentiles is a leitmotif of Matthew, and in their faithful response to God's visual revelation we see the firstfruits of their harvest. Strikingly, the Magi knew less than the others, but they acted on it to the fullest. Leaving homes and families, they began an arduous journey through alien lands, following a star for a year or more.[25] Some explore the

---

25 Traditional manger scenes can mislead. The Magi were not present at the manger (Should we put our Magi at the other end of the family room?); when they arrived, Jesus was in a house (Matt. 2:11). If even Herod would not kill toddlers without reason, the slaughter of infants up to the age of two implies that the Magi had followed the star for some time (2:7).

possible symbolic value of the Magi's gifts, but whatever Matthew and the Magi were thinking, they brought precious gifts suitable for a king: gold, which is the metal of royalty, frankincense, and myrrh, spices and perfumes worth thousands of dollars today. In today's idiom, they did not come bearing aluminum, Old Spice, and a fatigued pickup truck, but gold (still), a home-entertainment system, and a luxury car.

Observing these four responses to Christ's birth, readers must chart their own course. Matthew proposes the Magi, not Herod or the diffident Jews, as models of faith, and so they are. They knew little; they knew a king of the Jews had been born, and they only half understood that. Yet they acted on it to the uttermost. They spent time and money and followed a star that led them to Jesus. They worshiped and gave costly gifts, the stuff of their royal court, the cargo of their lives. They did not give what cost them nothing. Those who own Christ as king should do no less.

Let's review. First, we briefly stated the action of God. Second, we identified the several types of response to that action: an unbelieving Herod, the believing Magi, and two disappointing yet technically noncommittal responses. Third, while we explored the facets of belief, unbelief, and neutrality on display in the text, we sought to avoid a simplistic "Be like X, don't be like Y"; instead, we presented the anger and adoration as attitudes representing the whole spectrum of possible responses to God. Fourth, we tried to explain motives without lapsing into psychological guesswork. For this reason we avoided the temptation to speculate about the symbolic value of frankincense and myrrh or to guess the feelings of the Magi as they worshiped and gave gifts.

The Miracles of Jesus

The reader must judge if our two examples have successfully illustrated ways of finding the relevance of narratives, but we need to move to a greater challenge, the miracles of Jesus. We choose them because, dramatic as they are, they seem to pose a problem by making the same points over and over. They center on Christ, but do we simply say, "Believe in him," over and over? Before answering that question, consider what the miracles do emphasize.

1. *Jesus is Lord and God*—lord over men and nature, sin and disease, lord of Jew and Gentile, rich and poor, male and female. Noth-

ing exceeds his grasp: he cures disease and rebukes death itself. Demons cannot resist him. He commands nature and it obeys. His authority compels witnesses to contemplate Him. He feeds five thousand and they exclaim, "Surely this is the prophet who is to come into the world" (John 6:14, my translation). He calms storms, and the apostles ask, "Who is this? He commands even the winds and the water, and they obey him" (Luke 8:25; Matt. 14:33). People ask, "When the Christ comes, will he do more miraculous signs than this man?" (John 7:31).

2. *Jesus restores all things.* By temporarily reversing the effects of the curse, miracles prefigure the final condition of creation—freed from bondage to decay, free to be a supra-Edenic environment for mature humanity. Miracles are eschatological; they foreshadow the proper and future condition of humankind, free from sin and consequences such as disease and death. We will delight forever in what the miracles bestow for a season. In this way miracles unveil the scope of Jesus' redemptive work.[26]

3. *Jesus is compassionate.* The Gospels explain Jesus' motives in terms of his compassion and mercy. Compassion moved him to heal crowds (Matt. 9:36; 14:14), to feed four thousand hungry followers (15:32), to restore sight to the blind (20:34). There seemed to be no premeditation for some miracles; he simply saw a need and acted. When he came upon the funeral procession for the only son of a widow, he knew what that death meant. Moved by compassion, he raised the boy (Luke 7:11–17).[27]

4. *Miracles accomplish salvation.* Like its English counterpart, the Greek term for save *(sōzō)* has a large semantic field. In English we save leftovers, baseball games, money, and lives. In Greek, Jesus "saves" souls eternally (Matt. 19:25; Luke 19:10) and "saves" bodies temporally by healing them (Matt. 9:21; Luke 6:9). His authority to forgive sins, which he has both through his deity and through his atonement (Matt. 9:6; 8:17; see also Isa. 53), empowers him to reverse the curse and inaugurate a penalty-free humanity, including the full physical restoration we will enjoy eternally.

5. *Jesus meets needs.* This restates the last three points, but takes a

---

26 Howard Kee, *Miracle in the Early Christian World* (New Haven: Yale University Press, 1983), 150ff.

27 Many miracles from Old Testament history and Acts brought judgment, but all of Jesus' miracles benefited men.

human perspective on matters. We need restoration; we are pitiable; we need a Savior. Long ago people prayed—and do today—that God would extend his healing hand to them.[28]

6. *Miracles summon faith*. Signifying that the kingdom has arrived, that Jesus has vanquished sin, miracles ask, "Are you on his side?" Because Jesus healed mixed throngs and fed thousands, we know some unbelievers received miracles. He cleansed demoniacs and raised the dead, who could hardly exercise faith during their deliverance. Still, in Jesus' encounters with individuals, the faith of the individual or of his family comes up repeatedly. It seems that at least someone must have faith. So miracles are signs, given sometimes to prompt, sometimes to strengthen faith. Yet they do not compel it. For that reason Jesus refused to perform on demand for the Pharisees and Herod (Matt. 16:1–4; Luke 23:8–9).

This brief theology of the Gospels' miracles seems to confirm the view that the main lesson and main application of miracle narratives will be drawn from a cluster of closely related points: Jesus is Lord, compassionate, the Savior, the restorer who calls forth faith.

If we were to study Old Testament miracles, we would see many parallels to Jesus' miracles. They declare that Yahweh is Lord, that he is the compassionate and saving God, who restores all things and yet takes interest in the needs of his people; in this way he summons them and all peoples to faith in him. Some new themes would emerge, since God's wonders show his justice and holiness as well as mercy. Old covenant miracles are relentlessly theocentric. They announce the truth that Israel has a God like no other. This is what Moses teaches Pharaoh (Ex. 8:10; 9:14; 10:2), what Joshua teaches Israel (Josh. 4:24), what David teaches the Philistines (1 Sam. 17:46), what Elisha teaches Naaman (2 Kings 5:15), what Hezekiah asks God to teach Sennacherib (2 Kings 19:19).[29] The uniqueness of God is the message conveyed by all miracles.

---

28 The question, "Does God perform miracles today?" is outside the scope of this book. But even if he no longer performs miracles like those of Moses, Elijah, and Jesus, we certainly have the right to expect supernatural healing to this day, as James 5 shows.

29 The point is explicit in these texts, but implicit elsewhere (e.g., Gen. 40–41; 1 Kings 17–18). The prophets concur, teaching this to Babylon (Dan. 2:28, 47) and Israel (Mic. 6:5), until all nations know (Isa. 43:10; 45:3–6; 52:10).

Diverse Applications

At this point, a little voice (perhaps not our noblest part) protests, "But I can't stand up to make the same few points about *God* every week. It will grow tedious. People like variety. They want to hear answers to their problems, not theology lectures." This deserves an answer.

Let us admit at once that the voice has a point. People do want variety and relevance. But I can hardly think of anything Christians *need* more than an analysis of their *wants*. Perhaps they *want* an exhortation to live like the story's hero, that is, a call to works.[30] But they *need* true knowledge of God and his saving acts. There need be no tedium in that, for despite certain similarities, miracle stories do not all teach the same thing.

First, the acts of God are too deep, too complicated (from our perspective, at least) for us to weary of them. It is the Christian teacher's privilege to help people discover God's nature through his actions, that they may know themselves by knowing him.[31]

Second, while the lordship and love of Jesus never change, the form of human need does. Because our needs vary constantly, God's power and grace always find new expression.

Third, while the main point remains the same, the secondary points differ, as the characters in a narrative respond to God's acts in various ways. We do not preach the secondary characters in themselves, but they do represent types of response to God.

This then is the plan: to identify the central act of God in a narrative and to observe the way the characters in the drama respond to him. These become the avenues for the primary and secondary applications today.[32] The

---

30   That is what the sermon services, in print or on the Internet, offer.

31   "Man never achieves a clear knowledge of himself unless he has first looked upon God's face, and then descends from contemplating him to scrutinize himself"—John Calvin, *Institutes of the Christian Religion* (Philadelphia: Westminster, 1960), 1.1.2.

32   Good teachers sometimes do what is advocated here, but no other theorists specifically advance this proposal. Craig Blomberg in *Interpreting the Parables* (Downers Grove, Ill.: InterVarsity, 1990) advances something similar for parables. The interpretation of parables and miracles should be roughly similar, since both concern narratives. Miracle accounts often function like parables that actually occurred.

disciples, foes, and bystanders who encounter God respond to him roughly as believers, unbelievers, and bystanders do through the ages. We can test this proposal by seeing if it actually produces multiple lines of fresh applications for a couple of Jesus' miracles. The story of Jesus and the paralytic, with its strong characters and classic flow from setting to conflict to crisis to resolution, offers an ideal opportunity to test our proposed method.

The Healing of a Paralytic

The narrative of Luke 5:17–26 begins with several men carrying their paralyzed friend to Jesus to be healed. But Jesus was healing many that day, and the house was jammed. Blocked by the crowd, yet determined to get to Jesus, the men tied ropes to their friend's stretcher, tore a hole in the roof, and lowered him through it. Jesus, seeing *their* faith, unexpectedly says, "Friend, your sins are forgiven."

Since the men came seeking healing, not forgiveness, they were probably puzzled, but the Pharisees immediately recognized that Jesus was claiming deity. The reasoning goes this way: Only the person offended can forgive a wrong. If I offend John, it makes no sense to apologize to Mark. I must go to John, whom I offended. Therefore, it is senseless for Jesus to forgive a man he just met—*if* Jesus is merely a man. When he says, "Your sins are forgiven," he implies that the paralytic has sinned against him.[33] Thus, Jesus claims to be God, because only God is offended by every sin, and only God can forgive all sin (Isa. 43:25).

The Pharisees grasp this and decide that "this fellow" is blaspheming (Luke 5:21). Jesus, reading their thoughts, incites a crisis (vv. 22–23) by asking, "Why are you thinking these things in your hearts? Which is easier: to say, 'Your sins are forgiven,' or to say, 'Get up and walk' "? The answer to this question is not quite obvious. It is easier to *say,* "Your sins are forgiven," but it is harder to *confirm* it because it cannot be verified or falsified. "Get up and walk" is no harder to say, but it is riskier because open to verification.

---

33 The Jewish custom of using divine passives supports this reading. When, as in the clause, "Your sins are forgiven," a verb is passive, but no agent is specified, God is the understood agent. See Joachim Jeremias, *New Testament Theology* (New York: Macmillan, 1970), 10–11.

While the Pharisees ponder this, Jesus offers all the proof they could want: "But that you may know that the Son of Man has authority on earth to forgive sins . . . ," he says to the paralytic, "Get up, take your mat and go home" (v. 24). Whether the pause between Jesus' command and the rise of the paralytic lasted two seconds or two milliseconds, those moments constitute the climax of the narrative, for everything depends on what comes next. If the paralytic does not rise, then Jesus is indeed a blasphemer. But if he does rise, then Jesus does have the right to forgive sins and does indeed possess deity.[34] The pause is short; the paralytic rises at once and goes home (5:25). Thus in an instant the quest of the men of faith comes to a successful conclusion, and Jesus' critics see that he has authority to forgive.

This healing was one of the greatest public displays of Jesus' deity in his ministry, but when we see the story through the eyes of Jesus' allies, his adversaries, and the neutral crowds, the response is disappointing. A tool used in literary analysis will make this clearer. As narratives progress, they tend to subject characters to a test, a quest, or a choice. In a *test* the events put the character's mental, moral, or spiritual makeup on trial. In a *quest* the character pursues a goal, which may be obtained only by clearing certain obstacles. In a *choice* the character must decide between two courses of action, between covenant loyalty and disobedience.[35] A given drama may exhibit one, two, or, as in this case, all three elements.

For Jesus, the event tests his claim of deity. Is this the Son of God or not? Does he have the power to forgive sin and reverse its effects or not? In rising, the paralytic answers both questions. This becomes the episode's principal lesson: Jesus is Lord and deliverer, the restorer of creation, the forgiver of sins. Above all, the episode teaches readers to turn to Jesus—to God—for the forgiveness of sins. But how did the others respond to this revelation?

The Pharisees were apparently unmoved. Actually, Luke says nothing about their reaction, but the silence is deafening, since they grasped the situation and should have acclaimed Jesus' deity. As Jesus says, "He who is not for me is against me." To clinch the point, the Pharisees

---

34 Note the centrality of the dialogue in establishing the issues.
35 Ryken, *Words of Delight,* 48–49, 65–67, 110–13, 344–51; Doriani, *Getting the Message,* 67–68.

are soon plotting against Jesus (Luke 6:11). The Pharisees faced a choice. Having seen and understood the evidence, would they repent and believe or not? They did not.

The crowd's response seems more positive, initially. They were amazed, praised God, and declared, "We have seen remarkable things today." Yet, upon reflection, their praise is defective. Yes, Jesus does remarkable things, but that is not quite the point. Luke hints at their dullness when he reports that the crowd simply praised God and said, "We have seen remarkable things" (5:25–26).[36] It is not enough to find Jesus "amazing" or "great" (7:16). Both the Pharisees and the crowd encounter a choice in the narrative. If the Pharisees show the danger of rejecting the evidence for Jesus, the crowd shows it is equally deadly to be unaware that there is evidence. It is tragic to hold Jesus in high esteem but not believe.

For the paralytic and his friends, the drama is a quest. It takes no flights of fancy to imagine the group stirring one another to persevere when they find Jesus blockaded by the crowd. One conceives a radical plan and the others agree. We can see them, hear them, smashing a hole in the roof, clawing to enlarge it, tying ropes to the stretcher, and peering over the edge as they lower their immobile friend. "Seeing their faith, Jesus said, 'Friend, your sins are forgiven'" (my translation). Indeed their faith was visible; they proved their faith precisely by fighting through obstacles. This reveals a trait of genuine faith. When believers talk about seeking God's will, we often say, "We will wait and see if God will open a door or close a door." Perhaps. But this story suggests that sometimes the door is open, sometimes the door is closed, and sometimes we have to tear the door off its hinges, whether by ourselves or with the help of friends. The Bible's quest stories teach us that true faith fights through obstacles and temporary defeats.[37] The contemporary Christian willingness to look for open and closed doors reflects a commendable confidence in God's sovereign control of the course of history, but it forgets that there will be obsta-

---

36 The parallel in Matt. 9:8 agrees, reporting that the crowd "praised God, who had given such authority to *men*."

37 Robert Tannehill, *The Narrative Unity of Luke-Acts* (Philadelphia: Fortress, 1986), 1:111–27.

cles on the road to every great goal and that God wants us to fight through them.[38]

To review, the parties who saw Jesus heal the paralytic—the believers, Pharisees, and crowds—illustrate the various ways people respond to evidence for Jesus' deity to this day. The crowds' failure to see the evidence and the Pharisees' failure to accept the evidence warn people to cast aside doubt and believe, as the paralytic and his friends did.[39]

The Ten Lepers

Unlike the story of the paralytic, we study Jesus' healing of ten lepers (Luke 17:11–19) precisely because its relevance seems slight. The story's characterization and dramatic tension are minimal. Further, it manifests the various miracle themes described above, making it an ideal candidate for a boring exposition: (1) *Jesus is compassionate.* As Jesus traveled, ten lepers approached him, pleading, "Jesus, Master, have pity on us!" He did and healed them (17:13). (2) *Jesus restores things.* When Jesus cleansed the lepers, he restored them to both health and society, to the family and community they left when they fell ill. (3) *Jesus is Lord.* Ten lepers call Jesus Master (*epistata*), and one falls at his feet, praising God. (4) *Miracles summon faith.* Jesus is pleased that one returned to praise God, but wonders where the others are. (5) *Miracles accomplish salvation.* Jesus tells the returning leper, "Rise and go, your faith has saved you" (my translation). Despite the preponderance of familiar themes, perhaps the exposition will not be tedious.

The story begins when ten lepers see Jesus traveling between Judea and Samaria and plead for mercy, that is, for healing. When Jesus commands the men to go to the priests to prove that they have been cleansed

---

38 Think of Abraham's quest for a son and a land, David's quest for the kingship, Ecclesiastes' quest for meaning, and Gospel quests such as those of the Syro-Phoenician woman and the woman with the flow of blood. There is always an obstacle through which the faithful persevere. On the contrary, quests will end unsuccessfully—think of the rich young ruler—without a willingness to fight through obstacles.

39 I do not mention the common application that we should bring our friends to Jesus as the friends brought the paralytic. That assertion allegorizes the simple fact that the paralytic's friends carried him to Jesus. Strictly speaking, that application works only by equivocation: the physical act of "carrying to Jesus" is understood to mean "evangelizing."

(Luke 5:14; cf. Lev. 13:1–8), he implies that he will do something for them. The men have enough faith to obey; they are cleansed offstage, so to speak, as they walk to the temple. We already know that Jesus can cure lepers (Luke 5:12–14) and that he can heal at a distance (7:1–10).

Because Jesus heals the lepers at a distance, while they are on the road, the dramatic tension increases. Because the miracle occurs on the road, the lepers have three places to go. They should go to Jerusalem, that a priest may verify their cleansing and permit them to return to normal life. Or they may follow their presumed longing and go to their homes, families, friends, and livelihoods. But one leper realizes there is a third place to go—to Jesus, to thank him. Returning, he praises God in a loud voice, throws himself at Jesus' feet, and thanks him—the one time in the Gospels that someone directs thanks to Jesus rather than the Father.[40]

Notice the order of events. First, the leper prostrates himself, taking the posture of a worshiper. Next, with the leper at his feet, Jesus asks three questions: Ten were cleansed, weren't they? Where are the other nine? Did only a foreigner glorify God? *Then* Jesus invites him to rise, saying, "Go; your faith has saved [*sōzō*] you" (my translation). It is not hard to find the two theocentric—or, christocentric—foci of this narrative. First, the story reminds us that Jesus has mercy on sufferers, that he has power to heal by a word (Matt. 8:8, 16; Luke 8:25). Second, it has a striking testimony to his deity. No creature—no apostle or angel—can bear to see a fellow creature bowing before him in homage (Acts 14:8–15; Rev. 22:8–9). Yet Jesus not only permits it, he is pleased that a man lies prostrate at his feet, praising God. Indeed, he asks why there are not more!

The story sheds light on saving faith. All ten lepers had enough faith to ask Jesus for mercy and enough to obey a strange command, but only one had a faith that vetoed other options and returned to praise God. Thus we see that there is a faith and obedience that does not save, because it has no love of God, no passion to glorify him. The nine thankless men warn that one can receive gifts of grace without receiving salvation. Those who receive mercy should thank and honor God. The Samaritan knows this, but he also shows that the outsider, the unexpected one, may be the only one to honor God.

---

40 Robert Stein, *Luke* (Nashville: Broadman, 1992), 434.

To label our points in terms of chapter 4, the story has a *redemptive act* by Jesus, who saves both physically and spiritually. There are also an *exemplary act* of thanksgiving by the Samaritan, an implicit *doctrine* of faith and salvation, and, as an *ideal,* a summons to praise God for his grace. In the categories of chapter 5, the narrative presents our *duty* to believe and praise God, but also asks us to ponder what kind of man *(character)* would be willing to interrupt his journey to the temple and his home to return to thank Jesus.

Finally, this event and Jesus' other healings of lepers raise a question about the social aspect of Jesus' ministry. We might call Jesus' cleansing of lepers (Luke 5:12–14; 7:11–19) a social miracle since it restores its beneficiaries to society, not just health. Other miracles have social ramifications; Jesus healed a woman who suffered a chronic flow of blood that made her unclean (8:43–48). He also healed a Roman centurion's servant (7:1–10). If we link these miracles with his habit of befriending and dining with sinners and outcasts, we realize that Jesus habitually associated with the marginal and rejected members of his society. This pattern actually began when God chose tiny Israel to be his people. So, is the healing of lepers one aspect of Jesus' pattern of life that Christians ought to imitate? Can we say we ought to restore the rejected to society, touching the unloved and the unlovely, conveying the message that we accept them, as Jesus did?

Such a vast gulf separates us from Jesus that we dare not use "What would Jesus do?" to resolve all such questions. As John Murray said, "To aspire to be like God in one sense is the essence of virtue, to aspire to be like him in another is iniquity. To preserve this line of distinction is indispensable to all right thinking on truth and the right."[41] Here "right thinking" leads us to imitate the social aspect of this miracle. Radical social inclusiveness features prominently in Jesus' ministry. He would heal anyone, dine with anyone, talk to anyone, unrighteous or self-righteous, male or female, Jew or Gentile. In inviting a tax collector into his inner group, in teaching the rich to invite the poor, the crippled, the blind, and the lame to their feasts, Jesus made his will plain. Thus the healing of lepers is an image of his concern for those who are excluded from mainstream society and of his desire to restore them.

41 John Murray, *Principles of Conduct* (Grand Rapids: Eerdmans, 1957), 177.

SUMMARY

Since biblical narrative is common and potent, pastors should know how to preach it skillfully. This chapter has presented the main principles for applying narrative:

1. Identify the type of narrative: report, speech story, or full drama.
2. Find the main point at either the climax and resolution of dramas or possibly in actions or sayings that follow.
3. Formulate the theocentric theme, the way God is showing his redeeming love.
4. By examining the varied human responses to God's acts in the original context, determine which are exemplary and which are warnings to us. Point out any believing and unbelieving responses that persist to this day.
5. Draw out additional doctrinal and ethical implications.
6. Look for answers to all four of the questions people ask: What should I do? Who should I be? Where should I go? How can we see?

The tendency toward legal, anthropocentric messages lingers in the soul like a treatment-resistant bacterium. But if we focus on God's acts and the varied human responses to them, we should progress toward theocentric yet diverse applications.

8

Issues in Applying Narrative Texts

Humans are imitators. Heroes, whether chosen wisely or foolishly, possess an inexplicable influence over their devotees. Is this helpful? Does God want us to emulate heroes? The Bible's heroes? Does he want us to persevere as Abraham did, to flee temptation as Joseph did, and to confront authorities as Moses did? Is Jesus himself pleased with the question, "What Would Jesus Do?" Did Jesus intend his life to guide Christian conduct? Can narrative, by itself, guide Christian conduct? Or must we find an imperative to confirm every action modeled in narrative? Few issues touching the relevance of Scripture are more complicated than these. Ethicists and homileticians explore them at length.[1] Yet exegetes almost entirely ignore the relevance of narrative.[2]

THE DEBATE OVER NARRATIVE: CAN PAST ACTIONS HAVE PRESENT MORAL AUTHORITY?

Even if it is a bit naive, the question "What Would Jesus Do?" grasps that God's character is the standard of righteousness. Yet some deny

---

1 E.g., *Why Narratives: Readings in Narrative Theology,* ed. Stanley Hauerwas and L. Gregory Jones (Grand Rapids: Eerdmans, 1989).
2 Whether critical or conservative, high-caliber journals of biblical studies such as the *Journal for Biblical Literature,* the *Bulletin for Biblical Research,* the *Journal for the*

that historical narrative can have moral authority. Gotthold Lessing framed the objections succinctly. First, he said, any historical report may be unreliable. Second, reports of distant events, of people far away and long ago, cannot move us. Third, even if moving, past events cannot attain moral authority today, for, he said, "the accidental truths of history can never become the proof of the necessary truths of reason." Historical events are "contingent." That is, they could have turned out otherwise. If they had, they might convey a different moral lesson. But that is impossible, for moral truths are not contingent; they could not be otherwise. They are logically necessary and universally binding in the sense that offenses such as murder, theft, and treachery must be forbidden or society is impossible. So history may *illustrate* moral truths, but only reason can *establish* them. Thus between history and Lessing's (Enlightenment) era there had formed an "ugly, gaping ditch" that he could not cross.[3]

Today, few thinkers share Lessing's critique of biblical narrative, dominated as it is by his desire for a universal, rationally demonstrable ethic. Contemporary ethicists such as William Barbieri argue that a "well-woven story . . . facilitates reflection on questions of morality in a way that eludes traditional academic approaches." No principled argument, he says, can condemn war as powerfully as does Erich Maria Remarque's novel, *All Quiet on the Western Front,* or Peter Weir's film *Gallipoli,* or (I add) Eric Bogle's World War I protest song, "No Man's Land."[4]

Yet there are limits to narrative. Stories unleash emotion, reveal character, and convey ambiguity, but "they are not equipped to make the kinds of discriminations necessary for informed ethical decisions."[5] *All Quiet, Gallipoli,* and "No Man's Land" all protested World War I, a dreadful conflict in so many ways. But are all wars equally

---

Study of the New Testament, and the Journal for the Study of the Old Testament rarely consider these practical questions. On the separation of exegesis and relevance, see Moisés Silva, "Contemporary Theories of Biblical Interpretation," in *New Interpreter's Bible* (Nashville: Abingdon, 1994), 1:107–24.

3 Gotthold Lessing, "On the Proof of the Spirit and of Power," in *Lessing's Theological Writings,* trans. and ed. Henry Chadwick (Stanford, Calif.: Stanford University Press, 1957), 51–56.

4 William Barbieri, "Ethics and the Narrated Life," *Journal of Religion,* 78 (1998): 361.

5 Richard Lischer, "The Limits of Story," *Interpretation* 38 (Jan. 1984): 35–36.

dreadful? Do World War I protests condemn World War II? All wars?
Are there reasons—reasons that story cannot convey—why World
War II failed to stimulate the same sort of protests as did World War I?

So the thinkers line up, some favoring imperatives, some favoring
narratives. Some say, "Unless Scripture explicitly tells us we must do
something, what is merely narrated or described can never function
in a normative way."[6] But narrative theologians want to reconsider
narrative and ethics. They judge it naive to think we direct our behavior only by consulting laws and making rational decisions. Our choices
flow from our character and our experience—our past and our anticipated future. We choose from among the options our imagination (a
narrative-fashioning faculty) and our society offer us, from among the
"possible ways of being human in the world."[7] The question "What
am I to do?" relates to questions such as "Of what larger story do I
find myself a part? What community do I belong to? What are my roles
in it?"[8] We can learn character by asking, "Whom do I want to be
like?" as well as "What do I want to be like?" If we ask "Whom?"
rather than "What?" we are seeking guidance from narrative. When a
narrative world, whether historical or fictitious, seizes a reader, it
reveals new possibilities. Stories create habitable worlds, and narratives
become habitable texts; we can live in and by them.[9]

Today, most Christian ethicists agree that narratives possess a certain moral authority. They may prefer law, but they will appeal to narrative, with pride of place going to the Gospels and the hottest debate
reserved for Acts. In his theology of possessions, Craig Blomberg, a
sophisticated New Testament scholar, freely draws upon biblical narratives.[10] He uses the story of manna to prohibit hoarding, cites var-

---

6   Gordon Fee and Douglas Stuart, *How to Read the Bible for All Its Worth* (Grand
    Rapids: Zondervan, 1982), 97.

7   Kevin Vanhoozer, *Biblical Narrative in the Philosophy of Paul Ricoeur* (Cambridge:
    Cambridge University Press, 1990), 101-4.

8   Alisdair MacIntyre, "The Virtues, the Unity of Human Life, and the Concept
    of Tradition," in *Why Narrative?* ed. Hauerwas and Jones, 101-3.

9   Daniel Taylor, "In Pursuit of Character," *Christianity Today,* 11 Dec. 1995, 29–36;
    Anthony Thistelton, *New Horizons in Hermeneutics* (Grand Rapids: Zondervan,
    1992), 354–58.

10 Craig Blomberg, *Neither Poverty nor Riches: A Biblical Theology of Material Posses-
    sions* (Grand Rapids: Eerdmans, 1999).

ious kings to warn against profligacy and coveting, and views the rich young ruler and Zacchaeus as paradigms of the right and wrong attitudes toward wealth.[11] Aside from one early paragraph, Blomberg only considers the method when he discusses the sharing of wealth in the early Jerusalem church. He assumes that the practice is normative.[12]

The normative value of Acts is also a vital issue in the debates about miraculous gifts today. Is Acts primarily the history of the once-for-all birth of the church and spread of the gospel? If so, then the apostles' prayer for the ability to perform signs and wonders through the name of Jesus is not normative today (Acts 4:29–31).[13] But if Acts best demonstrates "what normal church life is supposed to look like," then we should pray for and expect to relive its pattern of miraculous gifts.[14]

Some say that narratives principally point to Christ. Reformed theologians such as Geerhardus Vos, Sidney Greidanus, and S. G. De Graff emphasize the centrality of God's redemptive purposes in narrative. God, they say, is the "prime agent" in every story. The Bible is his self-revelation, given so that he and his people will "exchange the deepest love of their hearts." Therefore, "God must be made central" in every exposition. Teachers must shun moral lessons; Scripture does not tell stories of Abraham or Solomon to show what sins to avoid! If we speak of Mary's love for Jesus, or Judas's hatred, we must not focus on Mary or Judas, but on "the One who awakened such love . . . [and] aroused such great hatred." To accent the roles of Mary and Judas as examples of love to be imitated or betrayal to be avoided is, De Graaf says, to stray from gospel into a man-centered religion.[15] These theologians will, hesitantly, reap moral lessons from narrative, but they decry "moralistic" readings of narrative. They say, "the highest practi-

11 Ibid., 38, 52–56, 138–41.
12 Ibid., 29–30, 162–63. In fairness, pages 29–30 do refer readers to Blomberg's earlier work on method.
13 Richard Gaffin, "A Cessationist View," in *Are Miraculous Gifts for Today? Four Views,* ed. Wayne Grudem (Grand Rapids: Zondervan, 1996), 37–38, 227–29. For the opposite view, see pp. 74–77, 88–91.
14 Jack Deere, *Surprised by the Power of the Spirit* (Grand Rapids: Zondervan, 1993), 114.
15 S. G. De Graaf, *Promise and Deliverance,* trans. H. E. Runner (Phillipsburg, N.J.: Presbyterian and Reformed, 1977), 17–23.

cal usefulness" of biblical narrative is to grant us "a new view of God" and to move people to faith.[16]

Even those who readily use narratives for guidance face quandaries. God is the ultimate standard of right and wrong, but how do we imitate Christ? To follow Jesus in his selflessness, compassion, and endurance is essential to discipleship. Yet to attempt to imitate Jesus' unique redemptive activities seems sacrilegious. Jesus commanded nature, forgave sinners, and, above all, died to ransom us from death. Theologians know they must distinguish between areas where we can and where we cannot imitate God, but they are slow to offer criteria.[17]

THESES ON THE ROLE OF NARRATIVE

Thesis 1: The Motto "Direct Teaching Has Priority over Narrative" Is Flawed.

Even if these matters should be solved, the question of the relative authority of narrative versus doctrinal/ethical teaching remains. It has been said that "unless Scripture explicitly tells us we must do something, what is merely narrated or described can never function in a normative way."[18] That is, precepts have priority over narratives, so that we cannot derive lessons from historical narratives unless we have explicit teaching to the same effect. Others, citing 2 Timothy 3:16, say "narrative supplies as much data for theology as any other genre."[19]

The heedless imitation of narrative, unsupported by moral directives, can certainly cause problems. Polygamous marriage (Gen. 29),

---

16 Geerhardus Vos, *Biblical Theology: Old and New Testaments* (Grand Rapids: Eerdmans, 1948), 18. Greidanus supports limited ethical use of narratives; see *The Modern Preacher and the Ancient Text* (Grand Rapids: Eerdmans, 1988), 157–87, 226–27.

17 When Douglas Moo argued for the distinction in a published interchange with Richard Hays, Hays said he could hardly understand Moo's point. See Douglas Moo, review of *The Moral Vision of the New Testament,* by Richard B. Hays, *Bulletin for Biblical Research* 9 (1999): 275; Richard B. Hays, "The Gospel, Narrative and Culture: A Response to Douglas J. Moo and Judith Gundry-Volf," *Bulletin for Biblical Research* 9 (1999): 292.

18 See n. 6.

19 Blomberg, *Neither Poverty nor Riches,* 163.

making decisions through lots or devices like Gideon's fleece (Josh. 7:14–23; Acts 1:23–26; Judg. 6:36–40), suicide with noble intent (Judg. 16:26–30), and reckless divestiture of possessions (Luke 18:22; 19:8) are a few.

But how can one argue that narrative is normative only if backed by explicit teaching? It is odd to grant ethical assertions priority over narrative when (1) the principle itself is extrabiblical and (2) Scripture is fundamentally a narrative account of God's redemption. The speeches of Moses, the declamations of the prophets, the letters of the apostles are not freestanding. They frequently comment upon or draw conclusions from narrative. When they do, the narrative is foundational and the ethic is derivative.

If we consider the Bible's most direct statements about God and the Christian life, a little probing shows that narrative leads us as much as direct teaching does. Scripture says that God is compassionate (Ps. 86:15) and it commands believers, "Be kind and compassionate to one another" (Eph. 4:32). But the doctrine and the command hardly take precedence over narratives that show his compassion. We discover what the compassion of God means through narratives that show it. The miracle narratives reveal that Jesus' compassion moved him to heal crowds (Matt. 9:35–36; 14:14), to feed hungry multitudes (15:32), to heal two blind men outside Jericho (20:34).

Or consider the episode at the gate of Nain (Luke 7:11–17). "Look!" says Luke, and we almost look through Jesus' eyes as we come upon the scene. They were carrying out a dead man, the only son of his mother, and she was a widow. Jesus focused on her. First her husband, then her only son had perished, so that fear for the future thickened her grief. Jesus took it in. Compassion led to action and he commanded the woman, "Don't cry." Next, he touched the bier, halting the procession, and commanded, "Young man, I say to you, get up!" Then the dead one arose. He began to speak, and Jesus gave him, perhaps just a lad, back to his mother. Whence this miracle? There is no hint that Jesus planned to teach his followers a lesson, no inkling that he had to fulfill prophecy. Compassion moved him. He saw, he knew, he felt, he acted. That is what "God is compassionate" and "Be compassionate" mean. The narrative defines compassion and directs it.

Similarly, narrative shows what it means for God to be loving (1 John 4:16), gracious (2 Chron. 30:9), faithful (1 Cor. 10:13), holy

(Ps. 99:9), merciful (Deut. 4:31), and righteous (Ps. 7:11). For example, we understand God's love via narratives demonstrating it in the exodus and the Gospels. Take a passage such as Romans 5:6–8: "When we were still powerless, Christ died for the ungodly. . . . While we were still sinners, Christ died for us." Which is better, to say, "The life of Jesus illustrates Romans 5," or to say, "The doctrine of Romans 5 comments on the life of Jesus"? We *see* Jesus sacrificing himself for the weak, for disciples too weak to pray with him for an hour, or stay loyal to him (Matt. 26:40–41, 69–74). Then we understand the doctrine, "While we were still powerless, Christ died for the ungodly." Then we know what God requires of us. Again, Jesus' encounters with Zacchaeus and the Samaritan woman interpret the doctrinal statement, "While we were still sinners, Christ died for us." Yet, temporally speaking, the life of Jesus precedes the doctrine. Without God's action, the doctrine is an abstraction. We know the mercy, faithfulness, justice, and salvation of God by his actions, as recorded in narrative.

We draw two conclusions. *Principle 1:* Narratives and discourses are mutually defining. We oversimplify if we say, "Narrative merely illustrates doctrine," or "We can never derive laws from narratives unless explicit commands verify them." Since all Scripture interprets all other Scripture, narratives help define doctrines and commands. *Principle 2:* When narratives show God acting in ways that manifest the attributes which, according to Scripture, we must share, we ought to imitate those character traits.

Thesis 2: Where There Is No Direct Teaching, Narrative Provides Guidance.

Narratives also provide paradigms for faithful conduct in areas that direct teaching never covers. For example, when national or state politics produce reprehensible public policies and private peccadilloes, Christians may debate whether it is still possible to serve in government. This spawns related questions about compromise at work. Can Christians work in the media? If their company was once "clean" but now acquires a trashy talk show, can they continue? Can we labor for a media conglomerate that produces both worthy and worthless magazines? Must an advertising worker quit if his company lands a beer campaign? Even if he does no work for it?

No ethical precepts directly address these questions, but the narrative pattern of Israelites working for pagans implies that total with-drawal is unnecessary. Israelites often worked for pagan kings. Many, laboring for pagans, did not suffer rebuke but served God, Israel, and the nations: Daniel in Nebuchadnezzar's and Belshazzar's houses, Nehemiah in Artaxerxes' house, Esther in Xerxes' palace. But the con-trast between Joseph serving one pharaoh to save lives and Moses refus-ing to serve another pharaoh, who took lives, indicates we cannot take every post. Further, the account of Daniel and his friends suggests how risky it can be to work for the godless and refuse them total obedi-ence (Dan. 1:11–16; 3:1–30; 6:4–24). Yet remember Obadiah, the devout governor of wicked Ahab's palace. He hid and fed God's prophets, showing what one man can do, even if surrounded by evil, if he is willing to risk everything (1 Kings 18:3–14). If Obadiah could work for Ahab, a murderer and idolater, then Christians can work in politics today. Paul's statement that Christians cannot cut off all con-tact with unbelievers (1 Cor. 5:9–11) supports the line of reasoning we derive from the narrative pattern.

Robert Roberts argues that moral rules need not be "action imperatives," since narratives present "paradigmatic individuals" to us. He says, "Virtually everybody's morality is guided, at some stage, by individuals who exemplify the virtues . . . [and who] function as moral rules."[20] Men such as Daniel and Obadiah confirm Roberts's point.

Similarly, there is little direct teaching on the exercise of civil lead-ership (Deut. 17:14–20), but far more from narrative. We can take warn-ing from Saul, who focused his life on retaining power (1 Sam. 18–26); from Solomon, who sank into self-indulgence (1 Kings 10–11); from Ahaz, who schemed in godless independence (Isa. 7–8). We can also learn from the godly kings, who did what was right and left the results to God. David spared Saul, although Saul burned to kill him (1 Sam. 24, 26). Hezekiah rid Judah of idols, knowing the mighty Assyrians would read his action as rebellion and attack (2 Kings 18–19). Josiah led Judah to repentance, though a prophetess averred that his reforms would never avert judgment (2 Kings 22–23).

---

20 Robert Roberts, "Virtues and Rules," *Philosophy and Phenomenological Research* 51.2 (June 1991): 326–28. Roberts effectively uses paradigmatic individuals and events in his work on ethics. See "The Balloon Stomp" in *Taking the Word to Heart* (Grand Rapids: Eerdmans, 1993), 156ff.

We draw three related conclusions. *Principle 3:* Where a series of acts by the faithful create a pattern, it guides believers, especially if God appears to bless the narrated actions. As the case of believers serving in pagan courts shows, this holds even if no law verifies the actions. *Principle 4:* But isolated acts, such as Gideon's use of the fleece, are not normative, especially if God does not approve them and if they cohere with no law. *Principle 5:* Where a narrative does not clearly commend or condemn an action, and where no pattern develops, we should hesitate to draw ethical lessons.

Thesis 3: Though We Must Critique Moralistic Uses of Scripture, Scripture Does Offer Moral Guidance in Narrative.

Scholars lambaste preachers for moralistic uses of narratives. They point out that biblical narratives show how God has acted in redemption "despite the acts of men as much as through them." So, the scholars say, to concentrate on human deeds in narratives is to abuse them, making the story of grace into a source for law and promoting an anthropocentric rather than a theocentric focus.[21]

There is truth in this charge. Yet to be against moralizing "is no more adventurous than to be against sin."[22] Everyone opposes proof-texting, but uses texts to prove points. Similarly, everyone opposes moralizing, but uses narratives to guide morality. So we need to stop posturing and define terms in order to determine whether narratives can teach doctrine and ethics, and, if so, how.

It is said that to moralize is to transform "the *de*scription of past people into *pre*scription for people today." Moralizing also applies the incidentals rather than the essentials of the text.[23] This helps only a little. The difficulty is that moralizing, which is scorned, overlaps with "identifying with" characters in the narrative, which is accepted. "Identifying" occurs when readers see in a narrative someone roughly like themselves, a character who illustrates righteousness or wickedness, a life shaped or not shaped by covenant truth.

---

21 John Goldingay, *Approaches to Old Testament Interpretation* (Downers Grove, Ill.: InterVarsity, 1981), 39–40; Greidanus, *Modern Preacher,* 157–66.

22 Goldingay, *Approaches,* 53.

23 Greidanus, *Modern Preacher,* 158–66.

Surprisingly, Leland Ryken regards it as a presupposition for narrative interpretation that "the characters in a story (especially the protagonist) are intended to be representative or exemplary of people generally."[24] But even more-cautious scholars believe authors *sometimes* intend audiences to identify with figures in narratives. Sidney Greidanus believes Israel recognized itself in the stories of Abraham, Isaac, and Jacob. The patriarchs' story "was *their* story; what God did for the patriarchs he did for *them*."[25] This does not mean, Greidanus qualifies, that they learned moral lessons about lying or conflicted relationships from Abraham. Rather they discovered their relationship with their covenant God. The people of Israel would also see themselves in the figure of Jonah and hear, through him, a rebuke of their attitude toward the Assyrians. While mindful of the changes brought by history and the new covenant, Greidanus thinks the church should still see herself in Jonah.[26] Israel might even see itself in Samson, not for moralistic lessons about fraternizing with and divulging secrets to enemies, but as an example of God's ability to use flawed men to advance his kingdom.[27] Samson, like Israel, violates his separated status and goes after foreign women, but calls again upon the Lord.[28]

Ernest Best said identification is valid if it directs us to identify with sinners who know their need of grace. "The Bible does not share our interest in the development of character" or character types. Rather, its stories awaken us to the judgment and mercy of God. Peter's failures do not prove Peter's weakness but God's mercy. Even the stories of Daniel and of Mary and Martha are "dominated by an interest in God rather than the characters themselves." If we forget this, identification leads to legalistic commands to do (or not do) as the character did. Further, if we depend on identification and there is no one like us in the story, application is thwarted and the sinner escapes.[29]

---

24 Leland Ryken, *Words of Delight: A Literary Introduction to the Bible* (Grand Rapids: Baker, 1987) 83.

25 Greidanus, *Modern Preacher,* 179.

26 Ibid., 180–81; John Stek, "The Message of the Book of Jonah," *Calvin Theological Journal* 4.1 (1969): 39.

27 Greidanus, *Modern Preacher,* 180.

28 Barry G. Webb, *The Book of Judges: An Integrated Reading* (Sheffield: JSOT, 1987), 179.

29 Ernest Best, *From Text to Sermon* (Atlanta: John Knox, 1978), 90–92.

Yet it is perilous to accept such broad generalizations without modification, for narratives are not monolithic. Numbers and Acts invite readers to draw theological or ethical conclusions. But Kings reads like an extended explanation of the exile.[30] Read straight through, Mark hurtles toward the cross, with a startling disinterest in moral questions. But Matthew slows down, applying his story to his interest in disciple-making.[31]

Principle 6: Biblical narrative dwells on redemption before ethics, yet narratives do invite readers to identify with characters and find spiritual direction or warning. We must honor each author's designs, drawing lessons from individual passages or from multichapter units (e.g., the Joseph narrative, the passion narrative) as the author intends. Thus, narratives do more than *illustrate* moral principles that legal passages *declare.*[32]

In fact, *Scripture explicitly instructs readers to find moral guidance in narratives.* Scripture itself demonstrates that narrative has immediate moral and spiritual value. The New Testament repeatedly draws lessons directly from narratives.

- In Matthew 12:1–8 Jesus tells the Pharisees that they should know from David's eating of the showbread when he fled Saul's court (1 Sam. 21) that God desires mercy and not sacrifice.
- Paul commanded the Corinthians to take heed from the rebellion of Israel in the wilderness: "Now these things occurred as examples to keep us from setting our hearts on evil things as they did." Therefore, Paul continues, "Do not be idolaters . . . [or] commit sexual immorality . . . [or] grumble, as some of them did" (1 Cor. 10:1–10). Hebrews brings a similar warning from those days (Heb. 3:7–4:11).
- Hebrews 11 summons old-covenant heroes as a cloud of witnesses who exhort the church not to shrink back but to con-

---

30 Gerhard von Rad, *Old Testament Theology,* trans. D. M .G. Tasker, 2 vols. (New York: Harper and Row, 1962, 1965), 1:342ff.

31 Goldingay, *Models for Interpretation of Scripture* (Grand Rapids: Eerdmans, 1995), 73–75.

32 "Narrative passages do not generally teach something directly; rather they illustrate what is taught directly elsewhere." Douglas Stuart, *Old Testament Exegesis* (Philadelphia: Westminster, 1980), 48; Goldingay, *Approaches,* 42–43.

tinue to run the race (Heb. 10:35–12:2). This sustained exercise in the art of drawing lessons from history shows how faith
looks toward God's future and past temporary burdens.
Hebrews lauds the faith and perseverance of Abraham, Moses,
and a host of courageous, suffering believers. Their pattern of
life bolsters a wavering congregation: "Since we are surrounded
by such a great cloud of witnesses . . . let us run with perseverance the race marked out for us" (12:1).

Scripture bases many ethical conclusions on narratives. Jesus learned
how to face temptation through the failures of Israel in the wilderness
(Matt. 4:1–11; Luke 4:1–13). Jesus' refusal to perform miracles on
demand had precedent in the ministries of Elijah and Elisha (Luke
4:23–27). James finds in Abraham and Rahab proof that faith without
works is dead (James 2:20–26). For James, Elijah illustrates effective,
righteous prayer (5:17–18). Jude cites Cain, Balaam, and Korah to
show that those who throw off authority suffer judgment (Jude 8–11).

Paul agrees by putting Old Testament figures to typological use.
In Romans 4, Abraham and David represent the justified believer and
the forgiven sinner. Yet they do not merely *illustrate* justification by
grace through faith; they advance the argument. Abraham is more than
"anyman" justified by faith; he is the father of the Jews. In view of his
great sacrifices, no one can claim justification by works more than he.
But if even Abraham was justified by faith, then who can be saved by
works? Abraham also deepens our understanding of faith. From him
we learn that justification has no relation to works or to circumcision
(4:9–11), that faith perseveres (4:20), that it trusts God despite contrary physical evidence (4:17–19), that it empowers obedience (4:21),
that it leans on God's person and promises (4:17, 21).[33]

Likewise, David is no random example of God's mercy. God remits
David's sin with Bathsheba, though he committed it publicly, deliberately, and callously, to the harm of many, against knowledge and
despite lack of need (2 Sam. 11:2–15; 12:7–10). This shows that no
sin exceeds the perimeter of grace. God pardons the most flagrant sin.

33 C. E. B. Cranfield, *The Epistle to the Romans* (Edinburgh: T. & T. Clark, 1975),
1:224ff.; Leonhard Goppelt, *Typos: The Typological Interpretation of the Old Testament in the New,* trans. Donald H. Madvig (Grand Rapids: Eerdmans, 1982), 136ff.

The same holds for Paul's use of Jacob and Esau, of Adam and Eve. Paul "regards Adam and Eve as historical persons, but also as archetypes of the human race."[34] Further, Jacob and Esau represent election (Rom. 9:10–13), and Adam and Eve represent the roles of men and women (1 Tim. 2:12–15). Paul even uses his own conversion to demonstrate the extent of God's mercy and patience (1 Tim. 1:15–16).

Since many narratives lead readers to find moral guidance in them, we must seek clues that the author intended a protagonist or antagonist to set a precedent. Yet we honor Scripture's design when we refrain from spiritualizing incidentals. This means we look for principles behind actions rather than mindlessly imitating details from biblical times. So we do not wear robes and sandals to mimic Jesus and the disciples. But we do follow Jesus' example of welcoming sinners. Dining with someone expresses acceptance today as then, so we might eat with sinners today too. Yet we need not dine in a reclining position, for that was simply the ancient custom for formal meals. Again, we should greet our brothers warmly when we meet, but hugs or handshakes may replace the holy kiss. These decisions seem obvious, but the judgments behind them rest on case-by-case analysis.[35]

Thesis 4: The "Imitation of Christ" Motif Uses Narrative to Guide Behavior.

Since Luther, Protestant theologians have been wary of the "imitation of Christ" motif. We associate it with literal, sentimental, and subjective interpretation. We align it with works-righteousness and exaggerated confidence in human ability.[36] Yet we cannot erase the motif from Scripture.[37] Jesus himself commanded his disciples to fol-

---

34 J. N. D. Kelly, *The Pastoral Epistles* (London: Black, 1963), 68.

35 Among other examples: (1) The Mosaic law requiring parapets (= railings) on roofs inspires life-preserving safety regulations. (2) Not muzzling an ox while it treads grain means we are to pay laborers what they deserve. (3) Head coverings (1 Cor. 11) establish modesty and submission to authority. For additional cases and the principles facilitating them see Michael Griffiths, *The Example of Jesus* (Downers Grove, Ill.: InterVarsity, 1984), chap. 5.

36 E. J. Tinsley, "Some Principles for Reconstructing a Doctrine of the Imitation of Christ," *Scottish Journal of Theology* 25 (1972): 45ff.

37 Although my case for imitation rarely intersects with his, see the evidence in Griffiths, *Example of Jesus,* 27–69.

low his example. They must be willing to work for the kingdom, as he was (Matt. 16:21–26; Mark 8:31–37; Luke 9:21–25). They must serve, just as he did not come to be served, but to serve (Matt. 20:28; Mark 10:45).

The apostles heard this lesson and developed it, explaining how and why believers are to imitate Christ. Conformity to Christ is our destiny (Rom. 8:29; 1 Cor. 15:49; 1 John 3:2–3); it is also our obligation. John said, if we claim to live in Christ, we must walk as Jesus walked (1 John 2:6) and lay down our lives for others as Jesus laid down his for us (1 John 3:16). Because God is light, we cannot walk in darkness (1 John 1:5–6). Paul set Christ's life as the pattern for love and forgiveness in the church (Eph. 4:32; 5:2). We must prefer the interests of others over our own, as Jesus did (Phil. 2:3–8). Christ's love is also a paradigm for the family; husbands should love their wives as Christ loved the church, sacrificing himself for her (Eph. 5:25–27). Regarding himself as an example to his churches (Phil. 3:17; 2 Thess. 3:7), Paul urges them to imitate him as he imitates Christ (1 Cor. 4:16; 11:1; Phil. 4:9). Thus godly leaders become, in turn, a pattern for the church (1 Tim. 4:12; Titus 2:7; 1 Peter 5:1–5).[38] Peter instructs his churches to suffer mistreatment with endurance, without hatred toward the oppressor. This is their calling, because with the same endurance and restraint "Christ suffered for you, leaving you an example, that you should follow in his steps" (1 Peter 2:18–25). In Hebrews, Jesus, our trailblazer and elder brother, cuts a path through suffering and finishes with glory. As members of his family, as followers of this trailblazer, we expect to follow a similar course (Heb. 2:5–14; 10:32–12:4).

Acts supports the imitation motif less directly. It implies that the disciples were changed, that they had become Christlike through their time with him, so that observers knew they had been with him (Acts 4:13). Acts also hints that the disciples patterned their ministry after Jesus'. Like Jesus, they healed all sorts of people, focusing intently on them, adding words to interpret their works, and charging nothing (e.g., 3:2–26; 14:8–18). Thus Jesus' disciples performed deeds like his, and greater (John 14:12).

This teaching is consistent with both human nature and Jesus' cul-

---

38 In the New Testament, only James and Jude lack this motif, a fact attributable to the theme of the former and the brevity of the latter.

ture. It is human nature to imitate. The counsel of 3 John 11, "Dear friends, do not imitate what is evil but what is good," assumes that all imitate, then urges wise choices. In addition, the culture of Jesus' time, and particularly the rabbis, promoted imitation.[39] Before books were available widely, rabbis gathered disciples who, by repetition and disputation, memorized and mastered every word of their leader's principal teachings. The best student was "like a well lined with lime, which loses not one drop."[40] Disciples were also expected to imitate their masters' lives, which incarnated their ethic. The rabbi was "living Torah." That is, "the life of the rabbi was itself Torah," hence suitable for imitation.[41]

On this point, Jesus and the rabbis agreed: Disciples should learn the teachings and follow the life pattern of their masters. Thus Jesus declared, four times over, that he expected his disciples to pattern themselves after him. Luke 6:40 says, "A student is not above his teacher, but everyone who is fully trained will be like his teacher." Because the goal was mastery of the teacher's every word, disciples could never exceed, but could be *like* the teacher. In John 13 Jesus washes his disciples' feet. Then he says that they ought to wash each other's feet, as he washed theirs. He assumes his disciples will follow his example and then declares, "No servant is greater than his master, nor is a messenger than the one who sent him" (vv. 15–16). John 15:20 says the same principle holds for the treatment Jesus received: " 'No servant is greater than his master.' If they persecuted me, they will persecute you also. If they obeyed my teaching, they will obey yours also."

Matthew 10:24–25 brings mastery of the teaching, imitation of conduct, and the expectation of similar treatment together: "A student is not above his teacher, nor a servant above his master. It is enough for the student to be like his teacher, and the servant like his master." At the center of a long discourse and in a culture that values memo-

---

39 The Mishnah dates from the second century and does not necessarily represent Judaism prior to the destruction of the second temple in A.D. 70. But many rabbis quoted in the Mishnah are from Jesus' era or earlier.

40 Mishnah, *Aboth* 1:1; 2:8; Emil Schürer, *The History of the Jewish People in the Age of Jesus Christ,* rev. ed., ed. Geza Vermes et al. (Edinburgh: T. & T. Clark, 1979), 2:333; Rainer Reisner, *Jesus als Lehrer,* 3d ed. (Tübingen: J. C. B. Mohr, 1988).

41 W. D. Davies, *The Setting of the Sermon on the Mount* (Cambridge: Cambridge University Press, 1964), 364, 455–56.

rization, Jesus first requires his disciples to master his words (cf. Luke 6:40).[42] But in context (Matt. 10:23, 25b) Jesus warns the disciples, second, that they must endure persecution as he did (cf. John 15:20). Third, "It is enough for the student to be like his teacher" (Matt. 10:25) implies that the Twelve should conduct themselves on their mission as he had conducted himself on his (cf. John 13). Notice how his directions in Matthew 10 require the disciples to do what they had seen him do:

- The destination Jesus went first to Israel; the disciples must too (10:5–6).

- The message Jesus proclaimed the kingdom (4:17), as must the Twelve (10:7).

- The proof Jesus had healed the sick (4:23), raised the dead (9:18–26), cleansed lepers (8:1–4), and driven out demons (8:28–34). The disciples receive the same fourfold commission (10:8).

- The manner Jesus gave miracles freely; so did the disciples (10:8).

- The provision Both Jesus and the Twelve counted on generous supporters (10:9–10).

- The travel Jesus kept moving (Luke 4:43), as must the disciples (Matt. 10:11–15).

- The conduct Jesus, shrewd yet innocent, knew when to withdraw or speak in parables; the disciples must be wary too (10:17).

- A result Rumblings of persecution had started for Jesus and his men (10:18–23).

Thus the assertion "It is enough for the servant to be like the master" governs Jesus' entire discourse. We conclude that Jesus does not simply declare that we must learn from narrative. His life constitutes the pattern for mission. Therefore, Protestants need to overcome their ret-

---

42 In Luke, the saying appears with scant context, in a loosely connected series of sayings, so that the meaning is less than certain; for the options, see I. H. Marshall, *The Gospel According to Luke* (Grand Rapids: Eerdmans, 1981), 269–70.

icence about imitating Christ. When Jesus says, "It is enough for a disciple to be like the Lord," he ratifies the imitation motif and confirms that we must learn conduct from narrative. Clearly, Matthew 10 shows that Jesus, the master, expects his life to be a pattern for his disciples.

But the imitation motif transcends Matthew 10. Indeed, Jesus, as he gave instruction to the disciples, embedded a self-reference in all five of his great discourses in Matthew.[43] In each block of teaching, *he exhorts his disciples to conform themselves to him.* In the first discourse, the Sermon on the Mount, Jesus is the archetype of the Beatitudes (5:3–10). In the second discourse, as we have just seen, he urges the disciples to pattern their mission after his. In the third discourse, the kingdom parables, he is the Sower (13:3–8, 37). He inaugurates the kingdom with a word, which is as easily destroyed or ignored as a seed. In the fourth discourse, Jesus is like the king who forgives a vast debt, setting an example for his disciples to show mercy to one another (18:21–35). In the fifth, eschatological discourse, Jesus is like a thief in the night, like a long-delayed bridegroom, like a master calling his servants to account (24:42–25:30). Clearly Jesus' habit was to include at least a brief imitation motif in all his teaching for the disciples.

So the "imitation of Christ" motif pervades the Gospels and Epistles. The Gospels certainly expect Jesus' life to shape the disciples' conduct. Jesus did good on the Sabbath and declared it right for everyone to do so (Matt. 12:9–13; Luke 13:10–16; 14:1–6). He valued children as members of the kingdom and expected his disciples to value them (Matt. 18:2–6; 19:13–15). He sat loose with possessions and urged his disciples to have a loose grip (Luke 9:58; 12:13–34). He was willing to break with his family (Matt. 12:47–50; Mark 3:20–21, 31–35; John 7:2–5) and expected the same of his disciples (Matt. 8:21–22; Luke 14:26). Above all, he knew that he must be crucified (Matt. 20:19) and that some disciples would follow him to a similar death (Luke 14:27).

Since the imitation motif suffuses the New Testament, every nar-

---

43   The five discourses are (1) the Sermon on the Mount: the heart and conduct of a disciple (5:1–7:27); (2) the Mission of the Twelve: the conduct of and outlook for missions (10:1–42); (3) Parables of the Kingdom (13:1–52); (4) the Christian Community (18:1–35); (5) the Olivet Discourse (24:3–25:46): Jesus on the future of Israel and mankind. Matthew marks each with a closing refrain saying, roughly, "After Jesus had finished saying these things . . ."

rative of Jesus' actions becomes relevant. When training select groups, we note that Jesus chose a core group of twelve. We befriend agnostics, deists, and polytheists because Jesus befriended sinners. We say, "Writing a check is not enough," and stress involvement in mercy ministries because Jesus touched the unclean.[44] We do not require an independent imperative to verify these points. Jesus' life is enough.

We even use Jesus' example to resolve exegetical disputes. Do we take Matthew 7:6, "Do not cast your pearls before swine," dialectically (sometimes you must not judge [7:1], but sometimes you must) or ironically (if you cast your so-called pearls before those whom you regard as swine, they will trample your pearls and tear you to pieces)? One way to resolve this question is to ask how Jesus' habits inform it. We observe that he never refused a pearl to a seeking sinner, though he did sometimes hide from those who thought themselves wise.[45]

Principle 7: Whether explicit (his prayers) or implicit (his fellowship with sinners), Jesus' life generally sets patterns for kingdom life. Those who imitate him also become patterns for righteousness.

Principle 8: We may not imitate Christ when he exercises the prerogatives of deity in his messianic office. As prophet, he speaks the truth on his own authority ("Truly I say to you"). As priest, he offers himself as a ransom for sin. As king he commands the wind and the waves and defeats Satan in solo combat. As judge, he reads hearts and judges the world. These acts we cannot directly imitate. So imitation of Jesus is more problematic when divine attributes such as omnipotence (raising the dead, calming storms) or omniscience (knowing thoughts) are prominent in texts. It is more plausible to imitate when his human qualities (hunger, tiredness) or actions (praying, asking questions) are predominant.[46]

Together, our eight principles suggest how the book of Acts guides Christians. Its pattern of open fellowship and generosity to the poor

---

44 N. T. Wright, *Jesus and the Victory of God* (Minneapolis: Fortress, 1996), 141–42, 148–49, 369–442; see also Robert Stein, *The Method and Message of Jesus,* 2d ed. (Philadelphia: Westminster, 1995), 25–26; Gerd Theissen, *The Historical Jesus* (Minneapolis: Fortress, 1998), 431–37.

45 Thomas Bennett, "Matthew 7:6—A New Interpretation," *Westminster Theological Journal* 49 (1987): 371–86.

46 For more-refined principles and detailed case studies relating to the "imitation of Jesus" motif, see Griffiths, *Example of Jesus,* and Tinsley, "Some Principles."

is Christlike (2:42–47). Acts has other patterns that rest on the teaching and conduct of the risen Christ, patterns that have implications for Christians today: (1) Mission is an essential task of the church. (2) Racial discrimination is inconsistent with the gospel. (3) God will raise and direct the church.[47] The summary narrative statements in Acts that describe the customary life of the Jerusalem church can also be understood as having applications for other churches.[48] Further, when males persistently take leadership roles in Acts, we may be take that as a pattern.[49] But where there is no pattern, and where we cannot replicate singular events, such as casting lots for Judas's successor (1:23–26), the didactic should guide our evaluation of the descriptive.[50]

Thesis 5: Biblical Narratives Guide Readers in Their Proper Use.

Old Testament narratives lack anything as compelling as the "imitation of Christ" motif. Since some books scarcely evaluate the conduct of their characters, they yield moral lessons reluctantly. Nonetheless, many have embedded moral and spiritual lessons in their accounts.

Genesis opens the invitation to draw conclusions from narratives. Clearly, God was displeased with Adam and Eve for rebelling against him (Gen. 3). He also punished boastful Babel, where men built a city and made a name for themselves instead of repopulating the earth (Gen. 11). But he blessed faithful Abraham, who followed the divine call into Canaan, endured circumcision, and offered his son Isaac to God (Gen. 12, 17, 22). The Angel of the Lord declared, "Because you have done this and have not withheld your son, your only son, I will surely bless you" (22:15–18).

Many Pentateuch narratives invite readers to evaluate Israel's actions. The readers of Exodus 32 recognize idolatry when the Israelites

---

47 F. F. Bruce, *The Acts of the Apostles,* 3d ed. (Grand Rapids: Eerdmans, 1990), 21–22; I. H. Marshall, *Acts* (Grand Rapids: Eerdmans, 1980), 49–50.

48 Alan Brehm, "The Significance of the Summaries for Interpreting Acts," *Southwestern Journal of Theology* 33 (Fall 1990): 39.

49 Barbara Reid, "Choosing the Better Part," *Biblical Research* 42 (1997): 23, 31. Reid, a feminist, convincingly argues that this is the view of Acts, then exhorts her readers "to learn to read . . . against the intent of the third evangelist."

50 John Stott, *The Spirit, the Church, and the World: The Message of Acts* (Downers Grove, Ill.: InterVarsity, 1990), 7–8.

fashion a golden calf while Moses lingers on Sinai (cf. 20:1–6). The following punishment justifies comparing Israel's behavior to covenant law (32:21–33). Deuteronomy also leads readers to find moral lessons when Moses reviews Israel's sins in the wilderness (e.g., Deut. 4:3–4, 10–14, 32–34; 6:13–19; 8:2–5; 9:7–22). For example, Moses says, "Do not test the LORD your God as you did at Massah" (Deut. 6:16). Israel had pitched a camp at Massah shortly after the exodus. The site lacked water, so the people grumbled and demanded water, asking, "Is the LORD among us or not?" That is, they imagined God had to prove his presence by producing water on demand (Ex. 17:1–7). Considering the signs they had already witnessed, we groan at their unbelief. Dozens of narratives allow similar comparisons to law or prophecy, even if readers must draw their own conclusions (e.g., 1 Sam. 2–3, 13, 15; 2 Sam. 9; 1 Kings 21; 2 Kings 22–23). Deuteronomy's list of the blessings for obedience and the curses for sin invites us to evaluate all subsequent narratives as instances of blessed or cursed conduct (Deut. 28–32).

Though many require subtle judgment, the histories from Joshua to Nehemiah also invite moral and spiritual appraisal. Joshua shows the success that follows obedience at Jericho and the failure following sin at Ai. Judges describes days when Israel worshiped idols and refused to obey (2:10–23). If even effective leaders like Samson had suicidal relationships with pagans, we hardly wonder that everyone did whatever seemed right in his own eyes (17:6; 21:25), including mercenary idolatry and gang rape (Judg. 17–21). Yet during the same period, Ruth illustrates that God's laws do work and bring blessing on those who obey him.

The books of 1 and 2 Samuel rarely make overt judgments, but the fate of Saul, the king like those of other nations, shows what God thinks. By the end, Saul is rebuked and remorseful, though not properly penitent; and God leaves him dead and heirless. The books of Samuel also portray David as a flawed yet often exemplary king, the man after God's heart. Initially the ideal king (2 Sam. 6–9), his fidelity to God set the standard for later monarchs (1 Kings 11:4, 6; 14:8; 2 Kings 16:2). Yet he became a flagrant sinner who struggled to retain control of his household (2 Sam. 11–20).

The books of 1 and 2 Kings can be indirect or direct. They offer terse evaluations of most monarchs ("he did evil in the eyes of the

LORD"), while withholding comment on individual acts. Further, the accounts of the fall of Israel and Judah summarize their sins (2 Kings 17:7–23; 24:1–4). If we recall the instructions for a king in Deuteronomy 17, we know that Solomon has strayed as soon as we see him accumulating treasures, wives, and concubines (1 Kings 10:14–11:3).[51]

The Gospels also make some explicit judgments, while primarily letting readers draw their own conclusions. In Matthew, four full-length dramatic narratives directly praise someone in the story. Jesus tells the faithful centurion in Capernaum, "I have not found anyone in Israel with such great faith" (8:5–13). He commends the faith of the woman with the flow of blood (9:20–22) and the persistent Syro-Phoenician woman (15:21–28), and he blesses the woman who anoints him in Bethany (26:6–13).[52] But Matthew typically withholds explicit judgment in his narrative.[53] I count only four dramatic narratives that offer no moral assessment of any character: the exorcism of the two demoniacs (8:28–34), the feedings of the five thousand and four thousand (14:13–21; 15:32–39), and the transfiguration (17:1–8).[54] Other narratives give skilled readers enough information to appraise the characters. By evaluating occasionally and giving information that allows evaluation, Matthew shows how we may profit from his narrative.

Mark, like Samuel, lets the narrative speak for itself. Luke, like Matthew, has few narratives with no evaluation (e.g., 4:31–37; 9:10–17), yet few, again, with explicit praise (e.g., 5:18–26; 7:36–50; 10:38–42; 17:11–19). He lets readers draw conclusions, especially in the accounts

51 Iain Provan, *1 and 2 Kings* (Peabody, Mass.: Hendrickson, 1995), 69, 84, 91.
52 Dramatic narratives are stories sufficiently developed to establish the character of new figures or to add to our knowledge of familiar ones (Mark Alan Powell, *What Is Narrative Criticism?* [Minneapolis : Fortress, 1990], 54–55). They contrast with (1) brief reports of Jesus' movements (e.g., Matt. 4:12–13), (2) reports of numerous healings without a detailed account of any one encounter (4:23–25), (3) accounts of preaching tours (9:35; Luke 4:14–15), and (4) records of conflicts or narrative frameworks that establish the setting for teachings. On narrative types, see Daniel M. Doriani, *Getting the Message* (Phillipsburg, N.J.: Presbyterian and Reformed, 1996), 62–64.
53 Of course, Jesus' teaching often praises or blames disciples (16:17, 23) or Jewish leaders (12:39–42; 23:1–36).
54 The leper in 8:1–4 could be a fifth case, although he makes a preliminary confession and is healed.

of the final week. When the disciples fall asleep in Gethsemane, when Peter denies Jesus three times, when judicial figures promote false witnesses, do we need Luke to say, "That was bad"? Must he comment when the crucified robber asks Jesus to remember him in his kingdom? With the principle "Whoever is not against you is for you" (9:50), the Bible ineluctably draws us to approve such a person. As then, so now, the response to Christ and covenant is paramount.

Principle 9: Explicitly or implicitly, biblical narratives give sufficient direction for readers to gain guidance from them.

Thesis 6: There Are Experiential Reasons to Believe Narratives Are Authoritative.

Beyond theoretical discussions about the relative authority of narrative versus doctrine or law, we know that actions speak louder than words. Which speaks louder: a golfer muttering on the fifteenth fairway, "I have been extremely frustrated by this round of golf," or a golfer slamming his club to the turf and tossing it into the lake beside the fifteenth? If the action speaks clearly, a well-written narrative of it will, too.

This explains the prophets' symbolic actions. When Jeremiah ruins a new sash and smashes a pot, the action shouts that Israel shall be ruined and smashed (Jer. 13, 19). When he buys a field in enemy-occupied territory, it trumpets that the exile will end, that his descendants will enjoy the land (Jer. 32). When Ezekiel refuses to mourn his wife's death (Ezek. 4–5, 24), his action warns that Israel's suffering will be beyond mourning.

Symbolic actions still speak. Suppose a church member ardently criticizes a building program. He contests budget plans, accuses the church of losing its focus, and brings lists of underfunded ministries. People may tire of him, but if he stays in official channels, his behavior is tolerable. But suppose he walks into church one Sunday, bowl in hand, and starts splashing water on the carpet, pews, organ, and piano, declaring, "I baptize you in the name of the Father . . ." Suppose he takes a wad of money and hurls it at the pulpit. We now have more than an annoyance. Actions can indeed speak louder than words.

Principle 10: Narratives can convey some lessons with singular power. When not engaged in theory, theologians often assume the moral and doctrinal authority of narrative. We build our theology of giving from narratives in Acts 2, 4, and 11. We fashion a concept of doubt from the narratives of Thomas and Job. Our goal is to refine these intuitions.

SUMMARY

People make decisions by flipping coins because Israel cast lots (Josh. 7:14–23; Acts 1:23–26). Like Gideon they lay out "fleeces," though Judges portrays Gideon as a weak man (Judg. 6:36–40). They divest possessions to imitate the early church and horde them to imitate the patriarchs.

The formula "Narrative illustrates doctrines and imperatives" is not so much false as too restrictive, because the lives of Jesus and the heroes of faith construct paradigms for Christian conduct.[55] But how do we know when a pattern is a paradigm? Can we distill criteria to preclude abuses?[56] We cannot formulate rules to bar every error and justify every valid use of narrative, but we can remember our guidelines.

1. Biblical narratives tell the story of God's work of redemption. They describe his person and work and his ways with people, especially the covenant people. Since God acts according to his unchanging nature, past actions indicate what he might do in parallel circumstances today. Since we are created in his image, narratives may also exhibit how his image-bearers should live. For example, the God who loved Israel, a band of aliens and outcasts, bids us to love outcasts.

2. Because they describe God's work, narratives summon responses. They also illustrate proper and improper responses to him. Cultures ever change, but human nature has certain constants, so that past stories of sin, redemption, and faithfulness speak across the centuries.

3. Yet, even in the case of those who stay longest on stage (Abraham, Moses, David, Peter), the Bible takes no interest in free-floating moral stories. Scripture is not a Dostoevsky novel, where the portrayal of events counts more than factuality. Historicity matters.

4. Narratives suggest when the author intends a protagonist to set a precedent. When people whom God blesses for covenant faithful-

---

55 Fee and Stuart, *How to Read,* 77–78, 99–101.
56 Lawrence Toombs, "The Problem of Preaching from the Old Testament," *Interpretation* 23 (July 1969): 303.

ness set a pattern, we have a precedent, even if we lack a proof-text. This is especially true if the pattern correlates with something permanent, such as God's nature, redemption, or creation norms.[57] Antagonists set precedents that warn or instill repentance in converse ways.

5. We admit limits to imitation. Because language, customs, and social structures change constantly, we apply ancient narratives with caution, doing our exegesis case by case. Wherever God's agents had power and knowledge unique to their office, we cannot imitate them; we cannot dry up the skies or call fire from heaven. When the point lies in the sweep of events (e.g., the life of Joseph, the passion), we honor their design, refrain from spiritualizing incidentals, and learn from the complete story.

History illustrates moral and spiritual truth, but it can do more. The Bible never quite commands, "Associate with outsiders." It never quite says believers have permission to work in places where their hands might get dirty, for example, in pagan governments or large corporations; but the pattern of involvement visible in the stories of Joseph, Daniel, Obadiah, Esther, and others does provide much needed direction. If we avoid moralizing and mindless imitation, narrative can guide us, whether we have independent verification or not.

57 See William Larkin, *Culture and Biblical Hermeneutics* (Grand Rapids: Baker, 1988), 109–12; Richard Pratt, *He Gave Us Stories* (Phillipsburg, N.J.: Presbyterian and Reformed, 1990), 311–33.

9

A Plan for the Application of Doctrine

Some things lend themselves to step-by-step instructions more than others. Cooking, filing taxes, sewing, and writing directions are a few things that occur in discrete steps. Other matters are more instinctive: fakes in athletic contests and self-analysis in spiritual contests come to mind. Contemporary Christians already harbor doubts about the relevance of doctrine, but when I add that no five-step technique can guarantee that stirring lessons will emerge from doctrinal sermons, I feel like a meteorologist predicting that freezing rain will follow snow.

Nonetheless, sound doctrine does fortify the church. Past church leaders were both theologians and pastors. Athanasius, Augustine, Anselm, Bernard of Clairvaux, and Calvin had a dual passion for people and theology. They believed theology edified the church and reformed society. So Calvin believed of Geneva, so the Puritans and the Wesleys hoped for England, so Luther believed of Germany. Pastors may deny it, but contemporary sermons by respected evangelicals prove them to be preachers of doctrine too. They use doctrine to offer salvation and restoration, to address hot topics, and to direct the directionless. Further, while no technique guarantees a successful switch from exposition to application of doctrine, we do not entirely lack plans.

The Nature of Doctrine

It may be disconcerting to hear that there is no technique for applying doctrine, but this chapter faces a greater problem: Doctrine is not a genre of Scripture in the sense that narrative, law, poetry, and wisdom literature are. Rather, every passage, whether narrative, sermon, epistle, vision, praise, lament, or legal code, generates doctrines. Indeed, since all Scripture describes or reflects upon God's acts of redemption, all of it has theological interests and doctrinal implications. Recently, evangelical theologians have been disinclined to define doctrine as propositional truths about topics such as the nature of God, humanity, and the church. They prefer to define it as the normative interpretation of God's acts of creation and redemption[1] or as the application of biblical truth to new situations.[2]

Thus we bring no special exegetical principles to bear on doctrinal passages. We follow the usual steps for determining the author's meaning and the audience's reception of it. That is, doctrines are not found in doctrinal discourses—texts recognizable by their abstract discussion about God, sin, angels, atonement, and judgment. All Scripture is doctrinal, not least the narratives of Genesis and Matthew and the laws of Exodus and James. Whenever God acts and his servants interpret Scripture, doctrine is there. In short, the doctrinal passages of Scripture differ greatly from textbooks of systematic, historical, or polemical theology.

If doctrine is the right interpretation of God's acts, we must not link narrative, ethics, and doctrine as three equal genres with their own content and rules of interpretation. Rather, narratives are foundational, doctrine and ethics derived. Doctrine and ethics emerge as the Lord interprets his actions, whether by direct divine speech or by guiding his spokesmen.[3] In ethics, we must act roughly as God acts in the narratives and grow into his character as he reveals it in history. In doctrine the Christian community is reflecting on the meaning of Jesus' ministry, death, and resurrection. Part of this reflection will focus on

1 This definition draws on Alister McGrath, *The Genesis of Doctrine* (Grand Rapids: Eerdmans, 1997), 1–5; Richard Lints, *The Fabric of Theology* (Grand Rapids: Eerdmans, 1993), 66–74; and conversation with my colleague Michael Williams.

2 John Frame, *The Knowledge of the Doctrine of God* (Phillipsburg, N.J.: Presbyterian and Reformed, 1987), 76–85.

3 Here we assume the dual authorship of Scripture. God, the primary author, sometimes exercises his prerogative of declaring, with a very voice from heaven, the meaning of an event (e.g., Gen. 22:12, 16–18; Ex. 32:7–10). More often, he guides his agents to speak for him (Gen. 22:14; 1 Sam. 17:45–47).

direct divine speech, as in Jesus' discourse on the road to Emmaus (Luke 24) and God's word to Moses from the burning bush (Ex. 3:4–15). Still, doctrinal formulations more often begin with prophets or apostles meditating on divine actions. We earlier called doctrines "the cardinal truths of the faith" and "the fundamentals of a Christian belief system." But the starting point for a Christian belief system is divine action, not speculation about God and the world.

Doctrinal statements often grow from efforts to bring the truths of God's acts and character to bear on new situations, so we can see them aright and behave correctly in them. Thus, books like 2 Timothy, Hebrews, and 1 Peter draw on the life of Christ to fashion a theology of suffering and an ethic of endurance. Similarly, the prophets view the godlessness of Israel as immorality, but more as infidelity to God who had redeemed and "married" her.

The view of doctrine presented here runs against an older notion that we formulate doctrines by gathering various texts, gleaning truths from them by induction, and arranging the results in their proper order around topical headings, such as the doctrines of God, creation, and the church.[4] At worst, unskilled teachers rip through a concordance, collect a skein a verses linked only by the appearance of a key word, strip them of their contexts, then summarize the results as "What the Bible says about topic X."

No one advocates such reckless use of Scripture. Still, the church needs its leaders to summarize the teaching of the whole Bible on key topics. Leaders must address hot topics in the culture (e.g., gambling, gender issues), controversies in the church (e.g. styles of music and worship), and personal questions (e.g., handling illness, divorce, or prosperity). No single text completely answers such questions. Yet because they are valid, we must know how to address them. We must not shirk difficult questions.

Two principles guide us. First, when no one text offers a complete answer, we must harvest ideas from texts that offer brief, partial, and tangential witness. That is, we do serve the church by conducting doctrinal inquiries in the form "What does the whole Bible teach about topic X?" Second, we must develop a doctrinal or topical lesson with interpretive skill. Even in topical studies, teachers must fol-

---

4   Frame, *Doctrine of God,* 76–78.

low sound principles of interpretation. Refusing to wrest passages from their contexts, we must use them according to their place in the unfolding process of revelation.

PATTERNS FOR DEVELOPING TOPICAL STUDIES

The Four Conditions of Humanity

At minimum, we organize and synthesize the truth via the four nodal points in humanity's relation to God: at creation, after the fall, after redemption, and in the new creation.[5] From creation, we detect God's original purposes and basic principles, the fixed points for every discussion. From the fall, we see the effects of human wickedness and the curse; we sense how things go wrong and how to restrain, regulate, and remedy evil. From redemption, we discover God's potent cure for sin as it unfolds in his covenants and climaxes in Christ. From the new creation, we gain hope in our labor and insight from the future as it begins to break into the present. This approach operates best with foundational institutions such as work and marriage, since we have information about them in all four states. Work provides a test case:

1. *At creation,* we see that work is good, since God ordained it from the beginning. In creation, God himself worked. He planned, created, and fashioned reality. He splashed flowers, animals, plants, minerals, sounds, and colors in the sky above and the earth below. During creation, he called things into existence, then formed and arranged them, so they proclaim his handiwork (Ps. 8:3; 19:1). Then he rested, establishing the cycle of work and rest. He still oversees his creation, tending and watering his domain (Ps. 104:10–22). This shows that work is good in itself, and that humans reflect the image of God when we work.

2. *After the fall,* work became toil, the sweat of the brow and the frustration of thorns and thistles. Sin pervades work today. Cars built on Monday mornings suffer from hangovers. Projects completed Friday afternoon suffer from haste. People cheat as they produce goods and deceive as they sell them. Designers overlook or cover up flaws in their products. Ignorance, laziness, and malice bring many a sorrow.

---

5 This material roughly follows Christopher J. H. Wright, *Walking in the Ways of the Lord* (Downers Grove Ill.: InterVarsity, 1995), 14–23.

3. *After redemption,* work regains some of its original glory. Sin and frustration remain, but work has purpose again. Like Paul, we can pursue God-given tasks with fervor. Like Jesus, we can take satisfaction in our accomplishments. As he said, "My food is to do the will of him who sent me and to finish his work" (John 4:34). In redemption, God begins to remake us in his image. That includes restoration to the task of tending and guiding creation for him. We are the king's vice-regents, the president's vice-presidents.

4. *In glory,* work, purged of sin and frustration, will continue. When Christ returns, the faithful will be "put in charge of many things" (Matt. 25:21, 23). "In charge of many things" surely means work, but since it is a reward, we understand that the toilsomeness of labor ceases.

The Flow of Covenant History

Though useful, the "four conditions" approach does not lend itself to topics that develop substantially over time or demand careful nuancing. For these, we trace biblical teaching as revealed progressively in covenants with Adam, Noah, Abraham, Moses, David, and Christ. Pastors are mindful that the covenants of Moses and David, at least, feature substantial internal variety. For example, the Davidic era had subepochs such as the divided monarchy, the collapse of the north, and the exilic and postexilic periods, to name a few.

We can apply this approach to a theology of government. Instead of dashing to Romans 13, we start with Adam and find that governing is fundamental for human beings, whom God charges to rule creation for him. In Noah's era, God placed nations and peoples within boundaries, thereby calling government into existence (Gen. 10; Deut. 32:8; Acts 17:26). Soon, however, evil concentrated itself in human government and raised its hand against heaven.[6] After the flood, God said, "Scatter," but Babel refused, trying instead to build a tower and a name for itself (Gen. 11:4). Later, Nebuchadnezzar boasted, "Is not this the great Babylon I have built?" (Dan. 4:30). Isaiah understood the state's tendency toward self-deification. In Isaiah, the Lord says, "I am the LORD, and there is no other; apart from me there is no God" (45:5); and Babylon mimics, "I am, and there is none besides me" (47:8).

---

6 Jacques Ellul, *The Meaning of the City* (Grand Rapids: Eerdmans, 1970).

Yet even within Israel, government is ambiguous. Moses gave rules forbidding kings to amass wealth or wives, or otherwise behave like oriental potentates (Deut. 17:16–20). Then, before God consented to institute a monarchy, Samuel warned that Israel's own kings would abuse power, seizing land, hoarding wealth, and taking slaves (1 Sam. 8:10–20). Other Mosaic laws anticipate and regulate the abuses of the powerful, forbidding bribery, favoritism, and (to our ears) the odd sin of accumulating fields and wealth.

There were godly kings, of course, but more were evil or feckless. The prophets often railed against the abuses of oppressive governments, yet Joseph, Daniel, Nehemiah, Esther, and others show that the godly may serve in godless places. Habakkuk protested Babylon's rapacity, but Jeremiah prayed for the city (Jer. 29:7). Clearly, we have a range of responses to government, not least the hope for a King who will reign with justice.

New-covenant teaching stresses both submission to government and conflict with it. Romans 13 commands and Acts shows that Christians submit to governing authorities. But John the Baptist and Jesus both suffered state-directed murder, and authorities threatened to punish the apostles simply for preaching. When forbidden to preach, they decided to obey God rather than men (Acts 4:29). Thus, the summons to submit to laws and taxes (Rom. 13) is balanced by the vision of government as the beast that blasphemes God and fights the saints (Rev. 13).

Studies like this suggest how each age adds to the light given in the preceding one. Truth slowly builds upon truth.

Using the Four Questions People Ask

A third strategy for doctrinal or topical studies is to organize them around the four questions people ask (chaps. 5–6). Especially for topics with clear ethical implications, we can promote balance by listing our duties, the character traits permitting their discharge, the goals that guide action, and suggestions for distinguishing the truth from its counterfeits. This approach facilitates thoroughness more than does the custom of organizing talks around the accidents of alliteration (and consequent struggles to make every point begin with "P"). Let's use the four questions to sketch three topical studies: leadership in the church, distinguishing wants from needs, and dating.

Regarding leadership, it is an elder's *duty* to make disciples, teach, and promote purity of doctrine and life. Yet the description of an elder in 1 Timothy 3 accents *character* more than activity. Godly character equips leaders to lead. The *goals* of an elder include the growth, purity, and peace of the church. But any study of leadership must also *discern* why churches tend to choose dominant and successful men for office, following corporate rather than biblical qualifications.

In the matter of wants versus needs, adults have a *duty* to meet basic needs for food, clothing, and shelter for themselves and their children. But both rich and poor are prone to the *character* flaws of avarice, worry, greed, and the ingratitude that promotes self-pitying comparisons to others who have more than we do. This complicates the task of separating wants and needs. After we meet our needs and celebrate God's bounty, it is our *goal* to use wealth to build God's kingdom and meet the needs of others. But to become generous, we must *discern* the cultural trends that push even wealthy Americans to feel poor and to fear losing all they have.

Finally, in dating, our *duty* is to remain sexually pure, but the problem is that purity is the last *character* trait some people want. Once we *discern* the corrosive effects of the Western dating culture, the way it promotes temptation, Christian parents and leaders need to join to achieve the *goal* of purity for our youth. A simple prohibition on dating may have little effect; providing diverse group-oriented activities for young men and women is more promising.

DEVELOPING DOCTRINAL LESSONS

Established Pathways

Having examined ways to generate content for doctrinal or topical studies, we must now consider the pastor's challenge of taking an existing doctrinal idea and showing how it is relevant for the congregation. Both church fathers and contemporary pastors tend to shift instinctively, without apparent methodological self-consciousness, from doctrine to its significance. Unconcerned about crossing the fuzzy boundary between ideas and their relevance, they work without visible method.

When asked how he came up with ideas, cartoonist Bill Watterson said he holds a blank sheet of paper, stares into space, lets his mind wander, then tries to see the results through his characters' eyes.[7] The work of a pastor with a doctrine may seem all too similar: stare at a doctrine, meditate, and see what comes to mind. Intuition is at a premium here; still, there is more to the application of doctrine than hoping for random insights. There are patterns for finding relevance. The backbone of application of doctrine is the summons to believe it and to think, feel, and act accordingly. We can organize the teacher's work under four rubrics: "This is reality"; "These are the implications of reality"; "This is a perennial issue"; and "This is who needs the message."

1. *"This is reality."* Most doctrinal sermons make statements about God's person and work, or the nature of humanity or creation, then let the hearers draw the conclusions. Consider the following statements, from sermons I listened to recently:

- The redeemed are children of the light, not the darkness. God made us to walk in his light.
- Christ is coming again, and the best way to prepare for his return is to walk with him faithfully day by day.
- The holy God sees and cares about all that we do, so that everything we do is invested with significance. The smallest act of kindness or selfishness matters because it matters to God.
- In biblical times, friends shared their values and aspirations. The Bible says anyone who is a friend of the world is an enemy of God. One cannot be a friend of both God and the world.

Observe, first, that these statements are truly doctrinal. They make first-order assertions about the person and work of the Triune God—he is the Redeemer, he will return, he is holy and omniscient. Second, although there are no commands, the statements feel relevant; assertions about God's person and work imply something about our beliefs, attitudes, or actions. Third, they rest on biblical authority. The teacher may need to demonstrate, clarify, or answer objections to their points, but the church is expected to believe what God says about the reality and act accordingly.

---

7 Bill Watterson, *The Calvin and Hobbes Tenth Anniversary Book* (Kansas City: Andrews and McMeel; 1995), 19–20.

2. *"These are the implications of reality."* A second type of application pauses to declare the implications of doctrine, whether obvious or obscure. Consider some examples:

- God created the world and entrusted it to humans. Therefore, care for it.
- Our bodies are the temple of the Holy Spirit. Therefore, glorify God with your bodies.
- Jesus offered himself as a perfect, final sacrifice for sin. Therefore do not attempt to atone for your sins, but accept the sacrifice of Christ.
- Jesus intercedes for us at the right hand of the Father, and the Spirit prays for us with wordless groans. Therefore, take comfort, knowing that all your needs are represented to the Father.
- Each of us is sinful through and through. Therefore, expect every human to disappoint you.

For the doctrine of sin, there are other clear implications—we must repent, seek God's mercy in Christ, be humble, and evangelize sinners. Additional thoughts come when we poke around ideas, asking who might need them and who would resist them. Take the notion that we should anticipate disappointment from sinners. New converts must learn from the accounts of Moses and Peter that even Christian leaders will disappoint them. Individuals with too much self-confidence must hear that they will disappoint themselves—in their actions, emotions, and meditations. Finally, everyone should strive to grow in holiness, but all should realize that every remedy for sin will fail in part, for final deliverance from it is God's work.

For each doctrine we have mentioned just one or two implications. But many doctrines permit entire series of inferences, as Calvin amply displayed. For example, after defining and defending the doctrine of God's providential governance of all things past, present, and future, Calvin takes eighteen pages to expound its ramifications "to our greatest benefit."[8] Even the preceding exposition inserts edifying

---

8 See also Calvin's extended remarks on Christian freedom (*Institutes of the Christian Religion* [Philadelphia: Westminster, 1960], 3.19.1–16). As he says, freedom is "an appendage of justification and is of no little avail in understanding its power" (3.19.1). See too 3.21.1–4 on election and 4.1.1–12 on the church.

asides. Thus he says that those who know God's power "safely rest in the protection" of the one who controls all the harmful things we fear.[9] Calvin's deliberately practical meditations then proceed to develop the following points (and more):

- Providence requires humility; we should not call God to account for his actions, but "reverence his secret judgments" and "consider his will the truly just cause of all things."[10]
- The godly will neither murmur against God's will, nor fatalistically give up planning. We order our affairs, knowing God employs our means to effect his providence. We submit our plans to his will.[11]
- Rather than straining against God's providence, find solace in it, since "the Lord watches over the ways of the saints with . . . great diligence." God cares for tiny sparrows. He has power to overrule the wickedness of humanity. This knowledge gives us "patience in adversity and . . . freedom from worry about the future."[12]
- The doctrine of providence helps in adversities. Remembering that God has willed them, we have an "effective remedy for anger and impatience." When wounded by wicked men, we can go to God, believing that "whatever our enemy has wickedly committed against us was permitted and sent by God's just dispensation."[13]
- Still, we should not neglect "intermediate causes." God grants benefits, but people are his agents. If we suffer due to negligence, we will ascribe it both to God's will and to our error. Therefore, we must take counsel, seek assistance, and draw upon all "lawful instruments of divine providence" when we undertake anything.[14]
- The godly mind must find felicity in the doctrine of providence. Dangers threaten at every turn—fire, weaponry, wild

9 Ibid., 1.16.3.
10 Ibid., 1.17.1–2.
11 Ibid., 1.17.3–5.
12 Ibid., 1.17.6–7.
13 Ibid., 1.17.8.
14 Ibid., 1.17.9.

animals, the hazards of travel, and the threat of famine. But instead of letting dangers terrify us, we trust that God rules all by his wisdom, letting nothing touch us but what he has ordained.[15]

Calvin's approach is the oldest, most common, and least methodical way to apply doctrine: state the doctrine, then meditate on it. Knowing human brokenness, preachers ask, "How does this doctrine heal?" Knowing human sinfulness, teachers ask, "How does this summon repentance and offer restoration?"

3. *"This is a perennial question."* The doctrinal portions of Scripture typically address perennial issues. One preacher may expound passages on the relation of faith and works from Galatians or Ephesians, then say, "As then, so now . . . this doctrine has implications today." Another may study Paul's missionary methods and draw conclusions about his view of pagan religions and their adherents. Because Paul encountered pagan polytheists and we typically meet either agnosticism or perversions of monotheism, we say, "As then, so now to some degree . . ."

Most biblical doctrines address perennial theological questions about God and humanity:

- What is God like? Who enjoys a good relationship with him? On what basis?
- Why can't I control myself? Why can I not simply do what I resolve?
- How can we make sense of the hardships of life, from death to the loss of a job? Is God interested in my sorrows? In my desire to provide for self and family?

Regarding the last point, the Bible does address the brevity and uncertainty of life, but since the forms of poverty change from culture to culture, it never tackles the exact phenomena of unemployment, downsizing, and pink slips. Still, if Scripture speaks to a situation similar to ours, we can readily make adjustments. We can ask, Given this biblical answer to a perennial question, what follows?

15   Ibid., 1.17.10–11.

4. *"Who needs this message?"* The Puritans mastered the art of applying a doctrine to people in varied stations of life. They would make a point about the home, then reshape it for husband and wife, master and servant, parent and child.[16] They would make one point about society and rework it for rich and poor, for magistrates, ministers and the military, for farmers and merchants.

In his famous sermon "Sinners in the Hands of an Angry God," Jonathan Edwards garners his listeners' attention this way. He warns that any of them may die and enter hell within the year. Then they will have leisure to rue their indifference to this very sermon for all eternity. Lest this threat fail to move them, he admonishes them generationally. The aged must know they have stored up wrath against themselves. Their "guilt and hardness of heart" are great, if they disregard God's mercy. Young men and women must seize the "extraordinary opportunity" to renounce "youthful vanities." Children must know hell awaits them too. "Will you be content to be children of the devil, when so many other children . . . are become the holy and happy children of the King of Kings?"[17]

Preachers can still march through groups by age or social position to good effect. For example, a theology of work, status, and leisure applies very differently to students, people in early career, mid-career, late career, and retirees. A theology of marriage and family applies differently to engaged couples; to newlyweds; to parents with babies, toddlers, small children, older children, teenagers, and grown children. A theology of stewardship works one way for the poor, another for the middle and affluent strata.

As we said, the methodological self-awareness of teachers may be limited. They meditate and pray with a nearly blank screen or page before them. They rely on intuition and observation. They indwell the world of Scripture yet inhabit their own age. They comment on the difference and propose ways of bringing the two worlds closer together. However inattentive they are to methods, we can yet distill their practice to give inexperienced preachers a starting point and aid mature communicators for the day when intuition runs dry.

16 William Gouge, *Of Domestical Duties* (London, 1622); John Dod, *A Plaine and Familiar Expositions of the Ten Commandments* (London, 1612).

17 Jonathan Edwards, *The Works of Jonathan Edwards* (Carlisle, Pa.: Banner of Truth, 1974), 2:11.

Checklists for Preachers

The instincts of master-teachers lead them to four paths of application: (1) This is reality; (2) These are the implications of reality; (3) This is a perennial question; and (4) This is who needs the message. But some preachers consciously use certain checklists to gain more options for application. One helpful speaker-oriented list uses the basic interrogative questions: who, what, when, where, why, and how? [18] These questions will work with narrative and ethical passages, but may work best on doctrine:

1. *Who* needs this doctrine? Individuals or groups? If groups, the nation, the church, business, a profession? If individuals, which ones? Christians or non-Christians? Young or old? The self-sufficient and self-righteous or the humble and brokenhearted? People struggling with relationships, spirituality, vocation, social behavior, money, or their thought life? In a different vein, who will resist or misunderstand this doctrine, and how can we counter their objections? If we introduce people to Calvin's doctrine of providence, we must address misconceptions (fatalism) and rejoinders (are people not free?) before we can hope to apply it.

2. *What does God require?* Recall that the form for applying doctrinal statements is: "If doctrine X is true, what follows?" If one were eager to practice this teaching, where would one start? What must we believe or do? How does the doctrine guide feelings or emotions?

3. *What does God promise?* His yes is yes, so that whenever he says he will do something, it functions as a promise. Christians benefit when we direct them to God's asseverations about who he is and what he will do.

---

18 See Bryan Chapell, *Christ-Centered Preaching* (Grand Rapids: Baker, 1994), 204–11; Gordon Fee, *New Testament Exegesis* (Philadelphia: Westminster, 1983), 132–33; Sidney Greidanus, *The Modern Preacher, and the Ancient Text* (Grand Rapids: Eerdmans, 1988), 182–87; William Klein, Craig Blomberg, and Robert Hubbard, *Introduction to Interpretation* (Waco: Word, 1993), 411–25; Grant Osborne, *The Hermeneutical Spiral* (Downers Grove, Ill.: InterVarsity, 1991), 347–53.

4. *When and where* do we incarnate this doctrine? Here pastors seek realism and situational specificity, with instruction so concrete it is hard to evade.

5. *Why* must we live out this doctrine? *How* can we live out what it teaches? This is the question of motivation. Here pastors must instill obedience not from guilt, shame, or raw duty, but from trust in our all-knowing, truth-telling Lord. Here we are to remind listeners that God's mercy leads us to obedience and a desire to work out our salvation with fear.

My personal checklist adds two additional points:

1. *Address the whole person*—head, heart, hands, and mouth. That is, what ideas, attitudes, emotions, actions, and expressions are consistent with the passage? For the mind, what truth should we believe? What contrary ideas reject? What intellectual compromises watch? Remember the explanatory power of doctrine. Which of life's riddles might this doctrine solve? For the heart, what fears or anxieties resist the teaching? What comforts or encouragements does it offer? For the hands, have we noted what to do and how to do it, and when and where? For the mouth, what speech must we shun? What words utter to God or others?

2. *Remember grace.* We should always remember grace, since doctrinal teaching, like ethical teaching, can skew the motives for Christian living. The formula for applying ethical teaching can become, "Do this because it is right so to do." The formula for applying doctrine becomes, "Believe and act this way because it puts truth into practice." These formulae are valid, as far as they go, but truncated. The ethical formula forgets that we do the right thing because God has forgiven us, remade us, bought us, and called us to union with Christ, to submission to his will, and to conformity to his person. The doctrinal formula forgets that theological truth is Christocentric. The doctrine of sin indicates our need of Christ. The doctrine of redemption recounts the work of Christ. The doctrine of God describes the character of the God who saves in Christ. The doctrine of the Spirit tells how he applies the work of

Christ to us. No doctrinal truth obtains in isolation from Christ and his grace.

CASE STUDIES

There is little innovation in the patterns and checklists we have just examined, but they do present an alternative to hoping for random insights and idly whispering to ourselves, "I wish I were more creative." Thus we could simply deliver a "reality sandwich" and let listeners see its significance for themselves. Or, if we wish to be more didactic and directive, we can use the lists above. Pastors seem to use these questions or techniques spontaneously as they walk about with open ears, minds, and hearts. By listing them, teachers can transcend their instincts.

Some passages are unmistakably doctrinal, directly describing the character and work of God. Others beget doctrine when we find it useful to synthesize teachings found throughout Scripture, or when difficulties with the interpretation of hard passages lead to ideas that conflict with Christian fundamentals.

But our model for application reminds us that just as some passages generate relevant doctrines, doctrinal teaching also begins when people bring their questions to the Bible. Of the four questions people ask—What should I do? Who should I be? Where should we go? How can I see?—all but the first invite doctrinal answers.

These points are not difficult at a theoretical level, but practicing them is another matter. Therefore, let us go through a few case studies to see how a doctrinal text and questions can create a variety of theocentric applications. The first addresses a question people bring to Scripture, "How can I be a good man?" The last exegetes a doctrine-laden passage, John 10, that has both obvious and hidden implications. Between these are vignettes of the way doctrine answers weighty questions.

The Doctrine of God Applied: The Good Family Man

Since my dissertation explored biblical teaching on the family and since I care deeply about the subject, it is no surprise that I have spoken and written about the family and manhood for many years. Since my first teaching experiences at age twenty-six, my approach has shifted dramatically. The exposition of biblical texts (e.g., Gen. 2:18–25; Eph. 5:21–6:9) and the odor of soft legalism dominated my early messages. I stressed what a godly man would do, should do, in obedience to God. The metamessage was, "Do these things, and God will bless you and your family."

As time passed, as I encountered ever more men with shattered marriages, careers, and confidence, and as I saw my disabilities more clearly, my emphases shifted. I began to turn away from rules that solve problems and to look to God's work and person as the first source of direction. Next, I explored human nature and society. Rules came third. I spoke of the culture's power to lead us astray, of our weakness, of God's grace, of his desire to remake us in his image. In short, I began to emphasize theology and relabeled my series on biblical manhood "A Man after God's Own Heart." Allow me, in brief compass, to epitomize its themes, inviting you to observe the way relevance springs from the doctrine of God.

We must begin with God's transforming grace and every man's need of it. As Paul says, "All have sinned and fall short of the glory of God" (Rom. 3:23). Paul here makes two points about our sinfulness, not one. First, "All have sinned" means we have violated God's law and trampled his commands, have offended God and humanity. Second, "fall short of the glory of God" means we have lost the glory God granted when he created us in his image and gave us the privilege of representing his glory to the world.[19] Men still seek glory, but in the wrong places, places to which our culture directs us—career, wealth, pleasure, achievement, status, or physical manliness. Some resist the culture and seek glory in nobler places, such as public service, the family, or even institutional religion. Whether noble or ignoble in themselves, if we seek glory in created things, we are practicing idolatry and will surely fail. Every man is a sinner seeking glory in the wrong places. No man has hope, save in God-given repentance and restoration to life.

---

19 This is the interpretation adopted by the majority of Romans commentators, such as William Sanday and Arthur C. Headlam, *A Critical and Exegetical Commentary on the Epistle to the Romans,* 5th ed. (Edinburgh: T. & T. Clark, 1902), 84–85; C. E. B. Cranfield, *The Epistle to the Romans* (Edinburgh: T. & T. Clark, 1975), 204–5.

But now, God has adopted as his sons those who have repented and believed. He is remaking them in his image, restoring them to true glory as they become like him. Re-creation in the image of God has become the dominant (though not the only) theme in my series on marriage, parenting, work, and friendships between men. Consider each one with me, seeing how our doctrine of God answers the question, "How can I be a good family man?"[20]

No book of techniques or seven-step plans can carry us through the ever-changing challenges of parenthood. Parenting depends more on who we are than on the techniques we master. Parents teach their children as they sit at home, walk along the road, lie down, and get up (Deut. 6:7) because our instruction flows from our character and convictions. Convinced of God's truth, we talk about it. Transformed by God's love, we love our children.

A godly father is, above all, Godlike. God describes himself this way in Exodus 34: "The LORD, the compassionate and gracious God, slow to anger, abounding in love and faithfulness . . . and forgiving . . . sin. Yet he does not leave the guilty unpunished." Love dominates this passage, and the facets of God's love cited here are precisely what a good father offers his children:

- Compassion is the empathy that lets us mourn when they mourn, rejoice when they rejoice.
- Grace is the Godlike habit of bestowing gifts upon children for the pure joy of it.
- Slowness to anger checks the temptation to demand too much, to rebuke too often.
- Faithfulness is the capacity to endure precisely when endurance seems most burdensome.
- Mercy is the ability to overlook error and forgive sin.
- Not leaving the guilty unpunished means that fathers will love their children too much to let them think their misdeeds have no consequences. That is, Godlike fathers are just.

---

20 I develop the next paragraphs in my forthcoming book, *A Man after God's Own Heart* (Wheaton, Ill.: Crossway, 2001).

Thus God reveals love, justice, and faithfulness as his prime attributes. Micah 6:8 verifies that God expects his covenant people—hence believing fathers—to conduct themselves as he does: "What does the LORD require of you? To act justly and to love mercy and to walk humbly with your God." The last phrase, "walk humbly," supplies an essential qualifier. Fatherhood is a "walk," a way of life, but it is a humble walk, for every human father fails, hence must humble himself before God and his children. This is the bare skeleton of a father's duties. Because love, justice, and faithfulness are the main traits of our heavenly Father, they are to be our main traits as he remakes earthly fathers in his image (Eph. 4:13–16, 20–24).

A man's work likewise benefits from meditation on God's character. We start well if we aspire to imitate the Father's pattern of working six days and resting one, if we know Jesus' joy (John 4:34) and resoluteness (Luke 9:51) in his work, if we aspire to give others rest through our labors (Matt. 11:28). Similarly, a husband has commenced his journey if he has understood how the love of Christ is to serve as the model for and illumine his love for his wife (Eph. 5).

The friendships of men also benefit from grounding in theology proper. Christian messages on friendship tend to start either with exemplary friendships in biblical history (David and Jonathan, Ruth and Naomi) or the friendship aphorisms of Proverbs. They typically end with "the traits of a good friend." Though such lists appear to be character-oriented, they can take a legal "You must habitually act this way" tone.

We come closer to the essence of friendship by analyzing the character of God as friend. Scripture uses the metaphor rarely, but whether the case is God's friendship with Abraham, Moses, or Israel or Jesus' friendship with his disciples, two features are constant: self-disclosure and helpful presence. In one visit, God helps Abraham, his friend (2 Chron. 20:7; James 2:23), telling him that he will have a son in a year and revealing that Sodom will be destroyed (Gen. 18:10–32). He helps Moses lead Israel out of Egypt and also reveals himself, speaking to Moses face to face, as friends do, at the tent of meeting (Ex. 33:7–11). Jesus mentions self-disclosure and help again, telling his disciples, "Greater love has no one than this, that he lay down his life for his friends. . . . I have called you friends, for everything that I learned from my Father I have made known to you" (John 15:13, 15). Along with affection, self-disclosure and helpful presence are the traits we most seek in friendship. Shared interests, proximity, mentoring, team-work, and mutual respect all contribute but fall short of genuine friendship if these two elements are missing.

Theology proper even illumines the emotional lives of men. Is the good man tough or tender, stoical or expressive? Behold Jesus, who wept in public over the death of a friend and over the fall of Jerusalem (John 11:35; Luke 19:41). See him moved to compassion again and again at the plight of the people (Matt. 20:34; Mark 8:1–2). See him dismayed by the hardness and dullness of his listeners (Mark 3:5; 9:19). If we add that God ascribes feelings such as love, wrath, and pity to himself in the Old Testament, the conclusion is obvious.

The method here is theological in the strictest sense. If we know who God is, we know what it means to be a real man. Our method is also grace-oriented, for we confess that we will never be the friend or father we ought to be unless God first becomes our friend and father. Thus theology proper answers a man's basic questions.

Vignettes of Doctrine Applied

Let us sketch the way doctrine applies to a few other practical matters:

1. *How shall we regard the poor?* Did they bring it on themselves? Will they waste whatever they get? Remember God's compassion for Israel. He delivered Israel when she was poor, miserable, and oppressed in Egypt. Therefore Israel must have compassion on the poor, by giving to the Levite, the alien, the fatherless, and the widow (Deut. 26:1–15).[21]

2. *How can I love someone whose flaws I clearly see?* In God, perfect knowledge and perfect love meet; his love and his knowledge are not distinct from one another, for God is love and knows all things. As C. S. Lewis observes, "We could almost say He sees because He loves, and therefore loves although He sees." If this is true of God, it should be true of us. Our love of a friend, a child, or a spouse is most won-drous when we love despite known flaws. True love has "a power of

---

21 Bruce Birch and Larry Rasmussen, *Bible and Ethics in the Christian Life,* rev. ed. (Minneapolis: Augsburg, 1988), 29–30.

seeing through its own enchantments and yet not being disenchanted." If God can see and love, then so should we.[22]

3. *What is the source of human dignity?* God created humans in his image (Gen. 1–2), and they retained it even after the fall (James 3:9).[23] It is our *duty,* therefore, to treat everyone with dignity, speaking respectfully and banning humor that degrades others. The *goal* of those with economic influence should be to create jobs that foster self-respect and pay decent wages. As for the *character* question, what kind of person treats all, not just members of his or her tribe, with dignity? Why do some speak harshly and condescendingly to children, the aged, and secretaries and talk ever so politely to the wealthy and powerful? What kind of person strives to please only his superiors? How can we learn to see the image of God in everyone we see, every solicitor who calls on the phone?

4. *How is the doctrine of sin relevant?* We must first believe that the doctrine of sin applies to us and to all whom we meet. Therefore, we must repent and seek God's mercy, in Christ, for ourselves and for others. We also expect everyone around us, whether base heathen or admirable Christian, to fail. We anticipate disappointment from ourselves and others. We expect sin to affect our bodies, emotions, and minds. Since sin taints our minds, sin will corrupt even our meditations on sin. We fool ourselves on every front. And we should seek remedies for sin on every front.

A Doctrinal Text Applied: Jesus the Good Shepherd

Our second extended study draws lessons from a theological text (John 10:1–18). The starting point must be a thorough exegesis of John 10 that thickly describes the text and places its most overtly theological moments—the "I am" formula and the "good shepherd" claim—in biblical context. The goal will be to apply John's points as he makes them, showing how Jesus meets the concrete needs of a fallen race.[24]

---

22 C. S. Lewis, *A Grief Observed* (New York: Seabury, 1961), 56–57.

23 See Anthony Hoekema, *Created in God's Image* (Grand Rapids: Eerdmans, 1986), 11–32.

24 D. A. Carson's pellucid commentary on John models a style of exposition that offers timely theological judgment and hints leading to application to the church. See *The Gospel according to John* (Grand Rapids: Eerdmans, 1991), 379–90.

Wise pastors can apply general points to specific local situations.[25]

Before considering what Jesus meant when he said, "I am the good shepherd" (10:11, 14), we should note that we are predisposed to read it as a promise to rescue us in distress. For example, if a newly licensed teenage driver gets lost or accidentally winds up at a dubious party or gets in a minor accident, but comes home unscathed, Christian parents think, "The Lord is her shepherd." We think of the Lord as shepherd when we confront illness, chaos at work, or a difficult decision, and that is correct. But the good shepherd does more than deliver us from crises. When Jesus says, "I am the good shepherd," he claims to be the mighty caretaker of Israel, both strong and tender.

1. *The precursors of the good shepherd.* From Genesis onward, God announced that he is the shepherd and rock of Israel (Gen. 49:24). Jacob, thankful that God "has been my shepherd all my life" (Gen. 48:15), asked that God continue to shepherd his family after his death. As shepherd, God promised to lead his people, "to go out and come in before them," so they "will not be like sheep without a shepherd" (Num. 27:17). God also appointed undershepherds for Israel (Ezek. 34). When Israel's leaders came to crown David, they reminded him that even when Saul was king, "you were the one who led Israel on her military campaigns. And the LORD said to you, 'You will shepherd my people Israel'" (2 Sam. 5:2). David was a strong shepherd—a warrior who also killed wild beasts with his hands (1 Sam. 17:36–37).

The link between shepherding and battle teaches that a good shepherd is tender yet powerful as he protects Israel from her enemies. As Isaiah says, "The Sovereign LORD comes with power, and his arm rules for him. . . . He tends his flock like a shepherd: He gathers the lambs in his arms and carries them close to his heart" (Isa. 40:10–11; see also 63:11–12). We love Psalm 23 for its promise that our shepherd will let us suffer no physical or spiritual wants. But the shepherd's rod also strikes our enemies. Thus we fear no evil, even when dining in their presence.

Application: Honor God for both his strength and his tenderness. Leaders of families, churches, and businesses, strive to emulate his

---

25 On the importance of specificity, see Chapell, *Christ-Centered Preaching,* 202–5, 213–17.

strong yet tender leadership, keeping enemies at bay while gently leading those under your care.

2. *The name of the good shepherd.* David and other good kings and prophets *functioned* as good shepherds when they led Israel faithfully. But when Jesus says, *"I am* the good shepherd" (John 10:11, 14), he claims this is his very nature, not just his function. "I am" is a name of God. In Exodus 3:6 he declares that he is the God of Abraham, Isaac, and Jacob, and proceeds to the absolute statement "I AM WHO I AM" (3:13–14).[26] God also adds descriptions of himself to the "I am" formula: "I am El Shaddai, the Almighty," and "I am he who blots out your transgressions" (Gen. 17:1; Isa. 43:25).[27]

Therefore, when Jesus says "I am," he speaks as God does, implicitly claiming deity. Sometimes his "I am" is absolute: "Before Abraham was, I am" (John 8:58; 18:6).[28] More often Jesus says "I am" and adds a predicate. He says, "I am" bread, water, light, a door, the way, or the good shepherd. *With each "I am" saying, Jesus directs longings and needs to himself.* He fulfills the promises of Judaism. For example, the law *gives* light (Ps. 119:105), but Jesus *is* the Light. The law *shows* how we should walk (Deut. 5:32–33), but Jesus *is* the Way. Kings and priests (sometimes) shepherded Israel, but Jesus is the good shepherd. Thus,

26 The Septuagint reads *egō eimi ho ōn.*
27 The Septuagint of Isa. 43:25 reads "I am 'I am' who blots out transgressions." This doubling may serve to reinforce the identification, "I am he, I am he who blots . . ." Or it may make *egō eimi* a name, "I am 'I AM' who blots out transgressions." Isa. 51:12 reads, literally, "I am I AM who comforts you" (cf. Isa. 52:6). So the Septuagint uses *egō eimi* with a descriptor to produce a new title or name for God here and at Gen. 17:1; Ex. 3:6 and 13–14 (Septuagint: *egō eimi ho ōn*). Thus *egō eimi* becomes a divine name, equivalent to Yahweh.
28 Critical questions about the authenticity of John's "I am" sayings should be deflated by similar sayings in the Synoptics and Acts. When Jesus walked to the disciples on the water, he said, "Take courage, I am [he]" *[tharseite, egō eimi]"* Matt. 14:27; Mark 6:45–50). At Jesus' trial, when asked, "Are you the Christ?" he said, "I am *[egō eimi]"* (Mark 14:62). When the disciples wonder if the risen one whom they see is truly Jesus, he assures them, "Look at my hands and my feet, I am [he] *[egō eimi]"* (Luke 24:39). When Jesus appears to Paul on the Damascus road, he identifies himself as *egō eimi* (Acts 9:5; see also 22:8; 26:15). There are roughly ten "loaded" uses of *egō eimi* in the Synoptics.

it is Jesus' very nature to satisfy our proper longings for light, guidance, and loving direction.[29]

Application: Examine the validity of your longings and aspirations. Desires for food, health, acceptance, dignity, companionship, and direction for life are valid, but none of them should become an idol, something we *must* possess for life to have meaning. Do you see how Jesus meets your desires, either directly or through his appointed means? Train yourself to turn to Jesus to satisfy your longings rather than seeking fulfillment in temporal things.

3. *The opposite of the good shepherd.* The message of John 10 actually begins in John 9, where Jewish leaders proved themselves evil shepherds of a blind man whom Jesus healed. Jesus restored the man's sight on a Sabbath, so the leaders tried to induce the man to incriminate Jesus. When he refused, they insulted him and cast him out of their fellowship (John 9:28, 34). Jesus found the man, told him about himself, and led him to faith (9:35–38). Jesus often used miracles to teach about himself. He fed thousands and said, "I am the bread of life." He healed a man born blind and said, "I am the light of the world." He raised Lazarus and said, "I am the resurrection and the life." Here he cares for a blind man and says he is the good shepherd. Because Israel's shepherds treated the man so poorly, they serve as a foil for Jesus, the good shepherd.

In John 10:1–13, Jesus distinguishes two kinds of failed shepherds: thieves and hired hands. Thieves and robbers (10:1, 8) are overtly wicked. They care nothing for the flock, for its sick and weak. They do not know the sheep, who refuse to follow them (10:5, 8). They only plunder and destroy (10:10; see also Ezek. 34; Jer. 23). The Jewish leaders who fought Jesus epitomize bad shepherding. By opposing Jesus, they destroy the flock. The hired hand (10:12–13) is more uncommitted than wicked. He cares, but his concern for the flock is attenuated by his greater self-interest. When wolves come, hirelings abandon the field. Hirelings care, but in the test, second-rate interest is hardly distinguishable from no interest at all.

Application: Christians, guard against both kinds of failed shepherd.

29   Gary Burge, " 'I AM' Sayings," in *Dictionary of Jesus and the Gospels* (Downers Grove, Ill.: InterVarsity, 1997), 356.

There is nothing more dangerous than a thief, that is, a wicked religious leader (Matt. 23). Pastors, examine yourselves lest you act like hired hands who perform your duties when all is quiet and you are well paid. Watch, lest you start thinking like hirelings—fretting about overwork, low salaries, and lack of recognition. Guard against becoming an underpaid workaholic, but also know that preoccupation with pay and ease are marks of the hireling. The test will come, when standing for the flock costs something. Then we must be ready to fight the wolves.

4. *The work of the good shepherd.* Jesus' statement, "I am the good shepherd," stands twice in the middle of John 10 (vv. 11, 14), but the whole unit recounts his care for the sheep.[30]

First, Jesus *protects* his sheep. He is the door, the gate at the entrance to the sheepfold (10:7, 9). "Whoever enters through me will be saved" (10:9) promises physical preservation. Jesus saves the sheep from wolves and other predators. But the promise "whoever enters through me will be saved" goes beyond the physical. That is, there is one way to eternal life, through the shepherd who bestows it upon all who believe in him (20:31). *Application:* Therefore let every man and woman enter life through Jesus.

Second, the good shepherd *leads* his sheep. Sheep are notorious wanderers; they need guides. When Jesus says that his sheep "will come in and go out" (10:9), he means that he will lead us through our lives. It is a pitiful thing to lack a leader; when Jesus saw amorphous crowds "he had compassion on them, because they were harassed and helpless, like sheep without a shepherd" (Matt. 9:36). *Application:* Let us confess that we need leadership, the leadership Jesus offers.

Third, Jesus *knows* his sheep, and his sheep know him (John 10:14–15). By virtue of his deity, Jesus knows us with a sweet and intimate knowledge. We know his voice; he knows our name (10:3–4). Jesus knows and loves all, but has a peculiar knowledge and love for his sheep. The idea that God knows *everything* about me—even my darkest thoughts—is frightening. He knows! But he loves us anyway—

---

30 The textual unit is 10:1–18. The doubled statement shows its centrality; see Daniel M. Doriani, *Getting the Message* (Phillipsburg, N.J.: Presbyterian and Reformed, 1996), 160.

enough to lead us, protect us, and die for us. And he offers us the privilege of knowing him as well. *Application:* If God knows our flaws fully, yet loves us perfectly, we have assurance of salvation. Since God knows the worst and loves us anyway, we should cast aside fears of rejection and rest in his imperishable love. The doctrine of God's knowledge also liberates our prayer. God already knows our sins, so we can confess our sins to him openly. Plead confidently for a covering for their guilt and for release from their power.

Fourth, the good shepherd *lays down his life* for the sheep (10:17–18). Here Jesus' metaphor transcends lifelike comparisons. In truth, sheep exist only for the shepherd's benefit—to be shorn or eaten. To protect his livelihood, a shepherd might risk his life for his sheep, as David did when he killed wild beasts. But shepherds never *plan* to die; just the opposite, for if they do, they gain nothing and the defenseless flock is destroyed anyway. But Jesus' death was not the accidental result of facing brutes and losing. He chose to lay down his life for his sheep; he offered his life as a sacrifice for them (10:11, 17–18). That is, he made an atonement. The sheep were in mortal danger from the sins that merited eternal death. But our shepherd sacrificed his life and by that death saved them. Then he took up his life and *now* shepherds the flock again (10:17–18). Thus Jesus is designated the supremely good shepherd. He provides all for the sheep, whatever the cost. *Application:* Let us believe in Jesus who died in history that we might live in eternity.

All of this attracts us to Jesus. Observe that John's Greek term for "good" in "I am the good shepherd" is *kalos* rather than *agathos.* This term "represents, not the moral rectitude of goodness, nor its austerity, but its attractiveness," says William Temple, who continues: "We must not forget that our vocation is so to practice virtue that men are won to it; it is possible to be morally upright repulsively."[31] *Application:* Jesus' moral probity was winsome, adore-able, aesthetically pleasing, as our moral goodness should be.

So far, beyond urging readers to believe that Jesus is the good shepherd, the applications of John 10 have simply answered the question, "If this is true, what follows?" That approach has borne fruit, but it is unstructured enough to leave some looking for a plan. Beyond the checklists above, we can return to the four questions: What should I

31 William Temple, *Readings in St. John's Gospel* (London: Macmillan, 1947), 166.

do (duty)? Who should I be (character)? Where should we go (goals)? How can we see (vision)?

First, it is our *duty* to treasure the doctrine that Jesus, our good shepherd, leads and protects us. Second, the passage probes our *character*, to ascertain whether as an independent and putatively self-sufficient lot we will admit we need a shepherd and follow him. Third, our comments on hired hands set a *goal*. The paid staff of the Christian community must together resist the professionalization of ministry, lest we begin to think and act like hired hands rather than God's undershepherds. We aspire to build the kingdom, but we settle for petty fiefdoms. We want to serve the Lord, but get distracted by professional concerns—degrees, work schedules, salaries, recognition, and puffy résumés.[32] Fourth, it takes *discernment* to see the hand of the good shepherd in our life's course. Even the happiest among us may confess that their lives could be construed as a series of accidents that took them where they would never have chosen to go. If at college graduation someone told me I would be the academic dean at a midwestern seminary in two decades, I would have choked. I planned to be a philosopher, not a theologian, and certainly not an administrator! Yet the good shepherd leads where he wills. Our youthful aspirations matter, but few do precisely what we plan. Walking where the good shepherd leads, we flourish more than if a celestial genie had granted every wish.

In reviewing this section, three familiar points reappear. First, if we have patience, we again find a surfeit, not a deficit, of ideas. Second, we must dare to be boring by restating familiar points. When freshly observed, old points still have power to rekindle our admiration for Jesus. Third, some lessons are so obvious that it seems pedantic to state them. With them, the boundary between exposition and application remains blurry. But we could miss many other points if we failed to stop and meditate.

SUMMARY

It is customary to belittle the value of doctrine today, but Christian leaders know it is vital to join Christian doctrine and Christian

---

32 Superbly dissected by David Wells, *No Place for Truth* (Grand Rapids: Eerdmans, 1993), 218–57.

living. Sound doctrine edifies the church. We find the relevance of doctrine through processes more meditative than methodical. Still, there
are pathways for preachers who wish to rely on more than intuition:

1. If a study originates from a text, begin with thorough exegesis, establishing the contexts, the structure of the passage, and
   so forth. Get the precise message, then meditate on it.
2. If a study rises from a question people ask, we should turn first
   to the person and work of God as a most fruitful source of
   lessons for life, second to our knowledge of human nature, third
   to our knowledge of society.
3. Attempt to use the four motifs of practiced preachers: this is
   reality; these are the implications of reality; this is a perennial
   question; who needs this message?
4. Also use the common questions: Who needs this doctrine?
   What does it require? When and where do we incarnate it?
   How and why do we live it out?
5. To ensure diversity, use all four of the questions people ask,
   touching duty, character, goals, and discernment.
6. Finally, remember to address the whole person, head to heart
   to hands, reminding the audience of the grace that calls the
   audience to repentance, the love of the Father that makes
   them want to live in a way that pleases him, and the life of the
   God who remakes us in his image.

It will never be simple to apply doctrine, but if God has bestowed
at least a measure of the gifts that fuel meditation, and if the supple-
mental methods suggested in this chapter are added to it, we may hope
to move from the sense of a deficit to a surplus of potential applications.

10

A Plan for the Application
of Ethical Texts

FOUNDATIONS FOR APPLYING BIBLICAL LAW

Modern life stimulates numerous minor moral enigmas that make us sigh, "I wish the Bible addressed *that*." What does Scripture say about an American penal system that incarcerates nearly two million citizens, declaring that they must pay their debt to society—but not to their victims—by sitting in a cell block for several years? Does the Bible speak to blended families and the obligations these fathers and mothers have to children who bear no genetic relation to them? Does it address stop signs that are so superfluous that local drivers regularly run them at fifteen miles per hour? What do we owe accident-prone people, those who perpetually spill and break things, including their own bones? This chapter shows that the Bible answers more of these questions than we might think, if only we learn how to look in less-than-obvious places.

To progress, we must recall the earlier distinction between principles and rules. Principles are broad commands such as "Do not fret because of evil men" (Ps. 37:1, 7); "You shall not covet" (Ex. 20:17); "Do good to all people, especially to those who belong to the family of believers" (Gal. 6:10); "Trust in the LORD with all your heart and lean not on your own understanding" (Prov. 3:5); "Humble yourselves before the Lord and he will lift you up" (James 4:10). Though we must always exegete passages from which we teach, principles need meditation more than explanation. If someone struggles with pride, he needs to meditate, pray, wait on the Spirit, and consult a wise friend. Though there are matters to explain even with the simplest principles, exegesis is a lesser priority. In other words, we do not need much theory to help Christians overcome pride, covetousness, fretfulness, or discouragement. Prayer and godly counsel are paramount.

Rules, however, reward close exegetical scrutiny. Take Moses' law, "When you build a new house, make a parapet around your roof so that you may not bring the guilt of bloodshed on your house if someone falls from the roof" (Deut. 22:8). By skillfully following a few basic steps we can apply this rule to contemporary questions:

1. Use the principles of exegesis to determine the meaning for the first readers. Note the literary context, the cultural setting, the logic of the passage under consideration, and so on.
2. Evaluate the specificity and transferability of the command. Is it workable as it stands? If so, heed it. If not, find the principle behind the command and apply it to new situations.[1]
3. Answer the four questions people ask (chap. 5): What should we do? Who should we be? Where should we go? How can we see? Further, who most needs the command?
4. Use the rule to lead people to God. How does the command reflect the Father's character, the Son's work, or the Spirit's ministry? If the law exposes sin, lead people to repent and seek mercy in Jesus.

This process is familiar. But to refine it, we observe that laws can apply (1) identically, (2) analogously, and (3) typologically. The principle of honoring fathers and mothers applies *identically* from Moses to the present. Yet we must determine how to apply the ideal in our culture and phase of life. For instance, how do children honor their

1 See Jack Kuhatschek, *Taking the Guesswork out of Applying the Bible* (Downers Grove, Ill.: InterVarsity, 1990), 33ff.; Daniel M. Doriani, *Getting the Message* (Phillipsburg, N.J.: Presbyterian and Reformed, 1996), 144–46; William Klein, Craig Blomberg, and Robert Hubbard, *Introduction to Biblical Interpretation*, 407; John Goldingay, *Approaches to Old Testament Interpretation* (Downers Grove, Ill.: InterVarsity, 1981), 51–55.

parents when they are a thousand miles apart? When longevity brings debilitating diseases? The rule requiring an owner to slaughter an ox who has gored someone (Ex. 21:28–32) applies *analogously*. Bulls were the ancient equivalent of heavy machinery. Thus the law requires us to use machines and to plan manufacturing and farming so as to protect human life. Laws requiring animal sacrifices apply *typologically*. They point to something fairly dissimilar. The laws for temple sacrifices point to Jesus' one sacrifice.

These assessments may seem hasty, but experience and exegesis lie behind them. They say, first, that ideals, such as "Live at peace with all men," tend to apply identically. Second, rules relate to specific cultures, so that laws about bulls and meat that has been offered to idols (1 Cor. 10) usually apply analogously. Third, commands that have been abrogated or seem to conflict with other biblical instruction tend to be typological. We can also analyze commands according to their place in redemptive history. A command that is a creation norm probably applies identically. One that regulates sin may apply analogously.

The Rule about Parapets

These are only general guides. There is no substitute for slogging through some exegetical mud associated with contexts, syntax, lexicons, and analysis of a discourse or narrative. But let us make the theory complete by using our principles to analyze the law about parapets.

The steps leading to the contemporary significance of the regulation on parapets are clear. First, we determine the original sense. Because they worked, entertained, and even slept on their roofs, the Israelites readily understood why they had to place walls or parapets around them. In the heat, this kept Joshua, that reckless child, and Aunt Abishag, an overactive sleeper, from tumbling off the roof and wounding themselves. The law prevented the "guilt of bloodshed."

Second, we seek principles. Because Westerners rarely climb onto their roofs, we do not require parapets today. But we must determine the original principle and its transferability. The law incarnates love for neighbor and preserves life by requiring precautions that prevent accidental injuries. Thus, Moses authorizes safety regulations. We apply the principle most closely today when we install safety railings on flat roofs and place banisters by staircases. We extend the principle if we

install speed bumps in residential neighborhoods.[2] The rule for parapets shows that we may extend the sixth commandment by preserving life actively; we have not finished with it simply by refraining from
murder and anger.

Third, we answer the four questions. Our *duty* is clear, but the parapet law also requires *discernment.* We must see ourselves as our brother's keeper, even if he is reckless and should know better. Our *goal* is
a life-preserving environment for our community, even if it costs us,
because it fits our values and *character* to expend wealth to protect others, even if they are prone to bring troubles on themselves.

Fourth, this law leads us to God's goodness and grace. Our concern to preserve life echoes the character of the life-giving, life-
preserving Lord. Moreover, God's concern for foolish, reckless, and self-
damaging people is the source of our salvation. Without God's interest
in the kind of people who need parapets, *we* would be lost. This law
summons us to imitate his compassion for all who suffer from self-
inflicted wounds.

Restitution for Thievery

The case law on thievery is more complex, partly because it moves
us from personal ethics (prominent in the Decalog and the Sermon
on the Mount) to civil ethics and penal codes. It reads, "If a man steals
an ox or a sheep and slaughters it or sells it, he must pay back five head
of cattle for the ox and four sheep for the sheep. . . . If the stolen animal is found alive in his possession—whether ox or donkey or sheep—
he must pay back double" (Ex. 22:1, 4).

Following our four steps, we see first that the original meaning is
fairly clear, though we wonder why the punishment varies from one
animal and situation to the next. The norm, repeated in 22:7 and 22:9,
is that a thief must make double restitution to his victim.

Second, double restitution is our transferable principle, for it constitutes a perfectly just recompense. The thief returns the stolen animal together with one of his own, so that he loses precisely what his
victim would have lost, one animal. His victim, in turn, regains his animal and gains precisely what he would have lost, one animal.

2 John Goldingay, *Models for Interpretation of Scripture* (Grand Rapids: Eerdmans,
    1995), 92.

The increased punishment for sheep and oxen that have been sold or slaughtered is puzzling, until we consult the contrasting case of the thief who repents and returns the stolen animal before he is caught. He adds only a fifth of the value of the animal (Lev. 6:1–5; Num. 5:5–8). The lighter punishment apparently rewards his admission of sin. This especially contrasts with the thief who, by eating or selling the animal, gets rid of the evidence. So the basic idea is double restitution, with heavier penalties, apparently, to punish aggravated offenses and lighter ones to reward repentance. There are theories, but no one knows why the penalty for theft of oxen is stiffer than for sheep; small riddles abound in the law.[3] Still, we have several ideas that are relevant today:

- Theft is punished by restitution, not incarceration or maiming. The punishments suit the crimes.
- Restitution is made to the victim, not the state (not that the state is disinterested).
- The restitution imposes just punishment on the thief. It is neither harsh nor lax.
- Penitence demonstrated before the perpetrator is caught is rewarded.

The code had other features, stated elsewhere (Deut. 19:18–20; 25:1–3), that spill onto the margins of our text. Offenders should be punished but not degraded. Penalties are the same regardless of the offender's social rank. Retribution serves as a deterrent.[4]

Third, we consider the four questions: We have already listed our *duties.* The *goal* of the penal code as a whole is to promote holy covenant life in society, to purge evil from the land, to inculcate fear of evildoing. Exodus 22 also requires *discernment;* the purpose of penal law is not to make criminals suffer or get them off the street, but to seek justice in the land for victim and perpetrator alike. We should test our laws' goals against the Bible's. The law also tests our *character;*

---

3 Guesses abound. To survey options, see James Jordan, *The Law of the Covenant* (Tyler, Tex.: Institute for Christian Economics, 1984), 261–71; and Gary North, *Tools of Dominion* (Tyler, Tex.: Institute for Christian Economics, 1990), 519–25, 633–34.

4 Christopher J. H. Wright, *An Eye for an Eye: The Relevance of Old Testament Ethics* (Downers Grove, Ill.: InterVarsity, 1983), 165–66.

do we care about justice for both victim and perpetrator? Finally, are we willing to examine ourselves, not in order to judge the public thief without, but to detect the private larceny within?

Fourth, Exodus 22 leads us to God, reminding us that he is the just judge who requites evil. Sinners rightly fear his justice! Yet this law holds hints of mercy too. God acknowledges the penitent and will give them less than full justice. This is only a faint shadow of Christ, but it does suggest that justice and mercy can meet, that sin may not receive all that it deserves.[5]

PRINCIPLES AND RULES IN A CHRISTIAN ETHIC

If the last few pages have been successful, we have the sense of a plan. Yet we must refine our understanding of the relation between principles, which guide behavior without specifying particulars, and rules, which dictate actions in specific settings.

In determining the relation between principles, we begin with the relation between love and law. The double command of love for God and for neighbor is the foundational legal principle. The Law and the Prophets depend on love (Matt. 22:37–40), but love does not abrogate other commands, for there is no conflict between love and the law. Love, justice, and faithfulness are weightier than others, but we cannot neglect lighter ones, such as tithing (Matt. 23:23). *Love has primacy within the law, not over the law.* It is the greatest, but not the only command.[6] Love does outweigh Sabbath regulations (Matt. 12:1–8), but we do not pit love against the Sabbath, for the Sabbath, properly observed, expresses love for God and others. Love for neighbor and obedience to the law both argue for a day of rest and for freedom to meet human needs on the Sabbath. True love and true obedience are one. In love the commands cohere. Love is a disposition and motivation that impels lawful actions.[7]

The Decalog embodies the love command. We love God through

---

5 See Vern Poythress, *The Shadow of Christ in the Law of Moses* (Phillipsburg, N.J.: Presbyterian and Reformed, 1995).

6 See Douglas Moo, "Jesus and the Authority of the Mosaic Law," *Journal for the Study of the New Testament* 20 (1984): 3–11.

7 See John Murray, *Principles of Conduct* (Grand Rapids: Eerdmans, 1957), 22–26;

worship, love parents via honor, love spouses by fidelity. We love neighbors by respecting their property, by telling the truth to them and about them, and by willing their good rather than coveting their goods. The Decalog is "the heart of covenant law."[8] Connected to Sinai, it is "the binding charter expressing the will of the divine Lord of the Covenant."[9] It is oft repeated in the Pentateuch (Ex. 20:2–17; Deut. 5:6–21; Lev. 19), the prophets (Hos. 4:1–3; Jer. 7:9–11), the Psalms (50:16–21), the Gospels (Matt. 5:21–48; Luke 18:20), and the Epistles (Rom. 13:8–10; 1 Cor. 6:9–11; James 2:11).

The love command, the Decalog, and a handful of commands such as the *lex talionis* and the creation mandates for work, rest, marriage, and procreation, are policy statements for kingdom life.[10] They are clear, but difficult to incarnate. "You shall not bear false witness" (Ex. 20:16), but cannot silence at times amount to deception? "Give to everyone who asks you" (Luke 6:30), but cannot indulgence of feckless freeloaders harm both them and us? The right use of these principles requires insight.

A chief source of such insight is the specific commands called "rules." They supply inspired examples of the way to embody broad principles. *Rules incarnate, illustrate, and clarify principles.* The legal sections of the Mosaic code seem comprehensive at first, but closer inspection reveals them to be case laws that illustrate general principles.[11] These rules are culture-specific, making them hard to translate from one culture to another. Yet they supply the particularity, the detailed embodiment of biblical rules, that we need.

We must underscore the idea that principles and rules define and explicate one another. This assertion counters the critical allegation that the biblical ethic harbors inconsistencies that emerge when we compare foundational principles to secondary rules. For example,

---

J. I. Packer, "Situations and Principles," in *Law, Morality, and the Bible,* Bruce Kaye and Gordon Wenham (Downers Grove, Ill.: InterVarsity, 1978), 151–67.

8 Gordon Wenham, "Law and the Legal System in the Old Testament," in *Law, Morality, and the Bible,* 27–29; see also David Jones, *Biblical Christian Ethics* (Grand Rapids: Baker, 1994), 103–9.

9 J. J. Stamm and M. E. Andrew, *The Ten Commandments in Recent Research,* 2d ed. (London: SCM, 1967), 39.

10 Murray, *Principles of Conduct,* 27–44.

11 Klein, Blomberg, and Hubbard, *Introduction to Biblical Interpretation,* 278.

some play the love command (Matt. 22) against Jesus' denunciation of the Pharisees (Matt. 23).[12] But if Matthew's description of the Pharisees is even roughly accurate, then Jesus acts in love when he warns, "Do not do what they do" (23:3). This harmony of principles and rules also challenges situation ethicists and their cousins, who assert the supremacy of the love command and reduce rules to useful but optional advice. Rather, principles set the parameters for godly conduct, while rules specify the particulars that actualize them. Rules so incarnate Israel's moral ideals that they become paradigms for just law in other societies.[13]

In a way, this only restates the idea that Scripture interprets Scripture. It is not special pleading, as some say, for scholars who study any authoritative document assume, at least as an initial strategy, that it will be internally consistent. They expect the parts of *any* work to cohere and explicate each other.[14] The Bible should be no different.

We can see how principles and rules interpret each other by examining additional property laws. The eighth commandment (Ex. 20:15) forbids theft, but if someone thinks he fulfills the law simply by refraining from robbery, Exodus 22 corrects him. We have already seen that Exodus 22 opens by specifying punishments for theft. Yet the next several rules regulate accidental damage to a neighbor's property. They require restitution for destruction by fire, for grazing on someone else's land, and for injury to animals (22:5–6, 14–15). Thus we realize that "No stealing" entails "No damaging."

In language reminiscent of Exodus 22, Deuteronomy 22 devel-

---

12 See Stephen Barton, *The Spirituality of the Gospels* (Peabody, Mass.: Hendrickson, 1992), 30.

13 Wright, *Eye for an Eye,* 43.

14 Readers of the U. S. Constitution assume that one statement by an author interprets another. Suppose an American president lies under oath about a personal affair. Some argue that perjury is impeachable under the "high crimes and misdemeanors" clause of the Constitution. A debate ensues; is lying under oath about personal misdeeds a high crime or a misdemeanor? The opposing parties turn to the Federalist Papers, written by several of the authors of the Constitution. The Papers list bribery as grounds for impeachment. The debate then turns on the question: Is perjury about a personal affair analogous to bribery because both involve the miscarriage of justice? Or is it not, since bribery involves the use of public office for personal gain, whereas the lie hid only a personal misdeed? Wherever people finally stand, they use one passage to interpret the other.

ops "You shall not steal" yet further, adding, "If you see your brother's ox or sheep straying, do not ignore it but be sure to take it back to him" (22:1). While Exodus 22 forbids us to *cause* accidental damage, Deuteronomy 22 forbids us to *permit* accidental damage. Return a straying sheep, it says. If the owner lives at a distance, hold it for him (22:2). Ignore nothing that a brother loses (22:3). Finally, the property laws require Israelites to help actively, assisting the fallen donkey of a friend (22:4) or even of an enemy (Ex. 23:5)!

Clearly, then, the eighth commandment says more than "Do not purloin." We must not cause damage to the property of a neighbor, must not permit damage to his property, must guard against damage to the property of a friend or even an enemy. Thus, the eighth commandment does more than prohibit. God wants us to protect and restore whatever belongs to another. To put it another way, fifteen minutes after finishing this paragraph I went running and encountered a motorist stuck in snow and ice. I knew what I had to do.

Property rules show how principles and rules cohere as we explore the significance of "You shall not steal." The principle helps us comprehend alien-sounding rules about sheep, parapets, and such. But rules clarify the principle. They prove that a concern for the property of others in the concrete exigencies of life is part of God's will for us and part of the love we owe each other.

This suggests a strategy for occasions when ideals and rules appear to conflict. For example, in the debate over women's role in the church, feminists vitiate the rule "I do not permit a woman to teach or to have authority over a man" (1 Tim. 2:12) by playing it against the ideal, "There is neither . . . male nor female, for you are all one in Christ Jesus" (Gal. 3:28). Stressing the contrast between Timothy and Galatians, they argue that 1 Timothy has been misinterpreted, or that it is a temporary ruling, or, more invidiously, that it strays from the genius Paul displayed in Galatians.[15] They implicitly deny that 1 Timothy and Galatians 3 are mutually defining. Traditionalists, on the

---

15 For evangelical rejoinders, see Andreas Köstenberger, Thomas Schreiner, and H. Scott Baldwin, *Women in the Church: A Fresh Analysis of 1 Timothy 2:9–15* (Grand Rapids: Baker, 1995); John Piper and Wayne Grudem, *Recovering Biblical Manhood and Womanhood* (Wheaton, Ill.: Crossway, 1991). For perhaps the best biblical exposition of biblical feminism, see Craig Keener, *Paul, Women and Wives* (Peabody, Mass.: Hendrickson, 1992).

other hand, reason that male and female have equal value and soterical status in Christ, per Galatians, but that Timothy and other texts explain that men and women, while equal, still have differing roles in family and church.

SEVEN QUESTIONS FOR HARDER CASES

The last example reminds us that teachers face harder teachings than those regarding parapets and theft. Some (e.g., head coverings) are so vexing we tend to ignore them. We cannot settle every conundrum, but we can propose principles for approaching hard passages:[16]

1. Does the book itself limit the application of the teaching? Both Job and Ecclesiastes have teachings that the author portrays as flawed, as a foil to the intended lessons.
2. Does later revelation limit the scope of a teaching? For example, Romans 13 says submit to the state, but when Revelation 13 links the state with Satan and the Antichrist, we realize that simple obedience is sometimes impossible.
3. Does the passage present a broad moral principle or a specific manifestation of one? Compassion for the poor is a general principle, gleaning laws a particular manifestation.
4. Do cultural conditions make it appropriate to apply a teaching in new ways for new cultures? No passage that regulates slavery or polygamy or warfare applies as is. Since the significance of hairstyles and head coverings varies from culture to culture, we need to observe only the principles behind Paul's rules for hair in 1 Corinthians 11:2–16: we should not obliterate gender distinctions, should respect customs, and should avoid causing brothers and sisters to stumble.[17]
5. If a cultural form in the text still exists today, does it have the same significance it once did? In the West today, kissing means touching lips, male to female, typically in romantic settings. In biblical culture, kissing meant touching cheeks, male to male

---

16 This list adapts Klein, Blomberg, and Hubbard, *Introduction to Biblical Interpretation*, 409–19.

17 Keener, *Paul, Women and Wives*, 19–69.

or female to female. Therefore, we obey "Greet with a holy kiss" with handshakes or hugs.[18]

6. Is a law rooted in something permanent, such as the creation order, the character of God, the Decalog, or the plan of redemption? Or is it grounded in something temporary, such as the permission Moses gave Israel to divorce due to hardness of heart (Deut. 24)? Interpreters of Paul's prohibition of women as teachers divide here. Is it grounded in creation (1 Tim. 2:11–13), making it permanent? Or is it grounded in the fall (2:14), so that redemption may reverse it?

7. Is the command contrary to the standards of the day, part of a biblical protest against ungodly standards? If so, it is probably binding. We tend to think the *lex talionis* ("an eye for an eye") is passé, because it sounds vengeful. In fact, it forbids violent vengeance and ordains proportional punishment overseen by authorities. Because "an eye for an eye" challenges some standards of the day (especially in its protections for slaves), it is binding.[19]

Test Case 1: The Rebellious Son

Using these principles, we turn to the case of the rebellious son (Deut. 21:18–21):

> If a man has a stubborn and rebellious son who does not obey his father and mother and will not listen to them when they discipline him, his father and mother shall take hold of him and bring him to the elders . . . [and say], "This son of ours is stubborn and rebellious. He will not obey us. He is a profligate and a drunkard." Then all the men of his town shall stone him to death. You must purge the evil from among you. All Israel will hear of it and be afraid.

---

18 On kissing and gleaning, see Doriani, *Getting the Message,* 144–46, 148–49.

19 Yet it is not utterly different from other legal codes. See Umberto Cassuto, *A Commentary on the Book of Exodus,* trans. Israel Abrahams (Jerusalem: Magnes, 1967), 277–78; Victor P. Hamilton, *Handbook on the Pentateuch* (Grand Rapids: Baker, 1982), 219–20.

This unsettling text seems to exemplify the alleged cruelty of Old Testament law. Yet by interpreting in context, noting unique cultural conditions, seeking enduring principles, and factoring in later revelation, we find that it has important lessons for all ages.

Our interpretation begins with the context. Deuteronomy 21:15–17 protects the rights of firstborn sons by regulating a problem arising from polygamy. If a man has two wives and two sons, it says, the father must give the actual firstborn the double portion that is his right by law, even if he prefers the firstborn of the second marriage.

This law may seem utterly irrelevant today, but its comments on failed experiments with polygamy apply to our failed experiments with serial monogamy. In each case, children may suffer injustice or deprivation due to a father's second marriage. God's will is plain. Fathers may not give preferential treatment on the basis of emotional affinity. Capricious action is forbidden. Parents must show equity to their children.[20]

By extension, this law prohibits all favoritism. Sadly, parents do prefer one child over another. We favor children who are easier to raise, warmer, more like us. We prefer children who look better, who run or think faster, who carry our genes. But God protects children of any former marriage, and, by implication, all other children who are out of favor. The law says, "Treat them with justice." Today, justice means equal provision. The law of primogeniture, which forbade the division of family land into parcels so small as to cause destitution (if land was scarce, younger sons took other professions), passed off the scene with national Israel and its agrarian culture. Today, we practice equity by providing equal food, clothing, education, and love for all our children.[21]

---

20 This exposition is indebted to E. Bellefontaine, "Deuteronomy 21:18–21: Reviewing the Case of the Rebellious Son," *Journal for the Study of the Old Testament* 13 (1979): 13–31; Christopher J. H. Wright, *Eye for an Eye,* 165–68; idem, *Deuteronomy* (Peabody, Mass.: Hendrickson, 1996), 235–38; P. C. Craigie, *The Book of Deuteronomy* (Grand Rapids: Eerdmans, 1976), 283–85; P. D. Miller, *Deuteronomy* (Louisville: John Knox, 1990), 166–68.

21 Equal treatment is not necessarily identical treatment. Parents may spend more time and money on a child who has, for example, a learning disability. The goal is to provide what each child needs in order to thrive.

But children have responsibilities to parents just as parents do to children. Deuteronomy 21:18–21 presupposes a long process of discipline that has failed to reform a stubborn, rebellious son. He is known as a glutton and a drunkard and refuses to amend (21:20). He squanders the family substance. If the firstborn, he endangers the family's patrimony, including what belongs to his siblings. If he behaves this way in his youth, with no hope for amendment, what will follow? He is intolerable and incorrigible; he has repudiated parental authority and social decency.

In Israel, fathers did not have the right of life and death over their children, as they did in some cultures. Nor could a harsh father, by himself, charge his son. *Both* parents, having exhausted all efforts at discipline, had to feel compelled to summon the elders and prosecute the case against their son. The execution of the death penalty fell to the community (21:21), for the rebellion had become a civil matter. Society had an interest in family matters, if troubles were grave enough to threaten the community.

The death penalty is stark, but recall that under some circumstances violation of any command of the Decalog, save coveting, could lead to a death penalty.[22] The son has committed covenant crimes, violating God's laws. His rebellion against the fifth commandment bespeaks his "resistance to divine direction as mediated through parental authority and teaching."[23] Acts that threaten to bring judgment on the community must be purged (21:21).

Today, the death penalty for this type of crime is rescinded.[24] In the Old Testament world the penalty fit within a series of capital crimes, discussed in Deuteronomy, for which death was not necessarily "an eye for an eye." Instead the rationale for the capital sanction, in cases including aggravated sexual sin (22:20–24), kidnapping (24:7), false prophecy (13:5), and idolatry (17:2–7), was to "purge the evil" from the covenant community. But in the church we purge evil not by exe-

---

22 Only exceptional violations of the eighth and ninth commandments merited terminal punishment: man-stealing (Deut. 24:7) and false witness regarding a capital offense (Deut. 19:16–21).

23 Miller, *Deuteronomy,* 167–68.

24 See Tremper Longman, "God's Law and Mosaic Punishments Today," in *Theonomy: A Reformed Critique,* ed. William S. Barker and W. Robert Godfrey (Grand Rapids: Zondervan, 1990).

cution but by excommunication, which is akin to spiritual death (Matt. 18:15–18; 1 Cor. 5:1–8, which echoes the language of purging). So the statute appears to be passé. Further, it may never have been enacted in Israel; there is certainly no record that it was. But whether it was practiced or not, it serves as a lighthouse, warning children that the result of ultimate rebellion is death (see Prov. 15:10; 19:16).

The passage presents several important social principles:

1. Juvenile criminality is a serious matter, affecting the whole community.
2. Juvenile crime merits a strong response. Punishment can deter crime.
3. Christian parents need not face rebellion alone. They may call the church to assist with open rebellion. Excommunication, on rough parity with capital punishment, might be fitting.
4. Discipline is the responsibility of both parents. "This son of ours is stubborn and rebellious" shows both parents owning their child's offenses and seeking to remedy them.

Finally, as legal as this passage is, it reveals God to us. It manifests his justice, a justice that protects children from unloving parents and a justice that protects society from ungovernable children. This justice shows that the wage of sin is death. Yet even the law of the rebellious son hints at God's grace. We have all been guilty of rebellion. All could have become incorrigible. But the Lord does not repay us according to our iniquities (Ps. 103:10).

Test Case 2: Sex with a Betrothed Slave Woman

Our second test case comes from Leviticus 19:20–22:

> If a man sleeps with a woman who is a slave girl promised [betrothed] to another man but who has not been ransomed or given her freedom, there must be due punishment.[25] Yet they are not to be put to death, because she had not been freed. The man, however, must bring a ram . . . for a guilt offering

---

25 The translation is difficult. Literally, it reads, "there will be *biqqōret*." This could possibly mean "investigation" but more likely means the punishment that fol-

> to the LORD. With the . . . guilt offering the priest is to make
> atonement for him . . . and his sin will be forgiven.

This unusual law is alien enough to strike contemporary Western readers as sub-Christian.[26] Yet, like all of God's law, it merits study because of its authority.[27] The first step is to place this law in its social and canonical contexts.

Socially, we must distinguish slavery in Israel from slavery in America and in the Greco-Roman era. A discussion of slavery lies outside the purview of this book, but we must note that while Israel's slaves were poor (unlike some Greco-Roman slaves), they had legal rights and the guarantee of freedom lacking in other systems. Specifically, slavery lasted a maximum of six years, unless the slave *chose* lifelong service (Ex. 21:2–6; Deut. 15:12–18).[28] The law in Leviticus 19 assumes the institution of slavery, which was universal in antiquity and still exists in many parts of Asia and Africa.[29] Unlike cultic prostitution or child sacrifice, God did not prohibit slavery outright. Rather, as with polygamy and divorce, the law tolerated and regulated it, so as to remove its worst features. The law protected slaves and undermined essential features of the slave system. Contrary to other nations, Israel's masters did not have absolute control over the life or body of slaves. It was illegal to kill, seduce, rape, or maim them. If a master even

---

lows an investigation. By analogy with Ex. 22:16–17 and Deut. 22:28–29, which require financial payment for the seduction of a virgin, the punishment is probably a monetary payment. See Gordon Wenham, *The Book of Leviticus* (Grand Rapids: Eerdmans, 1979), 270–71.

26 Not unlike the law permitting usury with Gentiles (Deut. 23:19–20). For a survey of the interpretive options, see Robin Wakely, "ḥrp," in *New International Dictionary of Old Testament Theology and Exegesis,* ed. Willem A. VanGemeren, 5 vols. (Grand Rapids: Zondervan, 1997), 2:283–85.

27 Principles for studying difficult laws can be found in Goldingay, *Approaches,* 56–61; idem *Models,* 96–103.

28 On slavery in the ancient world, see S. S. Bartchy, "Slave, Slavery," in 1098–1102; and "Greco-Roman Slavery," in *Anchor Bible Dictionary,* ed. David Noel Freedman (New York: Doubleday, 1992), 6:58–73; James Jeffers, *The Greco-Roman World of the New Testament Era* (Downers Grove, Ill.: InterVarsity, 1999) *Dictionary of the Later New Testament and Its Development,* ed. Ralph P. Martin and Peter H. Davids (Downers Grove, Ill.: InterVarsity, 1997), 220–36.

29 Gary Haugen, *Good News about Injustice* (Downers Grove, Ill.: InterVarsity, 1999.

knocked out a slave's tooth, the slave went free (Ex. 21:26–27). Slaves enjoyed the Sabbath rest; they could not be oppressed (Ex. 20:10; 23:9). Ordinarily there was one code for slave and free, though there were a few exceptions (Ex. 21:20–21, and here), showing that slaves did have slightly lower legal standing.[30]

Canonically, Leviticus 19:20–22 is a variation of biblical law requiring death for adultery (Lev. 20:10).[31] More specifically, because a betrothed woman was for legal purposes considered already married (Matt. 1:19), sexual relations between a man and a free betrothed woman was a capital offense (Deut. 22:23–24).[32] Since Leviticus 19 sets a milder penalty for a sexual sin with a slave, the *result* seems merciful, because no one dies, but the *reasoning* offends. Does it imply that God places a lower value on the slave? Is Moses saying, "It's not so bad, she's only a slave"?

With contexts set, we can examine the law more closely. It says that an act that would be adultery if a woman were free is not adultery if she is a slave, even if she would soon be free. The law accentuates the legal significance of slavery. Since the woman is still a slave, she remains the property of her master. A slave cannot be a wife, only a concubine; hence adultery with her is impossible by definition. Yet there is an ambiguity. The woman is a slave, yet, because she is betrothed, free in principle.[33]

The ruling matches the marginal nature of the case. It is arguably a case of adultery, and arguably not; it is neither clearly adultery, nor clearly not adultery. The law prescribes a payment because there is a property violation. The slave woman has lost value (cf. Ex. 22:17). Yet the case is like adultery. God is offended; therefore there is a sacrifice. The law, accepting the existence of slavery, views the woman as prop-

---

30 On slavery in Israel, see Wright, *Eye for an Eye,* 175–82; Richard Bauckham, *The Bible in Politics* (Louisville: Westminster/John Knox, 1989), 105–11.

31 Historically, there are signs that adulteresses and prostitutes were punished by public stripping and shame rather than death. See Isa. 32:11; Ezek. 23:10–30; Hos. 2:3–10; Nah. 3:4–7.

32 Some commentators think the passage protects female slaves from violation by owners (e.g., R. K. Harrison, *Leviticus* [Downers Grove, Ill.: InterVarsity, 1980]. But since it does not mention force, it appears to regulate consensual acts.

33 Bauckham, *Bible in Politics,* 34; Jacob Milgrom, "The Betrothed Slave-Girl, Lev. 19:20–22," *Zeitschrift für die Alttestamentliche Wissenschaft* 89.1 (1977): 49.

erty, damaged by extramarital sex. But it also views her as a person. Therefore the sexual act violates covenant standards. Sins committed with or against slaves offend God.

This law seems strange, and wherever slavery has been abolished, it seems irrelevant, too. Yet it expresses several principles relevant for Israel and the church. First, it encourages us to distinguish between sins and crimes. At the civil level, the case in view is merely a property offense, one remedied by financial punishment (Lev. 19:20). But it also offends God, so the sinner must bring a guilt offering so a priest may atone for his sin (19:21–22). In fact, a sin may offend God even though it is liable to no civil penalty at all. An act can be perfectly legal and utterly immoral.

Second, this law suggests that sin creates marginal cases that strain the legal code. Improper acts such as this sexual sin force decisions that fully satisfy no one. Pastors must be ready to address hard questions just as God did through Moses. If we say that adultery and desertion are the two grounds for divorce, we should realize that sin-wrecked marriages will create hard questions. Does violence to a wife or children constitute grounds for divorce? Is it a form of desertion to so mistreat a spouse that she must leave to preserve her life? Desertion can be marginal, too. One can leave and return repeatedly. A spouse can retreat to another part of a home, with separate bed, board, and finances, for years. Sin creates marginal cases and hard decisions.[34]

Third, Leviticus 19 shows that the law starts where society is. It acknowledges that societies inevitably decline from God's ideals. Without accepting evil, the law may attempt to effect *social* change incrementally. With *personal* sin, on the other hand, we are responsible to put it off and clothe ourselves in righteousness at once. But we have limited control over others, over society. Therefore sometimes we must be content to change what we can, little by little.

The Law as Restraint of Sin

Many laws and institutions exist only to regulate or limit sin. Armies, judges, penal codes, and clothing all exist due to sin. In covering Adam and Eve, God both instituted clothing to remedy our

---

34 On the difficulty of marginal cases in the area of divorce, see Jones, *Biblical Christian Ethics,* 202–3.

shame and concupiscence and demonstrated his willingness to ame-
liorate sin.[35] Later, when God chose Israel, it was already a historical
entity habituated to sin; ignorance and lawlessness ruled. God then matured Israel incrementally. Some practices, such as polygamy and slavery, were neither condoned nor outlawed. Instead, the law regulated
and restricted them; and narratives portrayed them as causes of dis-
cord and trouble (Gen. 29–30; 1 Sam. 1; 1 Kings 11). Jesus concurs
when he interprets Moses' divorce regulation (Deut. 24; Matt. 19). Men
had divorced their wives freely in antiquity, to their detriment. Moses
restrained divorce by restricting a man's right to remarry a wife he
had divorced. But, because of Israel's hard hearts, he still permitted divorce on the vague grounds of "something indecent." That is, because
they could not yet tolerate God's ideal, their wickedness was restrained, but not eradicated. Figure 15 may help.

A similar situation holds for oaths. Pagans lied whenever it served
them. Moses restrained this by requiring Israel to take oaths in God's
name. But ideally, disciples are so truthful that the need for oaths disappears. Likewise, regarding vengeance, some pagans extracted whatever their strength allowed (Gen. 4:23–24). Moses then limited retribution to an eye for an eye (Ex. 21:22–25). But ideally, disciples turn
the other cheek to those who strike them (Matt. 5:38–42).

Thus, Moses' law supports the adage that civil laws compromise
between what is feasible and what is desirable. Sometimes the law only
regulates institutions such as slavery, leaving their abolition for another
day. While the world slowly comes under God's lordship, laws make
fallen institutions such as slavery operate "with as little injustice as is
possible."[36]

This is an important principle for social reform. We need both
patience and zeal, a reformer's passion and a wise man's restraint. What
can be changed varies from age to age. When it was impossible to abolish slavery, the Bible ameliorated it. Centuries later, the time came to
abolish it. As I write this, the abolition of abortion seems impossible.
Therefore, we seek to regulate it, curtail it, and stigmatize it. We educate and persuade, focusing on abortions executed in gruesome ways,
for the most despicable reasons (e.g., gender selection), but the goal

---

35 Murray, *Principles of Conduct,* 41–42.
36 Goldingay, *Approaches,* 59.

Fig. 15.
THE TOLERABLE AND THE IDEAL IN MATTHEW 5

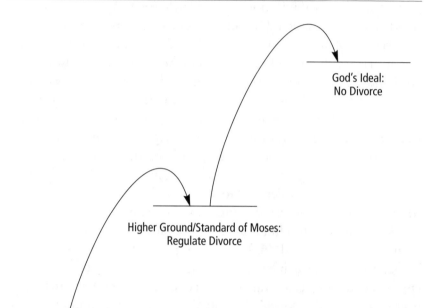

God's Ideal:
No Divorce

Higher Ground/Standard of Moses:
Regulate Divorce

Slough of Paganism:
Rampant Divorce

is always the abolition of abortion. Similarly, we cannot expect biblical standards for divorce to become national law tomorrow. But we can collaborate with anyone who opposes no-fault, autonomous divorce because of its devastating effects on women and children.

To recapitulate, sin complicates application of law by creating corrupt institutions and baffling cases where evil behavior is tolerated yet controlled. Here we learn that we cannot simply declaim moral absolutes from on high; we must engage the dirty cases. It is our *duty* to start where people are. It is our *goal* to eradicate evils incrementally. Finally, we must *discern* the time for frontal assaults on sin and the time when we can only restrain evils such as slavery and abortion.

Our engagement with hard cases leads us to Christ in two ways.

First, his incarnation models involvement in the grimy, complicated world of sinners. He engaged people where they were, yet held to his principles. Second, there is a sacrifice for those who get tangled up in sin. The guilt offerings of the Old Testament point to Christ's offer of himself to atone for our sin.

SUMMARY

We could profitably examine additional laws, but only at the expense of shifting from interpretation to Christian ethics. Instead, let us review our plan for applying laws. We have advocated four processes, expecting teachers to shift from one to another as they work. First, using normal exegesis, we determine the meaning for the first readers. Second, we find the principles in the original commands and consider how to transfer them to individuals, to church, and to society today. Third, we avoid soft legalism by asking what the law requires us to be (character), seek (goals), or see (discernment), not just what we ought to do (duty). Fourth, we lead hearers to God. This too has several aspects. We consider how a law reflects the person and work of God. After seeing how we fall short of the command, we remember repentance and Jesus' mercy. Finally, when we comprehend how intractable evil is, we also long for the return of Christ to purify all things.

11

Issues in Application of Ethical Texts

Do not accept a bribe (Ex. 23:8; Deut. 16:19; Prov. 17:23).

Honor your father and your mother (Ex. 20:12; Deut. 5:16; Matt. 15:4; Eph. 6:2).

Do not cook a young goat in its mother's milk (Ex. 23:19; 34:26; Deut. 14:21).

The mere act of listing these repeated commands conveys something of the task of applying biblical law. Some commands (prohibiting bribes) are so clear and specific that study and method seem superfluous. We simply obey. Others (honoring parents) are clear, but teachers may labor to apply them to specific challenges in parent-child relations. Finally, some (cooking goats) are so difficult that even seasoned scholars struggle with them.

THE CHALLENGES OF BIBLICAL LAW

However many laws we comprehend, questions still abound for the genre of law. First, what is the purpose of biblical law? The law cannot save, but how does it help believers grow in grace? How shall we reconcile biblical teachings that assert both the necessity and the impossibility of law-keeping? Is law a blessing or a curse? Moses led the people to pledge fidelity to the law (Ex. 24:1–8), yet predicted that Israel would disobey it. Paul says the law is holy, righteous, good, and spiritual (Rom. 7:12–14), yet declares that none can follow it. What then is the relation between the law's demands and our inability? What effect does this tension have on our teaching?

Second, even when we know a law still holds today, we face the challenge of filling out its principles. Moses says, "You shall not covet" (Ex. 20:17), but when does aspiration end and coveting begin? Paul says, "Fathers, do not exasperate your children; instead, bring them up in the training and instruction of the Lord" (Eph. 6:4), but there are times when our children will be displeased with our proper admonitions and exasperated that we do not let them have their foolish way.

Third, biblical guidance on many ethical quandaries is elusive. We do not expect Scripture to address nuclear armaments, the privileges and plagues of mobility, or a video culture where some men find their peak experience vicariously in the achievements of sports heroes. We might expect something on domestic violence, boredom, and substance abuse, but even here we gain insight only by extrapolating from biblical principles.

Fourth, how do we determine which laws we should obey literally to this day, which we should obey with adjustments, and which we should not observe at all, if we would honor God? Is there a method for finding equivalence between ancient and contemporary applications of law? To answer these questions effectively, we must first establish a theology of law.

A Theology of Law

Guidance, the Benefit of Biblical Law

The Bible shapes a believer's life in various ways. Biblical narratives show us how God acts and portray wise and foolish ways of responding to him. Biblical theology describes the world, enabling us to see it God's way and to act accordingly. Biblical law shapes behavior more directly, by commanding. Legal rules state what God requires in tightly defined situations. Legal principles promote life-shaping values such as love, holiness, justice, and faithfulness.

Narratives motivate us by describing the divine drama in which we live. But stories alone cannot provide sufficient resources for ethical growth or social change. They inspire change, but do not equip us to make the distinctions necessary for hard ethical decisions. Narratives carry the greatest ethical punch when we are already immersed in biblical values.[1] We need the story of the good Samaritan *and* the command, "Love your neighbor." We need "You shall not make an idol" *and* Isaiah's mockery of the woodcutter who builds a fire with one half of his wood and builds an idol with the other (Isa. 44:12–20).

The presence of law in Scripture shows that people need moral guidance. This seems obvious, but some theologians see it differently. They say that we are not changed by new rules or instruction but by a transformed imagination. "The deep places in our lives . . . are reached only by stories, by images, metaphors, and phrases that line out the world differently" and evoke transformed listening.[2] They say that we need metaphors, not mandates, and that Scripture is addressed "to our imagination rather than our obedience."[3] So preaching should feed the imagination. It should capture the heart through story rather than offering theology and moral admonition.[4] Further, some say the renewed heart and mind have an intuitive sense of what is right, so they spontaneously do what they should. More rhetorically, we hear, "What people need is more strength, not more advice," or "What Christians need is not more instruction but more motivation."

Well, yes and no. Yes, rules never change the heart. Yes, narratives

---

1 Richard Lischer, "The Limits of Story," *Interpretation* 38 (Jan. 1984): 35–36; see also Terry Eagleton, *Literary Theory* (Oxford: Blackwell, 1983), 207–9.

2 Walter Brueggemann, *Finally Comes the Poet* (Minneapolis: Fortress, 1989), 85–90, 109–10; see also John Goldingay, *Models for Interpretation of Scripture* (Grand Rapids: Eerdmans, 1995), 56–61, 89–90. Brueggemann admits that obedience begins with commands, but he considers them inferior. He says it hardly matters whether the Jubilee laws of Lev. 25 on the release of slaves were ever implemented or not. The important thing is "that Israel thought this provision, asserted it, hoped it" (p. 102). I wonder how many slaves would agree.

3 Paul Ricoeur, *Essays on Biblical Interpretation* (Philadelphia: Fortress, 1980), 117; see also *The Philosophy of Paul Ricoeur*, ed. Charles E. Reagan, and David Stewart (Boston: Beacon, 1978), 223–29, 239–45.

4 Books on preaching with this emphasis include Eugene L. Lowry, *The Homiletical Plot* (Atlanta: John Knox, 1980); Wayne Robinson, ed., *Journeys toward Narrative Preaching* (New York: Pilgrim, 1990); Richard L. Enslinger, *A New Hearing* (Nashville: Abingdon, 1987).

and parables reach the imagination in ways that law cannot. Yes, only the grace of God draws us to love and obey the holy God. Yes, it is grace, not law, that "teaches us to deny ungodliness and worldly passions, and to live self-controlled, upright and godly lives" (Titus 2:11–12, my translation). And yes, indirect approaches work; stories and analogies do move people to think, feel, and act God's way. As Nathan's rebuke of David shows, the indirect style can be effective with mature or resistant listeners (2 Sam. 12). One *can* preach an effective sermon without uttering commands.

Nonetheless, "We need strength, not advice" is a false dichotomy, spawned by the ingrown chattering of the cognitive religious crowd. *Theologians* may know all they need, but they are long habituated to biblical laws and ethics. Because they are immersed in biblical law, they are free to underestimate the law. *In theory,* Christians might only need to follow the Spirit's leading, but life refutes the theory. Not all Christians who want to obey know how to do it.[5] If a renewed mind were a sufficient guide to behavior, why does Paul still propound commands? Why does he say, "I am not free from God's law but am under Christ's law" (1 Cor. 9:21)? Christianity is not a new law, but Christianity has laws. Thus, *however sophisticated we are, there is a time to tell people what to do.* Whoever denies this is wiser than Moses, the prophets, Jesus, and the apostles, none of whom hesitated to command.

The ministry verifies this. Christians seek godly counsel on myriads of issues: How should they train their children? How should they respond to a boss whose directives walk a tortured boundary between legality and illegality? People want to know how to restore a fracturing marriage, how to break the power of bad habits, how to be more humble, tender, and forgiving. People with such questions are often highly motivated, but they need counsel to attain their goal. The irreligious need instruction too. Because God created and sustains all humanity, even those who deny him can profit by knowing his will.[6]

If a theologian thinks people need metaphors and not mandates,

---

5 Ibid., 214.

6 Prov. 31 includes an oracle from the mother of King Lemuel, who was apparently king of the Arab kingdom Massa. See Gen. 25:14; Richard Bauckham, *The Bible in Politics* (Louisville: Westminster/John Knox, 1989), 42; and C. G. Rasmussen, "Massa," in *International Standard Bible Encyclopedia,* ed. Geoffrey W. Bromiley, 4 vols. (Grand Rapids: Eerdmans, 1979–88), 3:277.

he ought to get out more often. Work on a construction crew and wit-ness the debasement of women. Play in a men's sports league and hear the obscenities. Sit in a park and watch mothers slap their children and utter preposterous threats about splitting heads and backsides. Once when I was getting my hair cut, such nonsense poured from the cut-ter and customer next to me that I heard myself say, "Actually, that's not true. You see . . ." Amazingly, they were all ears; they *wanted* guid-ance. Both Christian and non-Christian need instruction.[7]

Grace, the Source of Biblical Law

When God heard the groans of Israel in Egypt, he did not give them laws and say, "Here, obey these and I will deliver you." Rather, because God loved Israel, redeemed her from slavery, and promised her a land, Israel followed his commands (Deut. 4:32–40; 6:20–7:11). *After* the Lord achieved the exodus, the law followed, as Israel became a nation. Even the Decalog begins not with a law but with grace, "I am the LORD your God, who brought you out of Egypt, out of the land of slavery" (Ex. 20:2; see also 19:4–6). From the beginning law-keeping has been a response to God's prior action. We love because he first loved us (1 John 4:19). If redeeming grace *inaugurates* the covenant, the sin with the golden calf, while Israel was still at Sinai, teaches that forgiv-ing grace *sustains* the covenant (Ex. 32). From the start, the covenant depended on God's faithfulness, not Israel's success at law-keeping.

7 An older challenge to this view came from Bonhoeffer and Barth, who said the quest for universal moral principles is impracticable and unproductive. To treat biblical commands as rules for today or general moral truths is senseless. It makes a living word spoken in the past into a dead letter that destroys freedom and kills today. "There are no ethical directions in the New Testament which we should have or even could have taken over literally. The letter kills, the spirit gives life. . . . The Holy Spirit is only in the present, in ethical decision, and not in fixed moral precepts." Biblical commands spoke in the past, but we live before God today. Therefore it is "slavish and unfree" to obey old commands literally. It is impossible to erect "generally valid principles because each moment, lived in God's sight, can bring an unexpected decision." So wrote Dietrich Bonhoeffer, *No Rusty Swords,* ed. and trans. Edwin Robertson (New York: Harper & Row, 1965), 44–45. Karl Barth reserves special animus for casuistry. He says Scripture's con-crete commands are to particular men in particular situations. They cannot be relevant for our decisions today. See *Church Dogmatics* (Edinburgh: T. & T. Clark, 1957, 1961), II.2. 673–76, 684; III.4.11–17.

Legalism is pernicious, but we dare not equate law-keeping and legalism. It is evil to foist man-made laws on people or to teach that God's pleasure depends on our performance. But it is good to teach children their Father's will, for the law describes God's values and character. It reveals his design for the world and limns the way of flourishing. As the psalmist prays, "Be gracious to me through your law" (119:29). When both are rightly understood, there is no tension between living by grace and living by the law of Christ. Obedience never earns God's favor or contributes to redemption, but if we love God we heed his commands (John 14:15). As God told Moses, he gives us commands that it may "go well" with us; he gives them "for [our] own good" (Deut. 5:29; 10:13).

Love, the Goal of Biblical Law

Legalism is pernicious, but there is no tension between law and love because the law embodies love. By worshiping God, making no images, and honoring his name, we love God. By refraining from murder, theft, adultery, and false witness, we love people. Law-keeping does not frustrate love, it expresses it.[8]

Indeed, God's law makes love easier, not harder. By following it we overcome the greatest impediments to loving decisions—our ignorance and our selfishness. Our *ignorance* makes it impossible to calculate whether our actions will have good or evil effects. (One must be omniscient to determine the full effects of any act.) So we obey and leave the results to God. *Selfishness* leads us to choose whatever is most advantageous for us. In following the law, we forgo the calculations that can take a selfish turn and simply obey. (Yet there is a subordinate place for consideration of the effects of our actions.) So the law embodies love. Christians need the law's guidance to live in love.

Godliness, the Heart of Biblical Law

Some think of law as an alien force that foists an unwanted hegemony upon people. But the law comes from our Maker, not an alien. Its content, motives, and blessings deepen our relationship with God.[9]

8 J. I. Packer, "Situations and Principles," in *Law, Morality, and the Bible,* ed. Bruce Kaye and Gordon Wenham (Downers Grove, Ill.: InterVarsity, 1978), 153.
9 This section is indebted to Christopher J. H. Wright, *An Eye for an Eye* (Downers Grove, Ill.: InterVarsity, 1983), 21–31.

God's character, not abstract decrees, constitutes the content of moral living. We must be holy because he is holy (Lev. 11:44; 19:2), just as he is just (Deut. 16:19–20; 32:4), forgiving as he forgives (Eph. 4:32). We must love as he loves (1 John 4:7–11; Eph. 5:1), must serve because he came to serve (Matt. 20:28).

God's character drives the Decalog. We worship no gods before him because (1) he is the only God, (2) he is a jealous God, and (3) everything is "before him," that is, in his presence. We make no idols, no images of him, because all images misrepresent him. They are lifeless, powerless, and speechless, whereas he lives, acts, and speaks. We make no image because God has already fashioned an image of himself—man and woman. We think, feel, plan, speak, and act morally, as God does and as idols do not. We use God's name honorably, because his name reveals his nature and it is honorable.[10] We rest on the Sabbath because he rested (Gen. 2:2–3) and gives us rest (Heb. 4). The life-giving God says, "You shall not kill"; the faithful Lord says, "You shall not commit adultery"; the generous God forbids theft and coveting, and the truth-telling God forbids false witness.

Because God's actions express his character, those actions also serve as a basis for laws:

- We rest because he rested.
- We accept no bribe because he cannot be bribed.
- We sustain aliens, widows, and orphans because he sustains aliens, widows, and orphans (Deut. 10:17–19; Ps. 146:9).
- We hear the cry of the afflicted because he hears their groans (Ex. 6:5; Ps. 72:12).
- Israel supports her poor, lending them money and protecting them from slavery, because Israel was destitute when God redeemed her (Lev. 25:35–55; Ex. 22:22).
- Israel even petitions that its king act as God does: "Endow the king with your justice, O God." If the king is Godlike in his rule, he will judge justly, pity the weak, and deliver the afflicted (Ps. 72:1–4, 12–14).

So then, *to keep the law is to live as the image of God*. When we live the law, we express God's character and reflect his goodness. Then we know God and our truest self.

---

10 Consider, e.g., Jesus' "I am" statements; chap. 9, pp. 234–35.

Blessing, the Result of Biblical Law

Because we violate it, the law has the unintended effect of threatening judgment (Deut. 28:15–68). But in itself law is good. God designed it "to demonstrate and safeguard the distinctiveness of . . . Yahweh's covenant people."[11] It promotes justice and mercy. It protects from the miseries of sin. After all, drunkards get hangovers and liars suffer distrust (Prov. 5:21–23). By his laws God tells us, "I come here to present myself to you as your guide and savior. I want to govern you. You are like my little family. And if you are satisfied with my word, I will be your King."[12] Psalms 1, 19, and 119 praise the law of God in the context of this loving, covenantal relationship. Therefore, Israel hopes for a day when the law is obeyed, when it is written on the heart, but not for a day when there is no law.[13]

Biblical law is theocentric. "It presupposes God's initiative in grace and redemption; it is framed by what he has done and will do in history; it is shaped by his character and action; and it is motivated by personal experience of God's love for his people."[14] So let us guard against legalism and remember the grace motivation for obedience, but never disdain the law of God.

THE USE OF BIBLICAL LAW

This paean to biblical law may correct our attitude toward it, but hard questions remain. First among them is the use of Mosaic law. Some thinkers adopt categories that can, in effect, divide the law into relevant and irrelevant sections. This we must resist, even if it comes indirectly via useful categories such as "the three uses of the law" or "the moral, civil, and ceremonial law."

Three Uses of the Law?

One path for organizing the law distinguishes three uses or functions of the law. The first use is the restraint of sin. The law restrains

---

11 John Goldingay, *Approaches to Old Testament Interpretation* (Downers Grove, Ill.: InterVarsity, 1981), 44.

12 John Calvin, *John Calvin's Sermons on the Ten Commandments*, ed. and trans. Benjamin Farley (Grand Rapids: Baker, 1980), 39, 45. See also Calvin, *Institute of the Christian Religion* (Philadelphia: Westminster, 1960), 2.8.1–15.

13 Goldingay, *Approaches*, 47.

14 Wright, *Eye for an Eye*, 31.

sin by threatening punishments, whether civil or spiritual, for harmful acts (Ex. 20:18–20; Deut. 5:29). The fear of God should restrain cruelty to the disabled (Lev. 19:14) and exploitation of the poor (Lev. 25:17, 36, 43). In this sense, the law is for sinners (1 Tim. 1:9–10).

The second use is to lead to Christ. That is, the law identifies and brands sin, so we see our misdeeds as wickedness that estranges us from God. By labeling certain acts sin, the law heightens our consciousness of it, until we seek mercy in Christ (Rom. 2:17–3:20; Gal. 2:15–3:25).

The third use is to provide moral guidance. A few theologians deny this use, but most agree that the law reveals God's moral will for believers and guides us in it.[15] To receive guidance we must heed the law's prohibitions and discover the positive purpose of each commandment. That is, the law promotes the opposite of what it forbids. For example, "You shall not kill" also means "Preserve life," and "You shall not covet" means "Be thankful and contented."

De Facto Neglect of Some Laws

The greatest challenge is to determine which Old Testament laws to follow literally, which to adapt on the basis of underlying principles, and which to view as fulfilled or superseded. Consider our haphazard-looking response to certain laws from Deuteronomy 22–25:

1. "When you build a new house, make a parapet around your roof [lest someone fall]" (22:8).
2. "Do not wear clothes of wool and linen woven together" (22:11).
3. "You may charge a foreigner interest, but not a brother Israelite" (23:19–20).
4. "If you make a vow to the LORD your God, do not be slow to pay it" (23:21–23).

---

15 Luther stressed the two negative uses of the law and seemed at times to deny that Christians are bound by Old Testament law, including the Decalog. Yet his catechisms contain expositions of the Ten Commandments. Calvin affirmed the third use of the law unequivocally, calling it the "proper purpose" of the law (*Institutes,* 2.7.12). See D. F. Wright, "The Ethical Use of the Old Testament in Luther and Calvin: A Comparison," *Scottish Journal of Theology* 36 (1983): 463–85; Donald Bloesch, *Freedom for Obedience: Evangelical Ethics in Contemporary Times* (New York: Harper and Row, 1987), 108–13, 126–38.

5. "Do not have differing weights in your bag—one heavy, one light. . . . You must have accurate and honest weights and measures" (25:13–16).

Of these five, we adapt (1) and (5), take (4) literally, but expand it to cover promises, and essentially disregard (2) and (3).

The problem recurs in the New Testament. In 1 Corinthians 11–12, Paul commands women to cover their heads (11:5–10), forbids gluttony at the Lord's table (11:20–22), and urges all to use their gifts for the common good (12:7–11). We pay scant attention to the first and second laws, but insist on the third. Why?

The problem is most acute with the Mosaic law. What theologians call the moral law—traditionally viewed as the Decalog and the bedrock principles of justice, mercy, and faithfulness (Matt. 23:23)—clearly remains in force. It rests on the character of God and epitomizes the covenant way of life. The prophets, Jesus, and the apostles all restate blocks of it (Jer. 7:9–10; Matt. 5:21–48; 15:19; Rom. 2:21–24; 1 Tim. 1:8–11).

Just as clearly, others laws do not remain in force. Jesus implicitly abrogates food laws (Mark 7:14–23, esp. 19), and Acts explicitly rescinds them (Acts 10:9–15).[16] Hebrews declares portions of the law obsolete. The regulations for the Levitical priesthood have been set aside because they are weak and useless (7:11, 18). The gifts and sacrifices prescribed for the tabernacle "are only a matter of food and drink and various ceremonial washings—external regulations applying until the time of the new order" (9:9–10). They are "only a shadow of the good things that are coming—not the realities themselves" (10:1). Therefore, to continue them, after Christ's sacrifice, would be detrimental, for it would obscure the final character of his work (10:2–18). Likewise, Paul says the practice of circumcision, once a prominent command in the law, no longer matters (1 Cor. 7:18–19).

In the New Testament, in 1 Corinthians again, we see that some laws hold in nonliteral ways. Paul could use the law literally, as he did

16 Mark's terse editorial aside in 7:19b—*katharizōn panta ta brōmata*—literally, "cleansing all foods," is translated expansively in most English versions. In the New International Version, "In saying this, Jesus declared all foods 'clean.' " In the Revised Standard, "Thus he declared all foods clean." In the New Living Bible, "By saying this, he showed that every kind of food is acceptable."

in 5:13 when he argued for the excommunication of an immoral brother with a literal use of the dictum, "Expel the wicked man from among you" (Deut. 17:7; 19:19; 21:21). In 1 Corinthians 9:9–10, Paul, citing the law "Do not muzzle an ox while it is treading out the grain" (Deut. 25:4), determines that apostles may receive payment for their labors. When he adds, "Oxen are not a concern to God, are they?" (my translation), we see that Paul has stretched analogy to its limits.[17] Somewhat similarly, Paul in 1 Corinthians 8:46 extrapolates from Moses' first commandment to resolve a social/spiritual question: "May Christians eat meat that has been offered to idols?" There is but one God; therefore sacrifices to other gods are nonevents (Deut. 4:39; 6:4–5).[18] We conclude that Scripture itself shows that some portions of the law should no longer be enacted, some should be obeyed literally, and some follow analogically.

Still, pastors must explain our interpretive decisions or we lose credibility when we insist on obedience to one command but ignore another. Moses and Paul accept both slavery and male headship in the home. In our culture, people will certainly ask why we abrogate one and perpetuate the other. That is, we know that we sometimes owe literal obedience, sometimes analogical obedience, and sometimes none (when a law is fulfilled in Christ), but we need principles to determine and explain which is which.

The Moral, Civil, and Ceremonial Law?

One solution to this problem is to sort out the authority levels of the law through the categories of moral, civil, and ceremonial law.[19] By this system, the *moral* law is the eternal, permanently binding

---

17   Gordon Fee, *The First Epistle to the Corinthians* (Grand Rapids: Eerdmans, 1987), 406–8.

18   Frank Thielman, "Law," in *Dictionary of Paul and His Letters,* ed. Gerald F. Hawthorne and Ralph P. Martin (Downers Grove, Ill.: InterVarsity, 1993), 535; N. T. Wright, *The Climax of the Covenant: Christ and the Law in Pauline Thought* (Edinburgh: T. & T. Clark, 1991), 120–36.

19   Origen spoke of ceremonial laws, and Augustine distinguished moral and "symbolical" precepts, but Aquinas apparently coined the three-part formulation. See his *Summa Theologia,* vol. 29, *The Old Law,* trans. David Bourke and Arthur Littledale (New York: McGraw-Hill, 1969), question 99, pp. 31–45; cf. David Jones, *Biblical Christian Ethics* (Grand Rapids: Baker, 1994), 111.

account of our duty to God and others. It consists of the Decalog and key principles such as love, justice, mercy, and faithfulness. It commands us to worship God and love other people. Scripture certainly sets apart the Decalog. God delivered it first (Ex. 20:1–17). It comes, uniquely, from his mouth.[20]

Scripture also distinguishes the Decalog from judicial or *civil* laws collected in the book of the covenant and applied to life in Canaan (Ex. 20:18–23:19). For example, the law develops the sixth command (murder, 20:13) by a series of laws listing penalties for bodily injury or accidental death (21:12–36). It expands the eighth command (theft, 20:15) by naming penalties for specific property offenses (22:1–15). Further, Deuteronomy's repeated phrase "in the land" suggests that the decrees God added to the Decalog show how to experience blessing in the land he gave Israel to possess (Deut. 4:12–14; 5:22–33; 6:1). The Westminster Confession of Faith (19.4) helpfully explains that God gave Israel the civil law "as a body politick." Its "judicial laws . . . expired" when Israel ceased to be a nation-state. They oblige us no "further than the general equity thereof may require." So the laws concerning land use, debt, slavery, war, and the judicial system embodied the principles of love, equity, and justice for Israel. We must heed the principles of its civil laws and learn from the way Moses' law fleshed out the principles in Israel's civil code. But, as we have seen, we need not literally obey every law.

The *ceremonial* law regulates worship, the priesthood, tabernacle, sacrifices, and other symbols that prefigure Christ's work. Jesus' redemption fulfilled this aspect of the Mosaic law. The holiness code, with its regulations for food, clothing, and disease, is also part of the ceremonial law, designed to purify Israel by separating it from the nations. Since Pentecost, separation from the nations is not a kingdom goal, so the holiness code is obsolete. Still, we seek its spiritual significance. As Augustine said, to wear a garment of wool and linen together (Lev. 19:19) "is not a sin now. But . . . to wish to combine

---

20 "The torah plainly distinguishes the Ten Commandments from the rest of the law in . . . the following ways: They have priority through the chronology of revelation, through the manner of revelation, and through their unrestricted extension"—Bruce Waltke, "Dispensational and Covenant Theologies," in *Theonomy: A Reformed Critique,* ed. William S. Barker and W. Robert Godfrey (Grand Rapids: Zondervan, 1990), 71–72.

opposite modes of life . . . is always sin." Again, "There is no harm in joining an ox with an ass where it is required [Deut. 22:10]. But to put a wise man and a fool together . . . cannot be done without causing offence."[21]

Besides these biblical warrants, the classification of moral, civil, and ceremonial laws has pedagogical benefits. To untrained readers, the law of Moses appears to jumble pertinent and impertinent, timeless and antiquated decrees together. The categories of moral, civil, and ceremonial law help readers organize the material. The classification also has polemical value. When Faustus the Manichean attacked the church for its failure to heed Mosaic laws that he stripped from their context, then ridiculed, Augustine replied that one must distinguish moral and symbolic precepts. The "symbolical precepts" are, he said, no longer binding since they prefigure "the things now revealed."[22]

Despite these advantages, the moral, civil, and ceremonial distinction has drawbacks as well. First, this division does not always assist interpretation. If we encounter a law that relieves poverty, we gain little by labeling it a civil law.

Second, the categorization jars with Scripture's habit of interspersing all three classes of law. For example, Leviticus 19 has moral laws about idols, theft, lying, and love of neighbors (19:4, 11, 18) beside civil laws demanding justice for the poor and the alien (19:15, 34). It intersperses moral laws of kindness to the infirm and aged (19:14, 32) with ceremonial laws forbidding tattoos and cutting the body (19:19, 28).[23] (Those who would seize on the law against tattoos should note that it follows one forbidding the trimming of beards [19:28].)

Third, the threefold schema obscures legitimate genre categories, such as the distinction between apodictic and casuistic law. Apodictic laws promulgate unconditional directives. They read, "You shall . . ." or "You shall not . . . ," or "Do" and "Do not," and often have divine blessings or curses attached. Casuistic laws, or "case laws" (see chap. 6, pp. 128–30), have an

21 Augustine, "Reply to Faustus the Manichean," in *Nicene and Post-Nicene Fathers,* vol. 4, ed. Philip Schaff (Grand Rapids: Eerdmans, 1989), book 6.9, p. 173.
22 Ibid., 10.2, p. 177.
23 For analysis of Old Testament law with comparisons to other ancient Middle Eastern legal codes, see Dale Patrick, *Old Testament Law* (Atlanta: John Knox, 1985), and J. N. Walton, *Ancient Israelite Literature in its Cultural Context* (Grand Rapids: Zondervan, 1989), 69–92.

"if, then" structure: "If someone does X, then society does Y." Case laws sometimes manifest exegetically significant characteristics, which skilled teachers watch: they may come in topical clusters; they can be very culturally specific; they often mention penalties.

Fourth, it is misleading to label one set of laws the moral law, since all laws express God's moral character. Further, even the Decalog (the moral law) has commands pertaining to ceremonial worship (commands two and four) and civil justice (six, eight, and nine).

Finally, the moral-civil-ceremonial schema hinders our ability to see the Mosaic law as Israel did. For Israel, the law was simply the God-given, comprehensive authority for each sphere of life, for family and society, for work and worship.

WRIGHT'S VIEW OF LAW

Christopher Wright's work on Old Testament law represents a group of scholars who seek approaches that reflect the character of Scripture and facilitate interpretation.[24] Wright urges that we locate laws in their redemptive-historical epoch: creation, fall, redemption, or new creation.[25] Thus, since *creation,* humankind has had laws for marriage and procreation (family law), for work and rest (economic law). The *fall* brought new conditions and laws, many of which exist only due to sin. For example, after the fall God clothed Adam and Eve. His action had the force of an ordinance (Ex. 20:26; 28:42–43), making clothing the first member of a fraternity—including divorce, slavery, oath-taking, the penal code, and warfare codes—as institutions that are necessary only due to sin.[26] *Redemption* brings the example of Christ and laws which promote Christian holiness and community (Matt. 20:28; Eph. 4:32). The *new creation* supplies a new perspective (not new laws), an irrepressible optimism based not on a naive trust in human goodness or progress, but on the certainty that God will complete his victory.

This approach encourages thematic studies that trace the devel-

24   Christopher J. H. Wright, *Walking in the Ways of the Lord* (Downers Grove, Ill.: InterVarsity, 1995); *Eye for an Eye* (1983); and *God's People in God's Land: Family, Land and Property in the Old Testament* (Grand Rapids: Eerdmans, 1990).

25   This paragraph follows Wright, *Walking in the Ways,* 14–21. See also Geerhardus Vos, *Biblical Theology* (Grand Rapids: Eerdmans, 1948).

26   John Murray, *Principles of Conduct* (Grand Rapids: Eerdmans, 1957), 41–43.

opment of biblical ethics on complex topics such as government, property, or marriage.[27] More important, by grounding law in God's redemptive plan it promotes a biblical holism. Wright says that the exodus gave Israel a fourfold freedom: politically, from the tyranny of oppressive power; socially, from the murderous disruption of their family life; economically, from the burden of slave labor; spiritually, from ignorance of God to covenantal knowledge and worship of him.[28] Jesus' work is comprehensive too, though he eschewed overtly political or economic activity. Politically, he pacified animosities by making disciples of every nation. Socially, he restored lepers, tax collectors, and sinners to public life. Economically, he liberated humans from Mammon. Spiritually, he atoned for sin and bestowed eternal life. If God has redeemed us from such a complete bondage, we will expect his law to guide us as individuals and a society in a complete restoration.

Taking the law as a whole, Wright considers how it shaped Israel into a paradigmatic society, "the kind of society God wants." That is, God redeemed Israel, in part, to order their social life "to make visible his moral requirements on the rest of the nations." As Israel lived in "freedom, justice, love and compassion . . . they would function as God's priesthood among the nations."[29] As Moses says, he taught Israel God's decrees, so that as she follows them, she "will show [her] wisdom and understanding to the nations who will . . . say, 'Surely this . . . is a wise and understanding people,'" blessed "to have their gods near them . . . [and] to have such righteous decrees" (Deut. 4:5–8).

In regarding Israel as a paradigm for other nations and eras, we seek the goals or effects of Israel's laws for every sphere of life. When we read a law, therefore, we do not ask if it is moral, hence binding, or civil, hence passé. We ask how an Israelite would view this law, how it would shape his society, and how it can shape ours.

Wright proposes that Israel's society-shaping laws can be placed in five classes: civil, family, cultic, criminal, and charitable law.[30] But he ultimately minimizes classification, arguing that all categories interpenetrate: Civil laws have criminal sanctions. Charity laws overlap with

---

27 Wright, *Walking in the Ways*, 22–23, 181–96.
28 Ibid., 18.
29 Wright, *Walking in the Ways*, 24, 33–34; *Eye for an Eye*, 40–45.
30 Wright, *Eye for an Eye*, 151–59. Patrick (*Old Testament Law*, 21–24) wants to

cultic law, for they express devotion to the God who loves the poor. Civil and familial laws support one another, since both promote marriage and the nurture of children.

Therefore, the question "What class of law is this?" fades and another rises: "How would this law shape Israel as a society that serves as a light for every other society?" This question assumes that all law is relevant. It encourages us to ask, "What principles do these laws embody? How can we express them in our culture?" rather than "Are these laws in a category that still holds or not?"

To recapitulate, we have seen that the moral-civil-ceremonial schema for the law has heuristic and apologetic value. But it can undermine the relevance of the law by exaggerating the line between various types of law. Instead of dividing the law, we see that all types of law promote devotion to God and his righteousness. For example, ceremonial laws govern worship, which is also a moral act. Again, civil laws embody the Decalog, which states the moral law. Rigid categories can also have the unintended effect of devaluing all but the moral law, especially when a law seems odd or archaic. Instead of devaluing some laws, we affirm that every law expresses God's moral nature and will, so that it bears careful reading.

Changes in culture and in the status of national Israel mean we cannot obey every law literally, but we must find and reapply the principles in every law. Because Wright's five categories of civil, family, cultic, criminal, and charitable law are more detailed, they may improve upon the traditional triad. But this matters more: since the line between classes of laws is blurry, what counts is patient interpretation, not classification. God's law for Israel is a paradigm of a blessed relation with God and humankind. For that reason, we should try to apply every law today. This implies that all laws retain some form of authority.

THE AUTHORITY OF BIBLICAL LAW

Law's Authority in the Old and New Covenants

No one disputes the authority of the law in the Pentateuch, but it is also prominent in the rest of Scripture. The historical books use

---

multiply categories along form-critical lines. Walton (*Ancient Israelite Literature*, 78) says major elements of biblical law defy established categories.

law to evaluate individuals and nations. They illustrate the blessings of obedience (Ruth) and the misery of disobedience (Judg. 17–21; 2 Kings 17), though they admit that faithfulness may also bring trouble (2 Kings 18–19). The prophets charge the people with disobeying the covenant, urge repentance, and threaten judgment on the impenitent. Wisdom writers extol the law, meditate on it, and develop its principles. They also lament rebellion, lampoon disobedience, and bless the obedient.

The status of law in the new covenant is more complex. First, Jesus could be construed as a critic of the law. He seemed to violate the Sabbath and associate with the wrong people: with women, children, and sinners. He appeared to criticize the law when he quoted Moses, saying, "You have heard that it was said. . . . But I tell you . . ." He also seemed to repeal laws concerning divorce, oaths, and food (Matt. 5:31–37; Mark 7:1–19). Paul sounds a similar note when he says the law leads us to Christ (Gal. 3), who has freed us from the impossible task of fulfilling the law (Rom. 7).

In Paul's parlance, the church is no longer *under* the law, beholden to obey every prescription or suffer the consequences (Rom. 6:14–15; 1 Cor. 9:20; Gal. 4:5; 5:18). Yet the church is not *without* the law (Rom. 3:31; 1 Cor. 9:21), which is holy, righteous, and good (Rom. 7:12, 14). Therefore, Jesus, Paul, and James remind listeners of laws suited to situations at hand (Matt. 19:17–18; Eph. 4:28; 6:2–3; James 2:11). Paul regards a capacity to fulfill the law as a benefit obtained by Christ and bestowed by the Spirit (Rom. 8:2–4). Thus disciples still uphold the law and meet its basic concerns (Rom. 3:31; 13:8–10). So Christ is the end of the law (Rom. 10:4), but not the end of commanding.[31] Jesus agrees. He came to fulfill the law by correcting abuses of it, by obeying it, and by teaching his disciples its true meaning (Matt. 5–7).[32]

The whole Bible declares that the proper home of law is the covenant, where God redeems his people and they respond in loving obedience. Because the law facilitated covenant life, ancient Israelites viewed it as a joy and delight (Ps. 19). But because the law was en-

---

31 Goldingay, *Approaches*, 48.
32 Commands are concentrated in Matthew and Luke, with about fifty in Matt. 5–7 alone. See Stephen Barton, *Spirituality of the Four Gospels* (Peabody, Mass.: Hendrickson, 1992), 15ff.

crusted with man-made traditions and viewed, by some, as a means of salvation, the New Testament is wary of legalism. Yet both covenants uphold the law's goodness and authority.

Law's Authority in Its Fulfilled Commands

All laws reveal God's nature and bear his authority, but some of them no longer bind us to obedience. We reverently *study* the laws for priestly sacrifice, but we do not *obey* them, for Christ fulfilled them. Jesus implied and Peter declared that all foods are clean (Mark 7:1–19; Acts 10, 15), because Jesus fulfilled the holiness code that separated Israel from the nations. Now, uncleanness is a trait of people, not things. Evil flows out of the heart. Defilement characterizes what goes out of us, not what comes into us.[33] In the old covenant, the unclean contaminated the clean, but now the clean pass their holiness to the unclean (Matt. 8:1–4). Bad company still corrupts good morals (1 Cor. 15:33), but Jesus' practice of welcoming sinners is an authoritative custom (Matt. 9:10; Luke 15:1–2; see also Acts 10–11; 1 Cor. 5:9–11). Therefore, laws designed to separate Israel from the nations no longer bind as they once did.[34]

Since no texts come labeled "holiness code" or "ceremonial law," we eye them one by one, humbly. No one knows what some rules mean. Does "Do not cook a young goat in its mother's milk" mean "Do not participate in Canaanite fertility rites" or "Do not be cruel to animals"? It is hard to be sure. But few laws are so difficult. For example, the purpose of the odd-sounding laws against planting fields with two types of seeds or wearing clothing of two materials is clear. They promote separation, hence holiness (Lev. 19:19; Deut. 22:9–11). God prohibits mixing to show that we must separate what he separates. "As God separated Israel from among the nations to be his possession, so they must maintain their holy identity by not intermarry-

---

33 Graham Stanton, *Jesus and the Gospels* (Oxford: Oxford University Press, 1989), 244; C. S. Mann, *Mark* (Garden City, N.J.: Doubleday, 1986), 316; R. P. Booth, *Jesus and the Laws of Purity* (Sheffield: JSOT, 1986), 202–6; cf. John Pilch, "Understanding Biblical Healing: Selecting the Appropriate Model," *Biblical Theology Bulletin* 18 (April 1988): 65–66.

34 C. E. B. Cranfield, *The Gospel according to Saint Mark* (Cambridge: Cambridge University Press, 1959), 244–45; Robert Guelich, *Mark 1–8:26* (Dallas: Word, 1989), 370, 380.

ing with the nations."[35] The division between clean and unclean animals mirrors the division of clean and unclean persons. Every choice of holy food reminds us of God's holiness and the need to be holy from the kitchen outward.[36]

Because all law is authoritative, we explore it all. We rarely find exact answers to contemporary questions in ancient laws. Yet even rules about wandering beasts and seduced virgins expose us to the moral world of Scripture, if we have skill and time to find it. As Winslow Homer once said, "What they call talent is nothing but the capacity for doing continuous hard work in the right way."

SUMMARY

This chapter develops an earlier claim (chap. 6) that Christians can present duties and give concrete guidance without descending into legalism. Whereas narrative reaches the imagination and doctrine shapes the mind, law addresses the will, with principles that govern the sweep of life and with rules that govern many of its specifics. In telling us how to live, the law inescapably presents our sin, which we can describe as the gap between our aspirations and our capacity or as the chasm between God's holiness and our unrighteousness.

In itself, the law is good. It provides guidance. Further, the law never simply says, "Do as God says" or "Be as God is." Before God gave the law, he redeemed Israel. Before Jesus gave commands, he called disciples to himself. Thus God's desire for a filial relationship with us causes him to reveal his will to us. The law spells out the way of love between God and humanity and between one person and another. The law describes God's nature. By obeying it, we conform ourselves to him, achieve our identity, and find his blessing.

35 Gordon Wenham, *The Book of Leviticus* (Grand Rapids: Eerdmans, 1979), 269; John Hartley, *Leviticus* (Dallas: Word, 1992), 318, 323.
36 Christopher J. H. Wright, *Deuteronomy* (Peabody, Mass.: Hendrickson, 1996), 182.

12

Christ-Centered Application

I cannot forget the Sunday night when, at twenty-one, I spoke in the church pastored by my future father-in-law. In a quest to reform my own speech, I had found dozens of verses on the topic of speech, strung them together, and slung them at the congregation for thirty minutes. I sat down, flush with excitement over all the good commands I had presented. But when my father-in-law stood up before closing the service, he said more than a little about Jesus' mercy for those who misuse words. I began to protest silently, thinking, "All this talk of Jesus' mercy is undercutting my message. He's making it sound as if we don't really need to keep the law."

I was thinking as (what I now call) a "class-four legalist." Class-one legalists are autosoterists; they declare what one must do in order to *obtain* God's favor or salvation. The rich young ruler was a class-one legalist. Class-two legalists declare what good deeds or spiritual disciplines one must perform to *retain* God's favor and salvation. Class-three legalists love the law so much they create new laws, laws not found in Scripture, and require submission to them. The Pharisees, who built fences around the law, were class-three legalists. Class-four legalists avoid these gross errors, but they so accentuate obedience to the law of God that other ideas shrivel up. They reason, "God has redeemed us at the cost of his Son's life. Now he demands our service in return. He has given us his Spirit and a new nature and has stated his will. With these resources, we obey his law in gratitude for our redemption. This is our duty to God." In an important way this is true, but class-four legalists dwell on the law of God until they forget the love of God. Worshiping, delighting in, communing with, and conforming to God are forgotten.

Class-four legalists can preach sermons in which every sentence is true, while the whole is oppressive. It is oppressive to proclaim Christ as the Lawgiver to whom we owe a vast debt, as if we must somehow repay him—repay God!—for his gifts to us. I count myself a member of the legion of recovering class-four legalists. We slide into a "Just Do It" mentality occasionally, dispensing commands just because they are right. We need to review this book's remedies for class-four legalists.

A REVIEW OF GOD-CENTERED APPLICATION

Reviewing Prior Chapters

The first chapter argued that the aim of Bible application is to enable people to know God and conform themselves to him. Each portion of Scripture leads us to personal knowledge of the Triune God. Once we know God, he begins to remake us in his image, especially his moral image. This was God's original purpose in Eden, his renewed goal at Sinai, and the goal of the Gospels and Epistles.

Chapter 2 showed that loving God and responding to him especially mean responding to Christ by believing in, listening to, imitating, and following him. There is an unmistakable egocentricity to Jesus. He is the definitive interpreter of the law: "You have heard that it was said, but *I* say to you." Moreover, he invites those who cannot keep the law to turn to him for aid and mercy (Matt. 11:25–30). He insists that prophecy spoke of him, especially his death and resurrection. He says he surpassed the ministries of Israel's leaders. He is greater than Abraham, for he is eternal (John 8:53–58), greater than Jacob, because he is the gateway between heaven and earth (John 1:51; Gen. 28:12). He surpasses Moses because he inaugurates a covenant of grace and truth and offers true bread from heaven (John 1:17; 6:32–35). He surpasses Solomon in wisdom that attracts the nations (Matt. 12:42). Jesus also completes old-covenant institutions. He is greater than the temple, for he is the very presence of God (Matt. 12:6). He is the final priest, giving access to God (Heb. 7–10). He is the great prophet (Luke 7:16, 26), the great king (Matt. 21:41–46), the final judge (Matt. 25:31–46), the wisdom of God (Luke 7:31–35). In his "Have you not read" questions, he critiques any reading of the Old Testament that fails to see him there.

Chapter 3 demanded the highest conduct of teachers, arguing that their quest for holiness both makes them better interpreters and makes people more willing to trust them. "Who is sufficient for these things?" we asked. But we saw that the demand and the offer of perfection meet. God first gives us righteousness, then requires it. We strive only to be worthy of the gift we have received. We seize righteousness because God first seized us. God solves the problem of his infinite demand with the gift of his infinite succor.

Chapters 4–6 pointed to God in two ways. First, they explored and corrected our tendency to think application equals finding laws and telling people to obey them. Rules and ideals are just two of the avenues to application; we also have doctrines, narratives describing redemptive and exemplary acts, images, songs and prayers. Second, and more important, while duty ("What shall I do?") is one of the four foci of application, we stressed the primacy of character ("Who shall I be?"). However completely we know our duties, we can perform only according to our capacity. But capacity is a gift of God, as he progressively remakes those who, by faith, are united to him and participate in his character. That is, he sanctifies us by grace as surely as he justifies us by grace through faith.

Chapters 7 and 8 promoted a theocentric reading of biblical narrative. We proposed that preachers identify the central act of God in a narrative, then observe the way the characters respond to him. We find the main point at either the climax/resolution nexus of a drama or in the remarks following it. The theocentric theme—the way God shows his character and redemption—leads to the primary application. Next, the responses to God lead to secondary applications. The disciples, foes, and neutral bystanders who long ago saw God act, responded to him roughly as believers, unbelievers, and bystanders do to this day. Thus their responses can be exemplary or cautionary.

I suspect that a fear of tedium, a fear of making the same few points about God every week, is one root of moralistic uses of biblical narrative. For this reason, we explored the diverse themes evident in biblical miracles. Old-covenant miracles show that Yahweh is Lord and God, that he is the compassionate and saving God who restores all things and yet takes interest in the needs of his people, so summoning them and all peoples to faith in him. With the necessary changes, all this holds for Jesus' miracles and the miracles the Spirit accomplished through the apostles in Acts.

Chapters 4 and 9 proposed a formula for applying doctrine: "If doctrine X is true, what follows?" Like narrative, doctrine is theocentric. Soteriology recounts God's work of redemption, hamartiology indicates our need of Christ, and so on. No doctrinal truth obtains in isolation from Jesus.

Chapters 10 and 11 show that even the law instills personal knowledge of God. The Decalog reveals God's character to us, for every law flows from his person. We worship no gods before him because (1) he is the only God, and (2) everything is "before him," that is, in his presence. We make no graven images of him, because all images misrepresent him. They are lifeless, powerless, and speechless, whereas he lives, acts, and speaks. We use God's name honorably, because his name reveals his honorable nature. We rest on the Sabbath because he rested (Gen. 2:2–3) and gives us rest (Heb. 4). The life-giving God says, "You shall not kill"; the faithful Lord says, "You shall not commit adultery"; the generous God forbids theft and coveting, and the truth-telling God forbids false witness. Thus, to keep the law is to live as the image of God, reflecting his character.

Because God's actions express his character, they supply the basis for some laws. We accept no bribe because he is not bribed. We sustain aliens, widows, and orphans because he sustains them (Deut. 10:17–19; Ps. 146:9). We hear the cry of the afflicted because he hears their cry (Ex. 6:5; Ps. 72:12). The penal code reveals God's nature too; the law requires restitution for theft because God, the just judge, requites evil.

But the law reveals God's grace and mercy too. The prologue to the Decalog reads, "I am the LORD your God, who brought you out of Egypt," and soon after the epilogue God himself installs a system of sacrifice to atone for our violations of the law, a system that points to Jesus' perfect sacrifice.

Reviewing Our Convictions

In promoting the God-centered, Christ-centered reading of Scripture, I join a swelling wave that promotes Christ-centered living. Christians are learning to articulate and to live out their once inchoate desire to savor grace daily. In theological language, we are beginning to understand that God's grace in sanctification is as sweet and necessary as his grace in justification.

In addition, half-subliminally, through case studies where exegesis precedes application, this book has promoted *exegetical* preaching. New Testament professors are expected to write books that rest on exegesis, but our agenda counters a tidal wave of topical, anthropocentric preaching in the evangelical world. Surveying hundreds of sermons published in prestigious preaching journals in the 1980s and early 1990s, David Wells concluded that the content and organization of the sermons were determined by the Bible text under consideration just 24.5 percent of the time, and that just 19.5 percent "related in any way to the nature, character and will of God."[1] Recent books on homiletics, so rarely promoting exegetical preaching, verify Wells's analysis. Topical, seeker-oriented preaching is in the ascent.

Of course, preaching must meet needs, must answer the questions people ask (chaps. 5–6), but a departure from exegesis has consequences. I will mention two. First, topics such as suffering for Christ or self-denial or hell, topics that are biblical but fail to meet "felt needs," tend to disappear. The teaching on hell, for example, is less refuted than ignored, not so much falsified as missing.[2] Generally, we have lost interest in proclaiming what Paul calls the whole counsel of God (Acts 20:27), seeking instead to meet the whole catalogue of human need.

Second, topical preaching may excel at *engaging* listeners through gripping descriptions of our problems and questions, but it often falters at *instructing* them. Topical preaching is prone to sameness and flatness. A few dozen subjects arise again and again, and preachers recycle the same solutions over and over. Even if pastors shun the ultimate crime of propagating falsehood, they flirt with the penultimate crime of making faith seem boring.

---

1 David Wells, *No Place for Truth* (Grand Rapids: Eerdmans, 1993), 251–53.
2 The disappearance of hell is a topic in itself. See Martin Marty, "Hell Disappeared. No One Noticed. A Civic Argument," *Harvard Theological Review* 78 (1985): 381–98. Theologians debate the issue, but exegesis is not always given its due. For critique, see D. A. Carson, *The Gagging of God*, 515ff.; Robert Peterson and Edward Fudge, *Two Views of Hell: A Biblical and Theological Dialogue* (Downers Grove, Ill.: InterVarsity 2000).

THE BIBLE'S MANIFOLD TESTIMONY TO GOD'S REDEMPTION

The tendency to homogenize the proclamation of repentance and faith, particularly by attraction to Pauline theology, deserves additional attention. I do not criticize Paul, of course. Rather, I want to advance the exegetical thrust of this work by affirming that every book of Scripture has its distinct voice and testimony to God. To focus just on the New Testament, we should discover the unique contributions that each gospel, that Acts, that each Pauline epistle, that Hebrews, James, Peter, John, Jude, and Revelation make to the faith. A century ago, a scholar said, "The Christianity of to-day is broadly speaking the Christianity of St. Paul."[3] This still holds. Paul dominates Christian theology, perhaps shaping the Christian mind even more than the Gospels do. This is not unreasonable since he wrote thirteen books, several of which lend themselves to systematic Christian theology.

But we must let the individual voices of every book speak if they are "to articulate a word that may contravene our own values and desires. Otherwise we may succumb to the temptation of flipping to a cross-reference to neutralize the force of any particularly challenging passage."[4] Important as Paul is, other authors present complementary perspectives on the faith. Paul's theology, shaped as it is by his work as an evangelist of the Gentiles and by their questions and needs, stresses justification and reconciliation to God by faith, not works. But Hebrews, written for readers steeped in Scripture, develops the high-priestly ministry of Christ. It also calls Jesus our hero, our trailblazer, who defeated Satan in single combat, delivering us from the fear of death and bringing us into the family of God (2:10–15). Revelation presents Jesus as warrior, the rider of a white horse who wages war with Satan and his allies and conquers them. Because he achieved victory over the beasts, the dragon, and the harlot, he receives worship and comforts the afflicted church, spurring her to endure to the end.

---

3   A. H. McNeil, *New Testament Teaching in Light of St. Paul's* (New York: Macmillan, 1923), vii ff.
4   Richard B. Hays, *The Moral Vision of the New Testament* (New York: HarperCollins, 1996), 188. Curiously, Hays's survey omits Hebrews, James, and Peter!

This riff on Hebrews and Revelation could lead to a survey of every book's testimony to God. But that would require another book.[5] Instead, we will present a few basic convictions, then offer sample studies examining the distinct testimonies to God's salvation in Samuel and James.

The biblical theology movement, associated with authors such as Geerhardus Vos, Sidney Greidanus, and Edmund Clowney, provides the foundation for God-centered preaching. This movement stresses the organic unity of God's covenantal, saving relations with humanity. Working first with Adam and the human race, then with Israel, from Abraham through Moses, David, and the prophets, God progressively revealed his plan of redemption. Each epoch of redemption has its distinct character, yet all tell the story of a race that rebelled against its Maker, who accomplished a great deliverance.[6]

A promissory structure unites the parts. God pledged the coming of one who would crush the serpent (Gen. 3:15), one through whom Abraham would bless the nations (Gen. 12:1–3), and who would sit on David's throne forever (2 Sam. 7:8–29). The goal of the promises is, "You will be my people, and I will be your God" (Jer. 11:4; 30:22; Ezek. 36:28; Ex. 6:7). Because the old covenant emphasizes faith in Israel's God and loyalty to him, because it contains only shadows of the Son, God-centered preaching from it will not always mention Christ by name. Yet each epoch of the old covenant moves toward its completion in Jesus the Messiah.

I stand with the classic understanding that the promise of one who would crush the head of the serpent (Gen. 3:15) constitutes the first promise of a Redeemer, who appears much later. In Exodus, God's

---

5 See the survey in Daniel Doriani, *Getting the Message* (Phillipsburg, N.J.: Presbyterian and Reformed, 1996), 174–84.

6 Geerhardus Vos, *Biblical Theology* (Grand Rapids: Eerdmans, 1948). For discussions of unity within the Old Testament, see Walter Eichrodt, *Theology of the Old Testament*, 2 vols. (Westminster: Philadelphia, 1961, 1967); Gerhard von Rad, *Old Testament Theology*, 2 vols. (New York: Harper, 1962, 1965). For unity in the New Testament, see C. H. Dodd, *The Apostolic Preaching and Its Developments* (London: Hodder & Stoughton, 1936); J. D. G. Dunn, *Unity and Diversity in the New Testament* (Philadelphia: Westminster, 1977); Leohnard Goppelt, *Theology of the New Testament*, 2 vols. (Grand Rapids: Eerdmans, 1981–82); John Reumann, *Variety and Unity in the New Testament* (Oxford: Oxford University Press, 1990).

redeeming grace *inaugurates* the covenant. After the sin with the golden calf, while Israel is still at Sinai, his forgiving grace *sustains* the covenant. Thus the covenant depends on God's faithfulness, not Israel's law-keeping (Ex. 32). The sacrificial system, from Exodus and Leviticus, shows the deadly consequences of sin and makes us yearn for a sacrifice to atone for sin once for all (Heb. 7–10). Certain psalms burst the banks of Old Testament expectations in ways that point to an eternal deliverer. Psalm 45, while praising a king of Israel on his wedding day for his strength in battle (45:9–11), exceeds the limits of praise for any king: "Your throne, O God, will last for ever and ever" (v. 6). So some psalms describe a regal deliverer whose greatness exceeds what mortals possess. Similarly, the Spirit moved the prophets to foretell future deliverance in terms that transcended any old-covenant event or deliverer. The apostles see these as prophecies of the Christ (1 Peter 1:10–12).

Of course, the testimony of many books defies misconstrual. Matthew wrote his gospel so that the church could make disciples of the nations (Matt. 28:18–20). John wrote so people might believe that Jesus is the Christ and have life in his name (John 20:31). Luke recounted the ministry of Jesus to strengthen his readers' faith and prepare them to preach forgiveness in Jesus' name (Luke 1:1–4; 24:46–49). Paul wrote Romans to share his gospel and produce fruit among Rome's churches (Rom. 1:8–15; 16:25).

Our goal, then, is to preach Christ in ways that honor the vision, the genius, of each author, instead of making leaps to Paul that annul that vision. To sample studies of harder books we now turn.

Case Study 1: Samuel's Testimony to God

In proclaiming Samuel, it is possible to present a call to faith that, while valid in itself, virtually ignores the thought patterns of the writer:

1. Saul and David were both sinners.
2. We are sinners, too. We commit sins like the ones they committed.
3. Jesus died on the cross for sins like theirs and ours.
4. We must repent, and trust in Christ who died and rose for our sins.

These assertions are true, but they hardly express, in Samuel's language, the goal of knowing God and conforming ourselves to him. The terminology and logic, while inspired and edifying, are Paul's. By jumping from the prophet to the apostle in this way, we miss the genius of Samuel's unique call to faith. By repeating the error, we may fall into the crime of repeating the gospel so routinely and predictably that it becomes tiresome.

Samuel's summons to faith in God turns on its place in redemptive history. Judges ends with a double lament and condemnation of Israel's miserable response to the theocracy: "In those days there was no king in Israel; every man did what was right in his own eyes" (Judg. 17:6; 21:25 RSV). But would a king remedy Israel's rebellion? Not if they requested—and got—a king "such as all the other nations have" (1 Sam. 8:5, 20). Israel's first king, Saul, was indeed like the kings of the nations: physically impressive, bold and magnanimous at times, but lawless and self-promoting to the core, contra Deuteronomy 17. Saul nearly presided over Israel's destruction (1 Sam. 31).

But God prepared David, the man after God's own heart (1 Sam. 13:14), to succeed Saul and led him to defend the nation even during Saul's reign (1 Sam. 17; 23:1–5; 2 Sam. 5:2). David was Israel's shepherd-king, strong yet merciful, zealous for God (2 Sam. 9; Ps. 69:9). His passion for God proved itself after his anointing, in the battle with Goliath, and after his coronation, when he brought the tabernacle to Jerusalem as his first regal act (2 Sam. 6). No wonder David became the measure for all kings who followed him. Yet, in one outburst of sin, this best king broke all ten commands.[7] He did so deliberately, callously, from a public position, and despite lack of need. His sin initiated a chain of events that plagued the nation with civil war. Only God's mercy spared David and Israel (2 Sam. 12:2–13). If even the best king so needed God's mercy, lest he die for his sin, if ruin threatened the nation even at its apex, then no earthly king or kingdom can suffice.

Thus the Psalms twice declare, "Do not put your trust in princes,

---

7 He coveted Bathsheba, lied to Uriah, stole another man's wife, committed adultery and murder, and shamed his parents. He followed another god, making his desires into an idol, and remained impenitent for a year of Sabbaths.

in mortal men, who cannot save" (Ps. 146:3; cf. 118:9). Though the psalm is not Davidic, the sentiment is not alien to him. True, David twice asked, "Who may ascend the hill of the LORD? Who may stand in his holy place?" and twice answered, "He who has clean hands and a pure heart" (Ps. 24:3–4; 15:1–5). Yet David twice hymns another gift, "Blessed is he whose transgressions are forgiven, whose sins are covered. Blessed is the man whose sin the LORD does not count against him" (Ps. 32:1–2; 51:1–9).

The whole canon echoes this, but 1 and 2 Samuel have a distinct voice. They call for a king who can lead Israel into holiness and covenant fidelity. Saul and especially David seem poised to fulfill that hope initially, yet both fail. Today we know that not even a king after God's own heart (David, 1 Sam. 13:14), not even a supremely wise king (Solomon, 1 Kings 3:9–12), would fulfill the hope for a truly good king. But the history-writing prophets had begun to cry out for a deliverer whose kingdom would endure forever (2 Sam. 7:12–29; Isa. 9:6–7; 11:1–4; Jer. 23:5–6; Pss. 2, 110). So, Samuel ultimately replies to Judges' plea for a righteous king by promising a future son of David. He will build God's house and establish the throne of his kingdom forever (2 Sam. 7:12–13). This initially refers to Solomon, of course, but Solomon ultimately proved as disappointing as Saul and David (1 Kings 1–11).

Samuel calls for a king with the love for God David had, but with the holiness David lacked. Israel needed a king with David's passion for God, but with an ability to control other passions. They needed a king with courage to face God's foes in battle, but with the ability to defeat Satan, not just his representatives. In short, 1 and 2 Samuel constantly turn their first readers' thoughts to God's mercy and deliverance. Thus 1 and 2 Samuel lead us past Saul, Samuel, and David to the Lord himself. In new-covenant terms, we see what was then obscure, that the promise of *a* son of David who would establish the kingdom is fulfilled in *the* Son of David, who inaugurated the kingdom and established it forever.

Thus the leap from Samuel to Paul (Saul and David were both sinners; we commit sins like theirs; Jesus died on the cross for such sins; we must believe in him) is true but impoverishing. It washes out roads to God and stultifies the mind by repeating a few Pauline themes and ignoring other ways to the gospel.

Case Study 2: James

No book's witness to Christ is more misunderstood than James's. Luther called it an "epistle of straw" because it does not mention the cross, atonement, or justification by faith. To this day, many biblical scholars neglect or dismiss James because of its apparent lack of doctrinal content and alleged contradiction of Paul.[8] Yet James enjoys high regard among ordinary Christians. "Its call to realize professed ideals in appropriate action has spoken with prophetic urgency to generations of readers who have found James's directives difficult to perform rather than to understand."[9] Paradoxically, James's stringent demands sustain its popular appeal.

The testimony of James: Jesus is Lord. James names Jesus only twice, but his presence suffuses the epistle, which constantly restates his teaching. James honors "our Lord Jesus Christ" (1:1; 2:1) who will come again as judge (5:7–8), who heals the sick (5:13–16), who expresses his lordship through his royal law (2:8). James restates the teaching of Jesus, especially from the Sermon on the Mount.[10] He says that moth and rust destroy riches (James 5:2–3; Matt. 6:19), that we should take no oaths (James 5:12; Matt. 5:33–37) and judge not (James 4:11–12; Matt. 7:1–5). James also says, "Love your neighbor" (James 2:8; Matt. 22:39), "rejoice" in trials (James 1:2; Matt. 5:11–12),

8   Martin Luther, *Table Talk,* trans. Theodore G. Tappert, in *Luther's Works* (Philadelphia: Fortress, 1967), 424–25. Luther expresses four main objections to James, repeated to this day. For detail, see Werner Georg Kümmel, *Introduction to the New Testament,* trans. Howard Clark Kee (Nashville: Abingdon, 1976), 403–16; and Martin Dibelius, *James,* rev. H. Greeven, trans. Michael A. Williams (Philadelphia: Fortress, 1920, 1976). The extreme brevity of the treatment of James by Bart Ehrman in *The New Testament: A Historical Introduction to the Early Christian Writings* (New York: Oxford University Press, 1997), 384–85, is itself a statement.

9   Luke Timothy Johnson, *The Letter of James* (New York: Doubleday, 1995), 3. Johnson has a positive appraisal, as do, e.g., Raymond Brown, *An Introduction to the New Testament* (New York: Anchor Doubleday, 1996); Donald Guthrie, *New Testament Introduction,* 4th ed. (Downers Grove, Ill.: InterVarsity, 1990); Donald Carson, Douglas Moo, and Leon Morris, *An Introduction to the New Testament* (Grand Rapids: Zondervan, 1992), 410–17.

10 Peter Davids, *Commentary on James* (Grand Rapids: Eerdmans, 1982), 47–48; Johnson, *James,* 55–57; Brown, *Introduction,* 734–36; Guthrie, *Introduction,* 729–31.

and "ask God" for good gifts (James 1:5; Matt. 7:7). He says we should do the word (James 1:22; Matt. 7:24–27), keep the whole law (James 2:10; Matt. 5:19), and guard every word (James 3:2; Matt. 12:36–37). He says profession of faith must lead to action (James 2:14–26; Matt. 7:21–23), and that we cannot please two friends or masters (James 4:4; Matt. 6:24). So James immerses his readers in the teaching of Jesus, the Lord.

The gospel of James: repentance and humility. In the past, scholars accused James of stringing ethical sayings together without structure or logic, but most now acknowledge that James used the conventions of ancient rhetoric to structure his epistle.[11] James 1:26–27 initiates his sustained summons to true faith, declaring that those who have true religion (1) control the tongue, (2) look after widows and orphans, and (3) remain unpolluted by the world. James structured the rest of his epistle to develop this triad. First, genuine believers care for the needy, giving them respect (2:1–13) and rendering assistance (2:14–26). Second, true faith controls the tongue (3:1–12). Third, true wisdom spares disciples from pollution by the world (3:13–5:6).

This structure is widely recognized. Still, readers puzzle over James's decision to open the body of his epistle with the apparently minor, tangential issue of favoritism in the church. But, with subversive wisdom, James uses favoritism both to initiate the discussion of the three tests of true religion and to intimate that his readers will fail them all. Thus he foreshadows his gospel, a gospel of repentance and humility before God.

Specifically, James forbids the church to favor the rich over the poor by giving the rich better seats (2:1–7). James begins with this minor issue, because minor issues best reveal the heart. Jesus remembers and judges even our casual words and deeds (Matt. 12:33–37; 25:31–46) because they proceed from the heart. The apparent insignif-

---

11   "The entire document lacks continuity in thought." It is "paraenesis," that is, "a text which strings together admonition of general ethical content," creating a work that is eclectic and inconsistent—Dibelius, *James*, 2–11. But see the rebuttals in Johnson, *James*, 11–15; Davids, *James*, 22–28; and Duane F. Watson, "James 2 in Light of Greco-Roman Schemes of Argumentation," *New Testament Studies* 39 (1993); 94–121; and "The Rhetoric of James 3:1–12 and a Classical Pattern of Argumentation," *Novum Testamentum* 35 (1993): 48–64.

icance of favoritism deepens James's lesson. Further, favoritism illustrates all three aspects of true religion. (1) True religion helps the poor, but favoritism harms them by demeaning them (2:5–6). At least in the church, rich and poor should be equal in status and dignity, for all are sinners and all are the image of God. But favoritism denies the poor this equity. (2) Favoritism is worldly. It rejects God's valuations and strives for the favor of the rich (2:4–5). (3) Favoritism abuses the tongue by commanding the poor to sit on the floor (2:3).

James raises the stakes by connecting this apparently minor issue to the question of obedience. Favoritism violates the royal law, "Love your neighbor as yourself." One who shows favoritism is a lawbreaker. He violates the whole law by the one sin (2:8–10). This seems counterintuitive, for we tend to place obedience in the category of things we can do partially, like eating breakfast. If someone asks, "Did you eat breakfast?" we can say, "Yes," "No," or "Sort of. I had half a bagel and a sip of coffee." Nibbling is not exactly a break-fast, but it is not fasting either. But James puts obedience in the "all or nothing" camp, as in a ballgame where the ball is either in or out.

The logic is twofold. First, all commandments are connected. Lying violates the ninth command but it also steals truth from others (the eighth), dishonors them (the fifth), and so on. Second, *deliberate* lies break the first command. Since God authors the whole law, deliberate violation is rebellion. Thus all action has a global element. Disobedience is not like removing one brick from a pile (of possible good deeds); it is like heaving a brick through a sheet of glass, shattering the whole.

Since we are all guilty of favoritism, since we all tend to offer pious platitudes rather than real relief (2:14–26), we *suspect* that we fail the first test of caring for the poor. But James *announces* that we fail the test of controlling the tongue (James 3). "Not many of you should presume to be teachers . . . because . . . we who teach will be judged more strictly. . . . If anyone is never at fault in what he says, he is a perfect man, able to keep his whole body in check." In fact, no one is perfect; hence no mere human can tame the tongue (though God can). It is fueled by hellish fires (3:3–6). It is irrational, blessing God, but cursing people made in God's image (3:7–12).

To review, there are three tests of genuine faith: caring for the poor, controlling the tongue, and staying unpolluted by the world (1:26–27).

First, James announced that spurious faith is useless, dead (2:20, 26). Second, he implied that we fail the test of caring for the poor and declared that we fail the test of controlling the tongue. Soon he will disclose our failure of the third, our pollution by the world, our lust for pleasure. Still, James does not leave us to despair. Earlier he said that God has given us (spiritual) birth through the implanted word that can save us (1:18, 21). God also bestows wisdom from above, which James juxtaposes with the unspiritual, demonic "wisdom" of this earth (3:15).

But we must taste more bitterness before we can savor the sweet. Envy and selfish ambition produce hedonistic lusts characteristic of the worldly wisdom that infects us (3:14–4:3). Unrequited desires rage within. Some are so obviously selfish that we dare not even pray for them (4:2–3). Or we do pray and suffer God's veto of our egotistical petitions.

Even pagans regarded envy as an ulcer that produces misery and strife. Yet if people derive their identity from possessions, then envy is truly an element of worldly wisdom. If there is no God, we should grasp whatever we can. If we do not guarantee our own interests, no one will.

God's peaceable, gentle, humble wisdom is the antithesis of the strife produced by worldly wisdom. God's wisdom teaches us to accept the gifts and the place God gives and to let him guarantee rewards. Then we can pursue God-given aspirations without the pangs of selfish ambition. Yet, James declares, it is hard to live out this wisdom. James's readers have married Christ, but adulterous longings—envy and ambition—plague them (4:4, 8). Double-minded, they want to love Jesus *and* the world. But we cannot befriend both God and world simultaneously, for "friendship with the world is hatred toward God" (4:4).

James concludes this section with a question in 4:5 that we can paraphrase this way: "What do you think of your passions and ambitions? Do you think God sent them? That he designed our spirits to be governed by cravings, envy, and ambition? Scripture rightly says our spirits tend toward envy." Human history is largely a tale of envious striving, as we can already see in the accounts of Cain and Abel, Jacob and Esau, and Joseph and his brothers, in Genesis.[12] But that is

---

12 Johnson, *James*, 279–83; Sophie Laws, *A Commentary on the Epistle of James* (San Francisco: Harper and Row, 1980), 178–79.

not why God implanted our drives in us. Therefore, he gives grace to tame us to teach us that "God opposes the proud but gives grace to the humble" (4:6).

If we have followed James's logic, we understand our desperate need for this word of grace. We have failed the tests of true religion; we have not cared for the poor, controlled our tongues, or remained unpolluted by the world. We need the gospel now, and James supplies it, not a gospel of the atonement, but a gospel of repentance. Again, "God opposes the proud but gives grace to the humble." Therefore repent. Submit to God. Resist the devil. Draw near to God. Grieve, mourn, and wail over sin. "Humble yourselves before the Lord, and he will lift you up" (4:7–10). That is the gospel according to James.

This survey of James, together with our study of Samuel, suggests how we may present Christ in all of Scripture without taking flights of fantasy. James and Samuel show how diverse the call to faith will be if we resist the temptation to leap to Paul's gospel. Yet even the notion of "Paul's gospel" can mislead, since Paul's presentation of Christ varies from book to book. Romans stresses the justification of sinners, the redemption of spiritual slaves, the reconciliation of enemies, and the propitiation of wrath. But Colossians honors the cosmic Christ, 1 Thessalonians emphasizes the returning Christ, and 1 Corinthians portrays Jesus as the wisdom of God and head of the church.

We could also analyze the varied testimony to God in the Pentateuch, in Kings and Chronicles, and in the prophetic books. Indeed, as much as they resemble each other, Matthew and Mark offer distinctive testimonies to Jesus. In both, Jesus is Son of God, king of Israel, and the sacrifice who ransoms many from their sins. Yet via subtle differences Matthew portrays Jesus as the teacher who labors to bring the disciples, whom he calls "men of little faith," to a maturity that will enable them to fulfill the Great Commission. In Mark, the disciples seem somewhat slower to understand (8:16–21), and the gospel hurtles toward the cross, which everyone in the story so clearly needs.

With these representative studies in hand, one summative task remains. We must gather previous scattered remarks that can help us determine how preachers should week by week present the saving work of God, especially as revealed in the work of Christ. How shall we, as chapter 1 put it, instill faith in God and conformity to his person? What strategies will promote our dual goal: (1) to present the one gospel faithfully and (2) to present it without tiresome repetition? How can teachers be orthodox yet creative? How preach one theme with sufficient variation? How present one solution to the endless diversity of human needs? How give up the vain quest for originality without becoming repetitious? How can we dare to be boring, that is, how can we give up false creativity, without actually being boring, by leaping to Paul or to traditional appeals to give one's life to Jesus? Dennis Johnson has surveyed several recent answers to these questions.[13] By adapting his categories, we can collect and deepen prior remarks on the issue.

BRIDGING REDEMPTIVE-HISTORICAL AND NEED-SENSITIVE PREACHING

Emphases of Redemptive-Historical Preaching

Redemptive-historical preaching (RHP) emphasizes the unity of the history of redemption and the centrality of Christ in that history. It places every passage of Scripture in its historical context and asks questions such as: Where are this event and text located in the history of redemption? What are the traits of the covenant that govern the era? What do the people know about God's character, redemption, and ethic? How does this text add to that knowledge?

RHP emphasizes the progressive, organic revelation of God's truth, disclosed ever more fully in successive covenants with Adam, Noah, Abraham, Moses, David, and Jesus, in whose death and resurrection biblical history reaches its climax. This approach relates old-covenant events and earlier phases of Jesus' life to that climax. Afterward, RHP reads Acts and the Epistles in light of the death-resurrection nexus. The doctrine of the Epistles is the doctrine of Christ's person and work.

RHP traces the unfolding of the plan of salvation, seeking hints of the Christ, though he may not be mentioned by name, in all Scripture, so as to proclaim him from all Scripture (Luke 24). In the Old Testament, this occurs via typology more than prophecy. Observing

13 I thank Dennis Johnson of Westminster Seminary in Escondido, California, for permitting the use of his unpublished paper, "What's a Young Preacher to Do?"

that the New Testament explicitly identifies Adam as a type of Christ (Rom. 5) and that Jesus is often called the Son of David, RHP seeks parallels between other old-covenant offices and the ministry of Jesus. Thus Jesus is the great prophet foretold in Deuteronomy 18. He is the royal Son who sits on David's throne forever (2 Sam. 7). He is the effective priest, interceding for his people and offering a final sacrifice for their sins. He fulfills old-covenant institutions such as the temple (John 1:14) and the sacrificial system (Heb. 7–10).

For RHP, ethics follows the indicative-imperative pattern. With Abraham, God first blessed and justified him (Gen. 12:1–3; 15:1–6), then said, "Walk before me and be blameless" (17:1). Again, the law, given in Exodus 20–24, rests on God's prior redemption.[14] He says, "I am the LORD your God, who brought you out of Egypt, out of the land of slavery," *then* delivers the law (20:2; see also 19:4). Paul also grounds his imperatives on the indicatives of salvation.[15] In Romans, Ephesians, and Galatians, doctrinal segments precede the ethical, so that laws rest on grace. Sometimes Paul places redemptive reasons immediately before or after imperatives. "You are not your own; you were bought at a price. Therefore honor God with your body" (1 Cor. 6:19–20). "Work out your salvation with fear and trembling, for it is God who works in you" (Phil. 2:12–13; see also Eph. 2:1–10; Col. 3:1–5).

Strengths and Concerns of Redemptive-Historical Preaching

Sensitive readers realize that we have fundamentally adopted the redemptive-historical approach. Chapter 1 began, "A God-centered approach to the relevance of Scripture has two foci: knowing the God who redeems and conforming ourselves to him." Chapter 4 observed that redemptive acts are a prime source of application. The teaching

14 On theocentricity in Old Testament ethics, see Christopher J. H. Wright, *An Eye for an Eye* (Downers Grove, Ill.: InterVarsity, 1983), 21–32.

15 On the indicative and the imperative, see Wolfgang Schrage, *The Ethics of the New Testament,* trans. David Green (Philadelphia: Fortress, 1988), 167–74; Herman Ridderbos, *Paul: An Outline of His Theology,* trans. John DeWitt (Grand Rapids: Eerdmans, 1975), 253–65. For a survey of views, see Michael Parsons, "Being Precedes Act: Indicative and Imperative in Paul's Writing," *Evangelical Quarterly* 88.2 (1988): 99–127.

of narrative must "focus first on the redeeming work of God and the divine self-revelation embedded in it," for God is "the central character in every Bible story," and every passage discloses aspects of his redemptive purpose. Chapter 7 noted that sound interpretation of narratives focuses first on the acts of God, who is always the main actor. Indeed, the Bible is one long drama that begins when God creates heaven and earth, and ends when he restores them. The intervening chapters describe God's achievement of his aims, not humans reaching out to God.[16]

Redemptive-historical preaching exalts the God who saves with infinite mercy. It opposes moralizing application, denouncing narrative expositions that focus on human participants as exemplars of good or bad behavior. It cannot tolerate sermons (and hymns) that fail to name and honor Christ, that propound general moral or spiritual instruction that any theist could find agreeable. It safeguards an essential of interpretation: it keeps the broad context of every Scripture firmly in view. Nonetheless, some forms of RHP are prone to certain errors:

- The desire to relate every passage of the Old Testament to Christ can generate fanciful, exegetically unverifiable forays into typologizing.
- The zeal to trace each passage to its culmination in Christ can obliterate the distinctiveness of particular passages. At worst, RHP repeats one sermon, albeit a very good one, every week.
- The focus of RHP is narrative, which constitutes over 35 percent of Scripture. It has not sufficiently developed its method for other genres, such as psalms of wisdom or lament, proverbs, prophetic oracles, or the ethical codes of Moses or Paul.
- Some advocates of RHP are wary of any specific application, fearing that calls to change behavior will usurp the Spirit's role in application and drift into anthropocentric moralism. Zeal to avoid moralistic readings of narrative leads some to refuse all moral uses of narratives. But narratives edify too (chap. 7). Indicatives precede imperatives, but there *are* imperatives.

16   See also Daniel M. Doriani, *Getting the Message* (Phillipsburg, N.J.: Presbyterian and Reformed, 1996), 174–84.

None of these weaknesses is intrinsic to RHP. Because of its theocentricity, this approach is the starting point for preaching historical
texts, old covenant or new.

Overview of Need-Sensitive Preaching

Need-sensitive preaching stresses that biblical preaching should
edify its hearers by meeting needs, by motivating listeners to know
God, to grow in holiness, and to strengthen relationships. Various
styles of preaching are need-sensitive. The Puritans had lists of "uses"
for their expositions of texts or doctrines. Theonomists want to see
Old Testament law reform church and society. Seeker-sensitive
megachurches and their clones believe preaching should meet the felt
needs of unchurched visitors. Counseling-sensitive pastors see the
pulpit as preventative medicine, forestalling problems before they start
or eradicating them before they become entrenched. Christ-centered
homileticians partially agree with this camp, since they claim all Scripture discloses our fallenness and need of Christ. Most preachers desire
to promote godliness in largely godless cultures.

Need-sensitive preaching has a respectable theological heritage.
The Westminster Shorter Catechism, questions 17–19, interweaves
remarks about our objective status as sinners and our subjective experience of the miseries of sinfulness:

> The fall brought mankind into an estate of sin and misery. . . .
> The sinfulness of that estate . . . consists in the guilt of Adam's
> first sin, the want of original righteousness, and the corrup-
> tion of his whole nature. . . . All mankind by their fall lost com-
> munion with God and are under his wrath and curse, and so
> made liable to all the miseries of this life . . . and to the pains
> of hell forever.

Jesus conducted a need-sensitive ministry. When the blind, bleed-
ing, and leprous came to him, when parents brought their children,
when Israelites brought the crippled and demon-possessed, he responded to their "felt needs." Sometimes he gave exactly what they
wanted, other times he redefined their needs. A young man in a crowd
thought he needed a redivision of his inheritance, but Jesus knew he
needed a warning about greed (Luke 12:13–21). A rich young ruler

believed he needed to do something to inherit eternal life, but Jesus saw his failure to heed the first command (Matt. 19:16–22). Similarly, the apostles met some needs, redefined others, and refused a few requests (Acts 5:15–16; 3:2–10; 8:18–23, respectively).

Need-sensitive pastors get important things right. The church is a hospital. It is a mission organization that seeks the lost and welcomes the found. It is a family, where protective parents clear the obstacles to a baby's first steps. Need-sensitive preaching knows that the journey to faith can begin with flawed desires for peace or acceptance. It knows that God accepts even sin-laden repentance; he even purifies our repentance.

Emphases of Need-Oriented Preaching

Need-oriented preaching (NOP) seeks to reach unchurched or slightly churched people in language that communicates effectively by addressing the feelings of need that they experience. It observes that strife, fear, unhappiness, alienation, greed, lust, malice, violence, resentment, envy, guilt feelings, hypocrisy, and self-loathing are all (1) consequences of the fall and (2) sources of distress in the lost. By addressing felt needs, NOP helps cure real needs, the need for reconciliation to God and re-creation in the image of Christ.

Reactions to Need-Oriented Preaching

NOP elicits passionate opposition. Critics accuse it of pandering to a consumerist culture that places supreme value on personal peace and prosperity. They say NOP twists the Christ-centered gospel into an anthropocentric counterfeit. It subverts God's order: people are no longer viewed as servants of God who owe him worship; God is the servant of humankind, meeting our felt needs. NOP must fail, critics say, because a fallen race cannot even appraise its true needs. We think we need happiness, freedom from pain, significance, and so on. But our true needs are deeper and our situation far worse than we imagine—and most people deafen themselves to the diagnosis.

When indicted for pandering, NOP says, "We call it serving." Armchair theologians assault NOP for its imperfect methods of evangelizing, but as one pastor replied to a critic (in a somewhat different setting), "You may be right about my problems, but I still like my *flawed* method of evangelizing better than I like your perfect method of *not* evangelizing."

Indeed, unalloyed NOP does invite distortions. Yet while RHP and NOP can be antithetical, they can also be complementary. RHP says every proclamation of Scripture must focus on Jesus Christ, who came to save sinners. Surely, through Jesus' incarnation and atonement, his death and resurrection, God meets our need for redemption, for justification and reconciliation to God. Yet, by satisfying these true needs, he gratifies certain *felt* needs. Redemption liberates us from the grip of sin. Justification begins to cure guilt feelings. Reconciliation to God induces peace with our fellows. When God adopts us into his covenant family, he meets our need for love and for acceptance in a healthy community. Indeed, if the essence of temptation is the invitation to meet legitimate needs in illegitimate ways, then every felt need connects to a genuine need, even if it skews it.

Dangers in Need-Oriented Preaching

If need-oriented preachers are drivers who disdain the safe pavement of churchianity and prefer the off-road world where they encounter real live pagans, we should expect them to slip into a ditch occasionally. The ditch is anthropocentricity; it has several expressions:

1. NOP can shift "the focus of the assembly from worship in which God is the audience to be pleased, to entertainment in which unchurched people are the audience to be influenced."[17]
2. NOP can narrow sermon topics to themes that meet felt needs. Then the congregation hears not the whole counsel of God but the whole litany of human complaint. At worst, NOP abdicates pastoral leadership. Forgetting the importance of setting the agenda, it simply answers questions. And whatever teachers say, bad questions *do* exist.
3. NOP risks compromise with our self-help, technique-oriented society. It risks descent into a moralism that offers three steps for better marriages, five to better parenting, seven for effectiveness at work, and twelve for recovery from addiction.

17 Johnson, "Young Preacher," 14. I follow this paper for the next several paragraphs.

4. Despite its contrary intentions, NOP can slip into class-four legalism (see pp. 279–80). It so accentuates obedience to the law and steps for growth that it eclipses the proper concern for character, goals, and discernment (chaps. 5–6).

5. NOP's focus on steps toward happiness can obscure the austerity of God's demands and can overshadow the grace of God that alone heals hearts and renews minds. NOP may forget that self-help is, finally, impossible, that we can do nothing to earn the Father's loving gaze or to avert the Judge's holy scrutiny. Critics claim that NOP fails to address mature Christians, but because of these gaps it may not even inculcate the humility and fortitude that form maturity in the first place.

Need-sensitive preaching can avert these hazards. First, healthy churches know the pastor hears their questions and struggles and will address them. When trust is strong, the people expect the pastor to preach on topics that may not initially seem relevant. They realize that *it is the pastor's sacred duty to know the church's needs better than they do.* Second, by practicing expository preaching, pastors can be need-sensitive without being need-dominated. Expository preaching is sometimes considered the foe of relevance. But if the expositor exegetes both the Bible and the audience, he meets needs yet purges the faults of NOP. The concentration on Scriptures restores our focus to God.

Three Bridges from Need-Sensitive to Redemptive-Historical Preaching

These criticisms do not invalidate refined versions of need-sensitive preaching, especially if we build three bridges between need-sensitive and redemptive-historical preaching. They are (1) a commitment to expository preaching, (2) a recognition that redemption is our greatest need, and (3) a commitment to critique needs, lest they be deified. Three preachers, Jay Adams, Bryan Chapell, and Tim Keller, have labored to build such bridges.

First, then, Jay Adams is committed to expository preaching that induces change and equips and edifies hearers. In *Preaching with Purpose* Adams says, "Your preaching is to honor God by building up his church" through addressing its "needs, failures and appetites." Preaching must declare the *telos,* the purpose of the text, the positive change the Holy Spirit intends to elicit through the message. The telos is more than the theme, which may be a doctrinal abstraction suited to the lecture hall. The telos is the effect God intends a text to achieve in its hearers to bring them into conformity to Christ, to put off sin, and to establish godliness.[18] "It is God's task to apply the Scriptures," but preachers must discover that application and translate [it] . . . into contemporary forms."[19] Preachers must do more than label sin and urge general holiness. They must propose concrete steps toward obedience.[20]

Adams's approach prompts questions. Could his emphasis on concrete steps foster legalism? The great majority of Adams's examples come from the Epistles and Jesus' teachings; do all genres—narratives, laments, prayers—lend themselves to preaching that instills behavior change? Can an emphasis on behavioral change adequately address the motives and roots of sin?[21] Yet Adams's advocacy of expository preaching purifies need-sensitive preaching by urging pastors to address needs the Bible recognizes with solutions the Bible offers.

Second, in *Christ-Centered Preaching,* Bryan Chapell bridges from a need-sensitive starting point to a redemption-oriented conclusion. Chapell asserts that every Scripture addresses sin, its consequences, and God's remedy.[22] Holding the doctrines of humanity's fallen condition and God's sovereign grace in equipoise, he believes all Scripture reveals an aspect of our fallen condition and an aspect of God's redemption, which is fully manifest in Christ. Chapell says sermons must have a "fallen-condition focus." They must focus on an aspect of the brokenness of humankind or creation that only God can fully address. Fallenness includes disobedience to the law and the character flaws that drive it—rebellion, greed, egotism, and hardheartedness. It includes individual and corporate evils and the lethargy, self-absorption, and blindness that let them flourish. Fallenness encompasses sin and the results of living in a sin-cursed world: the depredations wrought by

18 Jay Adams, *Preaching with Purpose* (Grand Rapids: Zondervan, 1982), 1–46; the quotations are from pp. 12–13, 21.
19 Ibid., 131–33.
20 Ibid., 123–29.
21 Johnson, "Young Preacher," 9.
22 Bryan Chapell, *Christ-Centered Preaching* (Grand Rapids: Baker, 1994), 40–44, 201–2, 231–36, 263–66.

illness, accidents, and bad leaders. It covers unrequited yearnings for companionship or significance. Thus, Christ-centered sermons typically "seek to excavate the 'burden' of the text that required its writing." They take felt needs seriously, yet they educate hearers to see that God's redemption in Christ meets our true needs. Our highest need is the saving, sustaining grace of God.[23]

Third, if we believe Jesus meets the greatest human needs, then need-sensitive pastors must keep lesser needs from inflating into demigods, for need-sensitive preaching can take an insidious turn. "Come to our church," the enthusiast tells her neighbor. "Our pastor will help you with your problems." Because Scripture describes the way God designed humans to function, biblical teaching can indeed help unbelievers shore up relationships at home and at work. It can foster self-understanding and self-discipline. But when people come to church to glean insights for better living, they not only miss the main point (worship), they may also become happier devotees of false gods. Like a golfer making marginal improvements in a radically flawed swing, non-Christians who assimilate moral counsel from the church may get slightly better at doing the wrong thing—serving their idols. The Epicurean learns that supreme sexual satisfaction occurs within committed monogamy. The narcissist thrills to hear that he is created in the image of God. The disciple of relational gods learns the value of asking and granting forgiveness.

Need-sensitive preachers must realize that even if someone satisfies every felt need, the heart can remain empty. *Felt needs are often unfelt idols.* Therefore, messages on work, money, self-identity, and relationships must say, "Career, wealth, significance, and loving relationships make excellent servants, but miserable masters." They do not satisfy our deepest yearnings (Eccles. 5:10). They woo us away from God (Prov. 30:8–9; Matt. 19:16–22). They fail at the hour of greatest need (Luke 12:13–21). Ecclesiastes says that the pleasure (2:1), laughter (2:2), achievement (2:4), wealth (2:7–8), sex (2:8), and wisdom (2:12–16) that we attain will not satisfy today, and tomorrow they will be gone (2:11, 14–16, 19–21).

Need-sensitive teachers must help unbelievers see that their idol is whatever they trust to take care of them, whether wealth, science,

---

23 Chapell, *Christ-Centered Preaching,* 263, and private conversation.

education, or society.[24] Whatever sets our priorities is our god. If a man is willing to lose his wife and children in the pursuit of his career, we know his idol. An idol is whatever gives our life significance, whatever we would rather die than do without. Respect is Leah's idol when she gives birth to a son and says, "Surely my husband will love me now" (Gen. 29:32). We see its vanity when Leah has *six* sons and still thinks, *"Now* my husband will honor me" (see 9:34; 30:19). Respect is also Rachel's idol when she says to Jacob, "Give me children, or I'll die" (30:1). It fails again when she dies in giving birth to her second son (35:16–19).

Tim Keller has developed helpful diagnostic tools to facilitate the disclosure of idols.[25] He urges people to complete these sentences: "Life has meaning only if . . .," or "I have worth only if . . ." We know the deity's name when someone answers: ". . . if I am recognized for my accomplishments"; ". . . if I have wealth, financial security, and fine possessions and experiences"; ". . . if I am loved and respected by certain people"; ". . . if I have mastery over my life." Keller also proposes that people ask, "What potential loss worries me most? What loss might make life meaningless? How do I comfort myself when life turns against me?" The answers to these questions reveal if someone worships demigods such as respect, pleasure, security, relational success, or even spiritual achievement.

Because the heart is, as Calvin said, an "idol-factory," need-sensitive preaching must depose false gods and enthrone the true one. Negatively, we expose spurious needs and show why idols are doomed to fail. Positively, we exalt the Father God who meets real needs. He meets our physical needs, if not our wants, granting us food, clothing, and shelter. He meets our need for love and security by placing us in human families and adopting us, calling us his beloved sons and daughters. He grants significance, bestowing the dignity accruing to royal off-

---

24 For an analysis of money, power, science, and technology as gods, see Jacques Ellul, *Money and Power,* trans. LaVonne Neff (Downers Grove, Ill.: InterVarsity, 1984) and *The Technological Society,* trans. John Wilkinson (New York: Vintage, 1964); also Herbert Schlossburg, *Idols for Destruction: Christian Faith and Its Confrontation with American Society* (Nashville: Thomas Nelson, 1982).

25 The views of Keller, pastor of Redeemer Presbyterian Church (Presbyterian Church in America) in New York City, are chiefly known through his pulpit ministry and conferences.

spring and the respect due to those with valued abilities. So God meets our needs. Yet this very list reminds us of our need for redemption, for we pervert each of God's gifts. God bestows physical gifts, but we worry, horde, and splurge. He grants significance, but we boast one hour and despise ourselves the next. He brings us into relationship, but we doubt God one day and presume upon him the next. But God forgives and restores us in Christ. He never leaves or forsakes us.

This is the architect's first sketch of a bridge joining redemptive-historical and need-sensitive preaching. It has three spans: expository preaching, a Christocentric focus, and a critique of need-based idols.

Summary

I hope that this book, despite its weaknesses, will facilitate a deepening of application in evangelical pulpits. I hope for application that is deep, varied, and specific, yet God-centered and grace-oriented. Yet as I review prior chapters one last time, I am constrained to hope in God more than books and readers. Pastors need integrity, but we never have enough integrity to merit the trust of our auditors. I think again of the four aspects of application—duty, character, goals, and vision—and rue our perversion of all four. Duties? We fail to discharge them, but when we do, we bloat with self-righteousness. Character? We fail to appropriate the new nature we have in Christ, but when we do, we puff with pride at our virtue. Goals? We dissipate our energies in the ephemeral and frivolous. Then, when we do find a noble task, we fail to enlist enough allies to make the work strong. Vision? We are half blind, but when we do see aright, we prostitute the vision by dreaming about the way others will revere us when they hear our precious insights. Behind it all, we realize we will never know God and conform ourselves to him. If we focus on our attainment, the situation looks worse than we thought. But if we focus on the Lord, who graciously makes himself known to us and conforms us to himself, it may be better than we dare to dream.

13
Selecting a Text

The proper selection of a text is a necessary, although not sufficient, condition for valid application in expository messages. If the chosen text is too small, teachers cannot help but fall into subjective and moralizing interpretations. If it is too long, the lesson has too many points, each developed only superficially, and people get lost.

Consider the case of a young assistant pastor who strode to the pulpit and read his text:

> In the time of Herod king of Judea there was a priest named Zechariah, who belonged to the priestly division of Abijah; his wife Elizabeth was also a descendant of Aaron. Both of them were upright in the sight of God, observing all the Lord's commandments and regulations blamelessly. But they had no children, because Elizabeth was barren; and they were both well along in years. (Luke 1:5–7)

That night's sermon identified Herod and explained the convoluted history of his clan. It described the system of priestly divisions in Jerusalem. It defined key terms such as "upright," "observe," and "blameless." The preacher explained that the barrenness of Zechariah and Elizabeth was tragic since children were so important in that culture. He showed that even righteous people endure disappointments, but they prove their faith by persevering when God withholds their hearts' desires.

Though the sermon was thirty-five minutes old, the congrega-tion was taken by surprise when it came to an end. Why? The pastor had spent his time introducing the prophecy of John the Baptist's birth and missed the central events: the angel's message to Zechariah (Luke 1:11–17), his doubts and punishment (1:18–22), and the beginnings of Elizabeth's pregnancy (1:23–25). Like a sportscaster who introduces the players and discusses possible team strategies only to see the net-work cancel coverage of the game itself, the speaker gave the context for the announcement of John's birth, but missed the event itself. Con-sequently, the sermon was actually a history lecture with a sub-Christian moralism at the end. It described the priesthood in Jesus' day, its structures, and the pressures toward secularization. It summed up, "Despite the pressures, there were some good priests. Still, God did not always reward their obedience at once. We too may not be re-warded at once when we are upright. Yet if we persevere, proving our fidelity, God may reward us as he did Zechariah." Sadly, the speaker missed the basic points of the text.

RIGHT-SIZED TEXTS

Like Goldilocks, we want texts that are not too long and not too short, but just right. Obviously, one can err in this process in only two ways, by selecting too many verses or too few.

Texts That Are Too Short

The sermon we have just described illustrates the disastrous con-sequences of choosing a narrative text poorly. By choosing to speak on Luke 1:5–7, the preacher excised the redemptive action of God. Since these verses described only a man and a woman, the speaker had no choice but to deliver an anthropocentric "be good" message. Once the preacher fixed Luke 1:5–7 as his text and determined to stick to those three verses, his application almost had to be moralistic and anthropocentric; there was no action of God to report. If a sermon on a narrative text stops shortly after we meet the characters, it inescapably focuses on those characters. Only by following the narrative to the end can we find the redemptive work of God. And only when we find that redemptive work can we call the church to respond properly to it.

One can justify preaching on a single verse or sentence if it contains a cardinal tenet of the faith. Great evangelistic texts such as John 3:16 or Acts 1:8 can sustain an entire sermon. Terse doctrinal pronouncements that crown long discussions or epitomize central doctrines also merit a whole sermon. Think of a sentence such as "Christ Jesus came into the world to save sinners—of whom I am the worst" (1 Tim. 1:15). A doctrinal sermon, grounded in one great idea and some surrounding context, is the result. Such sermons typically become topical (not exegetical) messages. Thus a sermon could plausibly explain John 1:5, "The light shines in the darkness, but the darkness has not understood it." But it would be a topical message on the light, its presence, its limits, and its opposition to darkness. The applications would then follow the course appropriate for any doctrinal talk. The danger is that a doctrinal sentence might beget a doctrinal lecture.

Worse things can happen with short texts. Some teachers use them to launch into personal hobbies. The topic may be too trifling to sustain interest; a fragment of a text will yield a fragment of a lesson. The sense can be perverted by loss of the context. At worst, a talk may expound an (inspired record of) uninspired speech, such as the counsel of Gamaliel or Job's friends. Thus, short texts beget distortions and moralizing at worst, and topical sermons at best.

Texts That Are Too Long

The selection of excessively long texts also wreaks havoc with exposition and application. Long texts may force lessons with too many points, each developed superficially. The preacher may skip vital explanations of important matters, or the sermon may drown in swamps of points and entangling subpoints.

Young pastors and teachers (my memory aches) tend to cover too much in one lesson. Multichapter lessons can provide beneficial overviews of the sweep of a book or a large topic, but surveys often bury the audience under an avalanche of information. As points proliferate, they become shallow because there is no time for development. Illustration and precise application shrivel. No single leading idea unifies the whole, and everyone goes home reeling. Just as one of Mozart's patrons allegedly criticized a prized work with the terse comment, "Too many notes," so listeners say of some talks, "Too many points." Imagine, for example, a one-lesson presentation of Paul's concept of the Christian life in Romans 6–8. There is a place for, say, one message on

Samson's life (Judg. 13–16), but it takes great skill to bypass secondary elements and weave the primary themes into a coherent message.

The hazards of wrong-sized texts are clear enough: moralisms, lectures, and pastoral chaff from short texts, and volumes of undigested data from long ones. The selection of right-sized texts, on the other hand, smooths the path toward applications that lend themselves to the forceful proclamation of one main point.

Difficulties in Selecting Texts

Few scholars promote the skill of choosing a text. Some argue that preachers do not need to know how to select a text, since they can follow a good commentary's decisions, the divisions of the Bible translation they prefer, or, in some ecclesiastical bodies, the lectionary. Others suppose that the needs of the church, the church year, public events, and the convictions of the pastor will lead to the right text.[1]

None of these points obviates the need to know how to choose a text. Leaving the matter to the heart of the speaker is an invitation to subjectivism. To urge speakers to leave the work to others runs against the grain of true interpretation. We are thinkers. It violates our constitution to follow slavishly the aging decisions of the church and its commentators on such matters. Further, the chapter and paragraph divisions of the Bible, though useful, entail problems.

None of the chapter, verse, and paragraph divisions of modern printed Bibles is inspired, for none belongs to the original text. Moreover, copyists and printers have divided the biblical text in many ways over the years. For example, a fourth-century copy of the New Testament divided Matthew into 170 sections, Mark into 62, Luke into 152, and John into 50. A fifth-century manuscript gave Matthew 68 headings, Mark 48, Luke 83, and John 18.[2] Chapter divisions as we know them were devised in the thirteenth century.[3]

---

1 John Stott, *Between Two Worlds* (Grand Rapids: Eerdmans, 1982), 213–20; John A. Broadus, *On the Preparation and Delivery of Sermons,* 4th ed., revised by Vernon L. Stanfield (San Francisco: Harper & Row, 1979), 31–35. Stott and Broadus have various suggestions for the selection of a text, but both completely bypass literary and linguistic data.

2 Bruce Metzger, *The Text of the New Testament: Its Transmission, Corruption, and Restoration,* 3d ed. (New York: Oxford University Press, 1992), 22–25.

3 F. F. Bruce, *The Books and the Parchments,* 3d ed. (Westwood, N.J.: Revell, 1963), 118.

The sixteenth-century printer and publisher Robert Estienne finalized the New Testament verse divisions we now use. Useful as they are for reading and reference, even a casual reader can see problems, such as verses beginning mid-sentence and chapter divisions that interrupt the flow of thought. In fact Estienne's divisions, though still in use today, were erratic enough to encourage the story that he marked the verse divisions while he was riding horseback, with misleading divisions occurring when the jogging of his horse jarred his pen at the wrong places.[4]

Today paragraph divisions vary widely from one translation to the next. Hundreds of verse divisions break sentences into two or more pieces, and faulty chapter divisions sunder unified topics. Some examples: The first account of creation runs from Genesis 1:1 to 2:4, the second from 2:5 to 2:25. Isaiah's song of the Suffering Servant is senselessly divided into two chapters (52:13–53:12). The discussion of the Christian home spans Ephesians 5:18–6:9. Jesus' eschatological discourse spans Matthew 24–25. Paul's theological discussions of sin, justification, and life in Christ each span two or three chapters of Romans.[5] Since we cannot simply trust the chapter, verse, and paragraph divisions in our Bible, we need to know how to recognize a right-sized text.

TOPICAL PREACHING

A bold inquisitor might ask if we need texts at all. Considering how often texts are abused, why not give up the game altogether and let pastors preach what is on their mind? Surely that would be no worse than the all-too-obvious tendency preachers have of forcing texts to say whatever they want, and of getting to the topics they wish to address, whatever the reading or official sermon series may dictate. Why not liberate them to preach on general biblical concepts or the contours of Christ's life without a particular text?[6] Paul certainly grounded

4 Metzger, *Text,* 104.
5 According to most outlines of Romans, Paul introduces his theme in 1:1–17, treats sin or the need for justification from 1:18 to 3:20, justification by faith from 3:21 to 4:25, and the life of the justified in chapters 5–8.
6 On preaching without a text see Ernest Best, *From Text to Sermon* (Atlanta: John Knox, 1978), 100–101.

some of his ethic, as well as his theology, in creative meditation on the ways of Christ. He pleaded for Christian unity on the basis of Jesus' pattern of putting others first (Phil. 2:1–11). He based a monetary appeal not on Old Testament tithing rules but on Jesus' giving of himself (2 Cor. 8–9). By this standard, a contemporary sermon on marriage could base an appeal for lifelong fidelity on Jesus' steadfast refusal to quit when his disciples disappointed him or when his career path turned tough and ugly.

No explicit biblical precept requires that sermons start with a biblical text. If the example of Acts has normative weight, a message can begin almost anywhere, as long as it is grounded in biblical truth. Peter's sermon in Acts 2 begins with a question, "Are these men drunk?" The opening for the message in Acts 3 is a miracle. Stephen surveys Genesis, Exodus, and other parts of Old Testament history in his sermonic defense against the charge of blasphemy in Acts 7. Paul's starting point in Acts 17:22–23 is a pagan inscription; a few verses later, he quotes pagan poetry. But these cases show only that sermons may begin with popular ideas or questions. Except for the last, every sermon in Acts brims with biblical citations. None formally exegetes a text, but all stand on a biblical basis.[7]

We conclude, therefore, that speakers may use topical messages to address contemporary issues. Topical talks that draw on general biblical principles are especially apt when addressing issues unknown to biblical times, such as the dangers of mobility, our culture's strange concept of adolescence, or the effects of technology on Christian faith. Since no text meets these issues directly, we gain integrity if we marshal general biblical principles rather than forcing a passage into an alien mold. If we can find no text that suits a proposed message, we should wonder if the message is valid. As a safeguard, there is the wisdom in grounding a topical message in a passage that presents several of its ideas.[8] A message on work and overwork may begin with the fourth commandment. For friendship, draw upon Ecclesiastes 4:9–12.

---

7 The New Testament may not have a single example of a sermon based on a text, although William Lane argues that Heb. 3 and 4 are a loose homily on Ps. 95:7b–11. See Lane, *Hebrews 1–8* (Dallas: Word, 1991), 83ff.

8 Daniel M. Doriani, *Getting the Message* (Phillipsburg, N.J.: Presbyterian and Reformed, 1996), 109ff.

THE NORM

Topical sermons are often beneficial, but throughout this book we have assumed that text-based teaching is the norm. Furthermore, pastors should ordinarily work through books of the Bible seriatim. By preaching through whole books, pastors more readily preach the whole counsel of God. Such an approach helps them abandon minor obsessions. It liberates them to handle sensitive topics such as sexual ethics, gossip, and money, and difficult doctrines, such as human depravity, with greater freedom. Provided that pastors have the custom of proclaiming whatever is in the text, they are exonerated. If someone objects to a theme, the speaker can honestly say, "I did not choose this topic, God did, for he put it in the text before us." He could even add, "It was as hard on me as it was on you; it cut across my human preferences as much as it did yours. But they were not my own ideas, you understand, but God's, as best I comprehend his word. Show me my error in interpretation and I will concede your point. If you cannot, you quarrel with God, not me."[9]

Series also let pastors and congregations more readily enter the mind, the thought world, of Scripture. Thus, when they work through a book, they follow (albeit imperfectly) the arguments given by God to sustain his instruction. Learning to think and see the world God's way is, of course, a vital, albeit neglected, facet of application.

Further, by watching teachers work through texts, the church learns, by example, how to handle the word. Pastors should never seek to handle Scripture so that their auditors marvel at their wit and ingenuity in finding things no one would imagine. Rather, they should instill confidence that Scripture is accessible to the diligent. Moreover, ministers slowly build biblical literacy when they preach through books. When Christians read texts on which they have heard skillful teaching, they will recall salient points from lessons heard years earlier.[10]

At a practical level, teachers save time by working through one

9 Broadus, *Preparation and Delivery of Sermons,* 21–22, based on Donald G. Miller, *Fire in Thy Mouth* (Nashville: Abingdon, 1954), 102–3.

10 For more, see Broadus, *Preparation and Delivery of Sermons,* 19–23; and Robert Dabney, *Sacred Rhetoric* (1870; reprint, Carlisle, Pa.: Banner of Truth Trust, 1979), 81–89.

book. They save hours choosing the next topic. They can plan messages weeks in advance, gathering relevant material from their readings, marking the relevance of their topic for church and society, and accumulating illustrations. They can research background issues in depth and enjoy the fruit for months. They can become acclimated to the syntax and vocabulary of the original text. Therefore, even if leaders speak topically and trust commentaries at times, they should remember the benefits of working through an entire book.

GENERAL PRINCIPLES FOR FINDING A TEXT

There is no single formula for determining the appropriate length of a text. The simplest ideal is to *choose a passage that makes one main point or tells one story.* A proper text has one distinct, unified message. It contains the whole thought of the author on one point, as expressed in one place.[11] The text may be self-contained or feature complex relationships with other parts of the book in which it stands. It may or may not have subpoints and side interests. Yet a well-chosen text and a well-crafted lesson make one main point.

If a unified text is too rich for one message, do not cut it in half, but draw on other options: (1) Limit yourself to the chief issue in the text. (2) Preach the same text two consecutive weeks. Survey the whole one week and return to special issues the next. (3) Treat side themes later. Most books have recurring themes, both major and minor, and there may be a better time to address what must now be skipped.

So the goal is to find a text that makes one well-developed point or tells one complete story. How then is a text with one point found?

1. *Right-sided texts have a prominent and coherent idea.* Single sentences are usually too short to convey a complete idea. They need the surrounding material to provide context and elaboration to create a complete concept.[12] A chapter may present so many ideas that coherence becomes elusive. Ordinarily, a right-sized text will have one to

---

11 John Beekman and John Callow, *Translating the Word of God* (Grand Rapids: Zondervan, 1974), 279–80; Dabney, *Sacred Rhetoric,* 101.

12 See John Lyons, *Introduction to Theoretical Linguistics* (Cambridge: Cambridge University Press, 1968), 412–23.

five paragraphs. A paragraph is a cluster of sentences marked by coherence and a prominent concept.[13] Coherence means all the sentences deal with one main idea or action. A prominent concept means that one idea is stressed, so that the others obtain unity by preparing for, explaining, or developing that chief idea. The goal, therefore, is to locate one or more paragraphs where one idea has prominence and subpoints develop it coherently.

2. *Unified texts have a distinct vocabulary.* Special terminology often signals a text unit. Continuity and change in vocabulary can be obvious or subtle. The topic of Mark 7 is obviously "tradition," for the term appears five times in verses 1–13. Does the passage therefore end at 7:13? No, for the special vocabulary relating to things clean and unclean begins in 7:2 but continues to 7:23, after which it too disappears. Thus, in Mark 7, vocabulary alone discloses the limits of the text.[14] In 1 Corinthians 1:17 to 2:13, Paul repeats the term "wisdom" sixteen times, then the term disappears, showing that wisdom is the theme from 1:17 to 2:13.

Luke 8 presents a more subtle case. The parable of the sower, with its explanation, seems to span 8:1–15, followed by the new topic of the lamp on the stand in 8:16–18. But upon closer scrutiny, the vocabulary of 8:1–15 continues in 8:16–18. Both sections include the images of seeing (8:10, 16), hearing (8:15, 18), and taking away (8:12, 18). Vocabulary also suggests that Luke views the visit from Jesus' family, in 8:19–21, as part of the same topic. When someone tells Jesus his mother and brothers are outside, waiting to see him, he replies, "My mother and brothers are those who hear God's word and put it into practice." The phrase "hearing the word" is also in the last clause of the explanation of the sower (8:15). English translations veil another parallel between the sower and the family visit. The verb for "bear fruit" in the parable of the sower (8:8) and the verb for "put into practice" in the record of the family visit (8:21) both translate the Greek verb *poieō*. All this distinct language disappears in 8:22, where the storm at

---

13 Peter Cotterell and Max Turner, *Linguistics and Biblical Interpretation* (Downers Grove, Ill.: InterVarsity, 1989), 193–95.

14 Confirming the clue given by vocabulary, Mark 7:24 begins with the geographical marker, "Jesus left that place...."

sea begins. The repeated use of key words shows that Luke 8:1–21 has one theme: responses to the word of God.

3. *Unified texts repeat key phrases or ideas.* Genesis 1 repeats the phrase, "There was evening, and there was morning—the _____ day." In the Sermon on the Mount, the repetition of a key phrase delineates several sections. Jesus' phrase "Blessed are . . ." marks the Beatitudes (Matt. 5:1–12). The phrase "You have heard that it was said . . ." sets apart the section developing the true meaning of the law (5:21–48). The phrase "Your Father, who sees what is done in secret, will reward you," unites the section on hypocrisy (Matt. 6:1–18).

A special type of repetition called "inclusion" (or inclusio) is the use of the same phrase at the beginning and end of a section. The statement "Everything is permissible, but not everything is beneficial" opens and closes Paul's discussion of Christian freedom in 1 Corinthians (6:12; 10:23). In Matthew 19:30 we read, "But many who are first will be last, and many who are last will be first." A parable about reversals follows, and concludes, "So the last will be first, and the first will be last" (20:16). Parallel concepts may also create an inclusio. For example, before and after giving the law, Moses says the commands are God's very words (Deut. 5:5, 32). The parable of the rich fool (Luke 12:13–21) opens and closes with the issue of who will get an inheritance. The scene begins with a man saying to Jesus, "Teacher, tell my brother to divide the inheritance with me." It ends with Jesus asking in effect, "Who will get the money when the rich fool dies? It is his now, but whose will it finally be?"

4. *A unified passage clearly fits within its larger context.* Every passage contributes to its larger section. The themes of sections and books are usually clear; each smaller unit should advance them. For example, Israel's need of a king is the theme of Judges 17–21, as the inclusio at 17:6 and 21:25 shows, "In those days Israel had no king; everyone did as he saw fit." Each particular text within Judges 17–21 develops that theme. Again, Romans 1:18–3:20 describes the sinful condition of the human race. Each subsection develops a topic such as the forms, origins, and significance of human sinfulness. Every coherent text belongs to a larger section. If no such connection is seen, the text being considered is probably not of the right size.

Luke 9:50 and 11:23 illustrate the importance of locating Scripture within its context. In 9:50 Jesus declares, "Whoever is not against you is for you"; in 11:23, "He who is not with me is against me." Both statements deny the possibility of neutrality toward Jesus. But the statements seem to take an opposite view of apparently neutral parties. "Whoever is not against you is for you" implies that the neutral parties side with Jesus. But "He who is not with me is against me" implies that they oppose Jesus. How can both be true? The answer lies in the larger units. In 9:46–50, the disciples debated which of them was greatest. Seeking to preserve their position, they urged Jesus to stop a man who was expelling demons in his name. Jesus advised them not to be suspicious of someone who seemed to share the ministry. "Do not stop him," he said, "for whoever is not against you is for you." But in Luke 11:23 Jesus had just cast out a demon, and his foes claimed he did so by the power of Satan. In the context of blasphemy, Jesus declared that anyone who remained silent must be reckoned with the enemy: "He who is not with me is against me."

To summarize our discussion so far, authors ordinarily need one or two paragraphs to make and qualify their points with precision. Therefore, a paragraph or paragraph cluster is typically an ideal text. The principles above hold for all kinds of texts. Some specialized principles will help speakers determine the boundaries of narratives and discourses. Again, the process of applying both narratives and discourses will be easier if the teacher is working with a right-sized text.

Finding a Right-Sized Narrative

Narrative texts tell one story, typically in one place and time, with one set of characters. A story ends when the action has been completed, when the tension has been released, when the protagonist achieves a goal, passes (or fails) a test, or makes a choice. There are several signs that a new story is beginning.

1. *New characters and geography.* Virtually every new narrative features at least one change of characters or a shift in location. In 1 Samuel 16–30, for example, David is constant, while Samuel and Saul come and go. In the Gospels Jesus is constant, the disciples are nearly constant, Jewish leaders come and go, while minor characters typically appear in only one passage.

2. *New time.* Sometimes a book mentions a specific time interval ("six days later"). A new episode may begin by referring to the last story—"After such and such happened . . ." Kings and Chronicles place stories in the reign of particular kings. The Gospels may establish a new unit by a reference to Jewish festivals. Even a vague expression, such as "after this," "then," or "one day" may indicate the start of a new event.

3. *Summary remarks.* Lengthy narratives often close with a sum-marizing remark. Acts concludes several sections that way. The first instance reads, "So the word of God spread. The number of disciples in Jerusalem increased rapidly, and a large number of priests became obedient to the faith" (Acts 6:7; see also 9:31; 12:24; 14:26–28; 19:20). Especially in the Old Testament, summaries may come in the middle or beginning of a narrative. The statement "Day after day Saul searched for David, but God did not give David into his hands" (1 Sam. 23:14b), encapsulates 1 Samuel 21–23. (See also 1 Sam. 15:33–34; 18:30; 1 Kings 13:33–34; 2 Kings 17:40–41.) Summary remarks may set off one story or a series that should be studied for several weeks.

Finding a Right-Sized Discourse

No one sign marks the beginning of a new unit of discourse. Look for any of the following indicators that an author may be starting a new subject in an epistle, speech, or prophecy.

1. *Terms of address.* New units frequently open with a direct address such as "my brothers" (James, Galatians), "dear friends" (1 John), "O Israel" (Deuteronomy, Isaiah, Hosea), or "my son" (Proverbs). There are hundreds of others, and not always complimentary ("You foolish Galatians," "You cows of Bashan"). Of course, authors can use direct address in the middle of a discourse.

2. *Rhetorical questions.* Rhetorical questions can wrap up sections by eliciting responses to events. For example, Mark 8:14–21 closes with the question, "Do you still not understand?" Such questions can open new sections by anticipating objections or investigating implications of recent ideas. Romans 6:1–14, a section on sanctification, begins by anticipating an objection to justification by faith, "Shall we go on sin-ning so that grace may increase?" Romans 8:31–39 initiates reflec-tions on God's salvation by asking, "What, then, shall we say . . . ? If God is for us, who can be against us?" The question "Is any one of

you in trouble?" prepares readers for a discourse on life's joys and sorrows (James 5:13).[15]

3. *Acts of communication.* Writers may urge their audiences to remember, pay attention, heed advice, or use their ears. They also pause to indicate what they want to accomplish; here they use phrases such as "I want you to know," "Don't be deceived," "I do not want you to be ignorant," "What I am saying is this," and "I write in order to . . ." Or writers may sometimes label their discourses, with phrasing such as "I plead with you," "I urge you," and "I appeal to you." These often stand at the head of a paragraph.

4. *Formula for conclusion.* "Therefore," "so," "finally," and "now" are terms that may conclude one unit or launch another. Individual authors develop their own styles. For example, when the author of Hebrews applies a theological discussion, he often uses the formula, "Therefore + since such and such is the case + let us do X" (2:1; 4:1, 14; 6:1; 10:19–25; 12:1, 28).[16]

5. *Multiple markers.* When several of the preceding markers converge, there is almost certainly a new unit. "Therefore, I urge you, brothers" (Rom. 12:1) contains a formula for conclusion ("therefore"), an act of communication ("I urge you"), and direct address ("brothers"); and a new unit does in fact begin in Romans 12. Notice multiple markers in other passages: "My dear children, I write this to you so that you will not sin" (1 John 2:1). "What good is it, my brothers, if a man claims to have faith but has no deeds?" (James 2:14). "I do not want you to be ignorant of this mystery, brothers, so that you may not be conceited" (Rom. 11:25).

6. *Other genres.* It would be tedious to discuss principles for delimiting texts in every genre of Scripture, since observational skills will discover most of what remains. For example, visions usually announce their beginning ("I saw . . ."). Prophetic oracles begin with something like "This is what the LORD says." Most psalms are best read as a single textual unit. The details can be acquired as necessary.

---

15 The New Testament has hundreds of rhetorical questions. See Beekman and Callow, *Translating the Word of God,* 229–48.

16 The Greek usually has a logical particle *(oun, dio),* either a causal or a concessive participle, and a hortatory subjunctive.

Art and Science

The foregoing clues enable readers to choose well on most occasions, but setting a text is not formulaic. Problems in beginning physics regularly say, "Assume a vacuum," or "Ignore friction," but professional physicists have no such luxury. The real world, including the world of interpretation, is complicated. For us, the greatest complication is a unit that is woven into a larger story that spans several chapters. For example, in the passion narratives, each evangelist connects Peter's denial of Jesus to other parts of the story. John links the threefold denial (18:15–27) to the threefold restoration of Peter (21:15–17), for John's concern is God's mercy despite Peter's failure. Luke links the denial (22:54–62) with Jesus' prediction of Peter's failure and promise of deliverance despite it (22:31–34). Thus Peter must hope in God's resolve, not his own—and we must too. Mark stresses Jesus' solitary obedience. The narrative cuts from Jesus' trial to Peter's denial: Jesus stands before his questioners, denying nothing, while Peter cowers before his questioners, denying everything (Mark 14:53–15:5).[17]

In the technique known as intercalation, authors intertwine two mutually interpretive stories.[18] In Genesis 37–45 the narrator appears to interrupt the story of Joseph to recount Judah's sin with Tamar. Judah's sexual sin and self-serving leadership (Gen. 38) make Joseph's purity (chap. 39) and gentle use of power (chap. 45) all the more striking. In Mark 5:21–43 the account of a woman with a flow of blood seems to interrupt the story of the raising of Jairus's daughter. The healing of the woman gives hope for the even more miraculous healing of the dead girl. In each case we must read the two stories together, since they are mutually interpretive.

While the selection of texts is not the wax nose of exegesis, many chapters can plausibly be divided several different ways. One could take Romans 12:1–13:7 as one unit on a Christian's social relations. Or one could study 12:1–2 as an overture to the Christian life, then take 12:3–8 as advice for the believer within Christian society, 12:9–16

17 Raymond Brown, *The Death of the Messiah* (New York: Doubleday, 1994), 1:587–626.
18 Intercalation occurs over a dozen times in the Gospels, including eight in Mark. See Robert Fowler, *Let the Reader Understand* (Minneapolis: Augsburg Fortress, 1991), 142–47.

as counsel for the believer in dealing with individual Christians, 12:17–21 as principles for relations with individual non-Christians, and 13:1–7 for relations with non-Christian society.

SUMMARY

We cannot always trust textual divisions as handed to us by chapter and verse markers, commentaries, or lectionaries. Short texts, so easily taken out of context, encourage subjective and moralistic application. Long texts try to do too much. We have suggested ways to establish textual units that tell whole stories and present complete ideas. The choice of a text remains an art as well as science, for many texts can be divided several ways. Still, wise choices promote precise interpretation and varied application.

Index of Scripture

13:13–14—137
13:14–15—47
13:18—49
14:12—202
14:15—125, 265
14:16–23—137
14:27—16
15:1–16—106n, 137
15:13—230
15:14—125
15:15—230
15:20—204
15:25—50n
16:33—16
17:3—13
18:6—234
18:15–27—318
18:32—50
19:24–28—50
19:36–37—50
20:9—50
20:31—13, 55n, 146,
    236, 286
21:15–17—318

Acts
1:8—307
1:23–26—194, 207, 211
2—166, 211, 310
2:17–18—137
2:23–24—146
2:42–47—137, 207
3—166, 310
3:2–10—298
3:2–26—202
3:18—50
4—211
4:11—53
4:12—162
4:13—202
4:29—218
4:29–31—192
4:32–35—137
5:15–16—298
6:7—316
7—310

7:11—269
7:18—269
8:18–23—298
8:30–35—59
9:5—234n
9:9–10—269
9:31—316
10—277
10–11—277
10:1—269
10:2–18—269
10:9–15—269
10:39–43—50
11—211
12:24—316
13—166
13:32–33—50
14:8–15—186
14:8–18—202
14:22—46
14:26–28—316
15—277
17:2—55
17:11—55
17:22–23—310
17:26—217
19:20—316
20:27—283
22:8—234n
23:12–21—117
24–26—166
26:15—234n
26:22–23—50
28:3–6—168

Romans
1:1–17—309n
1:2—55
1:8–15—286
1:16—50
1:18–3:20—314, 309n
1:29–31—134
2:17–3:20—268
2:21–24—269
3:21–4:25—309n
3:23—228

3:31—276
4:1–8—46
4:5—133
4:9–11—200
4:17—200
4:17–19—200
4:20—200
4:21—200
4:23–24—46
5—195, 295
5–8—309n
5:6–8—133, 195
5:8—127
6–8—106, 307
6:1–4—136
6:1–12—101
6:1–14—316
6:2—139
6:11—139
6:12–14—138
6:14–15—276
6:19–23—138
6:22—138
7—276
7:4–5—106n
7:5–13—125
7:8–11—132
7:12—276
7:12–14—261
7:14—276
7:18—26
8:2–4—276
8:29—13, 17, 46, 147,
    202
8:31–39—316
9:10–13—201
9:11—146
9:33—53
10:4—276
10:27–30—83
11:20–21—6
11:25—317
12—124
12:1—17, 123, 317
12:1–2—318
12:1–13:7—318

Index of Names and Subjects

Bible (*continued*)
dialogue with, 65–66
as doctrinal, 214
dual authorship, 214n.3
ethical teaching, 124
genres, 93
goals, 146
as God-breathed, 56
human authorship, ix
inspiration, ix
as instructive, 82
interprets us, 22
original meaning, 4
practical counsel, 2
relevance, 2–3, 4, 41
self-interpreting, 247
biblical history, 45–46
biblical theology, 19, 285
biblicism, 66n.9
Blamires, Harry, 99
blessing, 47–48, 267
blessings and curses of covenant, 137, 208
blindness, 114
Blomberg, Craig, 181n.32, 191–92
Blondel, Maurice, 70, 73
boasting, 140n.40
Bonhoeffer, Dietrich, 264n.7
boredom, 238, 281, 294
bread metaphor, 32
bribes, 260
Broadus, John A., 308n.1
Bruce, F. F., 50n.15
Brueggemann, Walter, 262n.2
Calvin, John, 73, 142, 143–44, 213, 221–23, 225, 268n.15, 303
cardinal virtues, 134
case laws, 273
casuistry, 128–30, 131, 264n.7, 272
promotes holiness, 130
promotes legalism, 130
categorical imperative, 103n.10
ceremonial law, 270–73, 277
Chapell, Bryan, 300, 301–2
character, 68–77, 78, 80, 94, 96, 98, 100, 102, 114, 118, 121, 132–43,

187, 218–19, 232, 238, 243–44, 259, 281
centrality of, 70
as definitive gift from God, 133, 142
and duty, 105, 107, 108–11
and humility, 69–70
and listening, 68–69
misuse of, 140
as progressive work, 133–34, 142
proper use of, 142
character development (in narrative), 167
charitable law, 274
choice (literary analysis), 183–84
Christ-centered living, 282
Christian life, 137, 139
Christocentric focus, 304
church, 137, 207
Church Growth movement, 19n.14
church history, 155
church planters, 38
circular reasoning, 71n.17
circumcision, 269
civil law, 243, 270–73, 274
as compromise between feasible and desirable, 257
climax (in narratives), 167, 188
Clowney, Edmund, 285
co-text. *See* literary context
coherence, in texts, 312–13
commands, 97, 103, 126
specificity and transferability, 241
communication, 19n.13, 34, 42–44, 68
community, 116, 152
compassion, 179, 194, 229, 249
conduct, 56–57
confidence in the flesh, 140
conflict (in narratives), 167
conforming to God, 13–18, 44, 202, 280
conscience, 130, 155
consequences, 149, 156
constructive trouble, 154
consumerism, 24n.24, 298
context, 4, 9–10, 158–59, 216, 239, 314–15

relevance, 19n.14, 23, 24, 38, 39, 41, 170, 181, 219–20, 300. *See also* application
repentance, 5, 100, 290–93
repetition, 168, 294, 314
reports, 165–66, 188
resolution (of narrative), 167–68, 188
responses to God's work, 45, 166, 176–78, 188, 280
restitution, 244
results, 149
retribution, 244
rhetorical questions, 316
righteousness, 56, 79, 140
Roberts, Robert, 196
rule utilitarianism, 157
rules, 82–84, 93, 241, 246–47, 248, 281
Ruth, 208
Ryken, Leland, 198
Sabbath, 52, 125–26, 245
Sadducees, 53
safety regulations, 242
salvation, 45, 123
Samson, 198, 208
Samuel, 286–88, 293
sanctification, 8, 17, 28–29, 281, 283
Saul, 208
saving faith, 186
Schlatter, Adolf, 67
Schleiermacher, Friedrich, 70
Schlusser Fiorenza, Elizabeth, 34
science, 36
secularism, 60, 154
seeker-oriented preaching, 283
seeker-sensitive megachurches, 297
self-criticism, 153–54
self-deception, 67
self-expression, 36
self-help, 299–300
self-understanding, 57
selfishness, 113, 135, 265
Seneca, 124n.3
Sermon on the Mount, 16, 103, 119–20, 205
sermon preparation, 3
service, 266

servile fear, 7
setting the stage (in narrative), 166
sexual sin, 255–56
shepherds, 234
sibling rivalry theme, 171, 176
significance, 19, 25–26
Silva, Moisés, 74
sin, 28, 47, 56, 111, 123, 125, 221, 228, 232, 258–59, 297, 301–2
sincerity, 78
situation, 100
situation ethics, 156–57, 247
skills, 30–31, 39–40, 61, 76, 158–59
slavery, 254–55, 257
slowness to anger, 229
small talk, 43
social critics, 155
social freedom, 274
social miracle, 187
social reform, 257–58
Solomon, 50, 209
songs, 91–92, 93
specialization, 112
speech, multiple purposes, 43–44
speech stories, 166, 188
spiritual formation, 74–75
spiritual freedom, 274
spiritual gifts, 111, 147
sports, 106, 112
stealing, 247–48
Stendahl, Krister, 19, 20, 22, 25
Stoics, 134
stories. *See* narrative
Stott, John, 308n.1
Stradivarius, 30
strength, versus advice, 262–63
structural pluralism, 116n.33
submission, to Bible, 66–67
suffering, 24, 48, 78, 202
summary remarks (in narratives), 314
symbols, 90–91
teachers, 22
technique, 28, 30, 213, 299
tedium. *See* boredom
telos, of preaching, 300–301
Temple, William, 237